SCREENSHOT SINGAPORE

A PHOTOGRAPHIC EXPLORATION

SCOTT SHAW

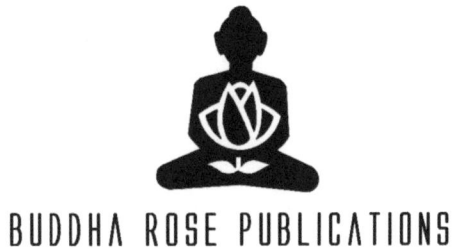

BUDDHA ROSE PUBLICATIONS

Screenshot Singapore
A Photographic Exploration
Copyright © 2019 by Scott Shaw
www.scottshaw.com
All Rights Reserved

First Edition 2019

No part of this book may be reproduced
in any manner without the expressed
permission of the author or the publishing company.

ISBN: 978-1-949251-17-3

Printed in the United States of America

10 9 8 7 6 5 4 3 2 1

SCREENSHOT SINGAPORE

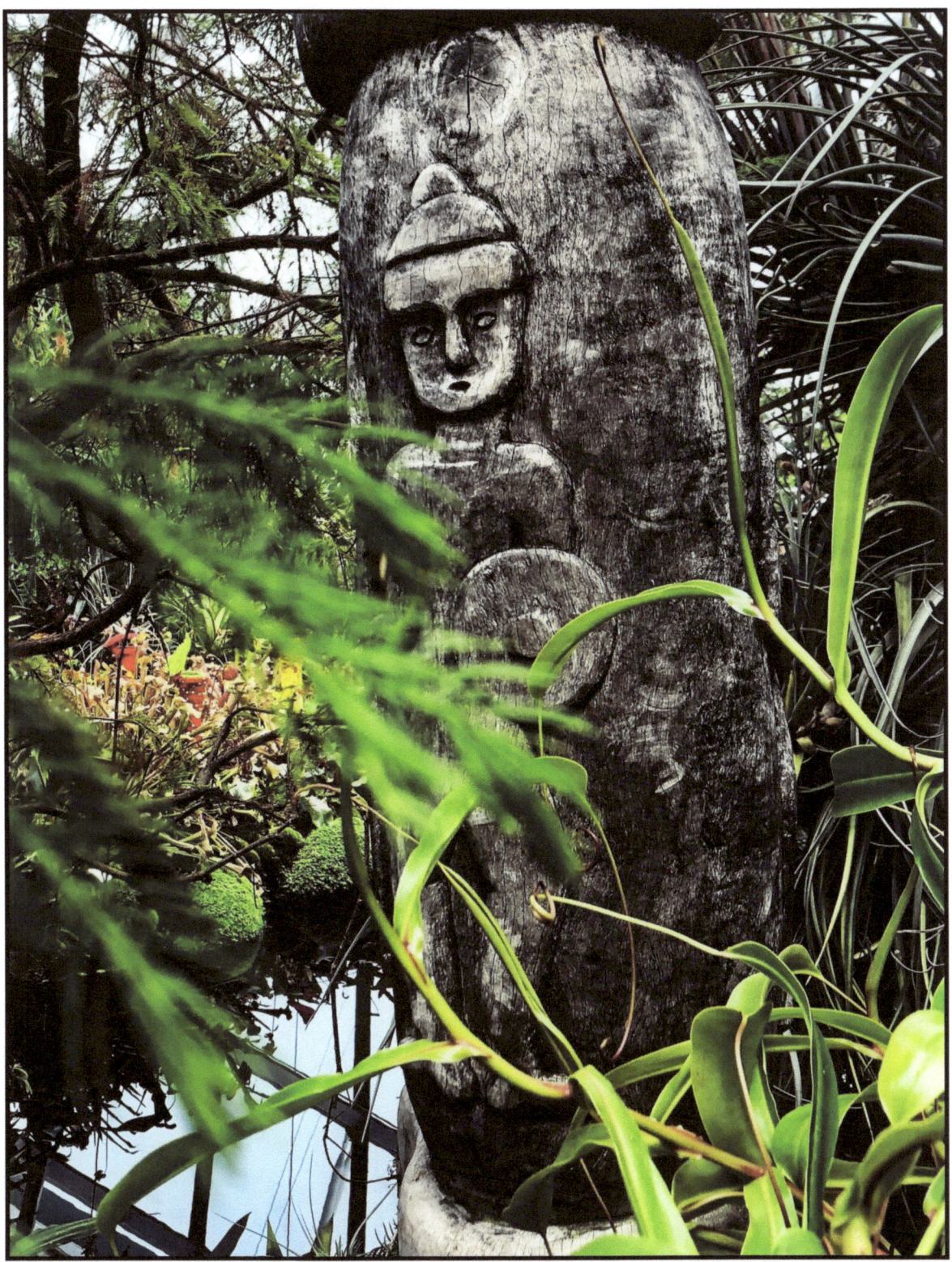

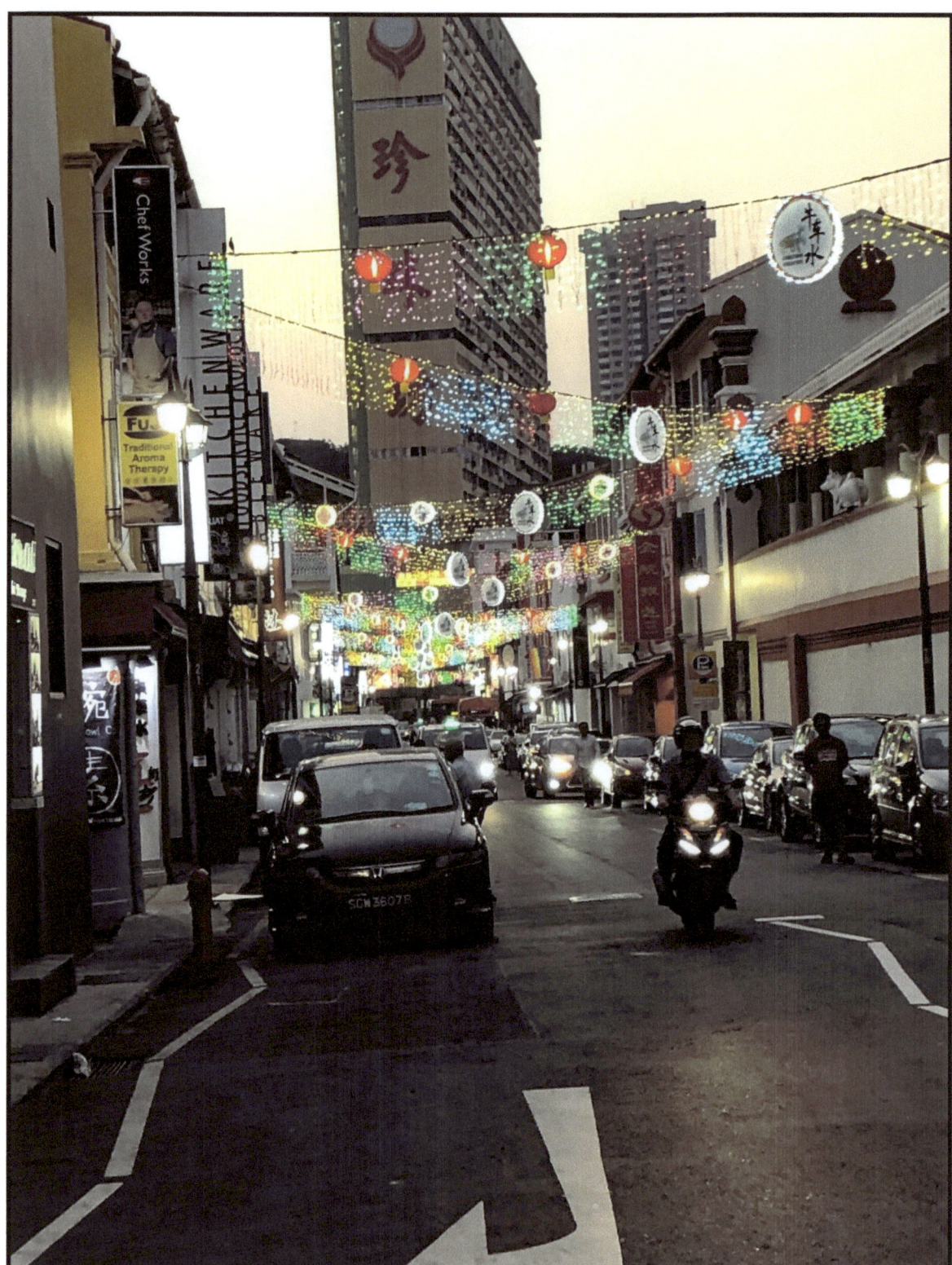

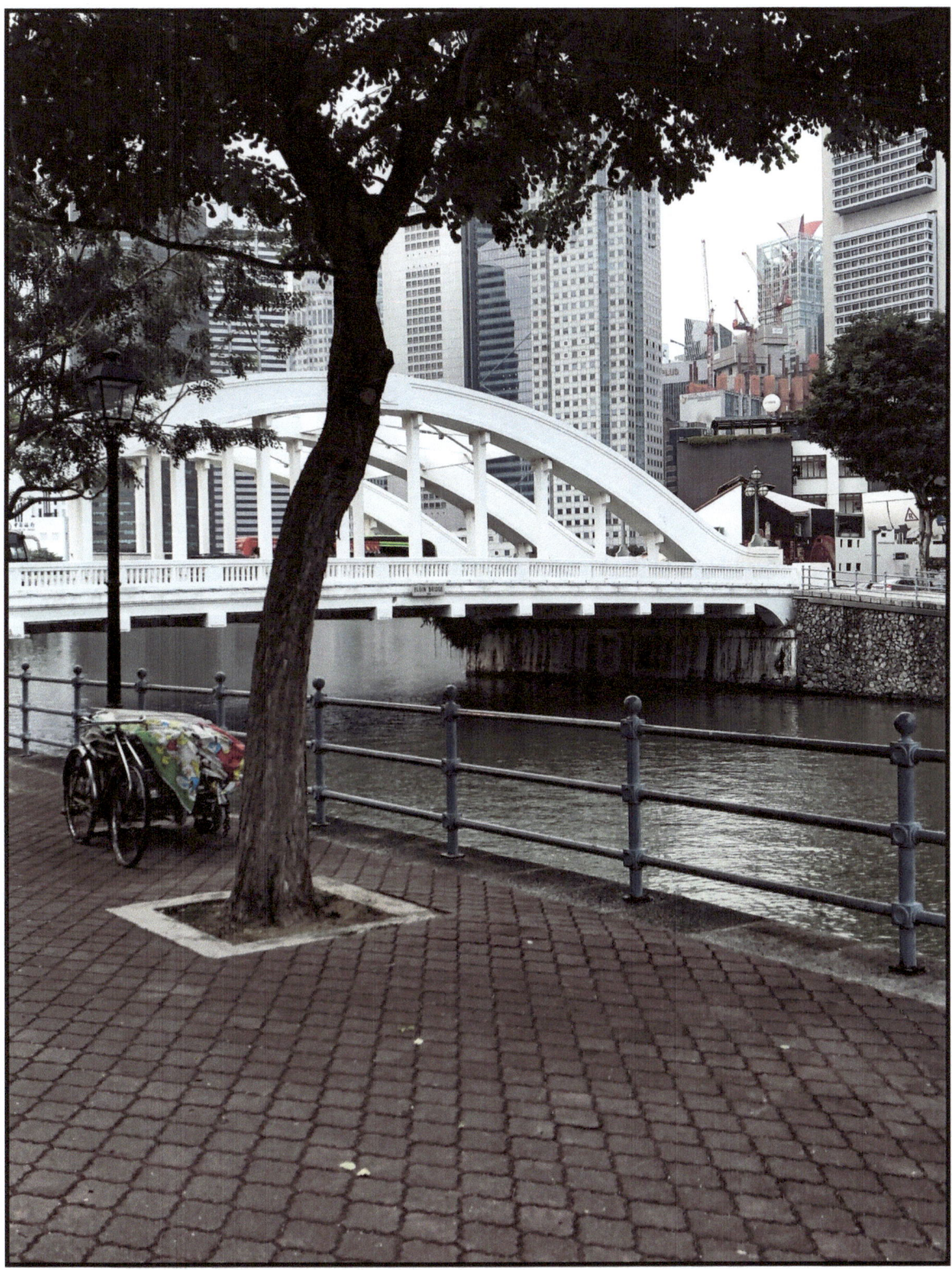

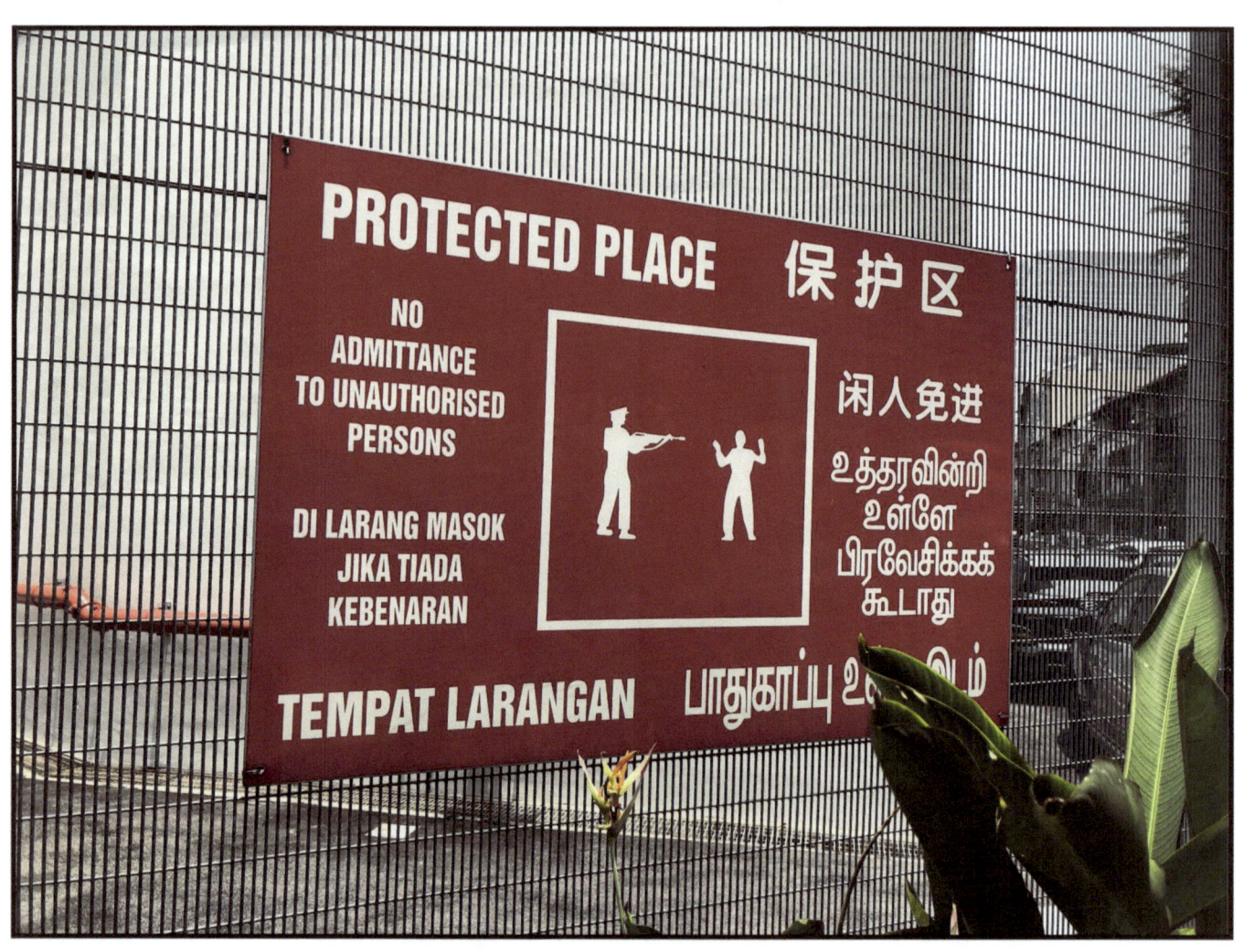

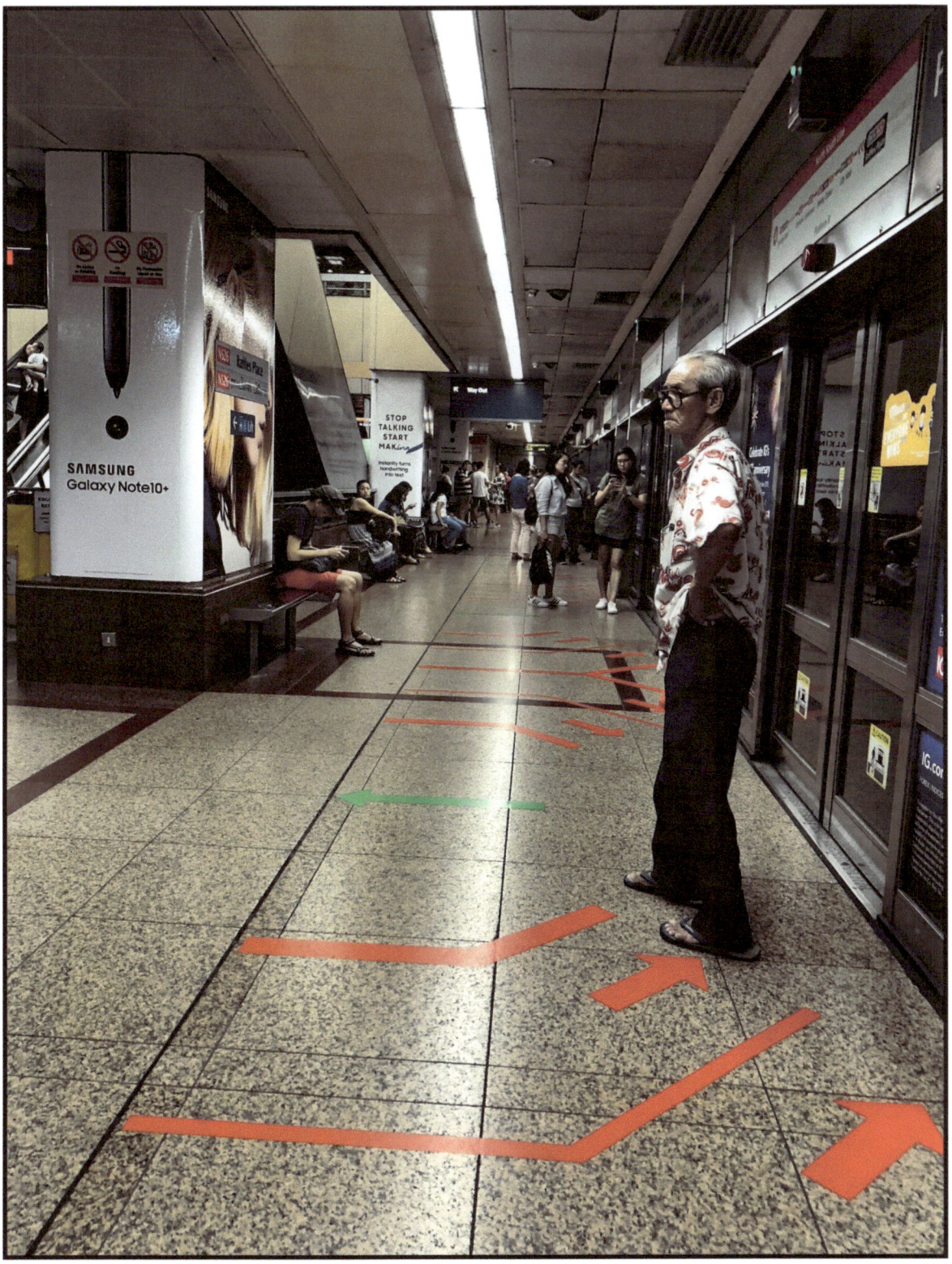

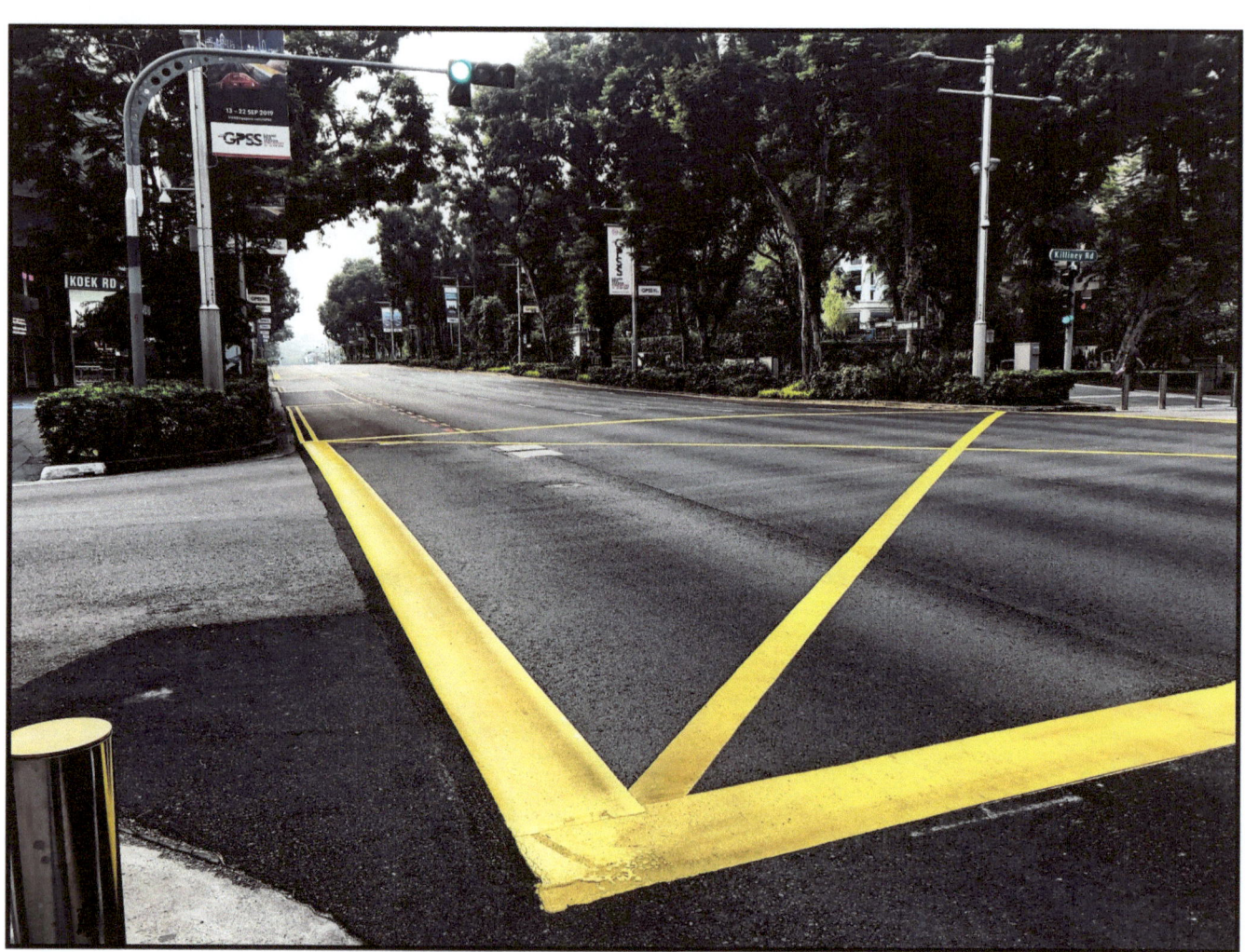

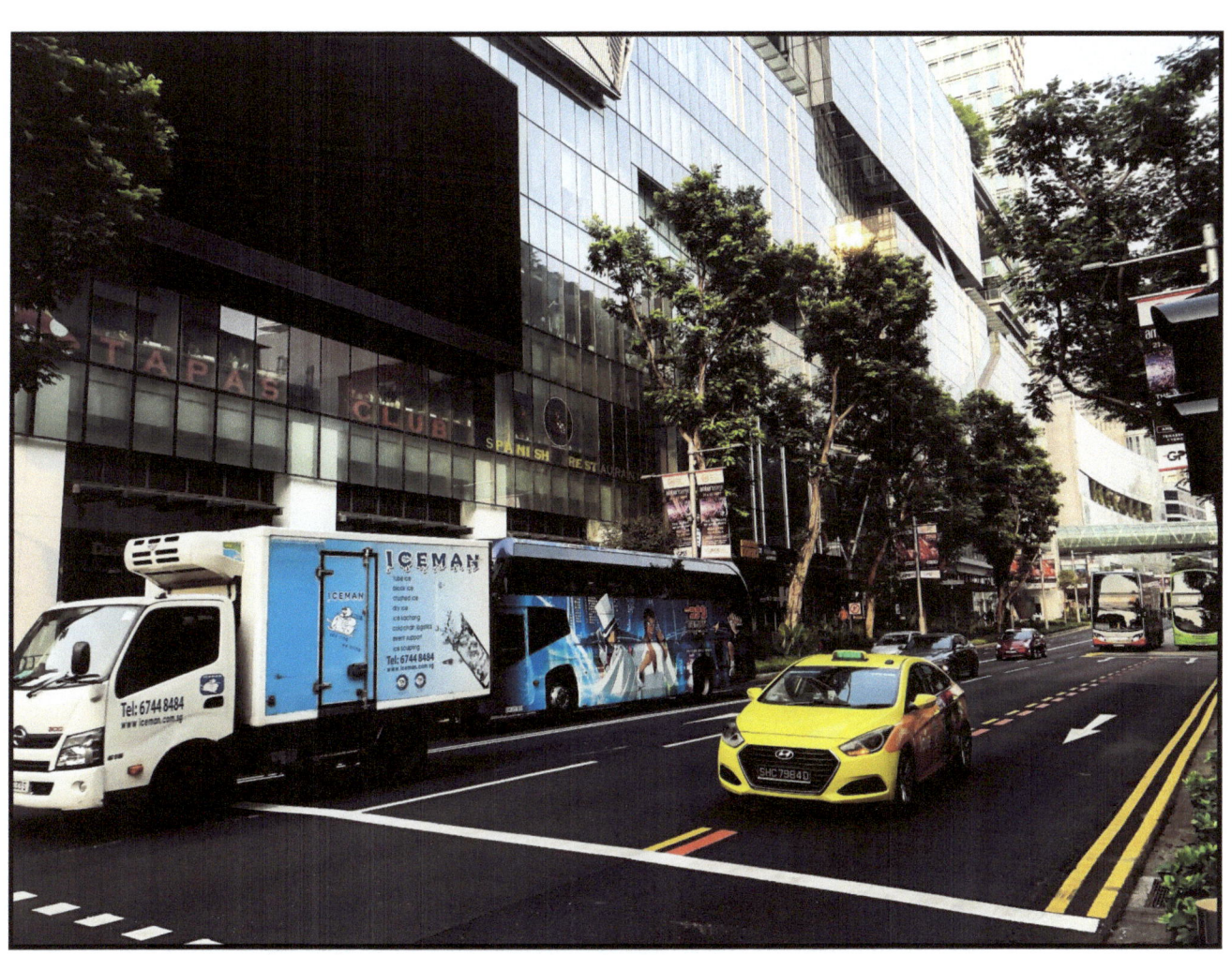

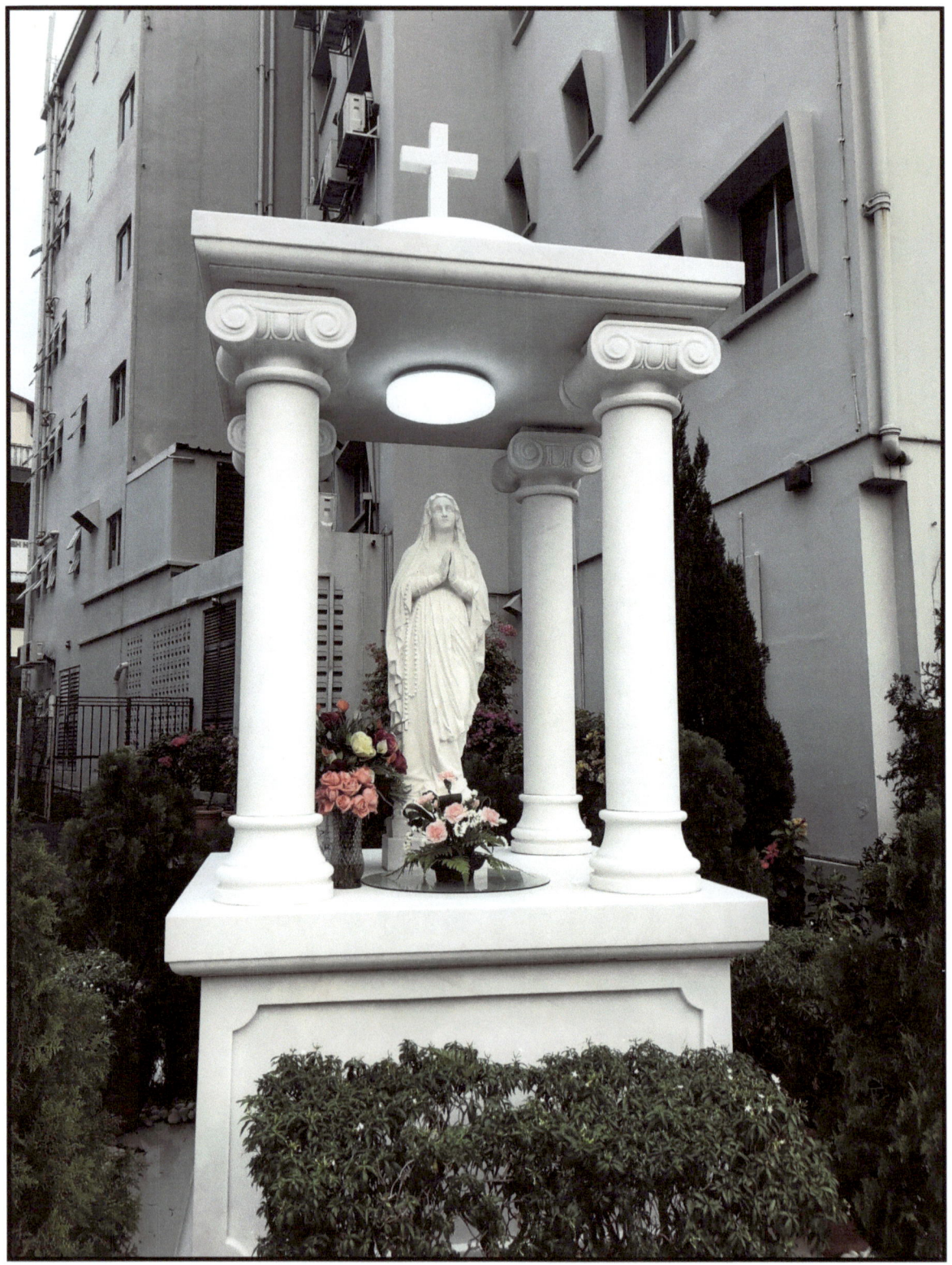

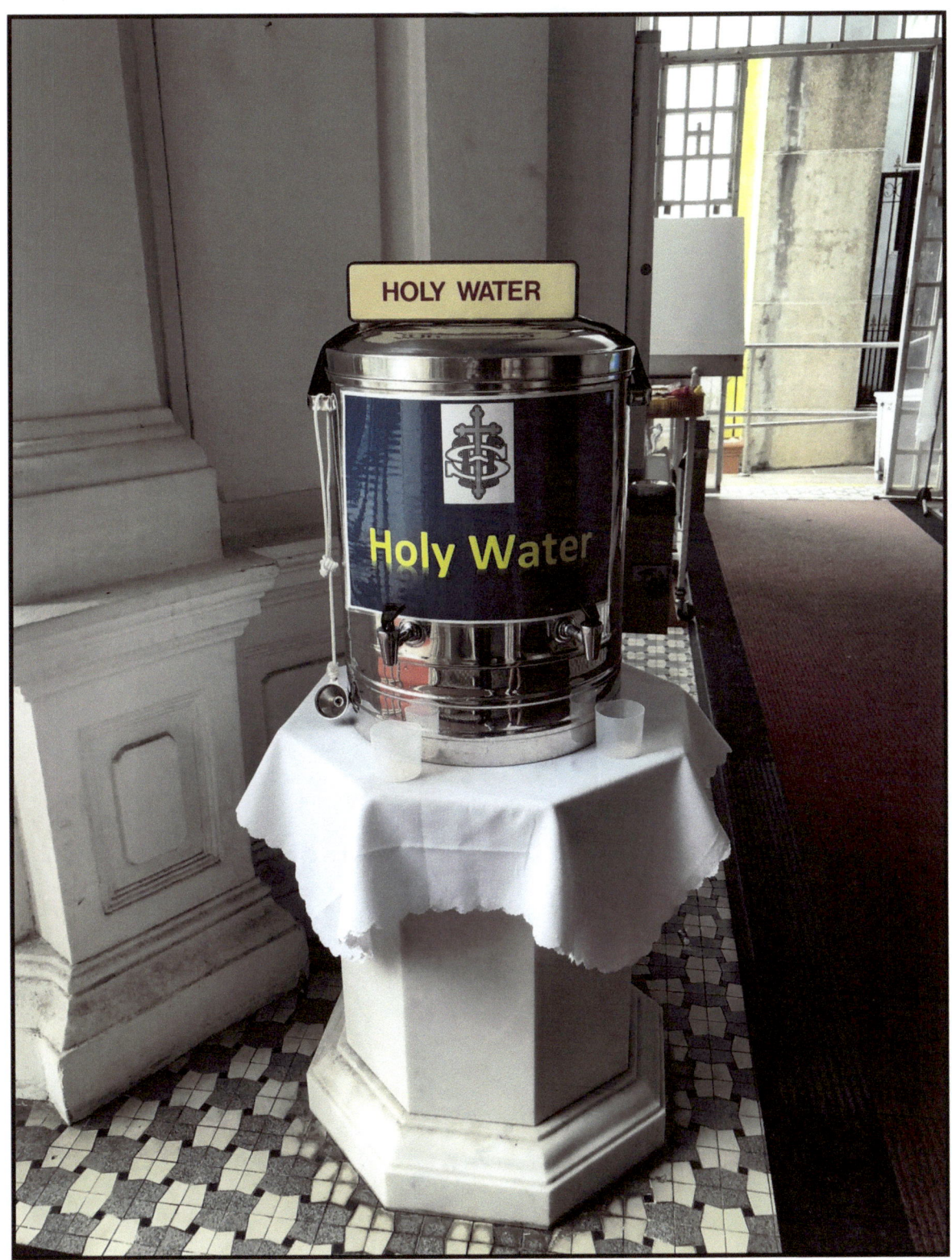

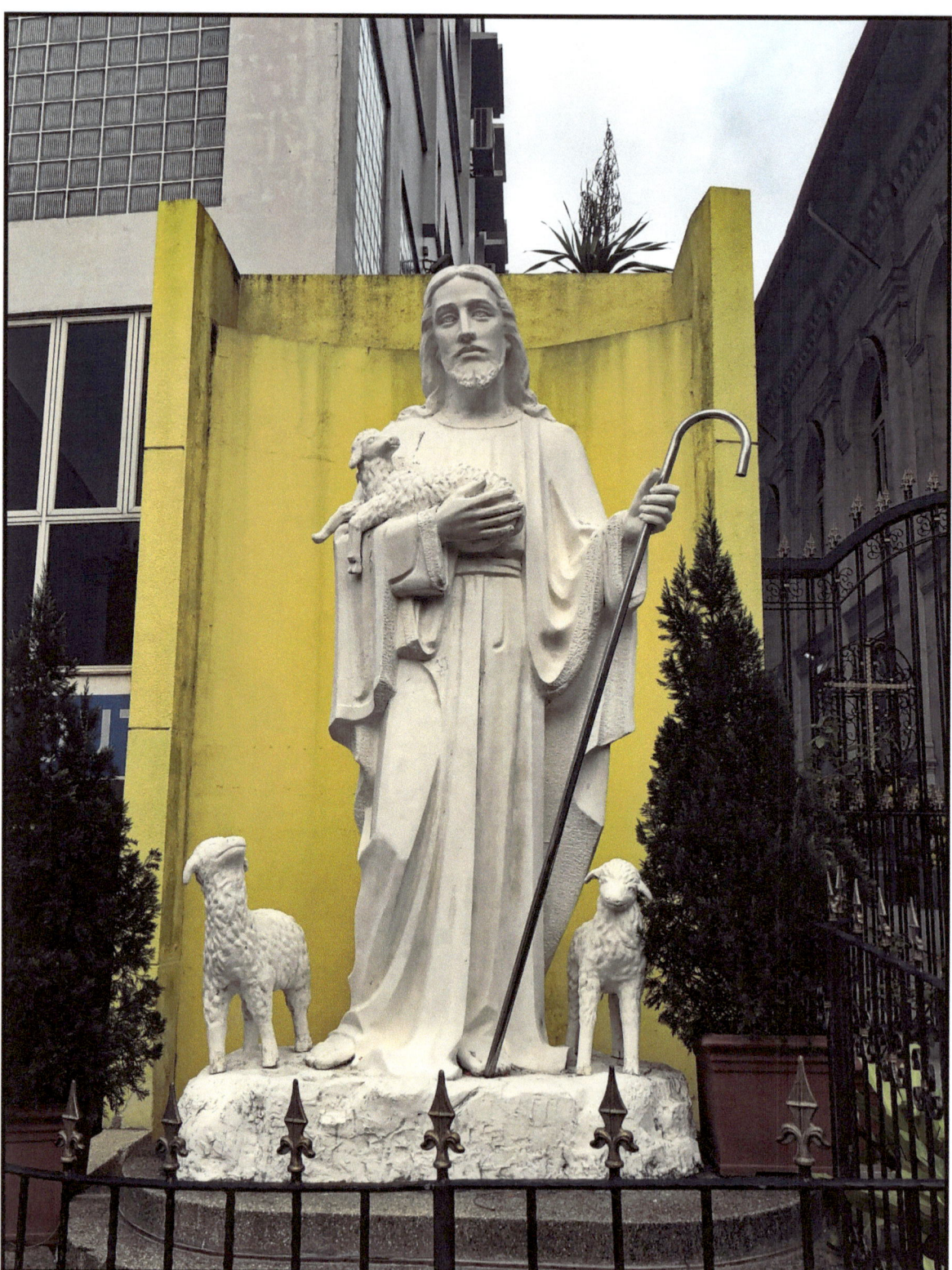

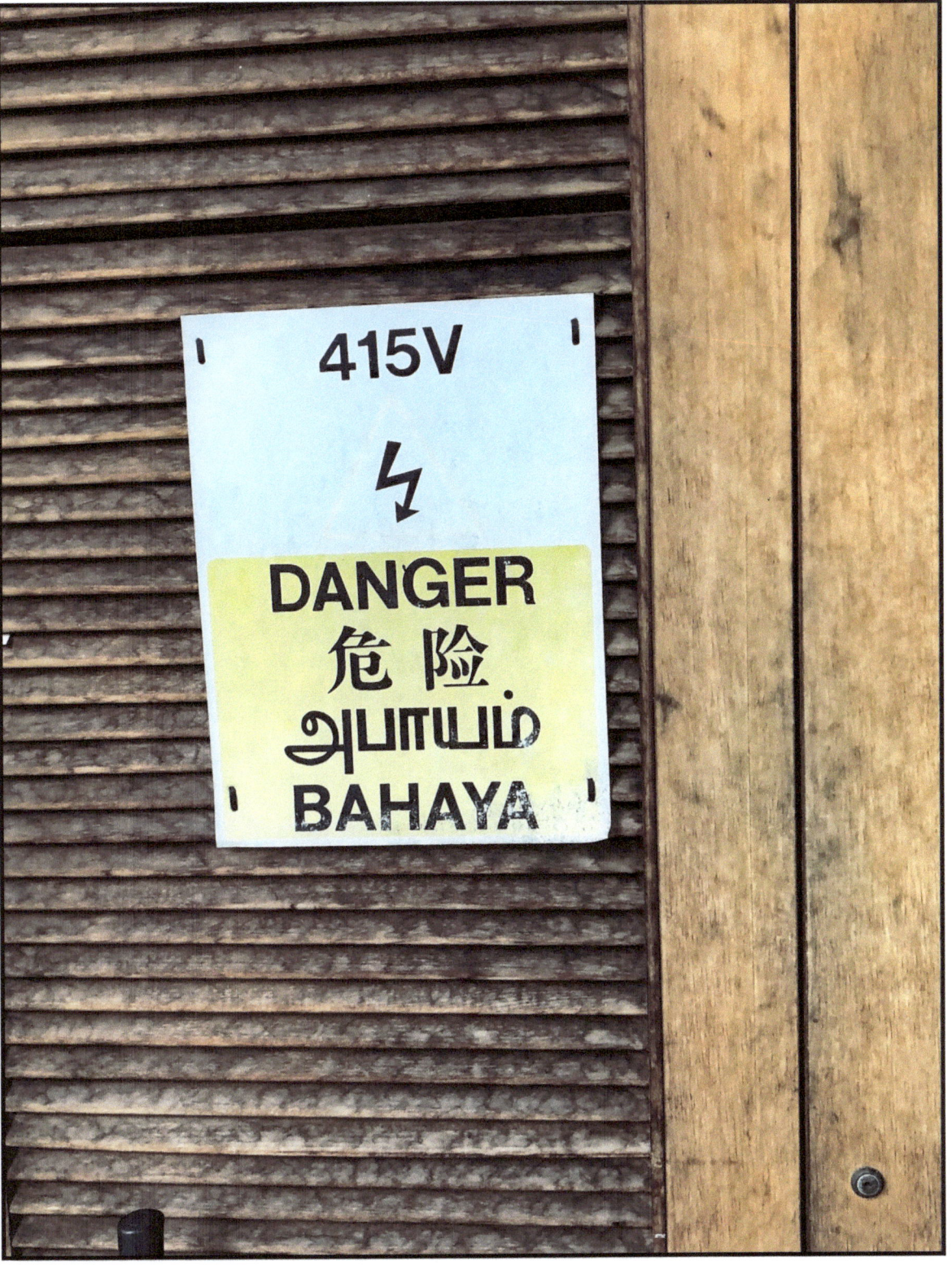

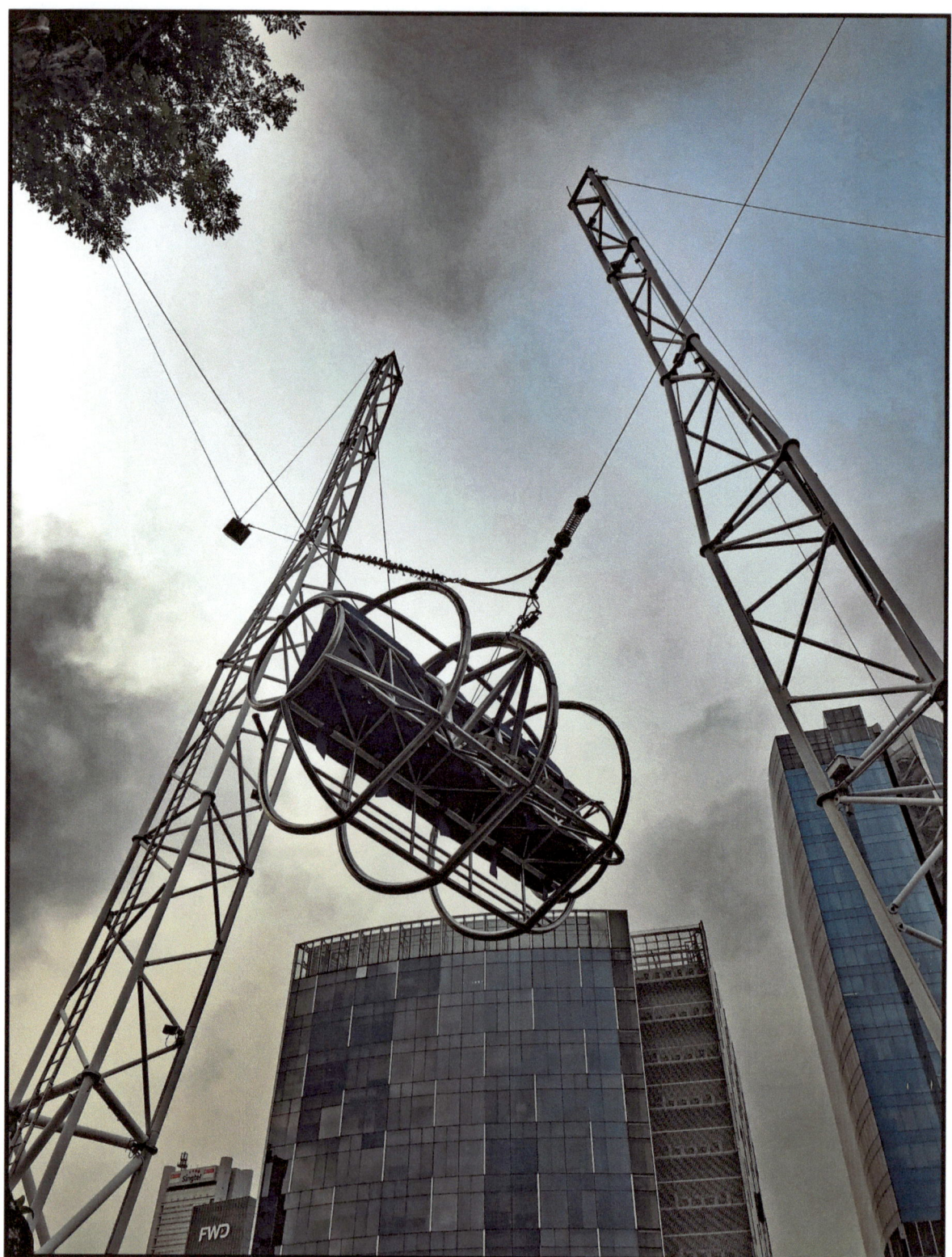

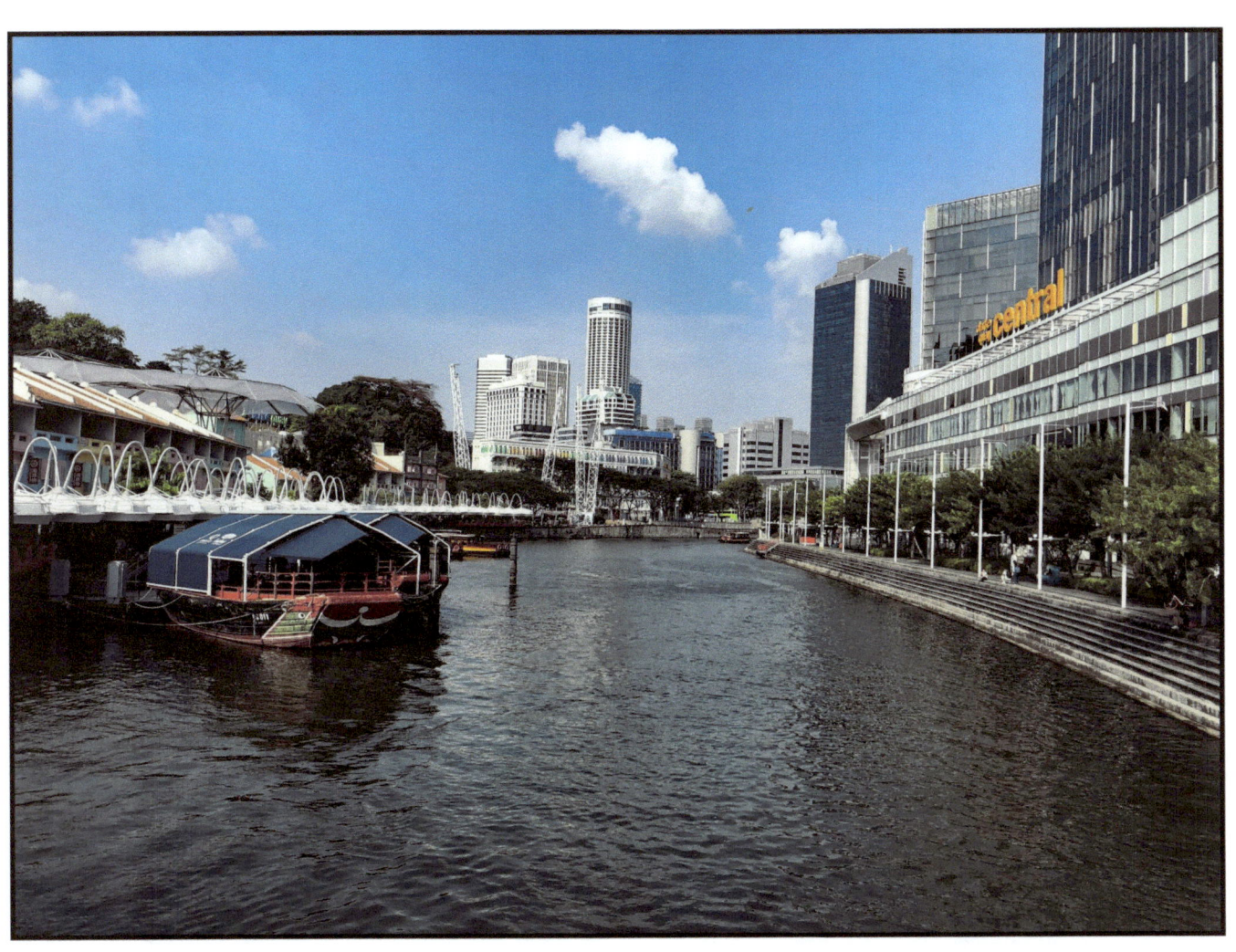

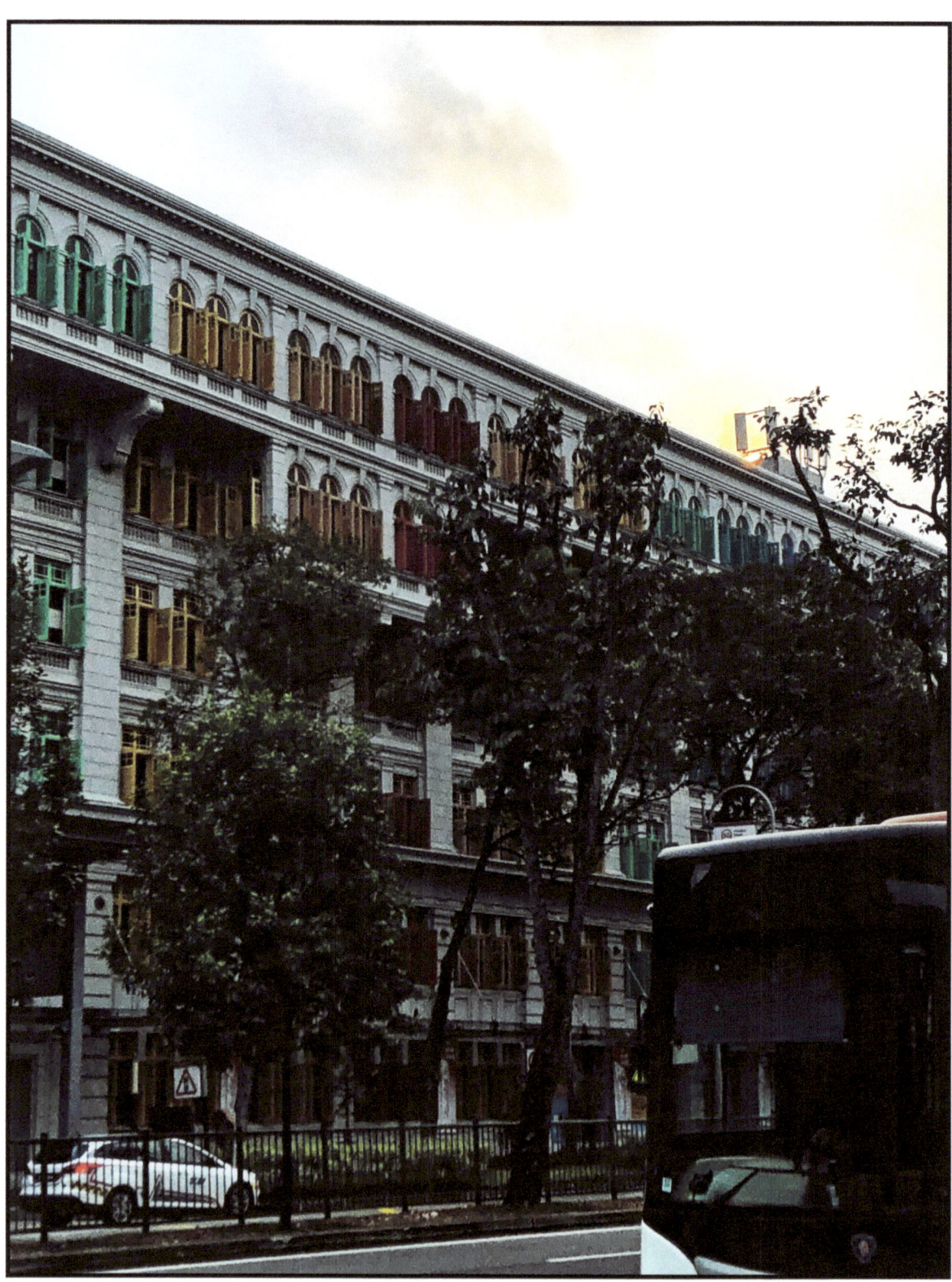

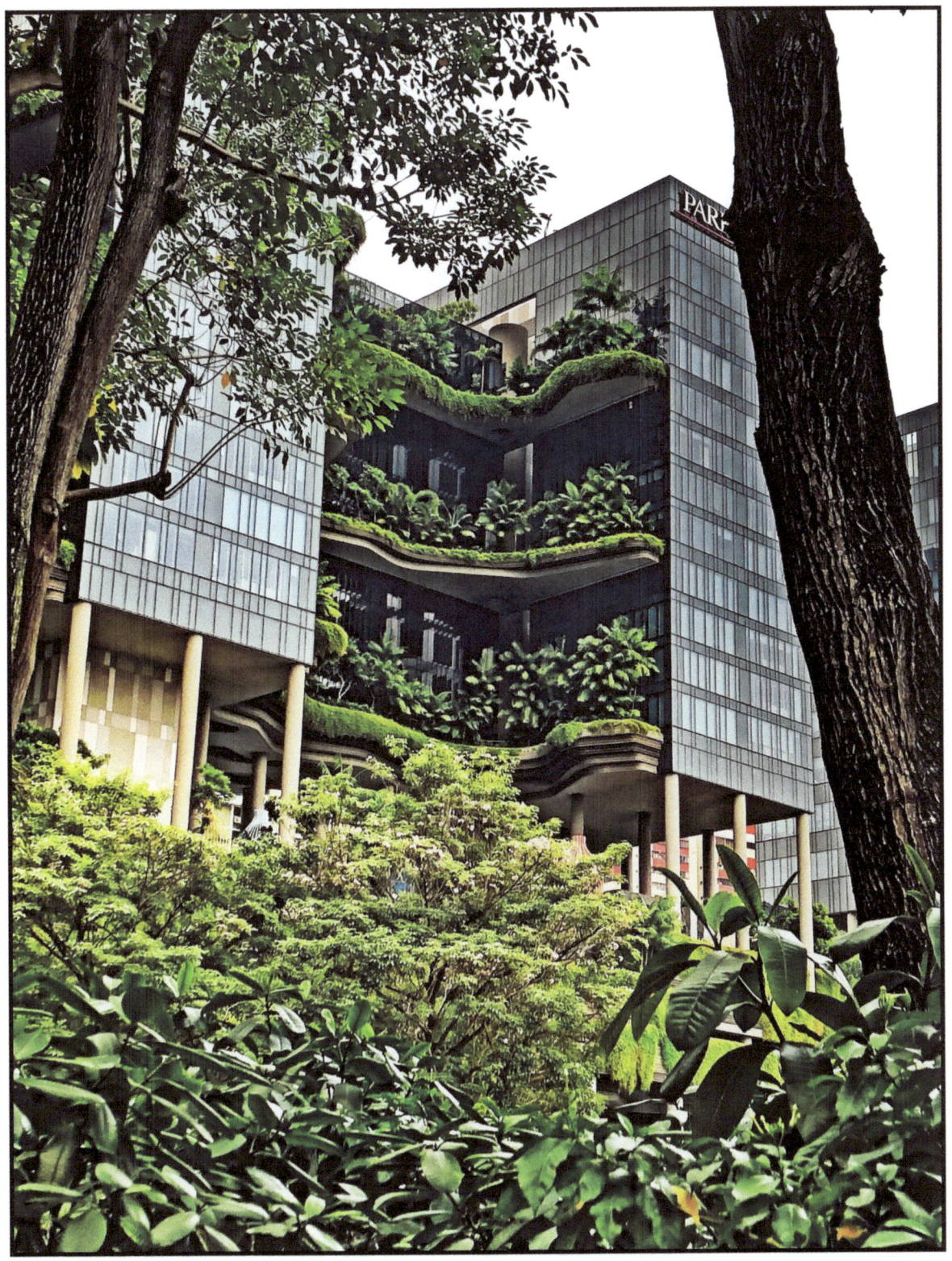

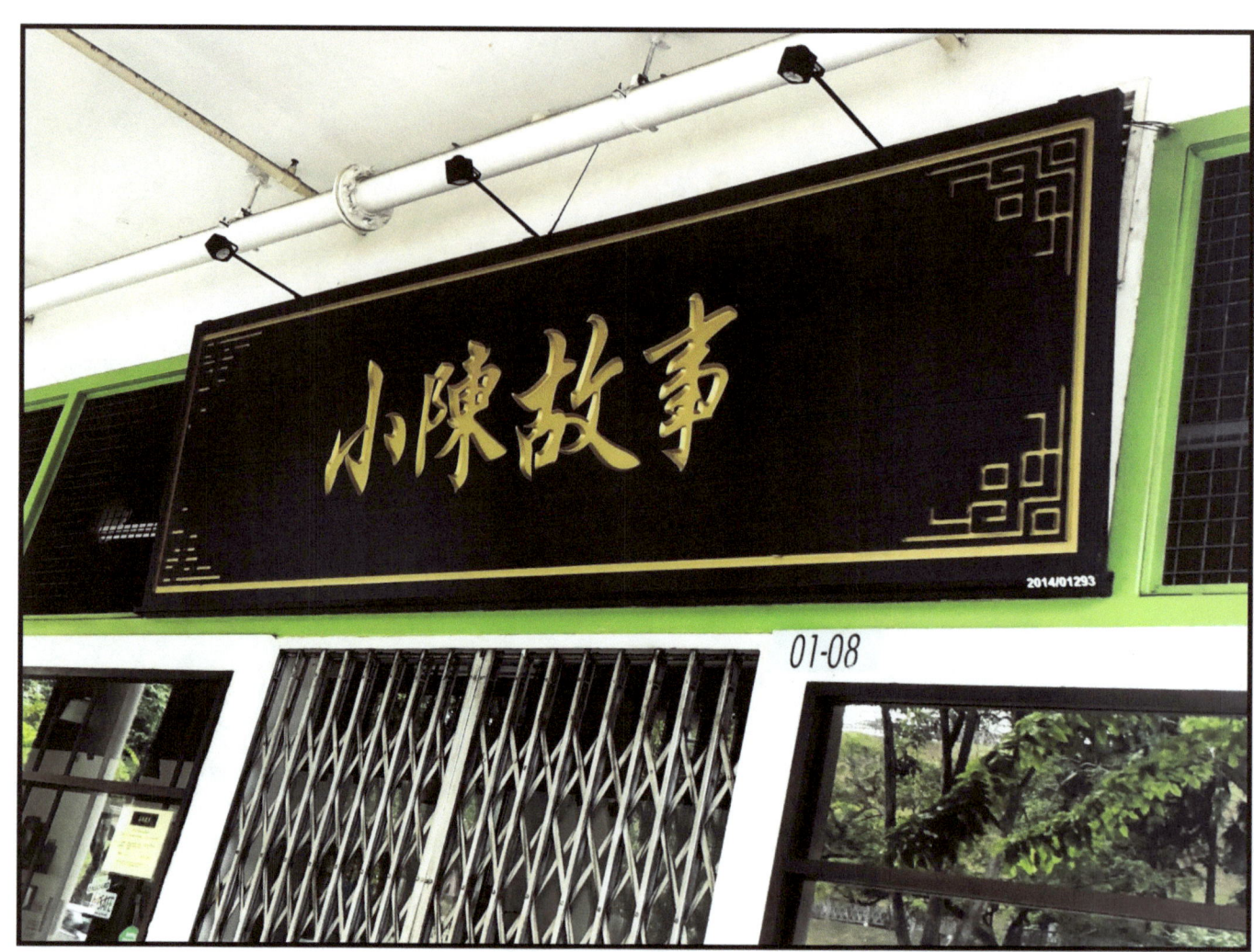

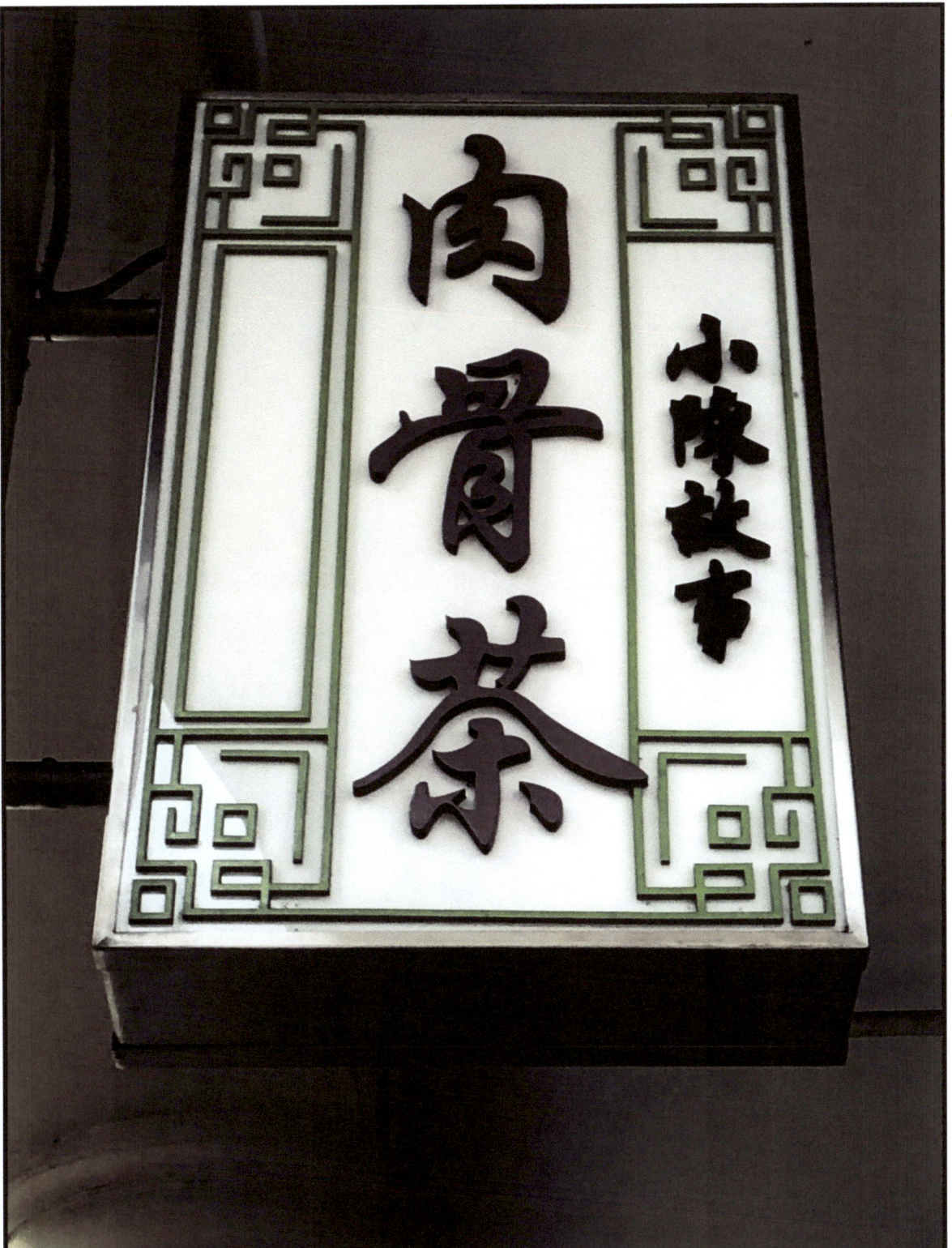

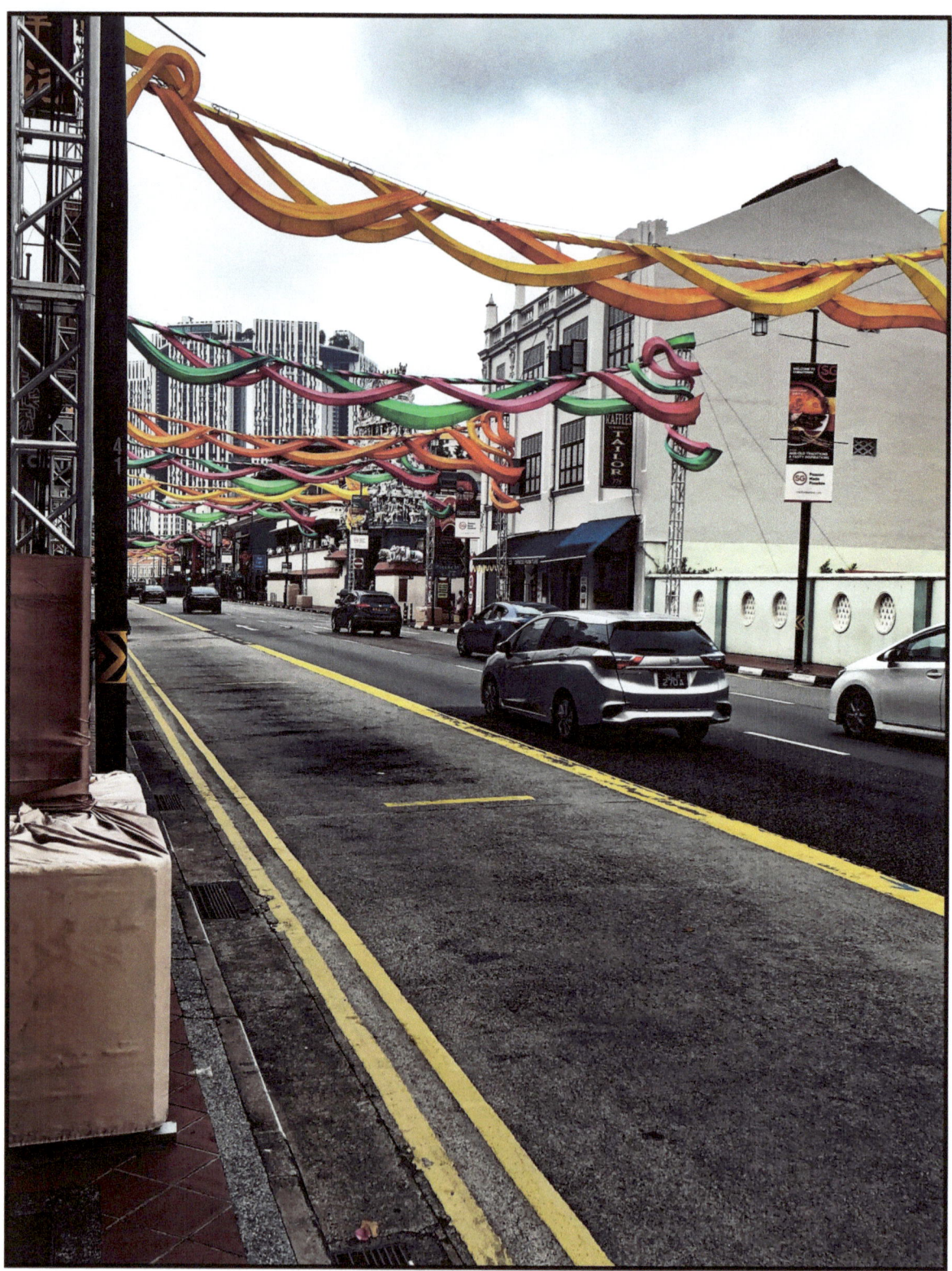

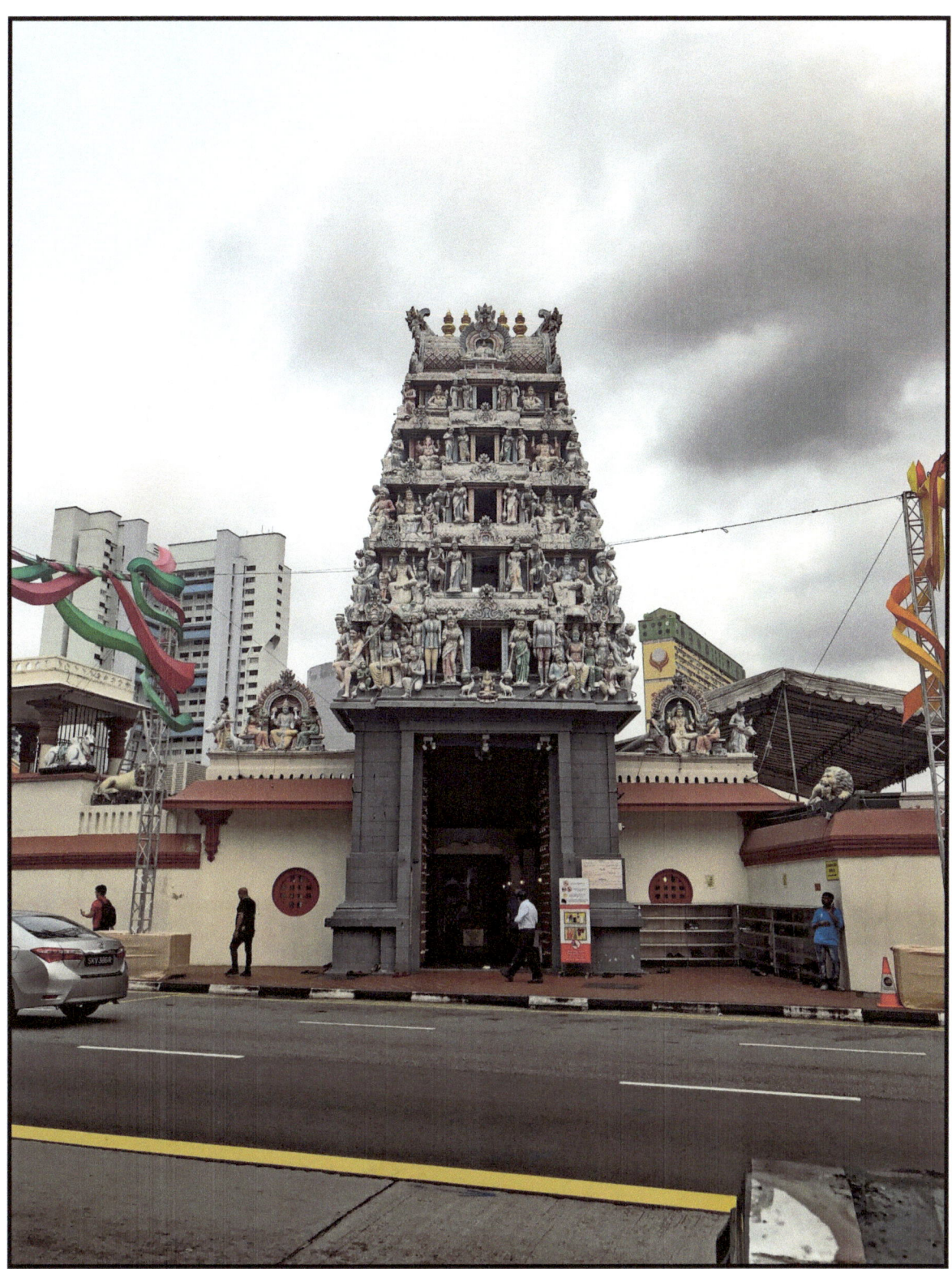

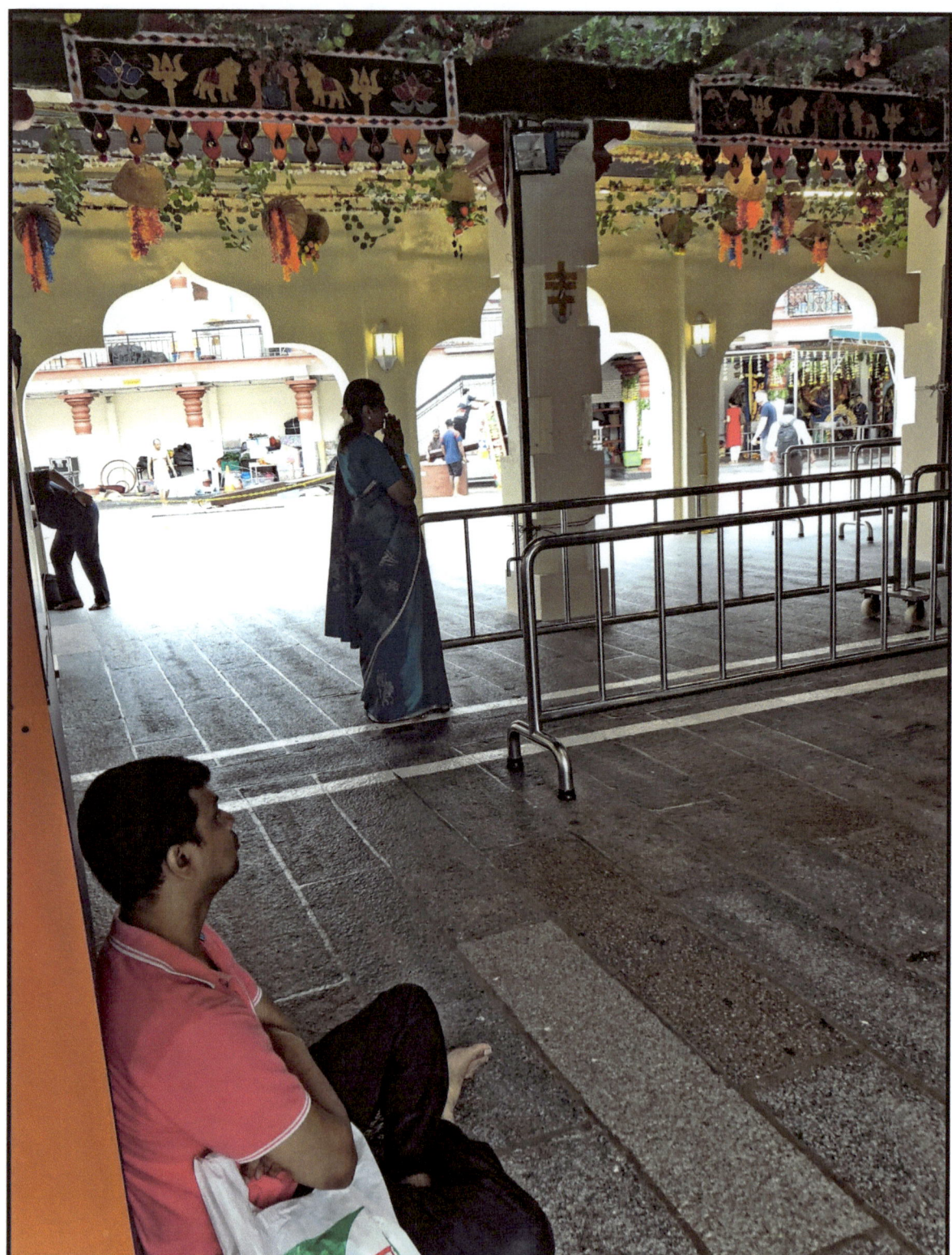

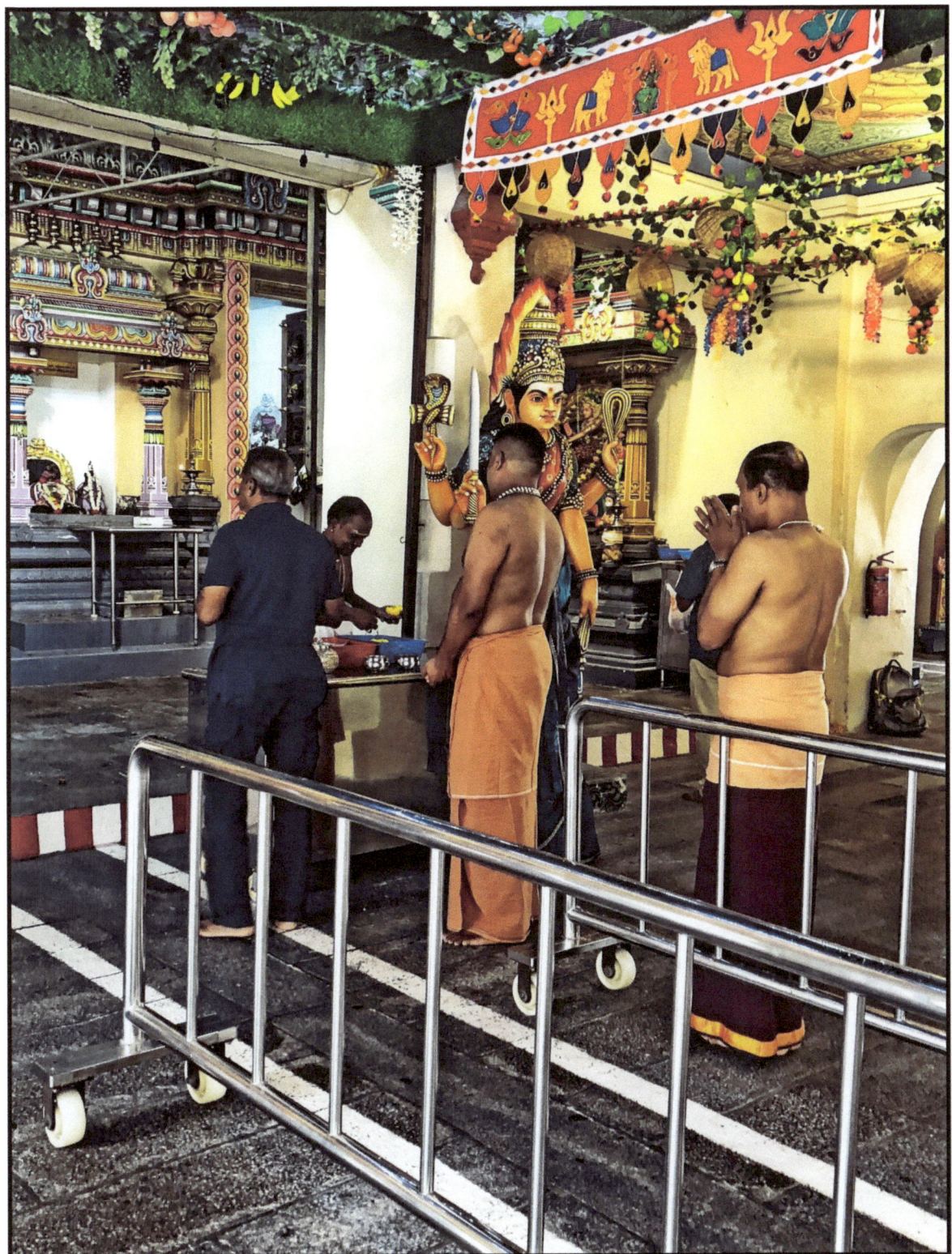

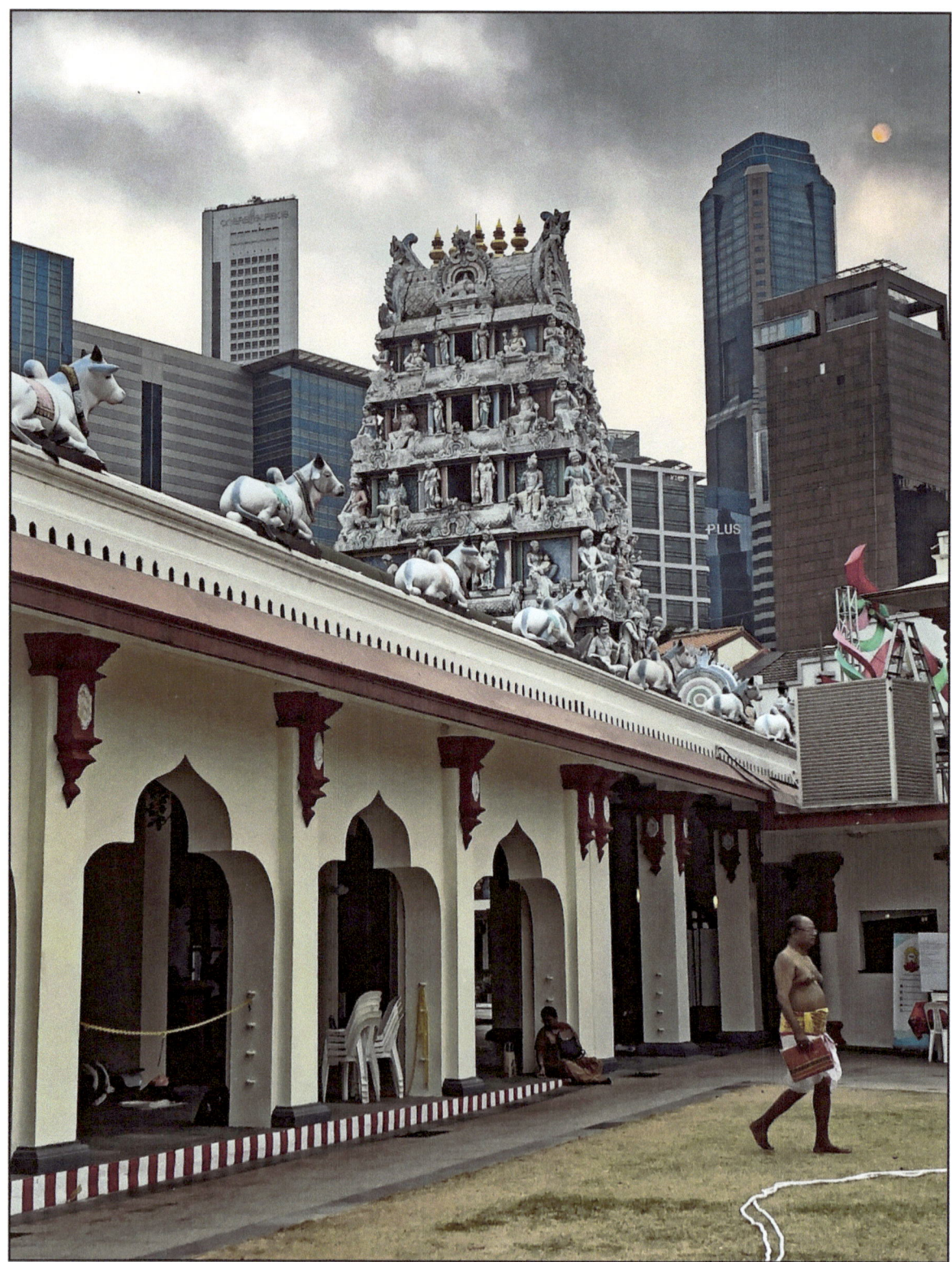

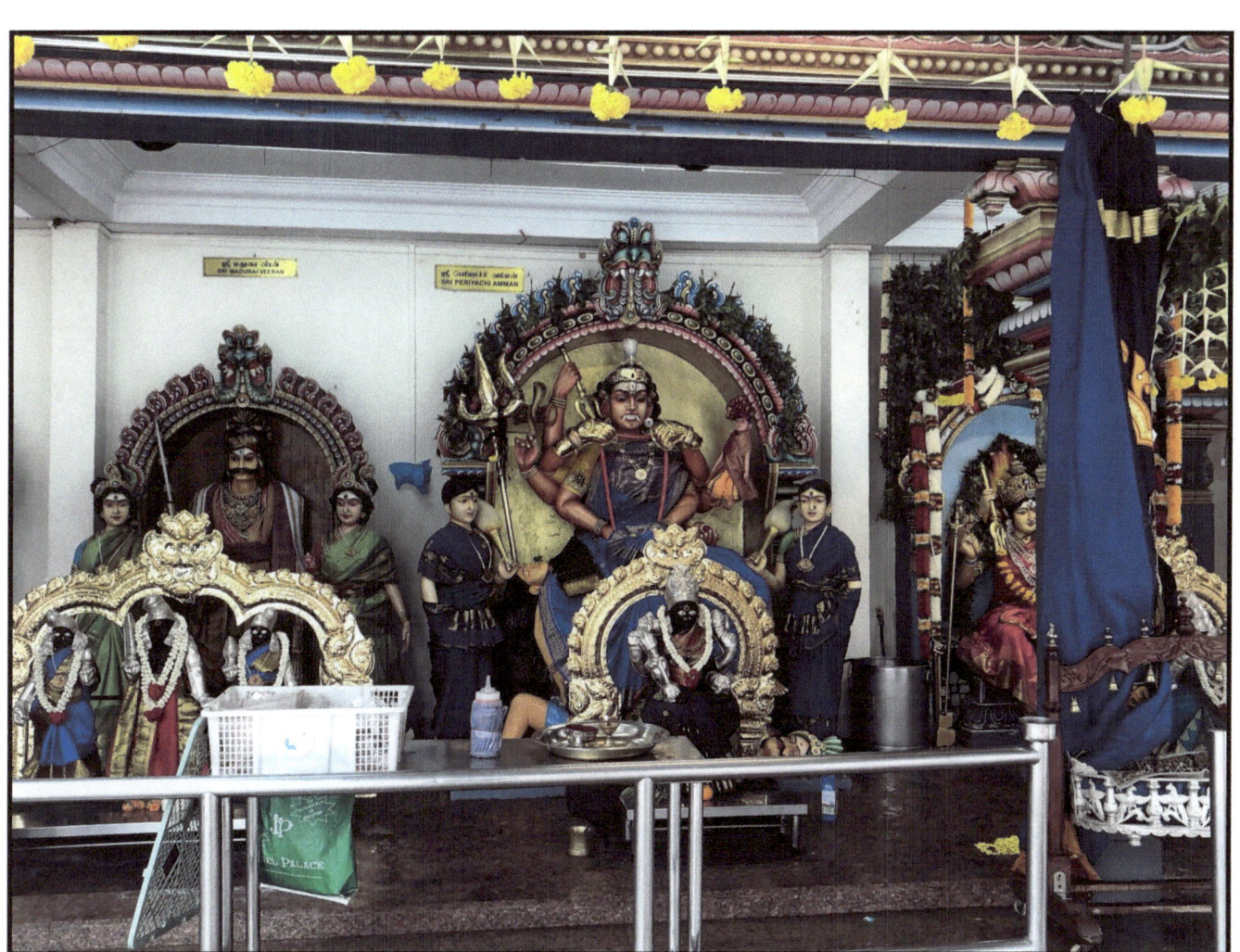

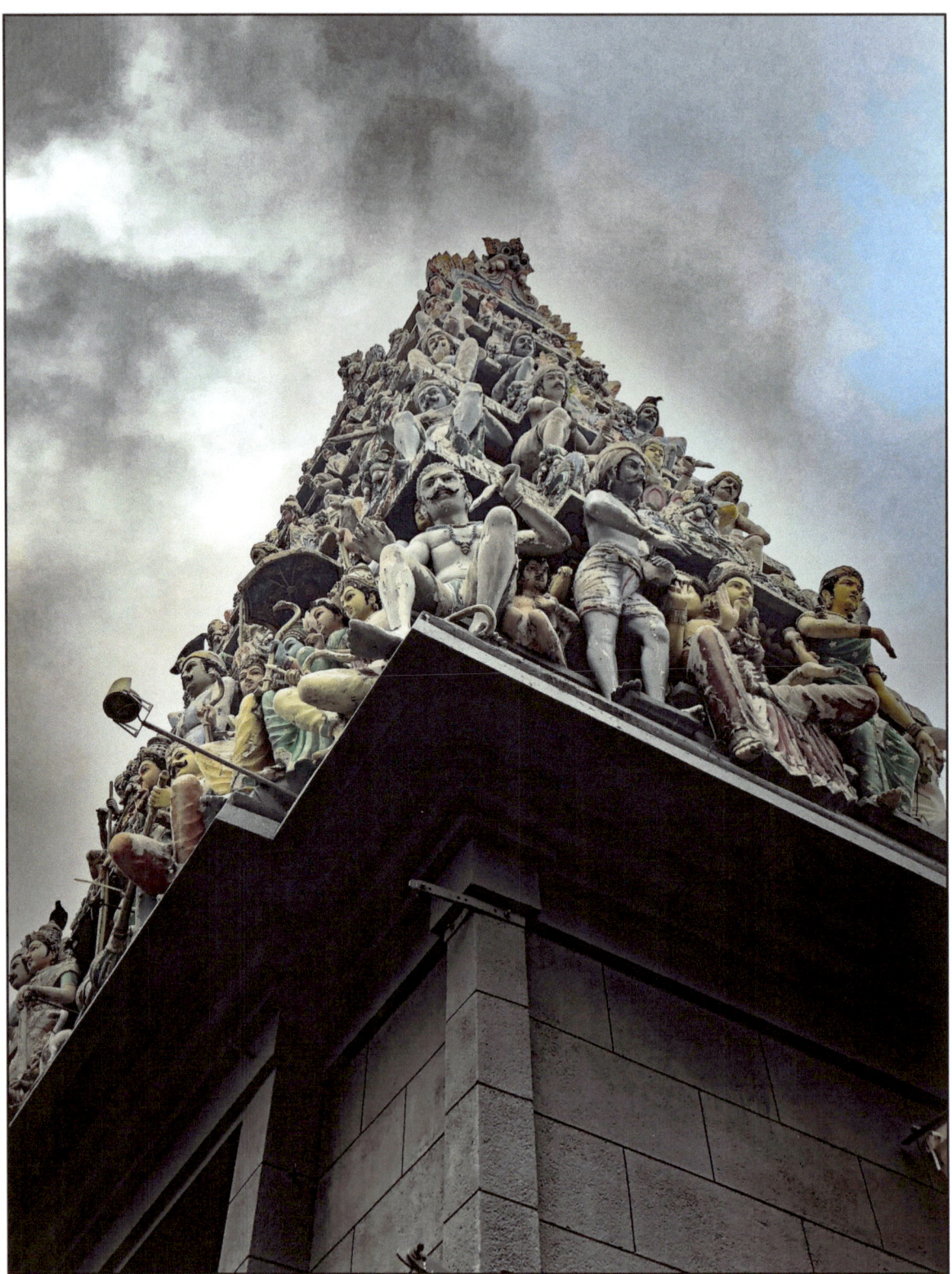

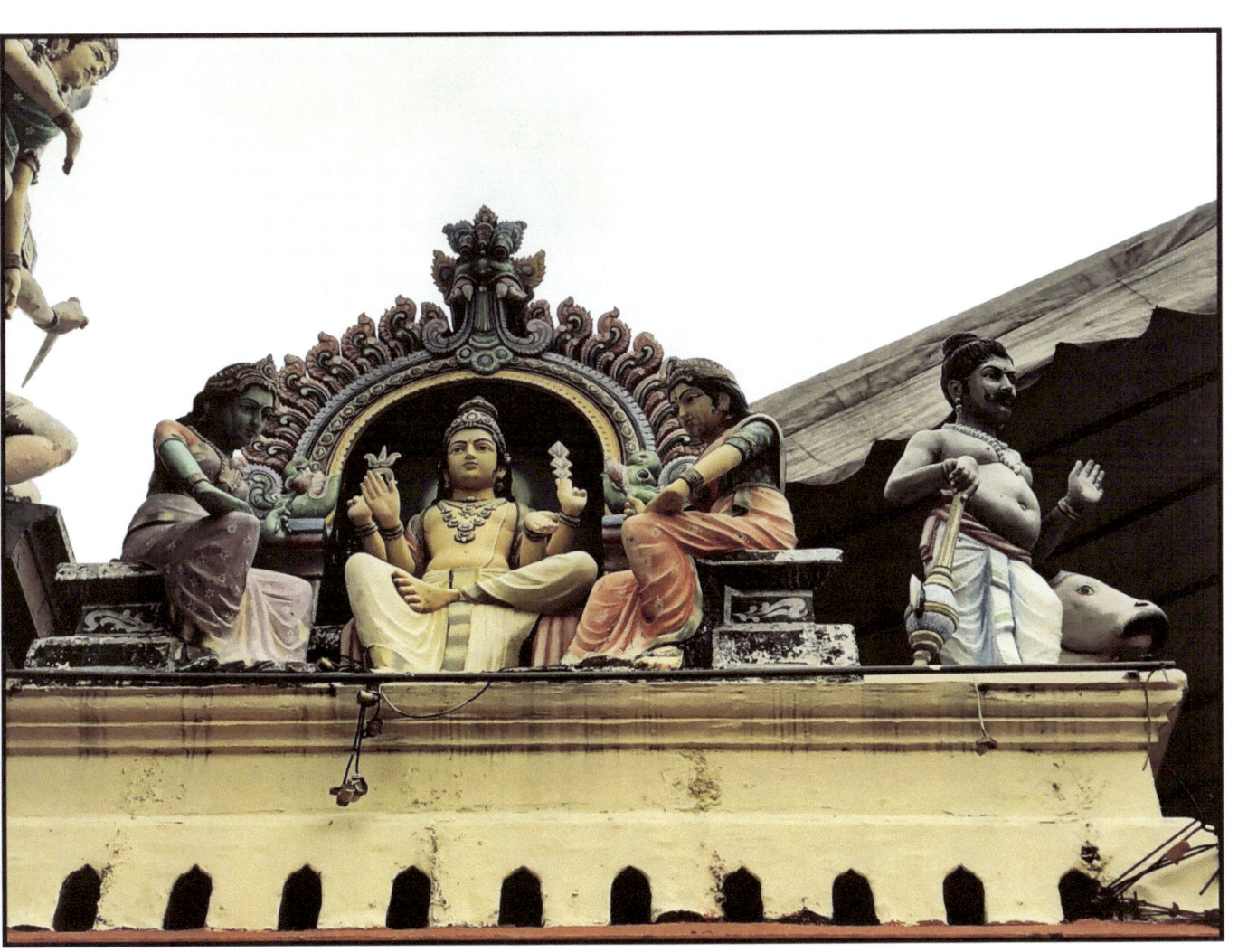

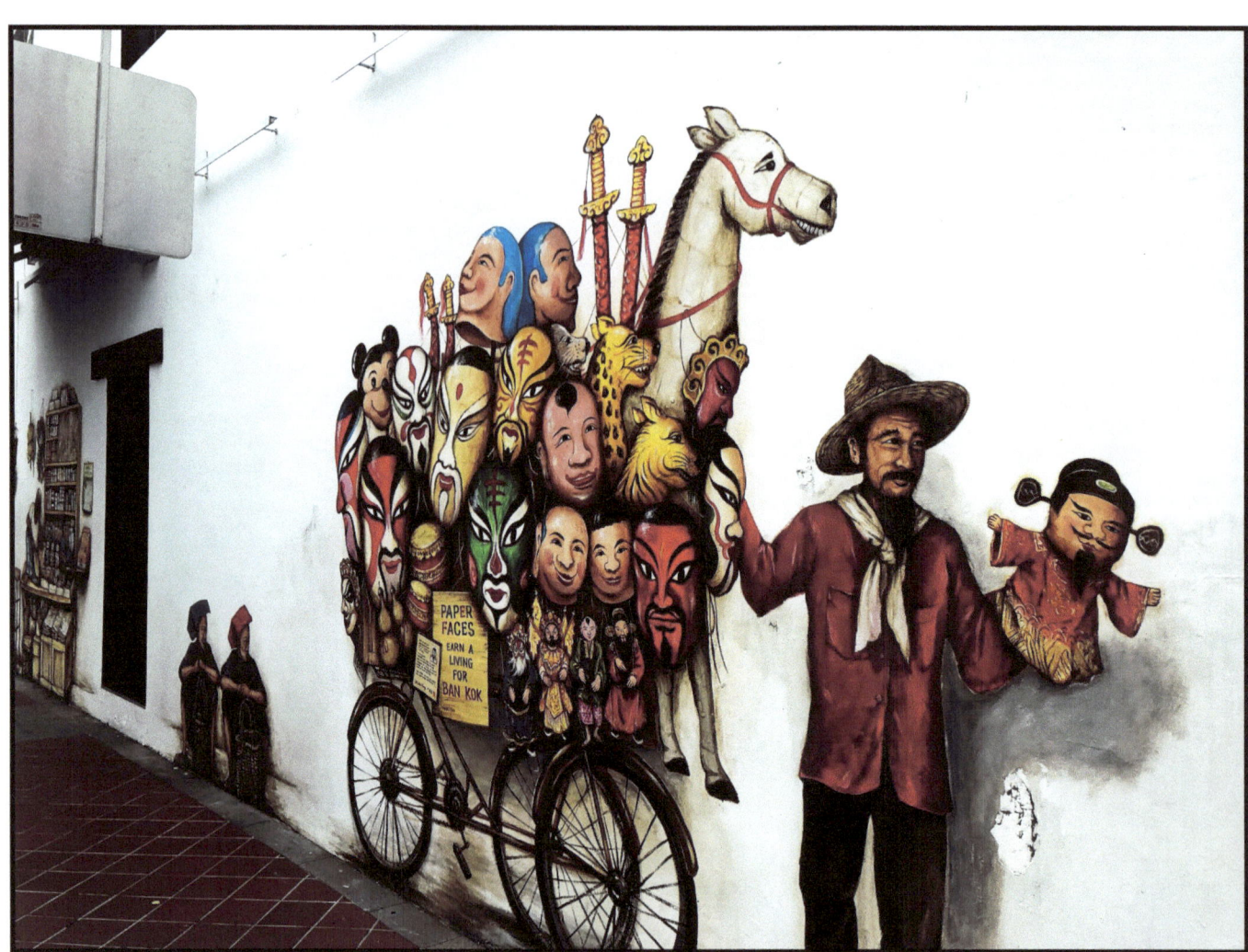

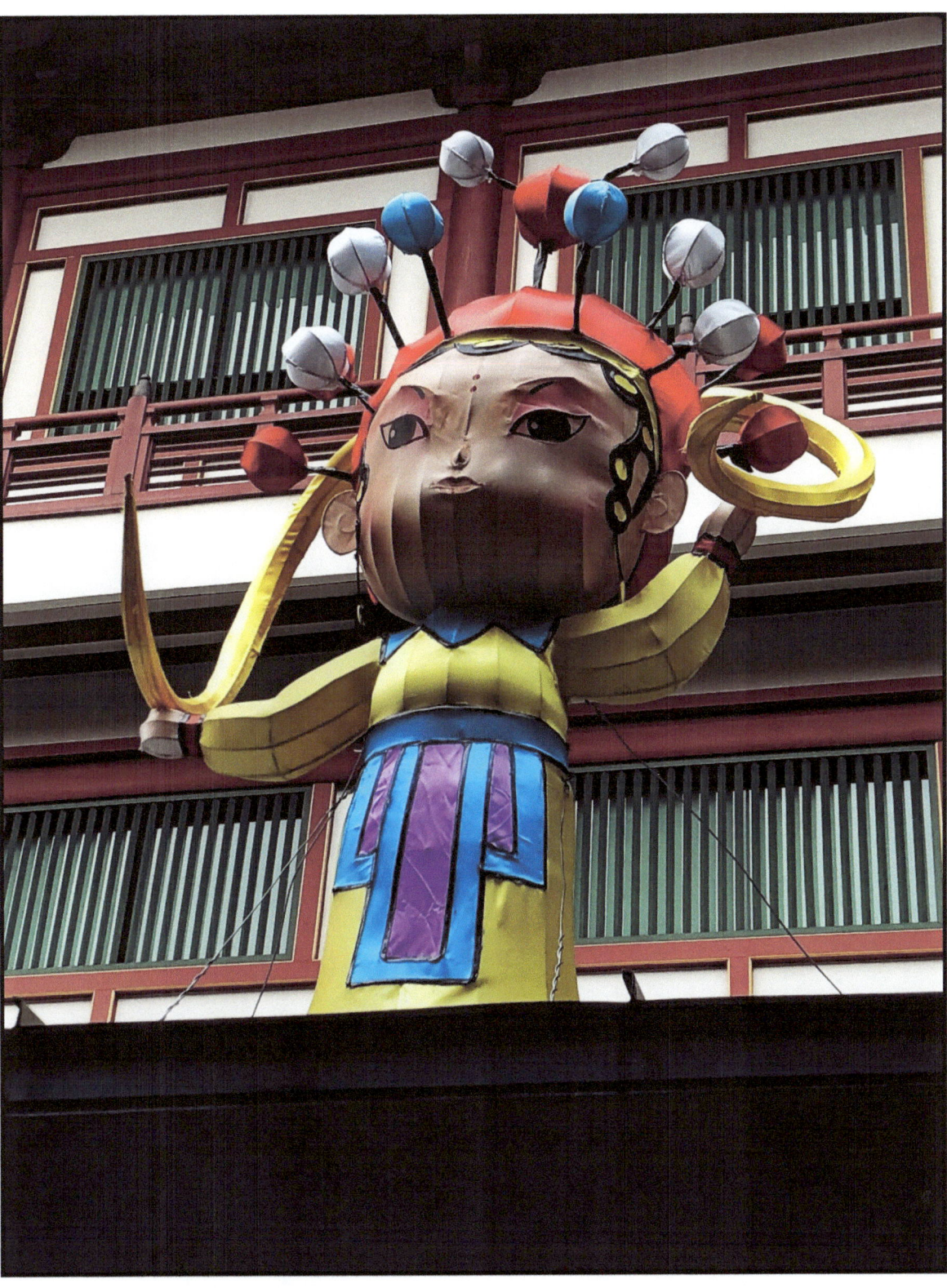

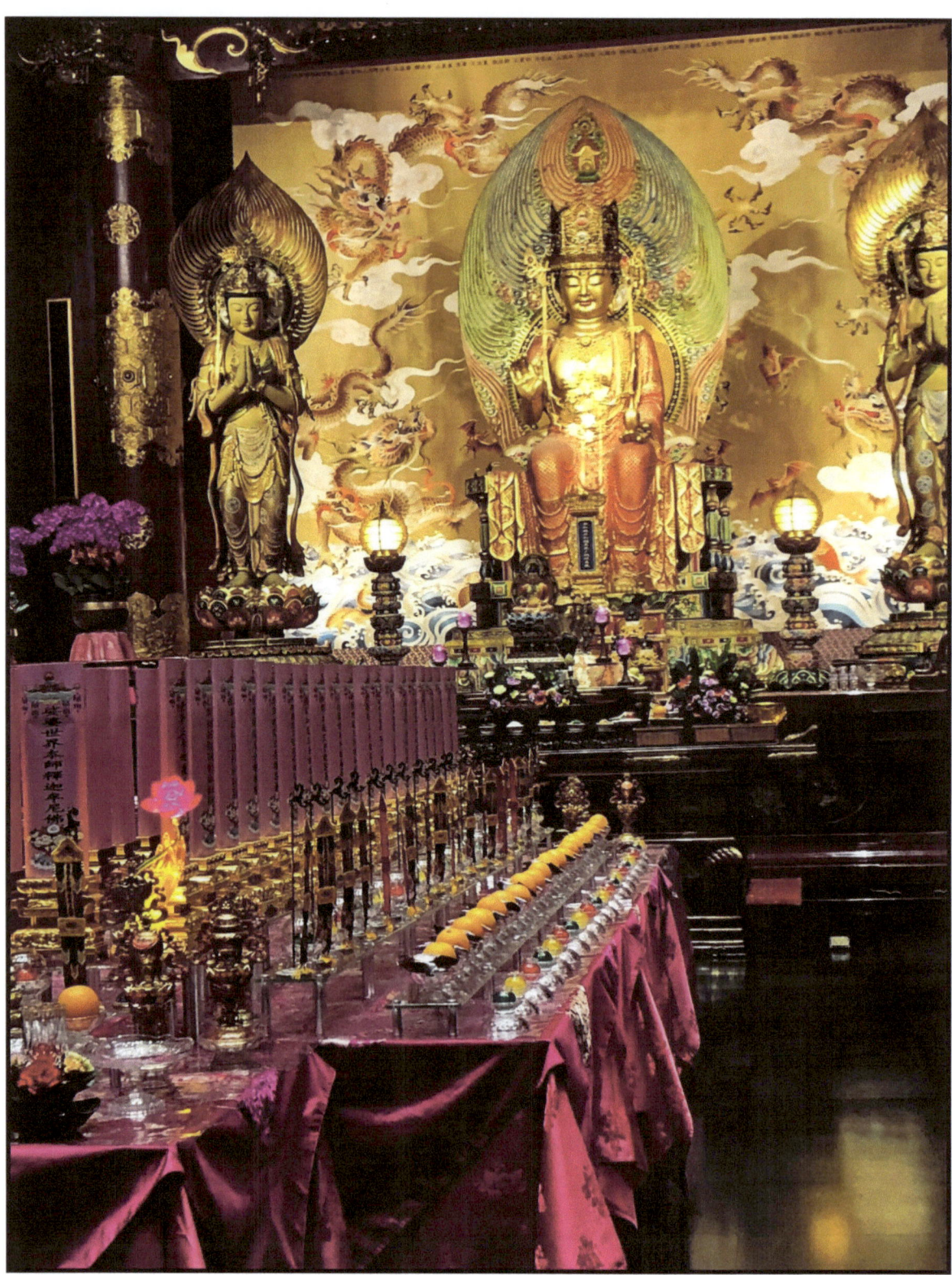

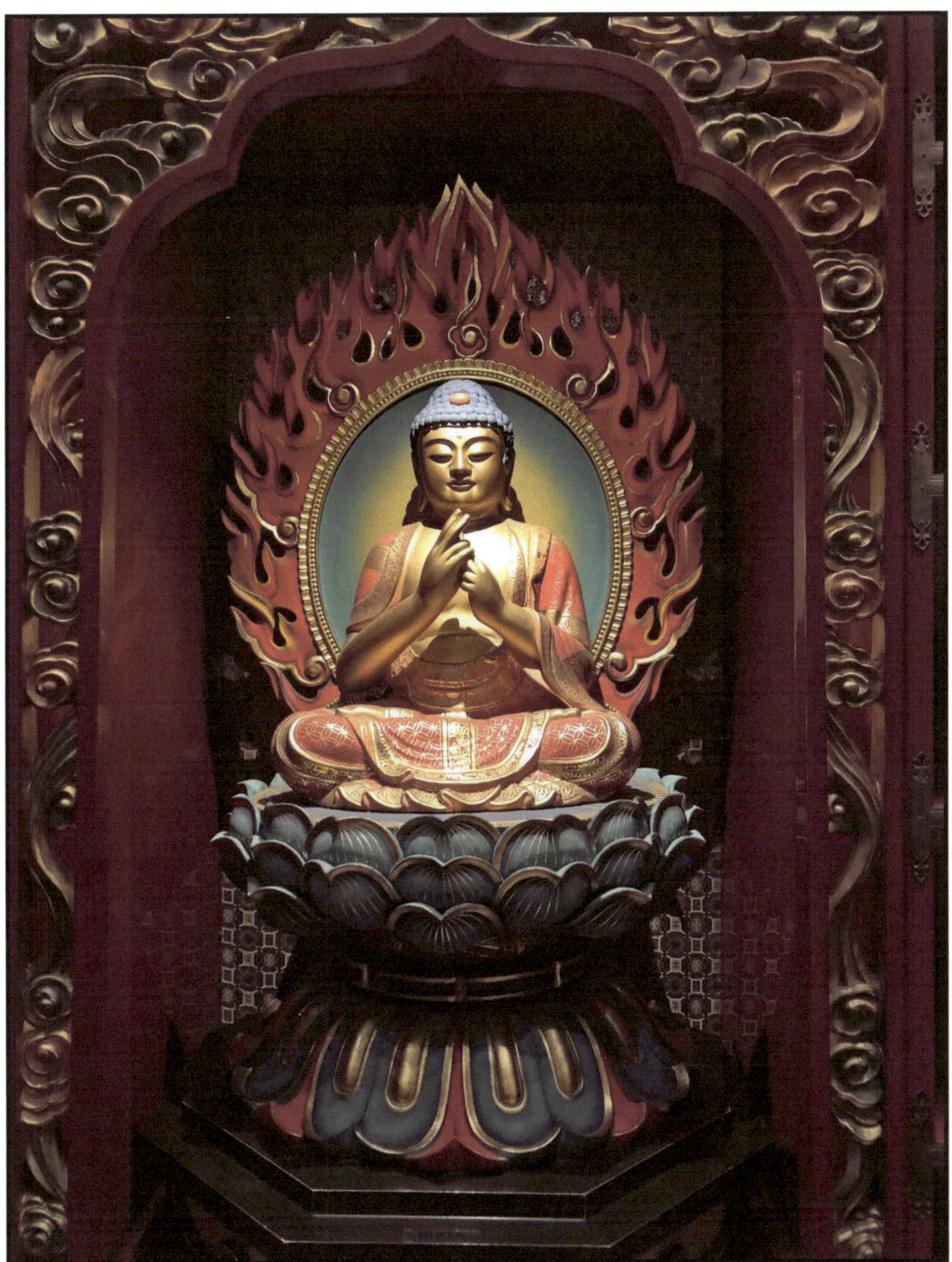

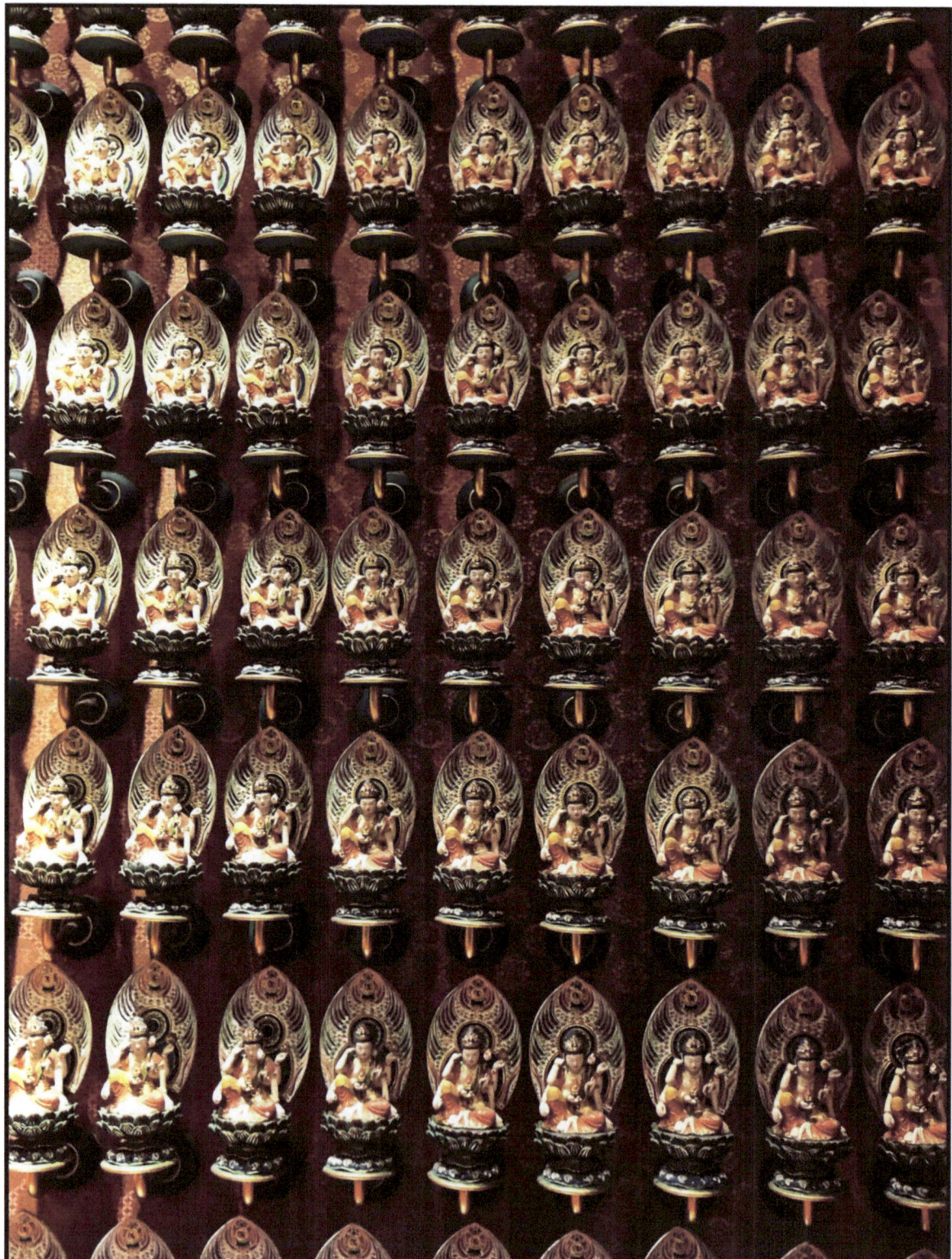

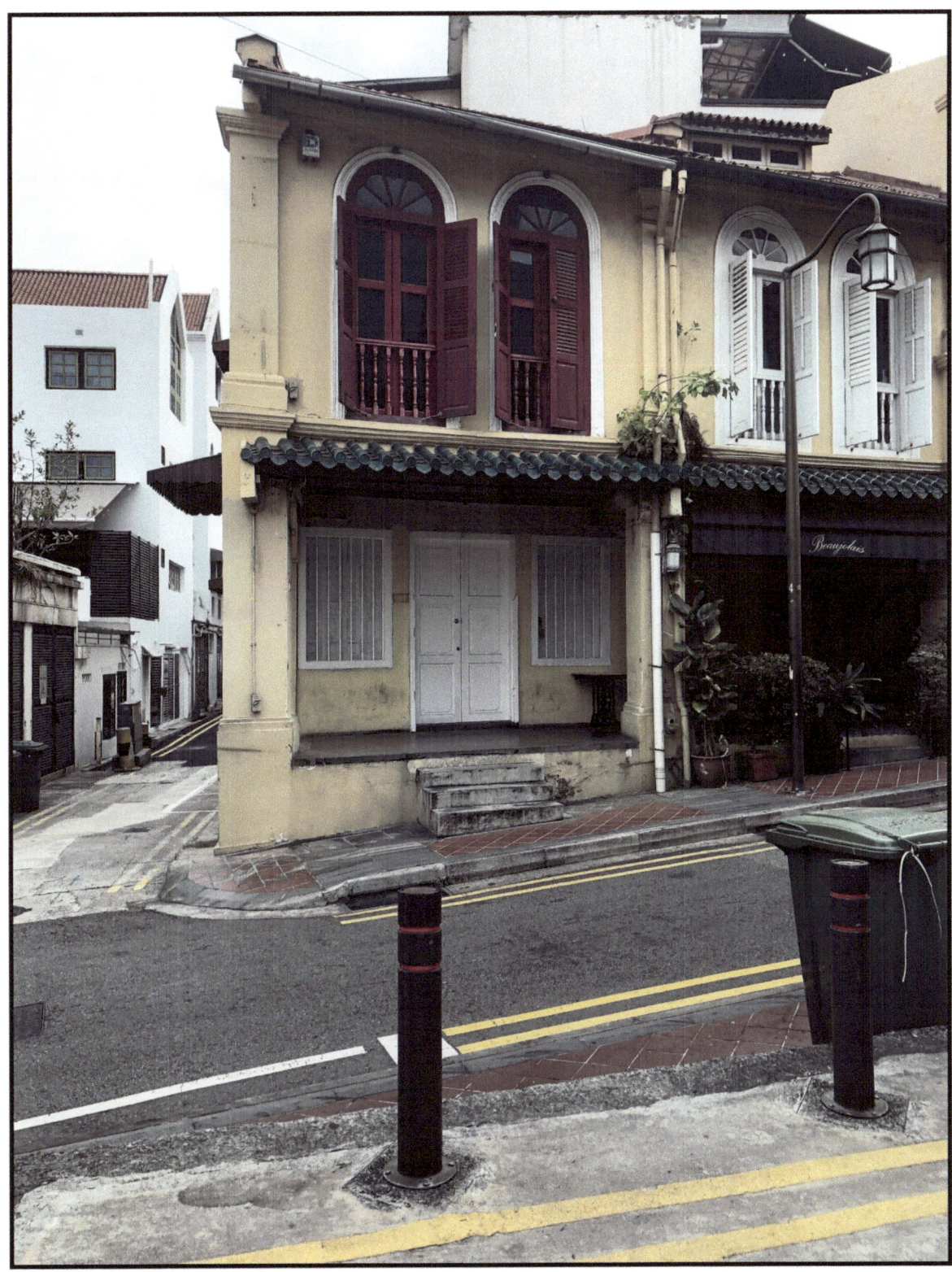

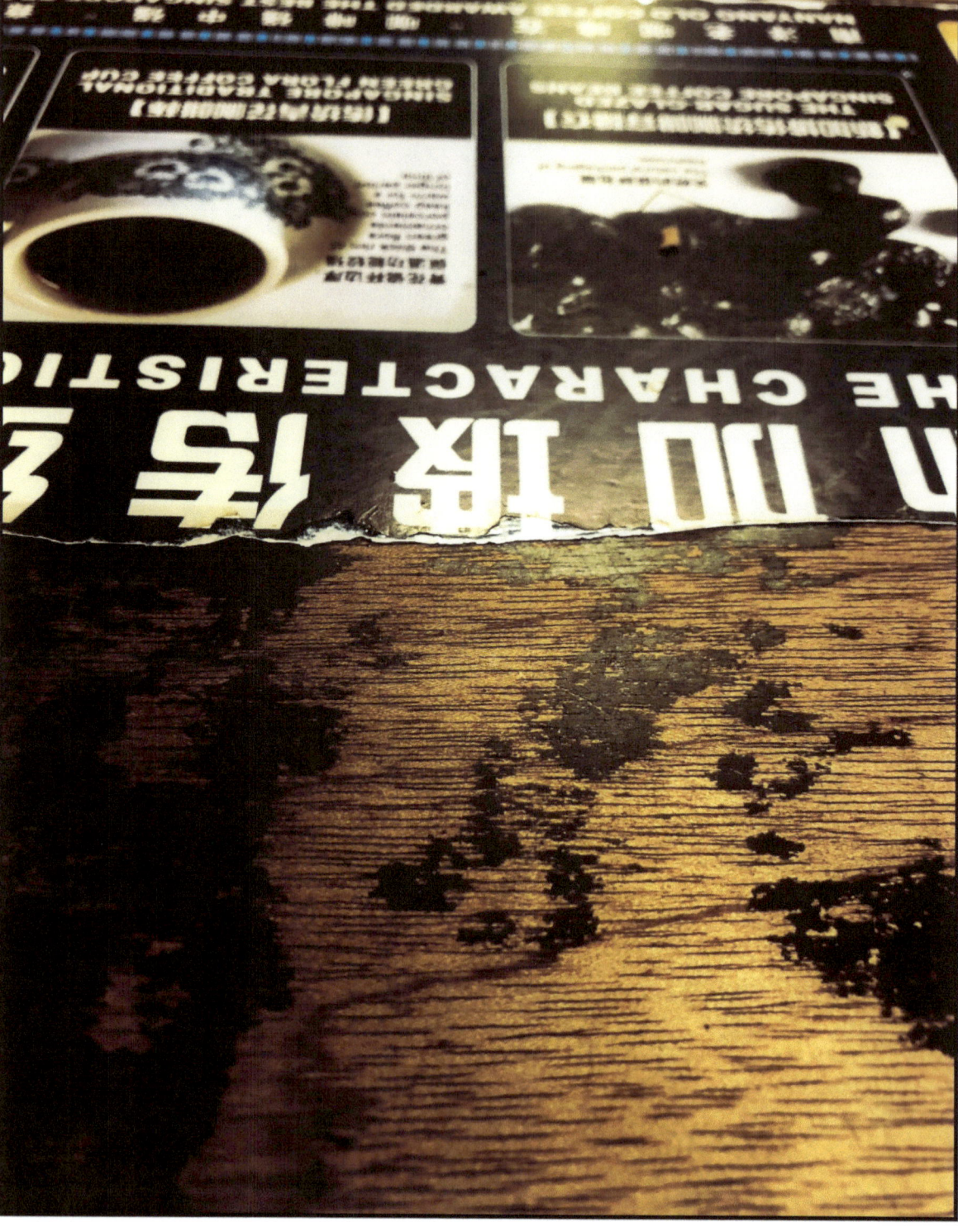

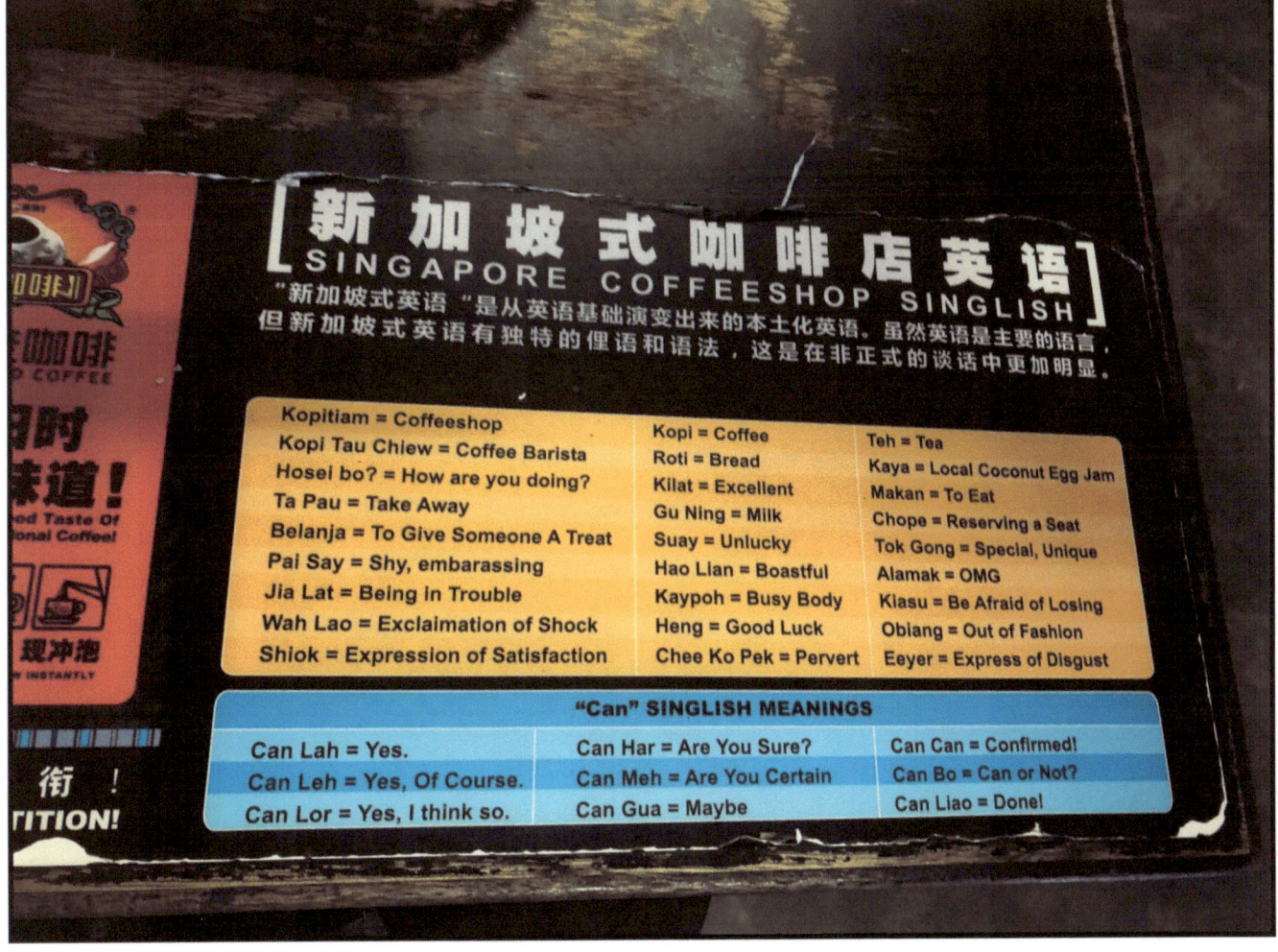

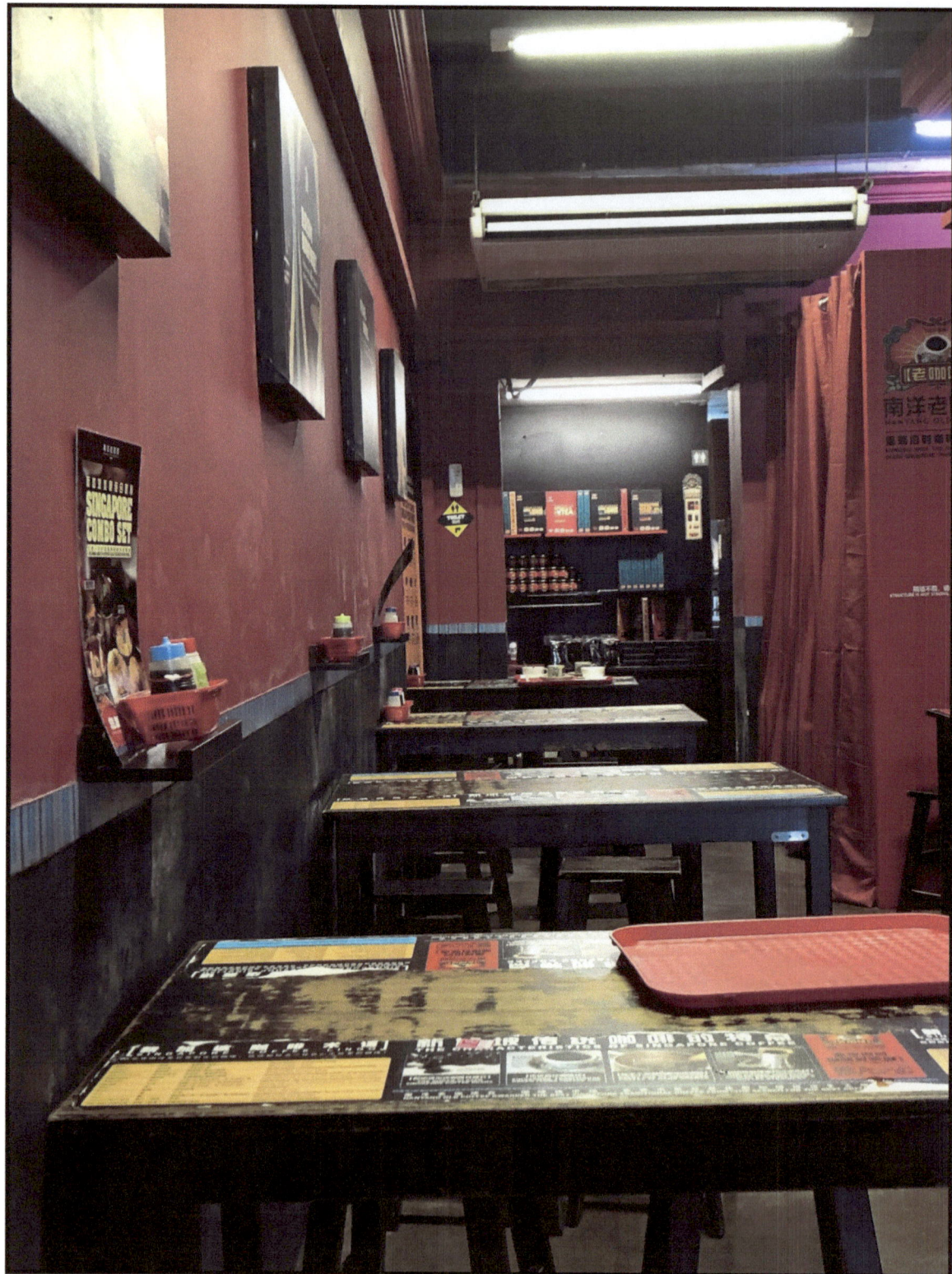

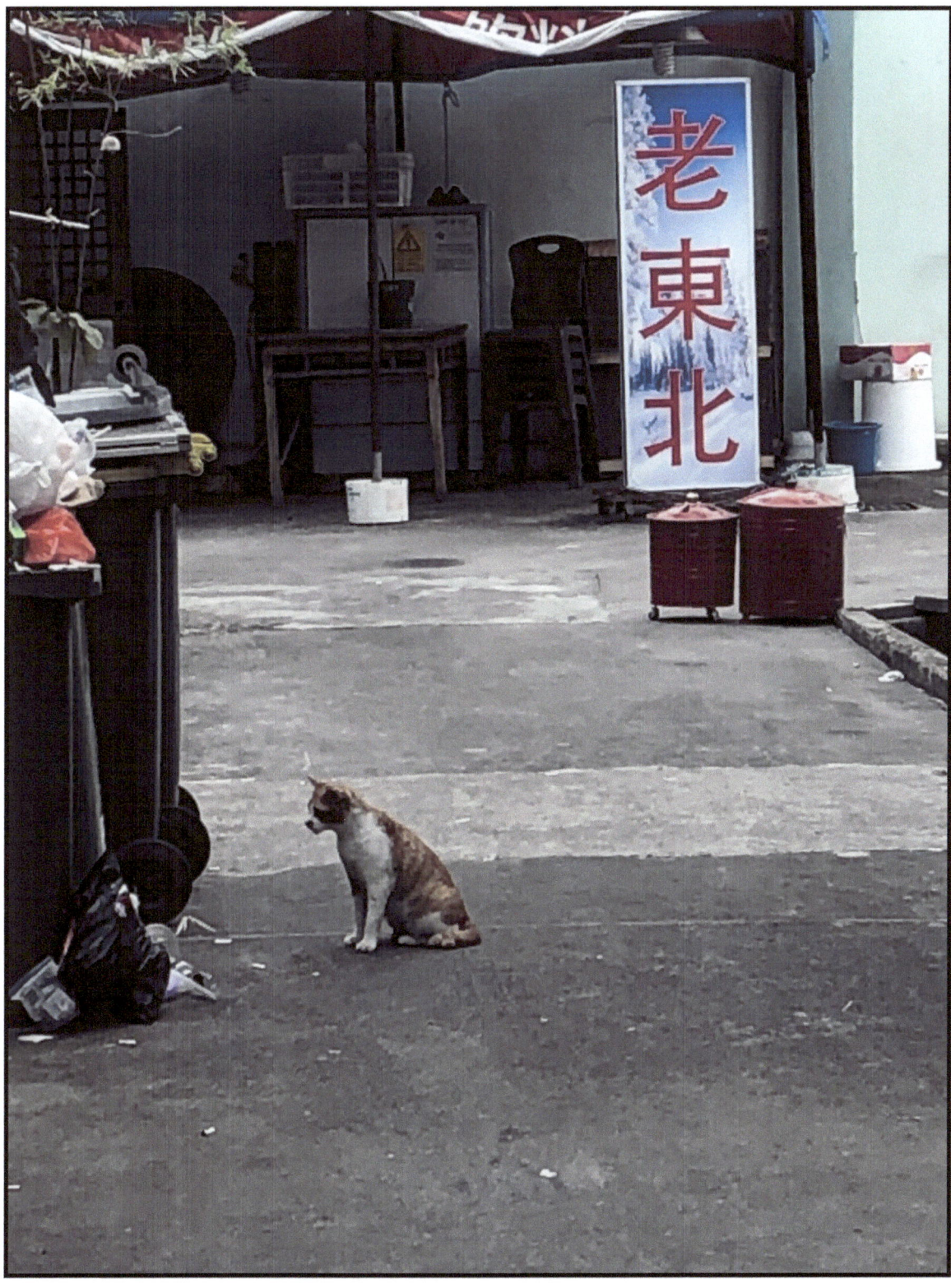

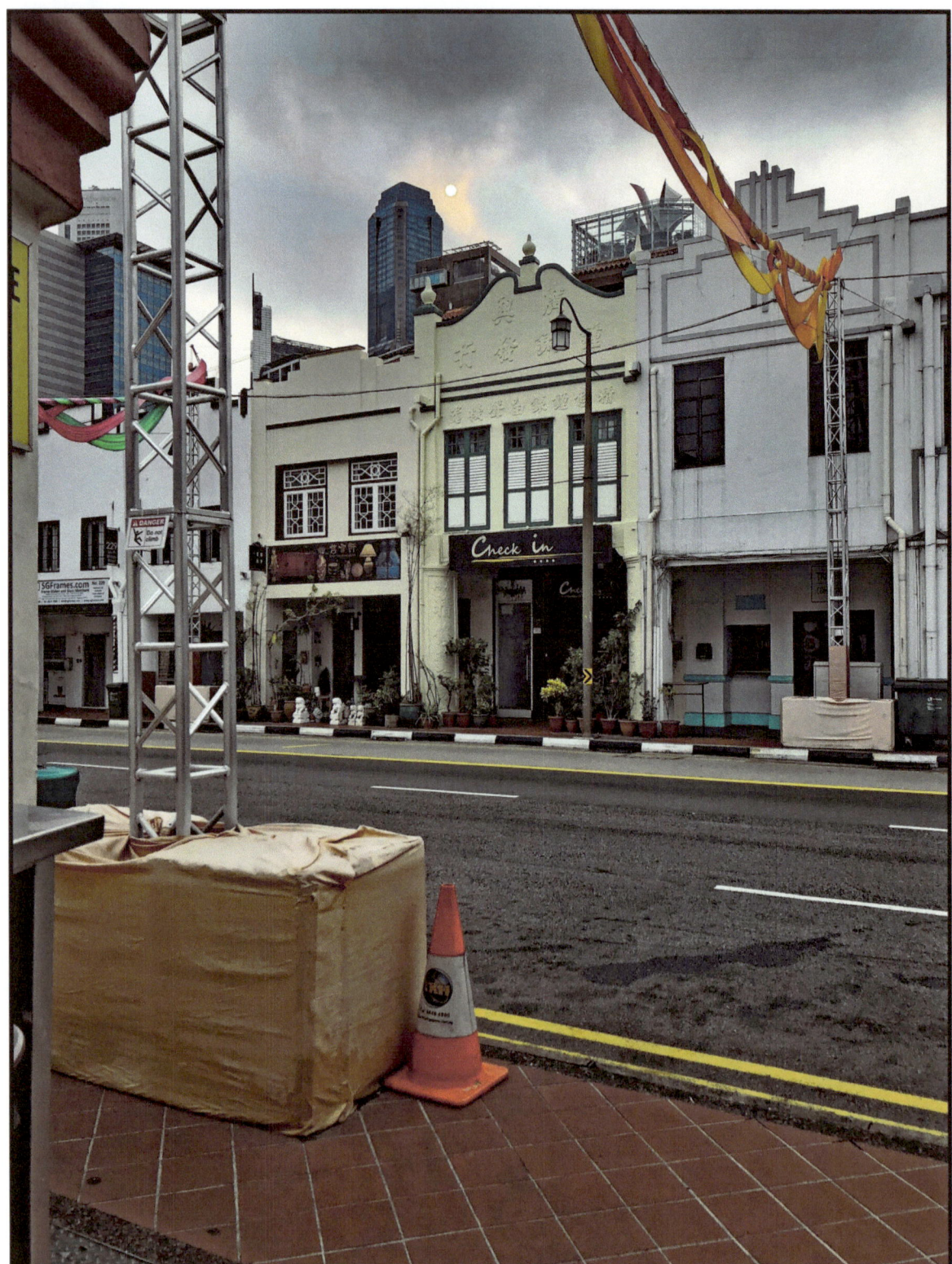

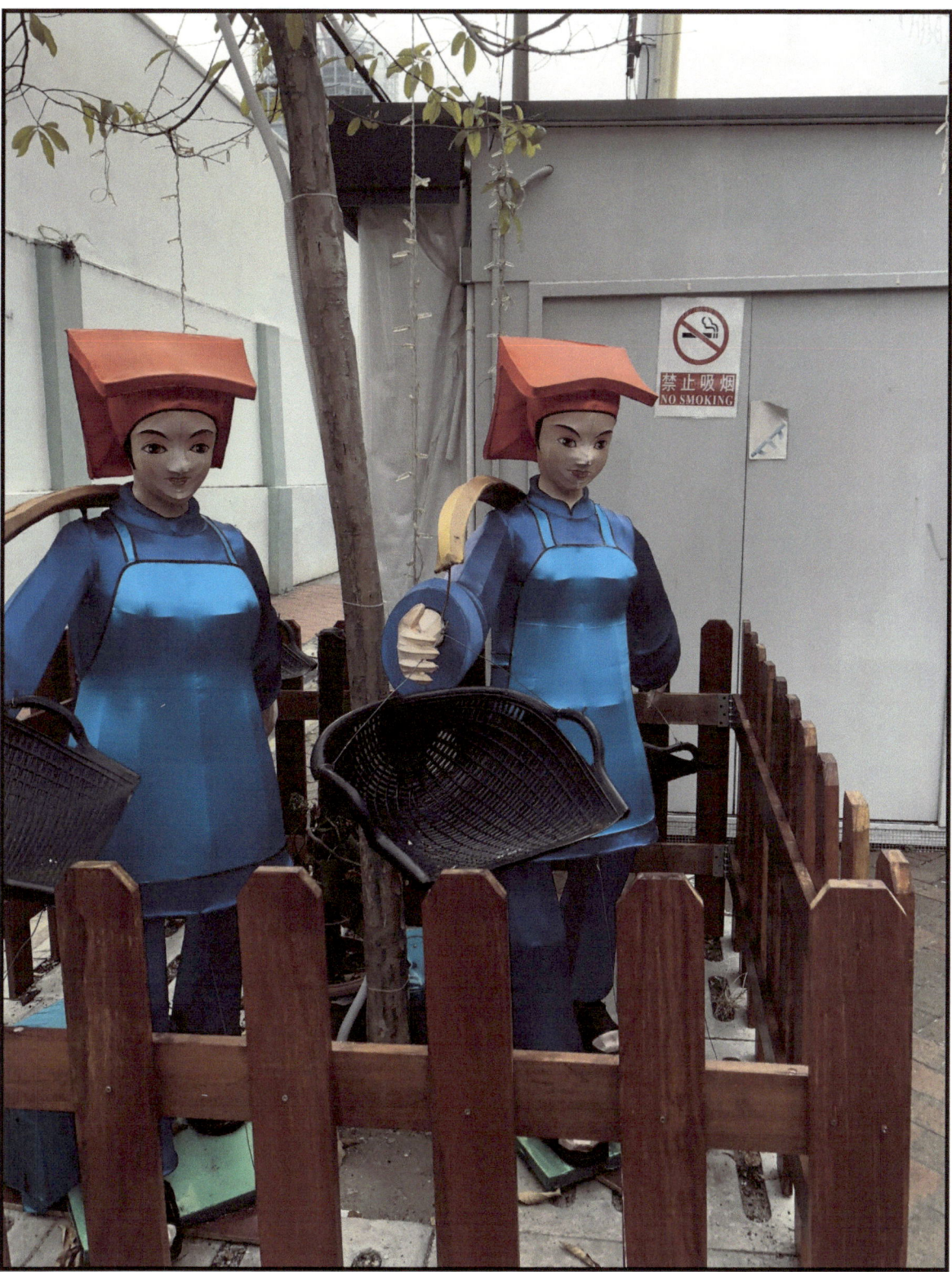

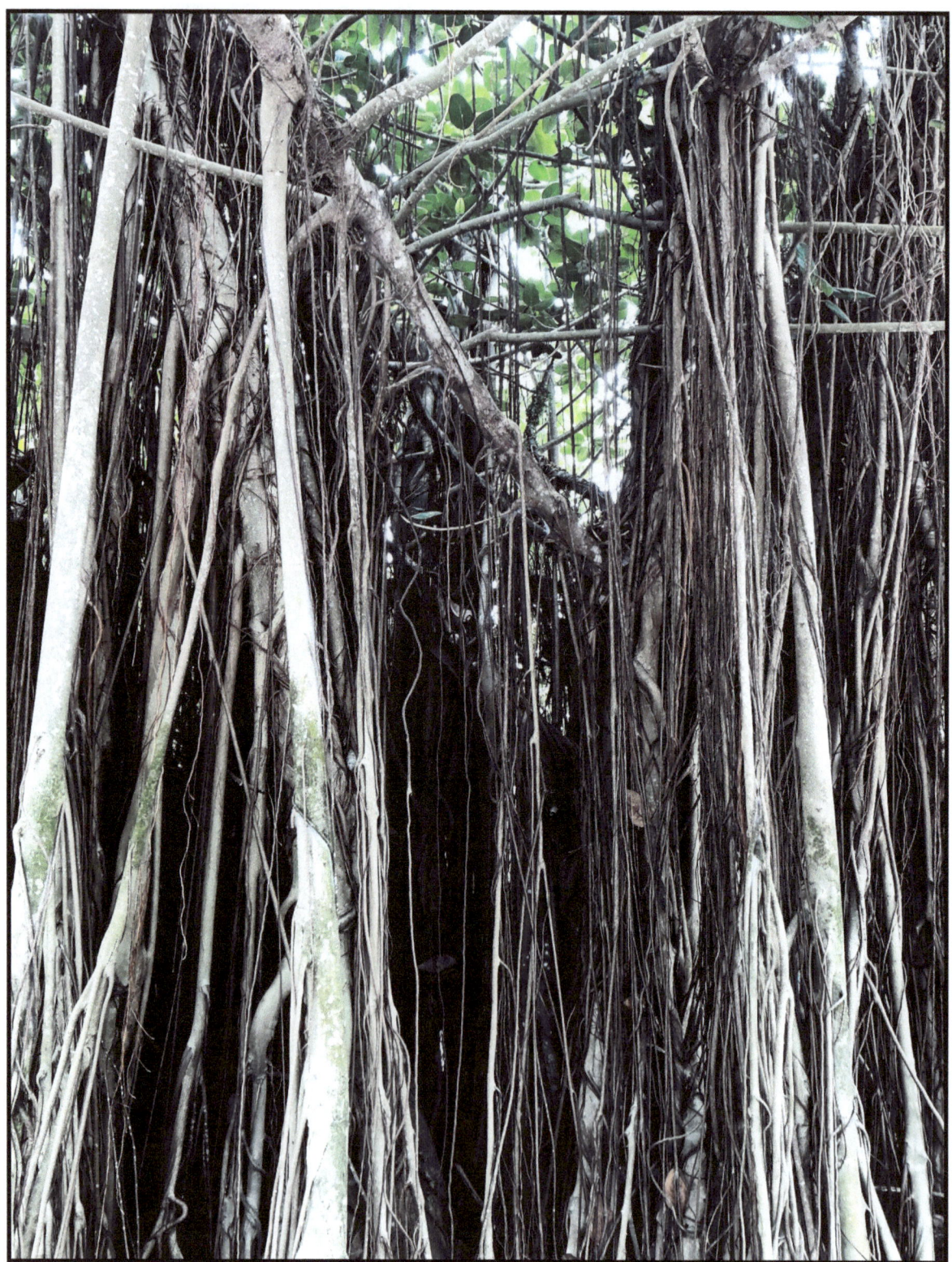

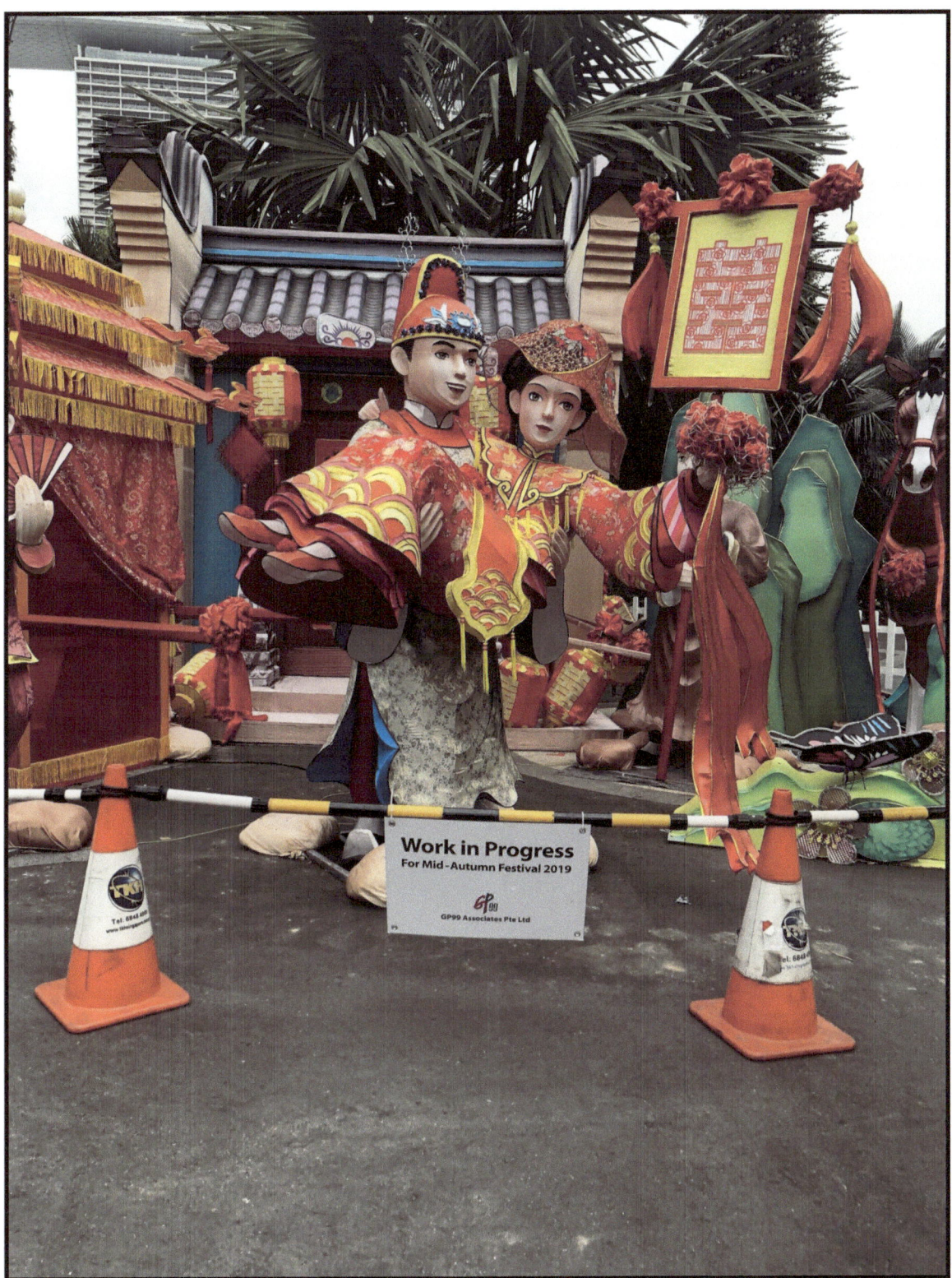

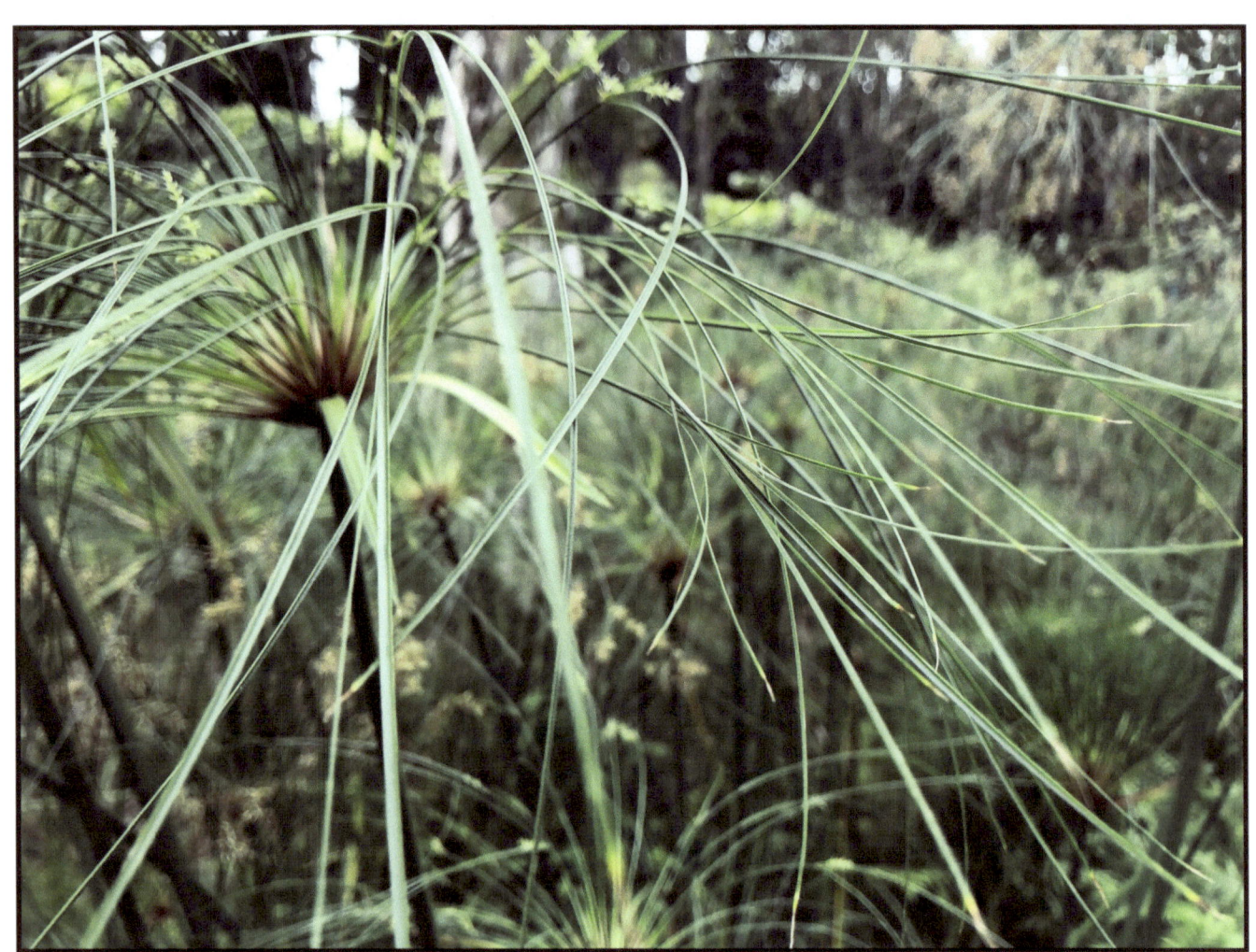

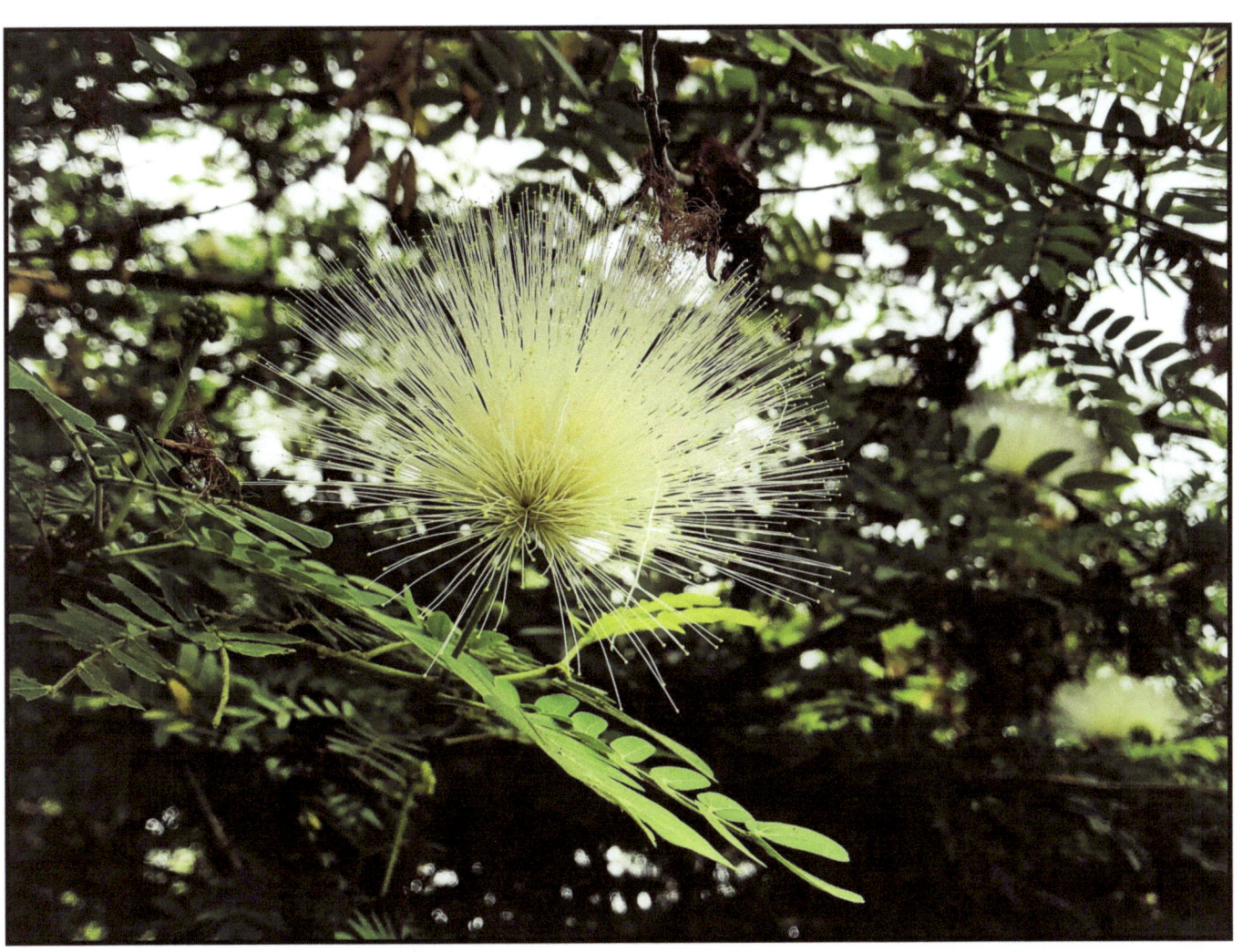

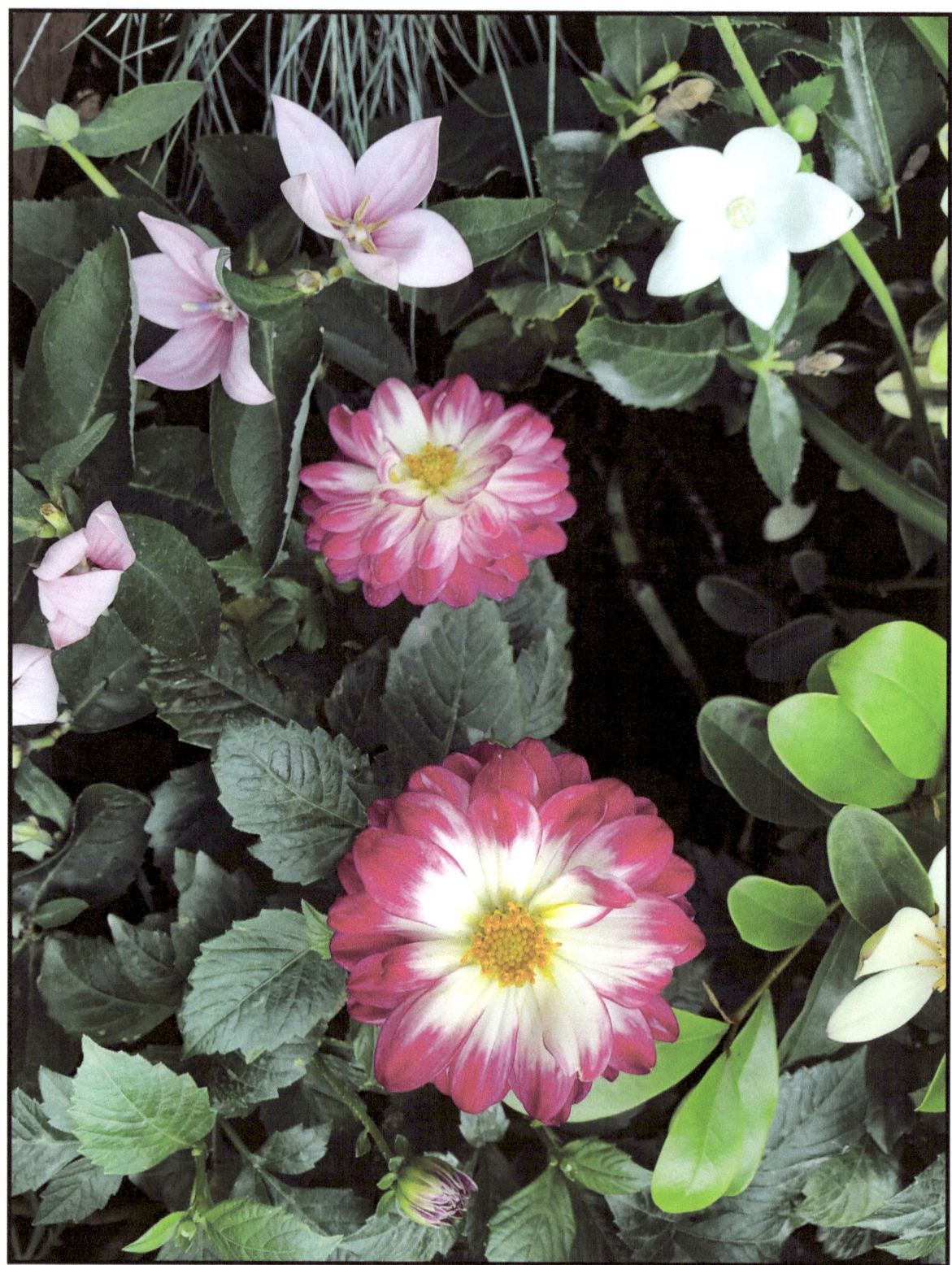

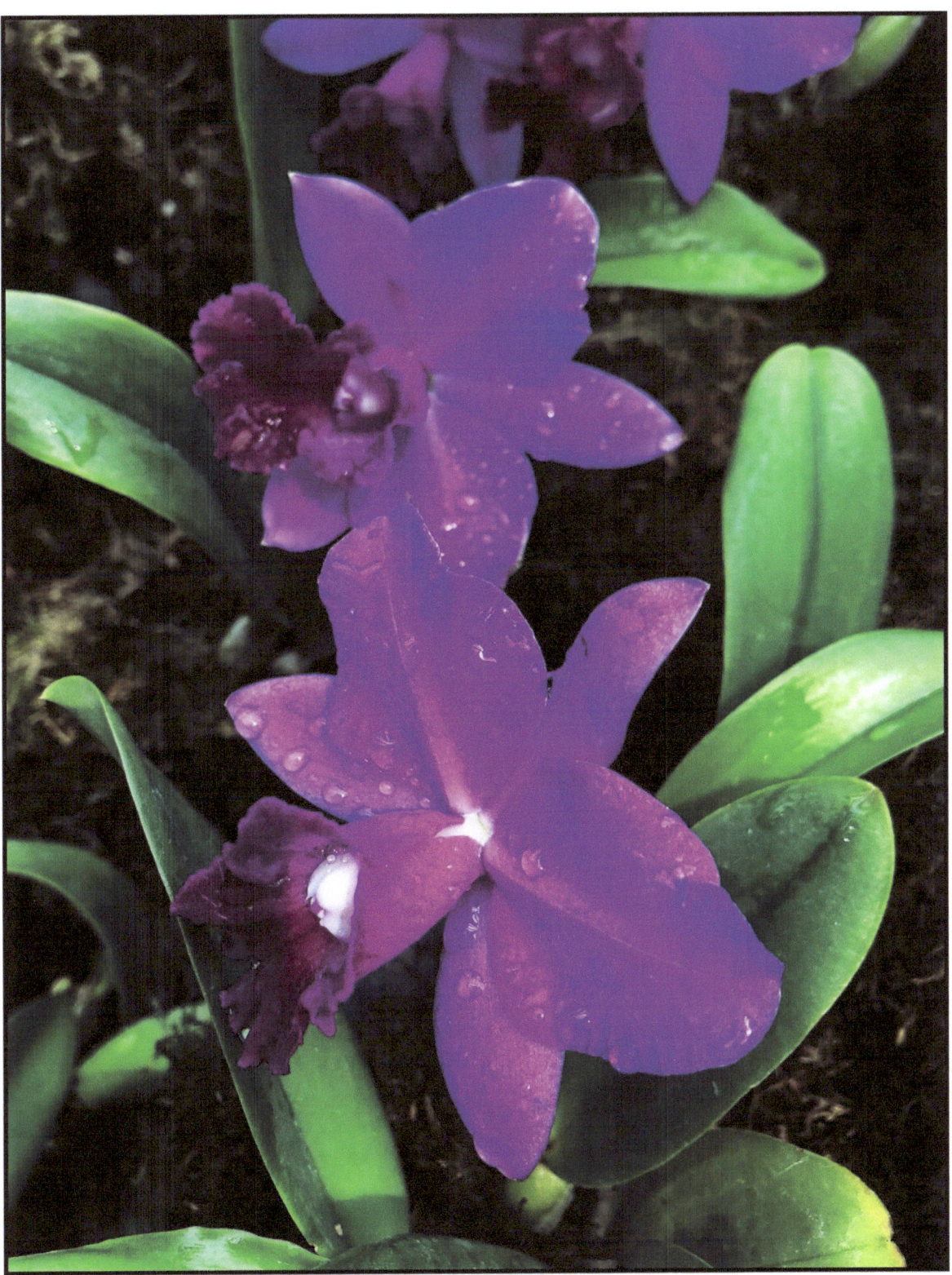

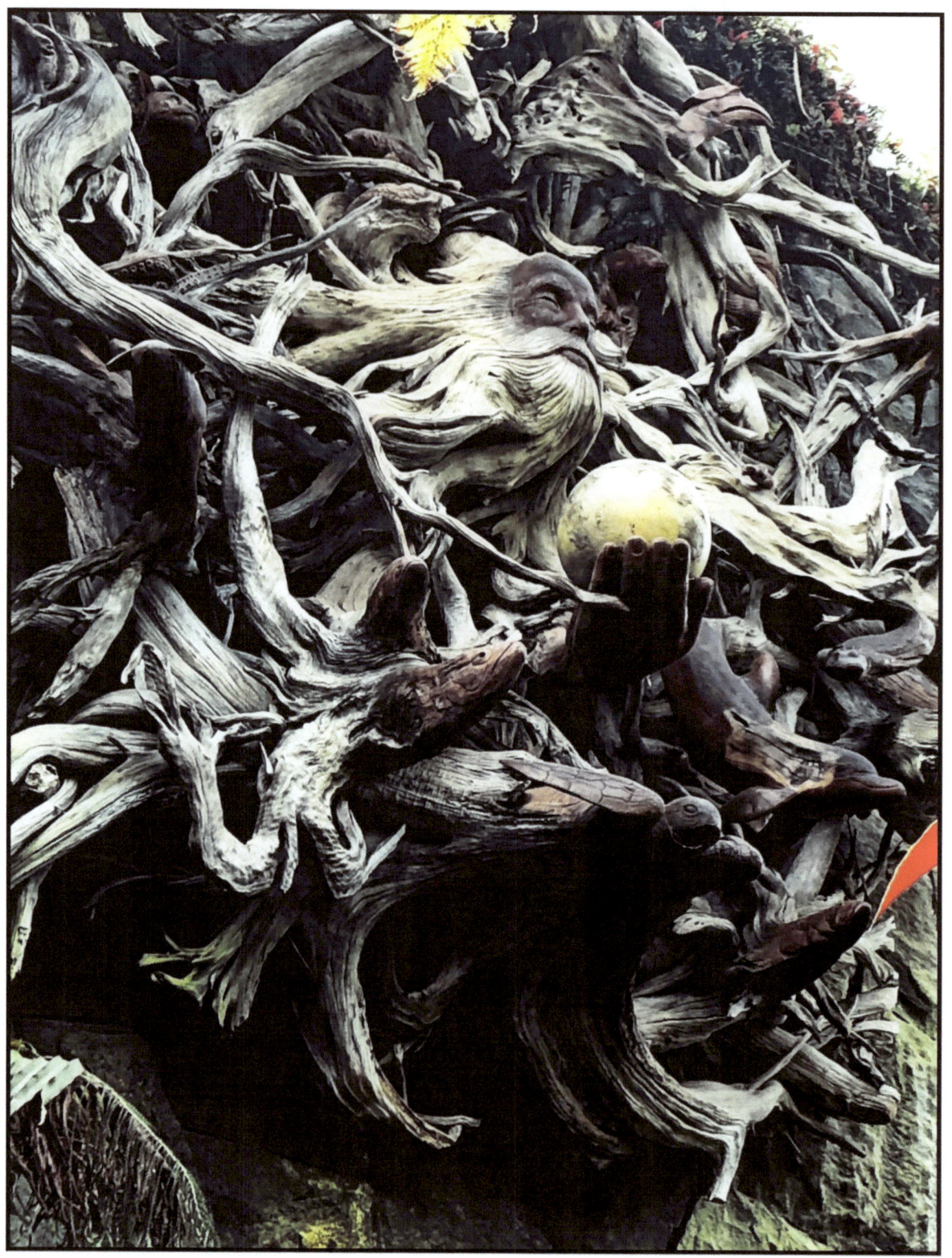

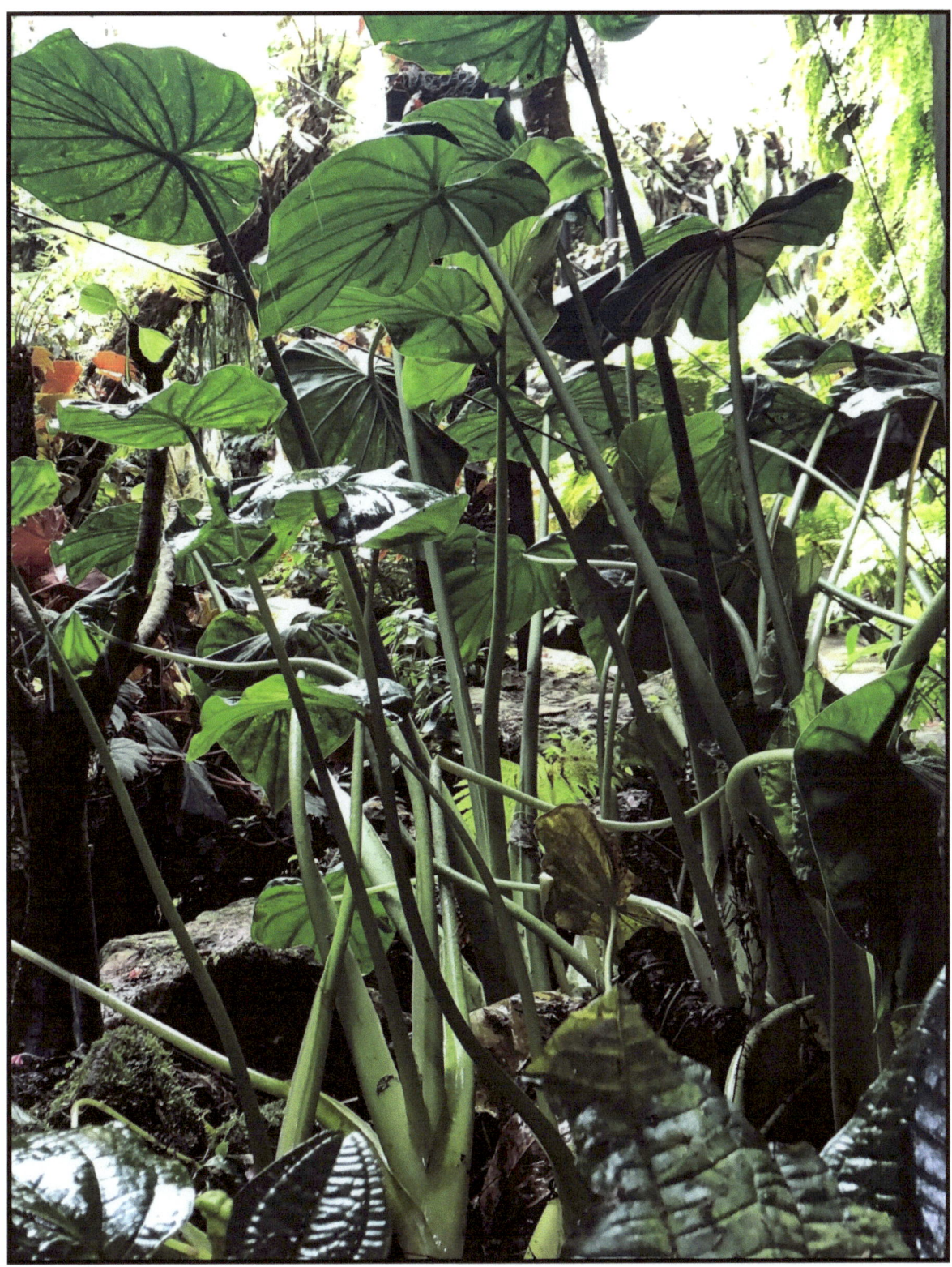

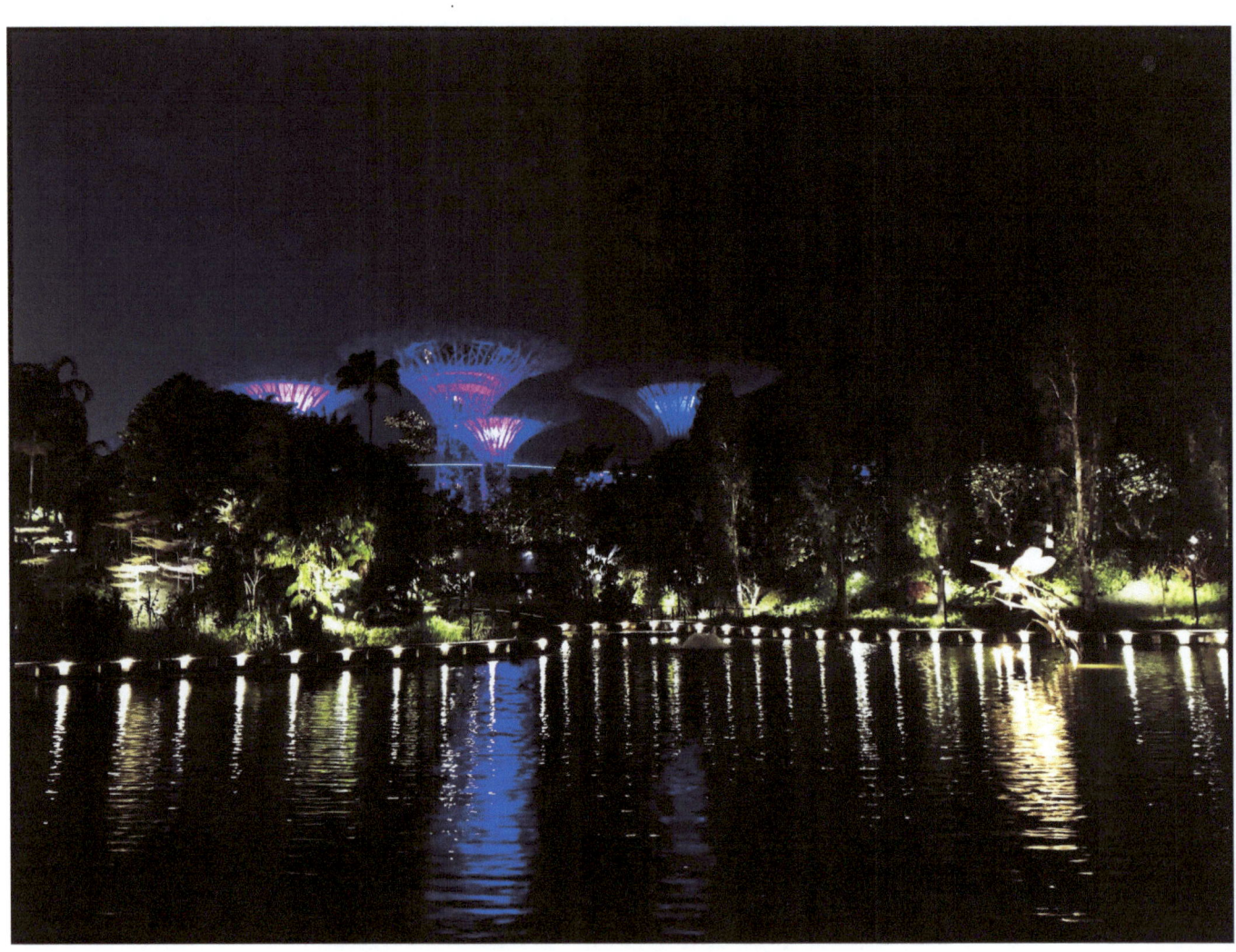

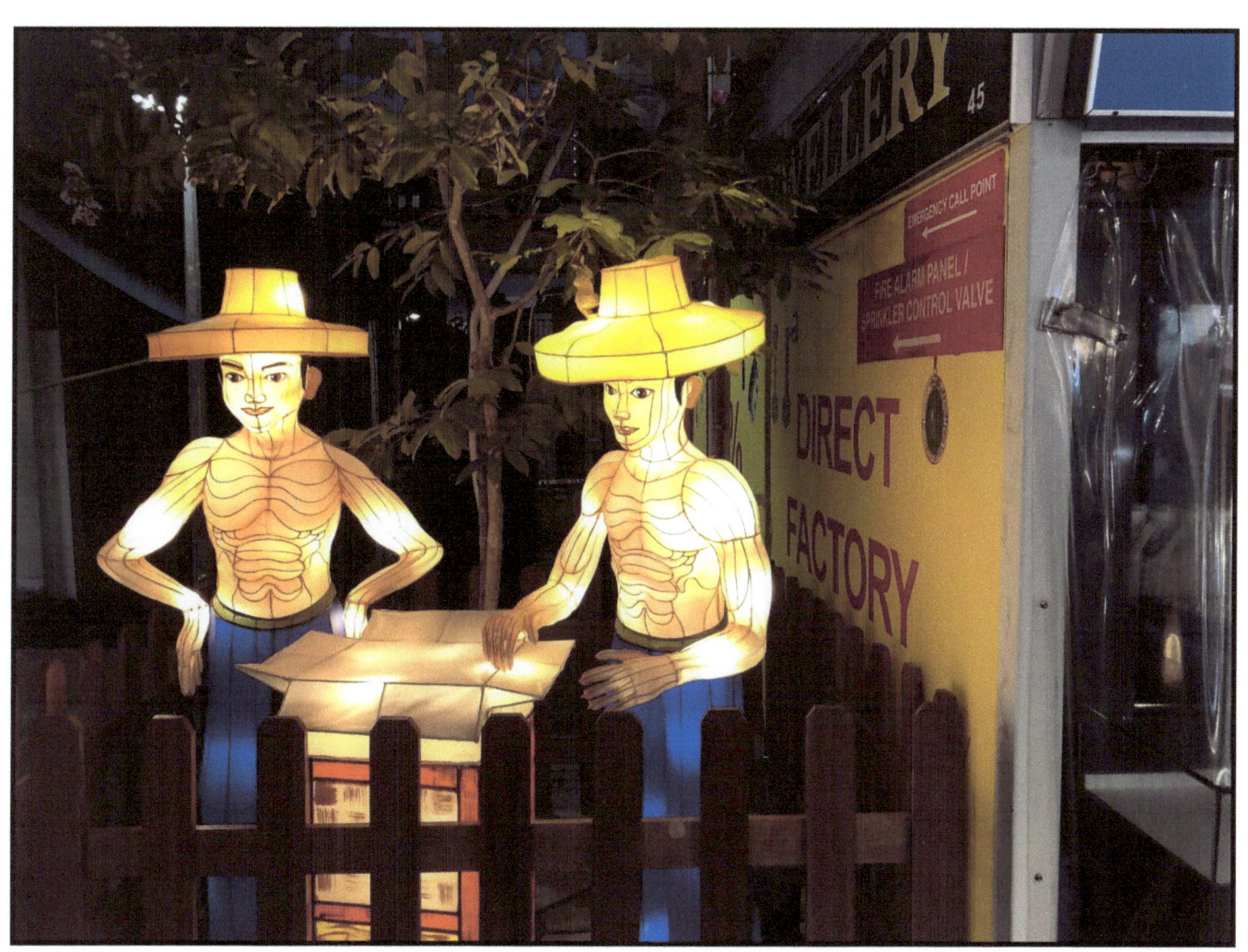

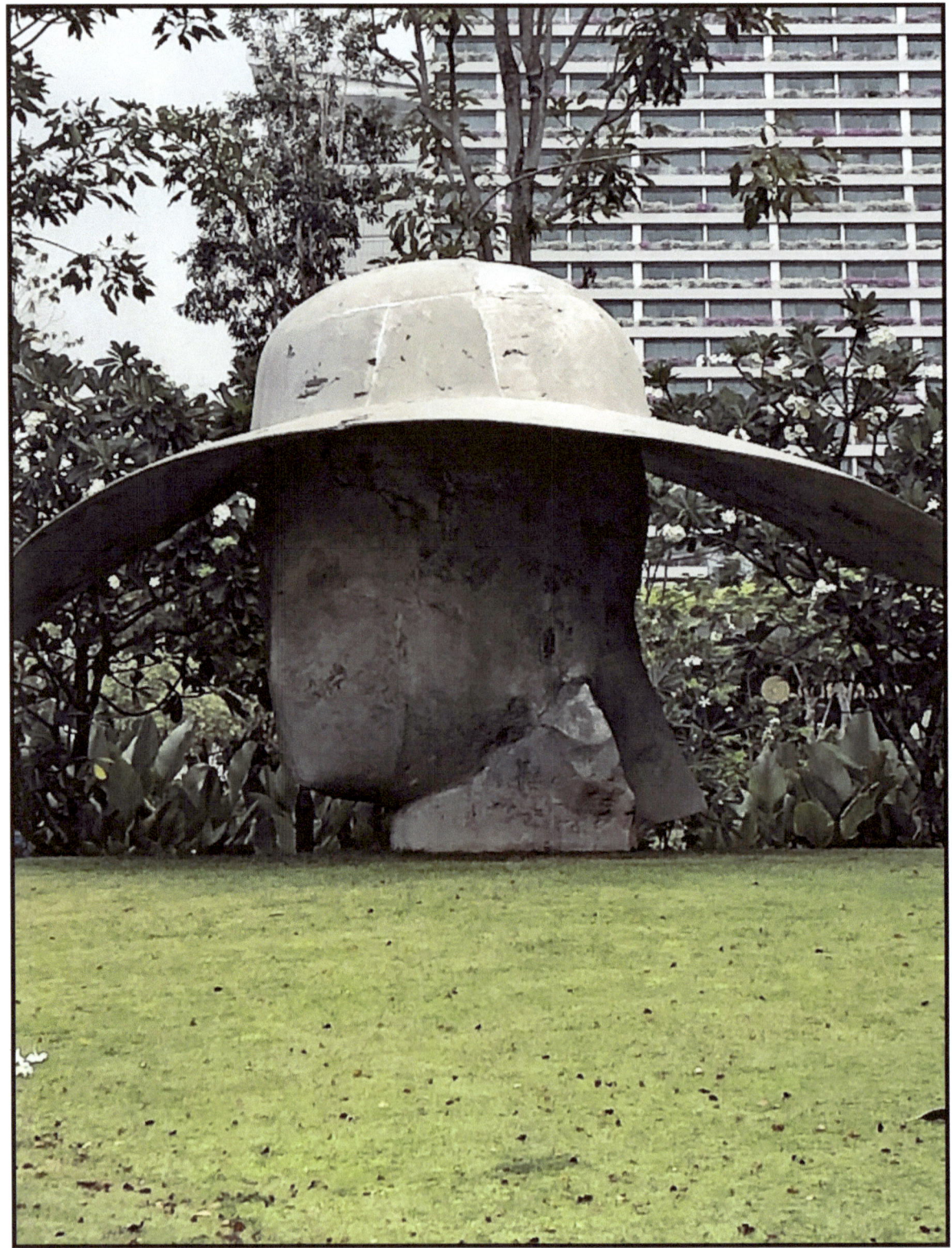

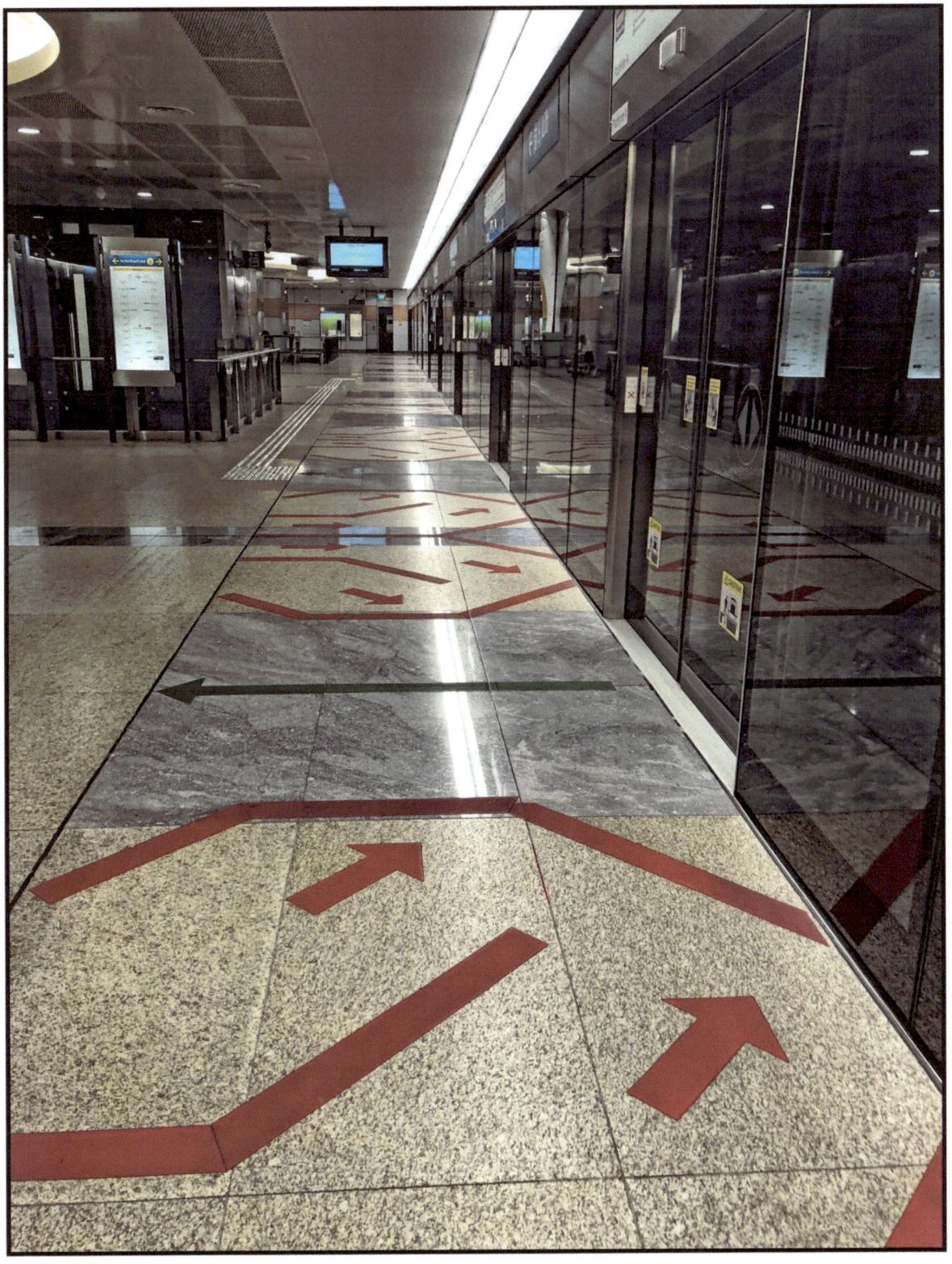

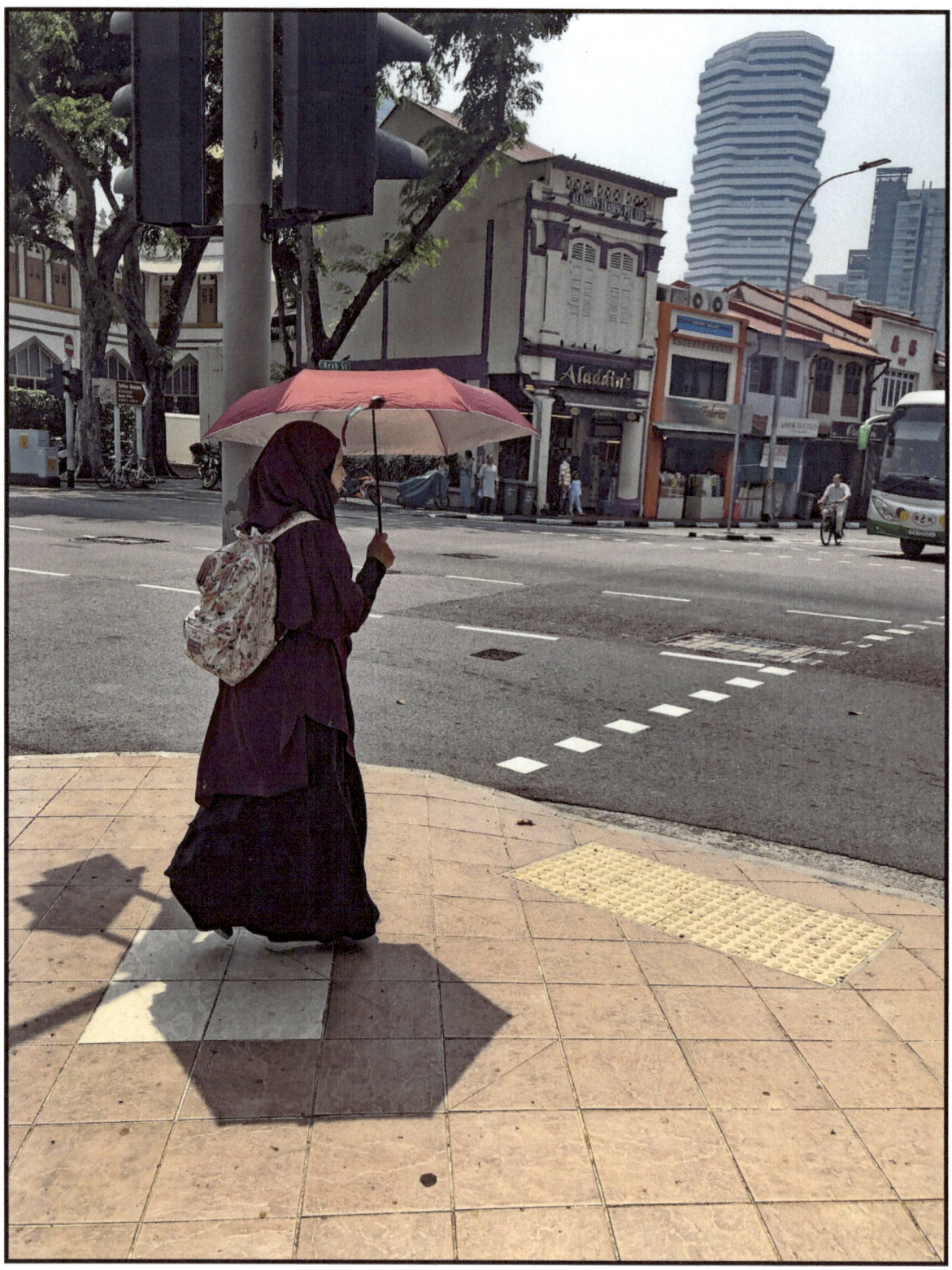

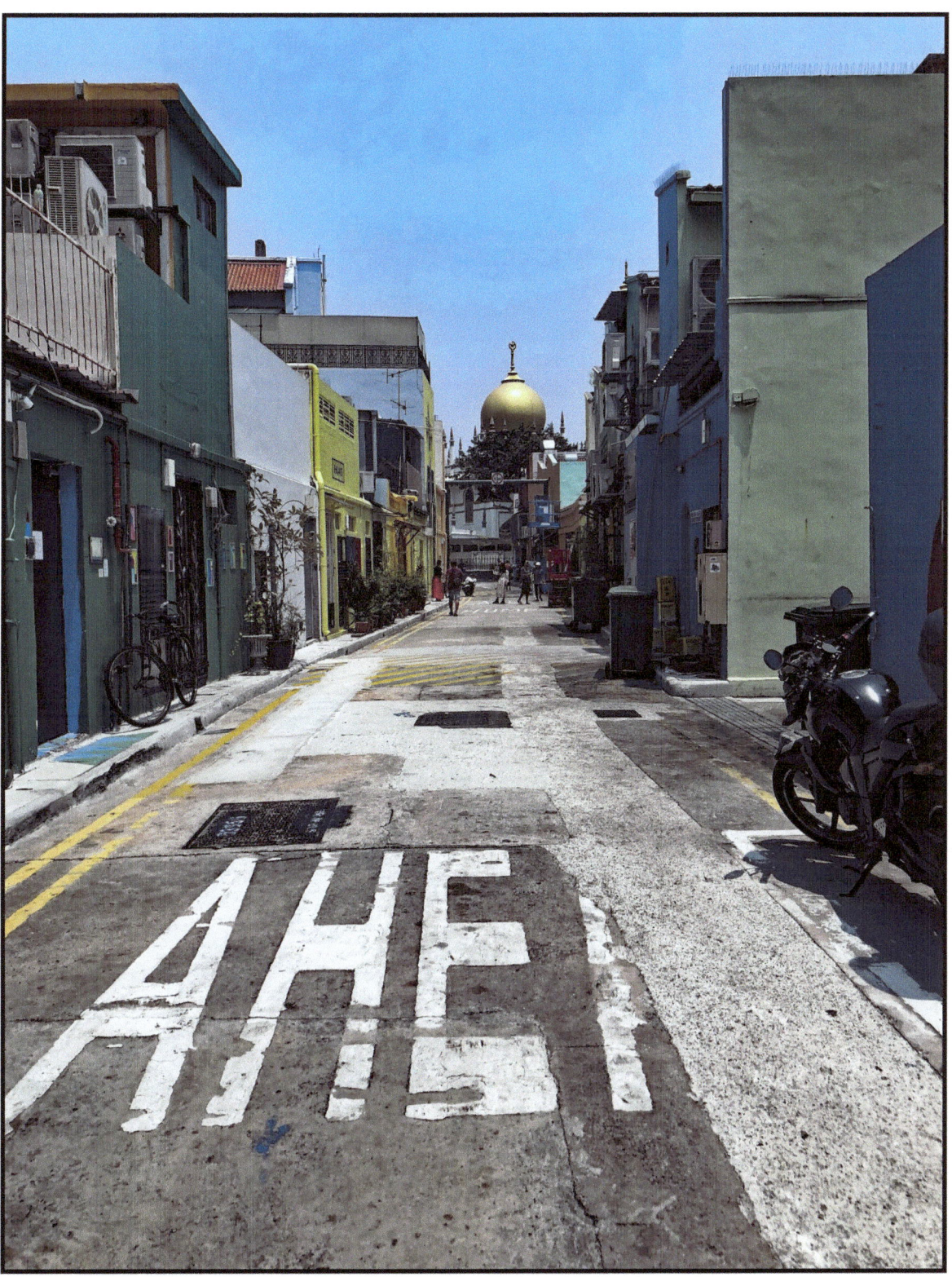

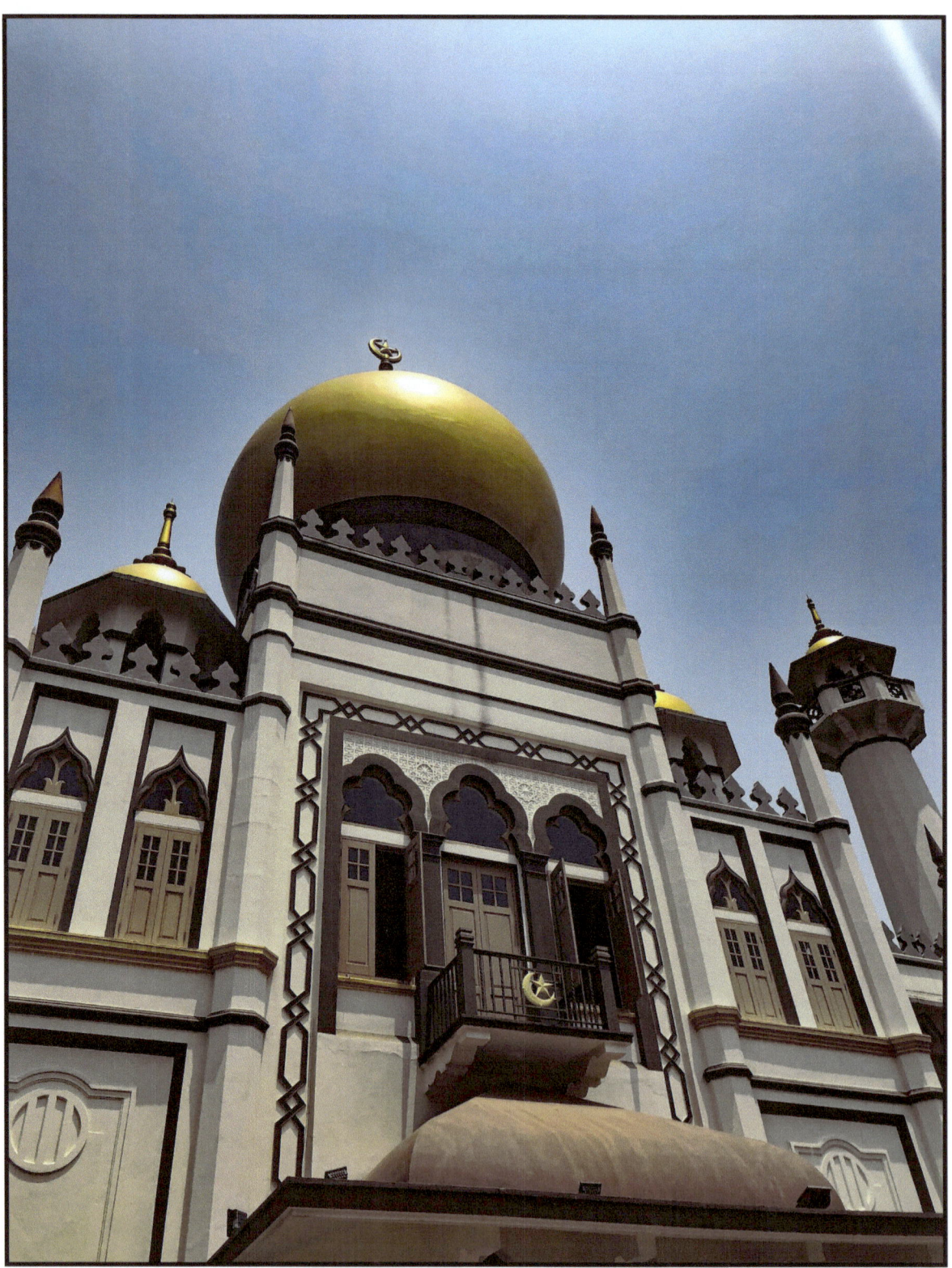

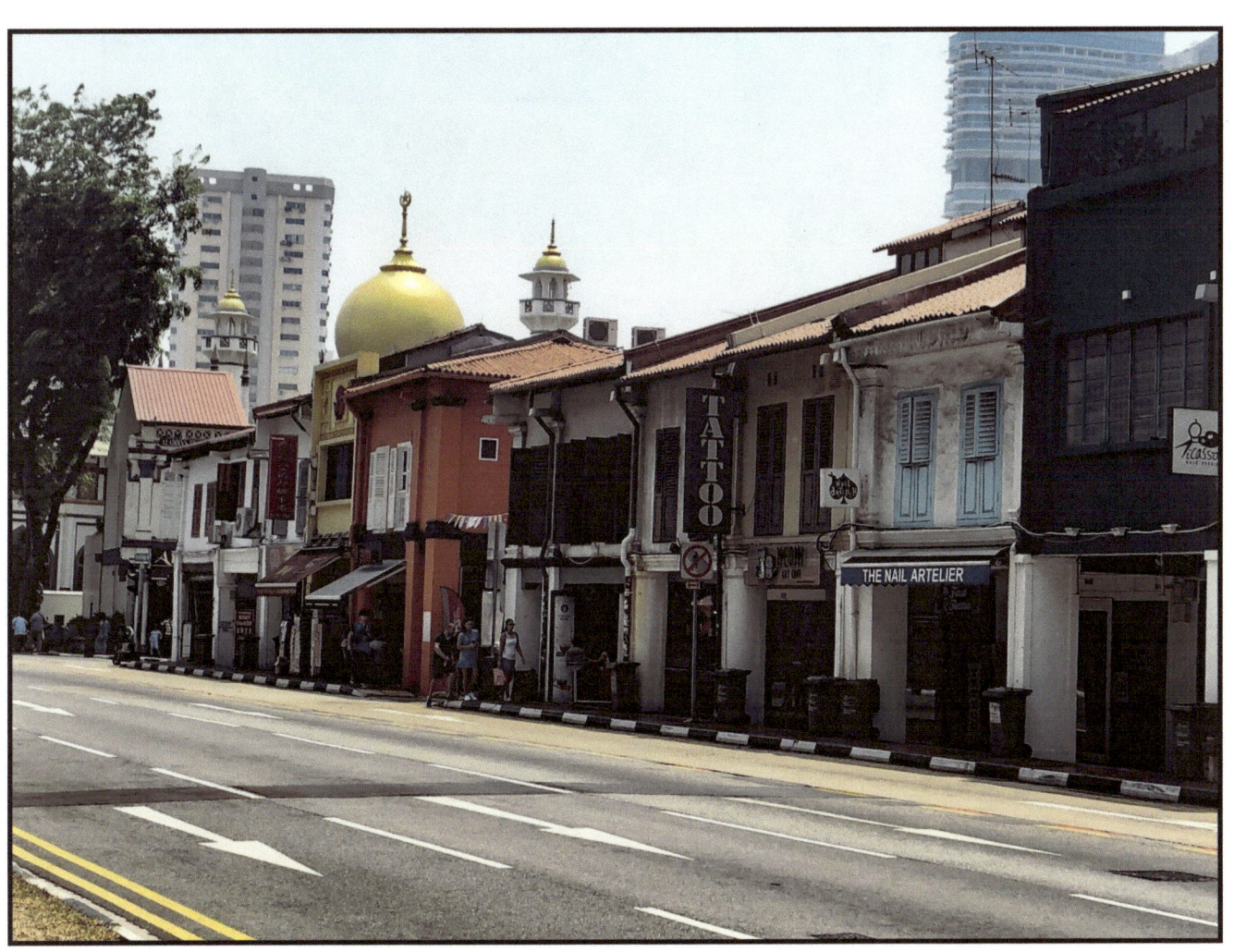

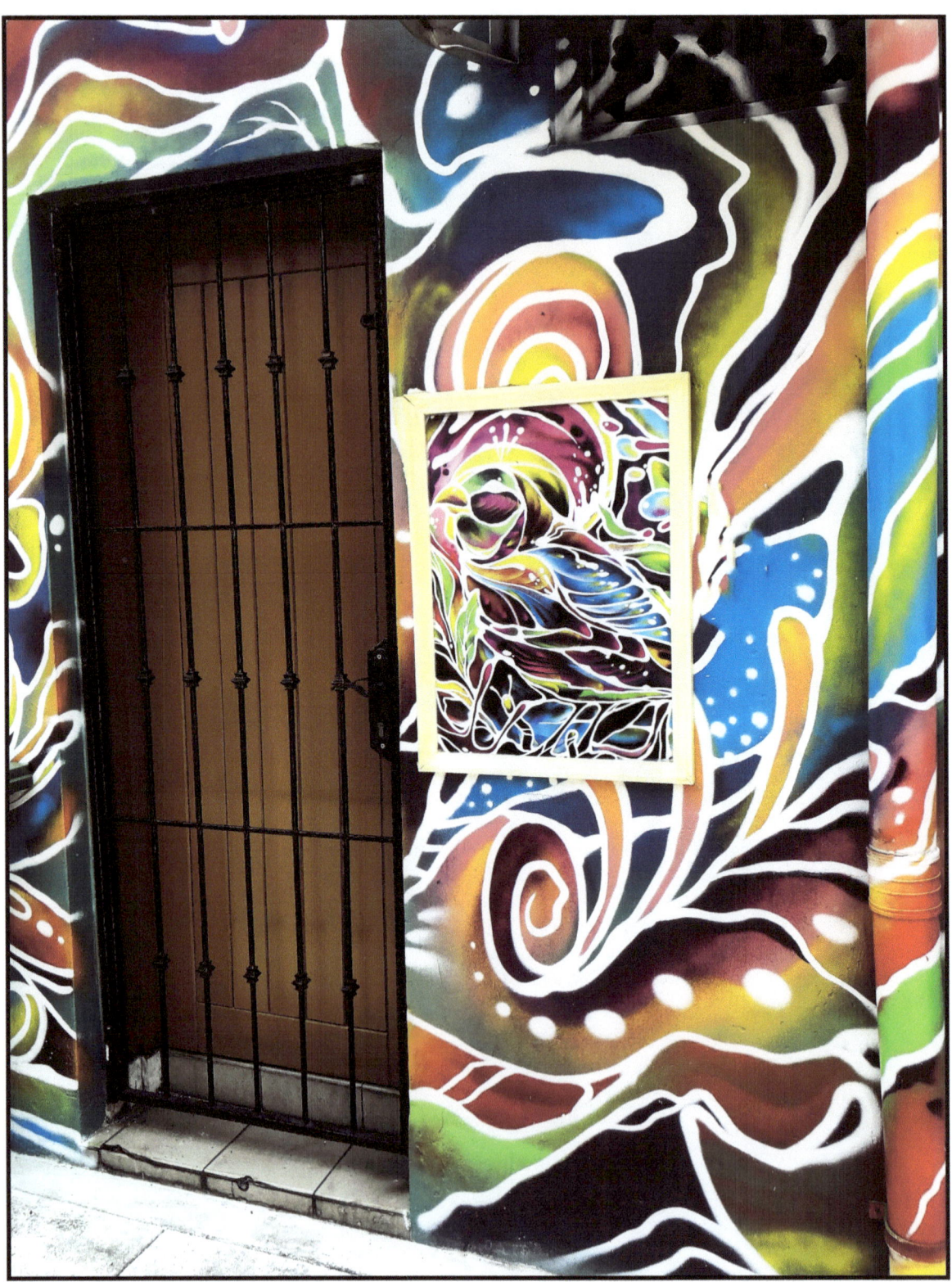

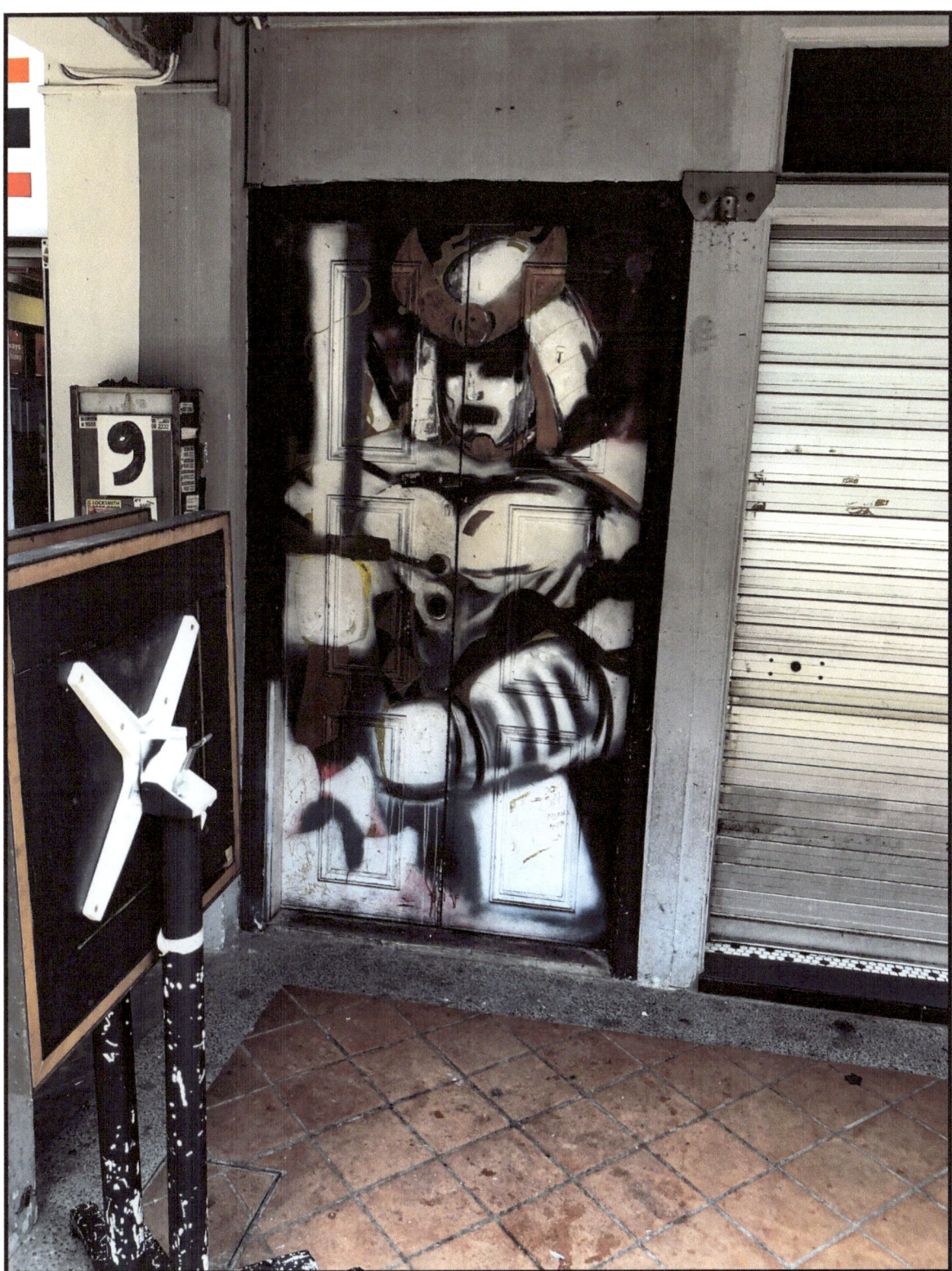

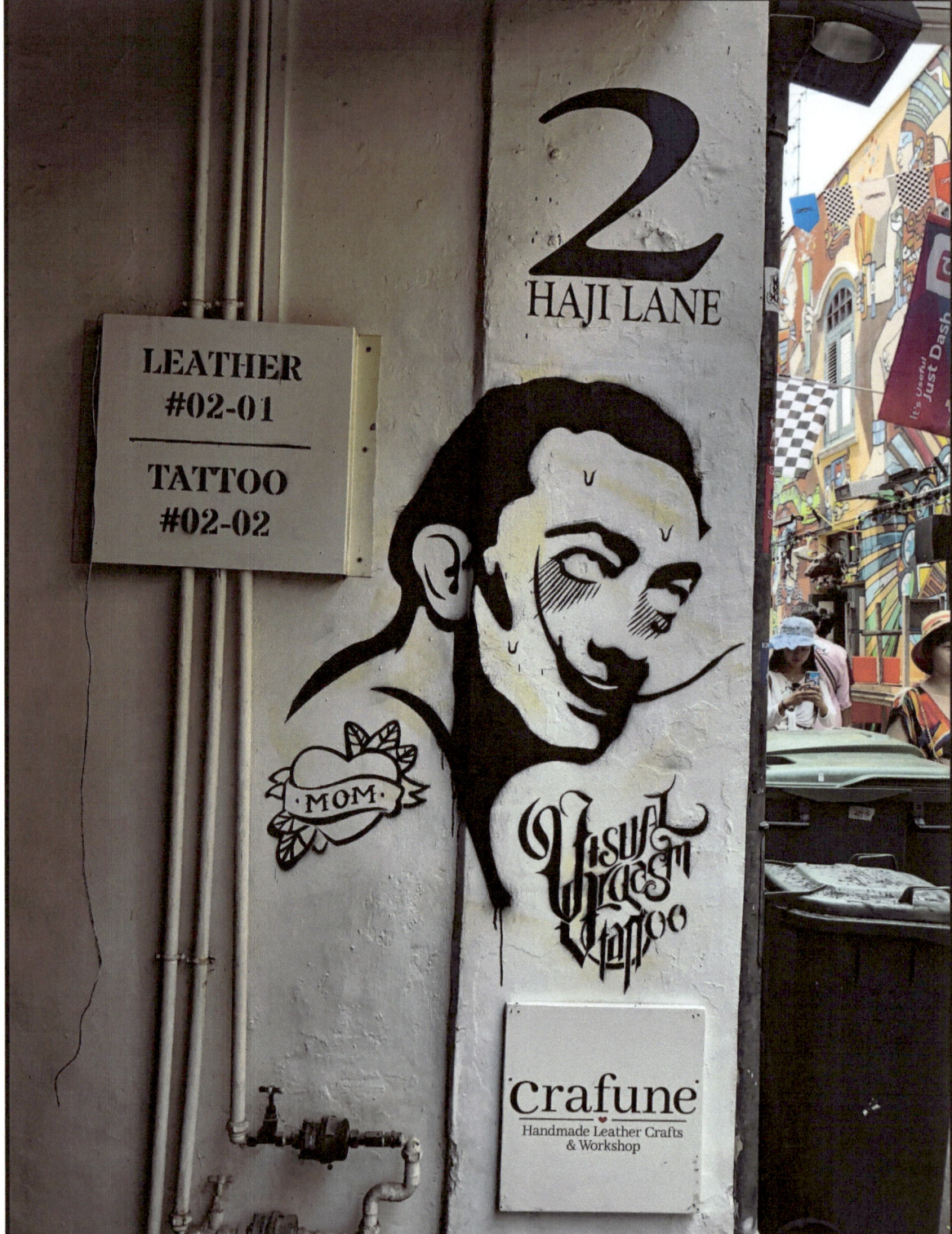

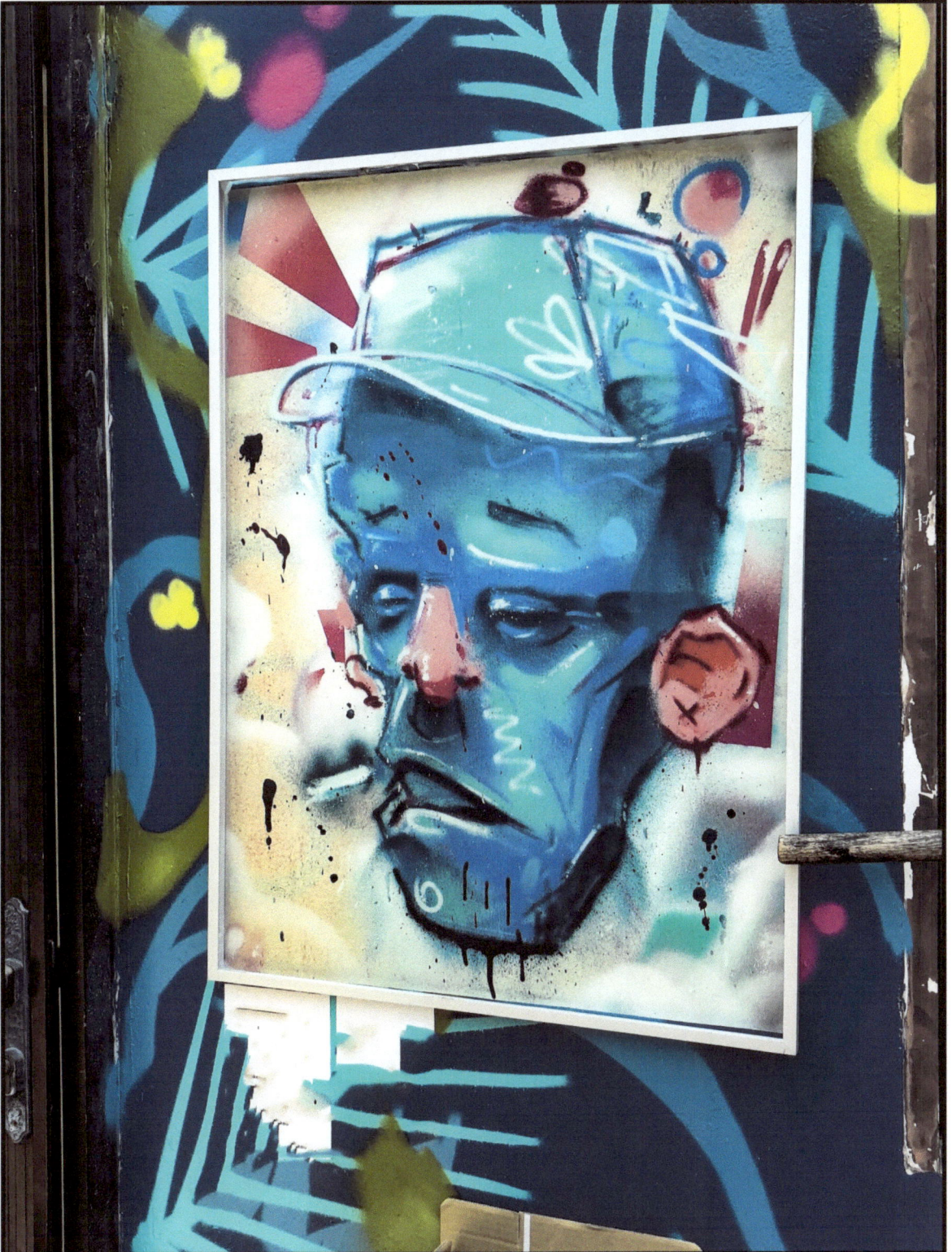

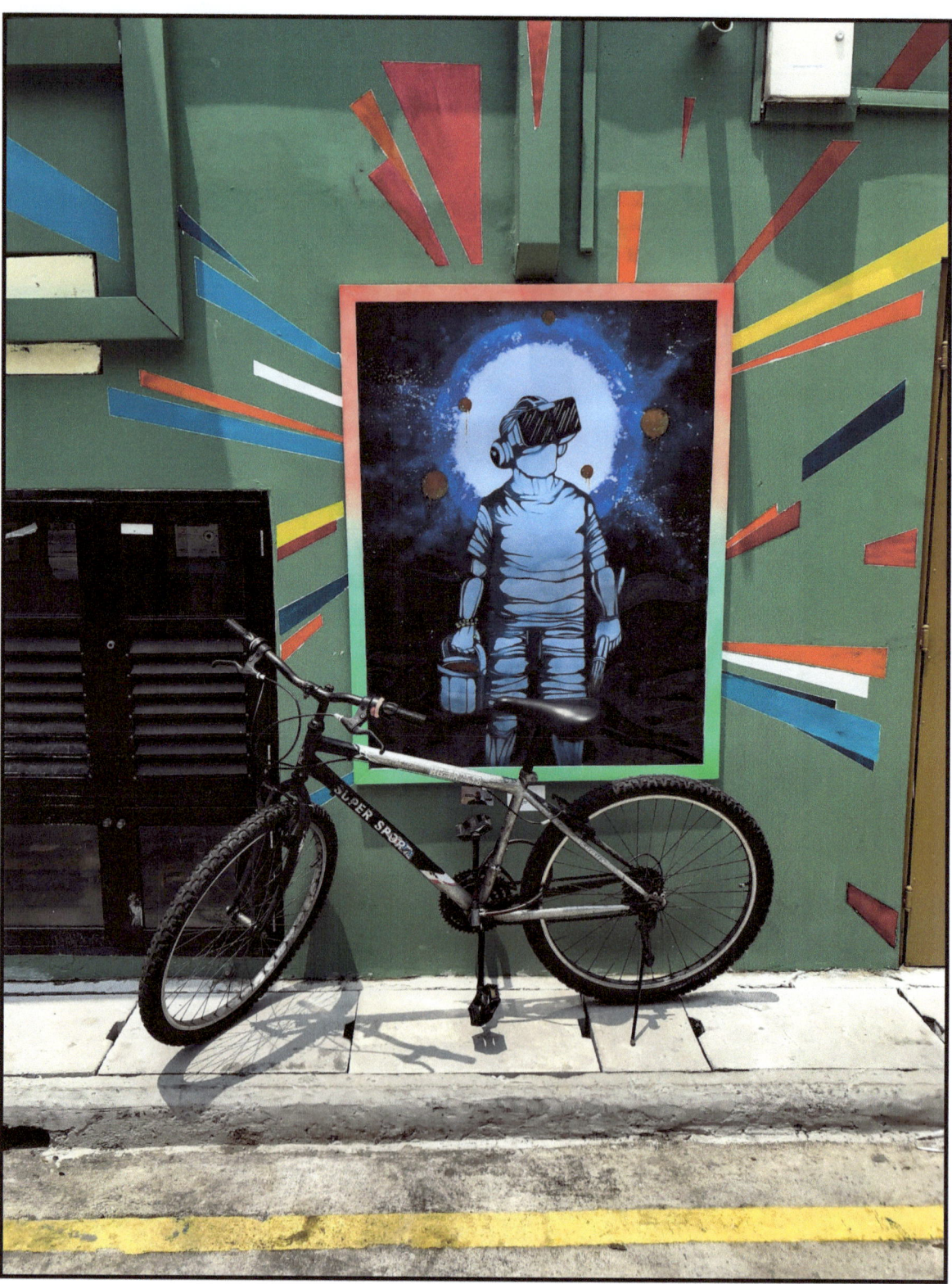

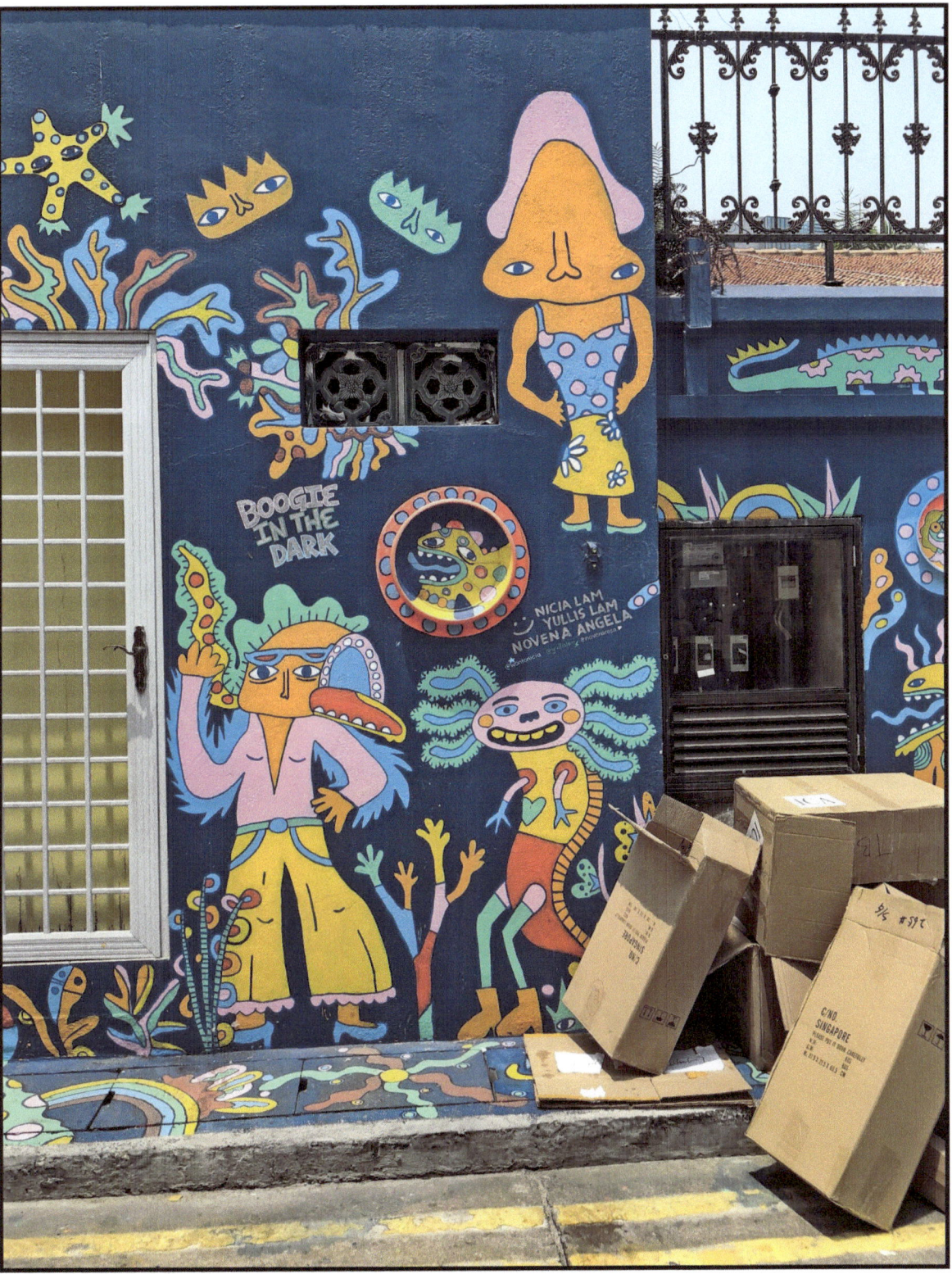

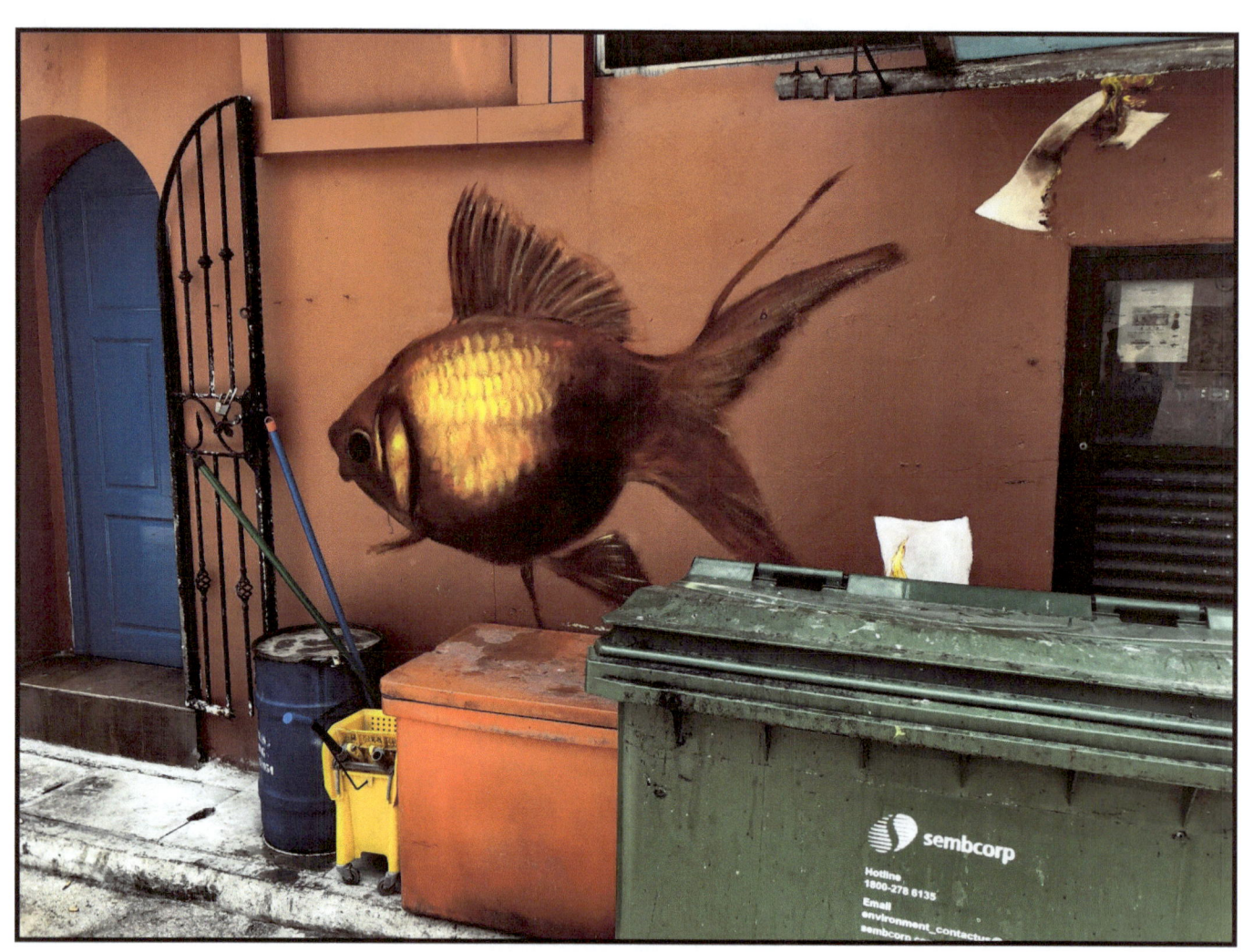

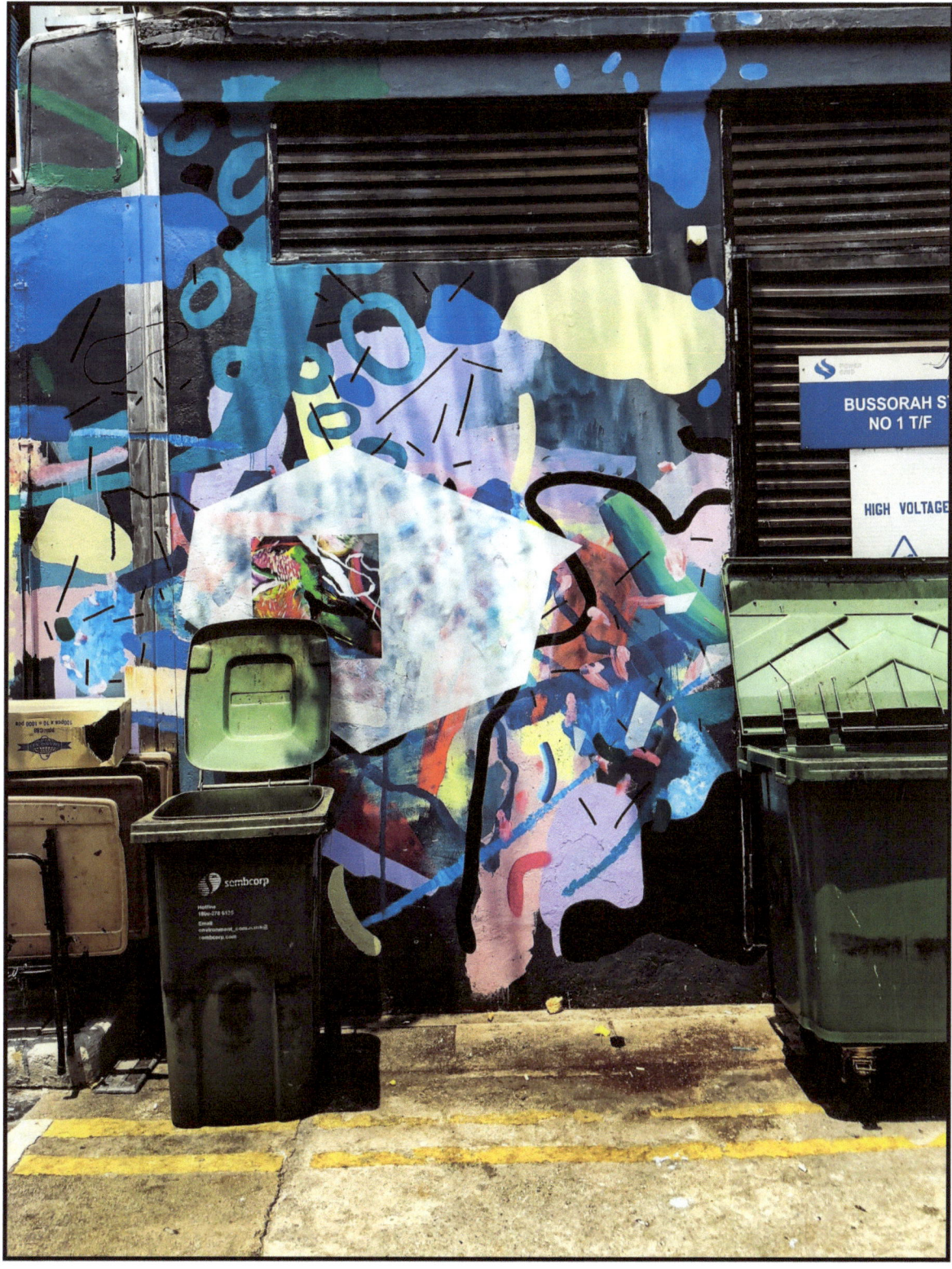

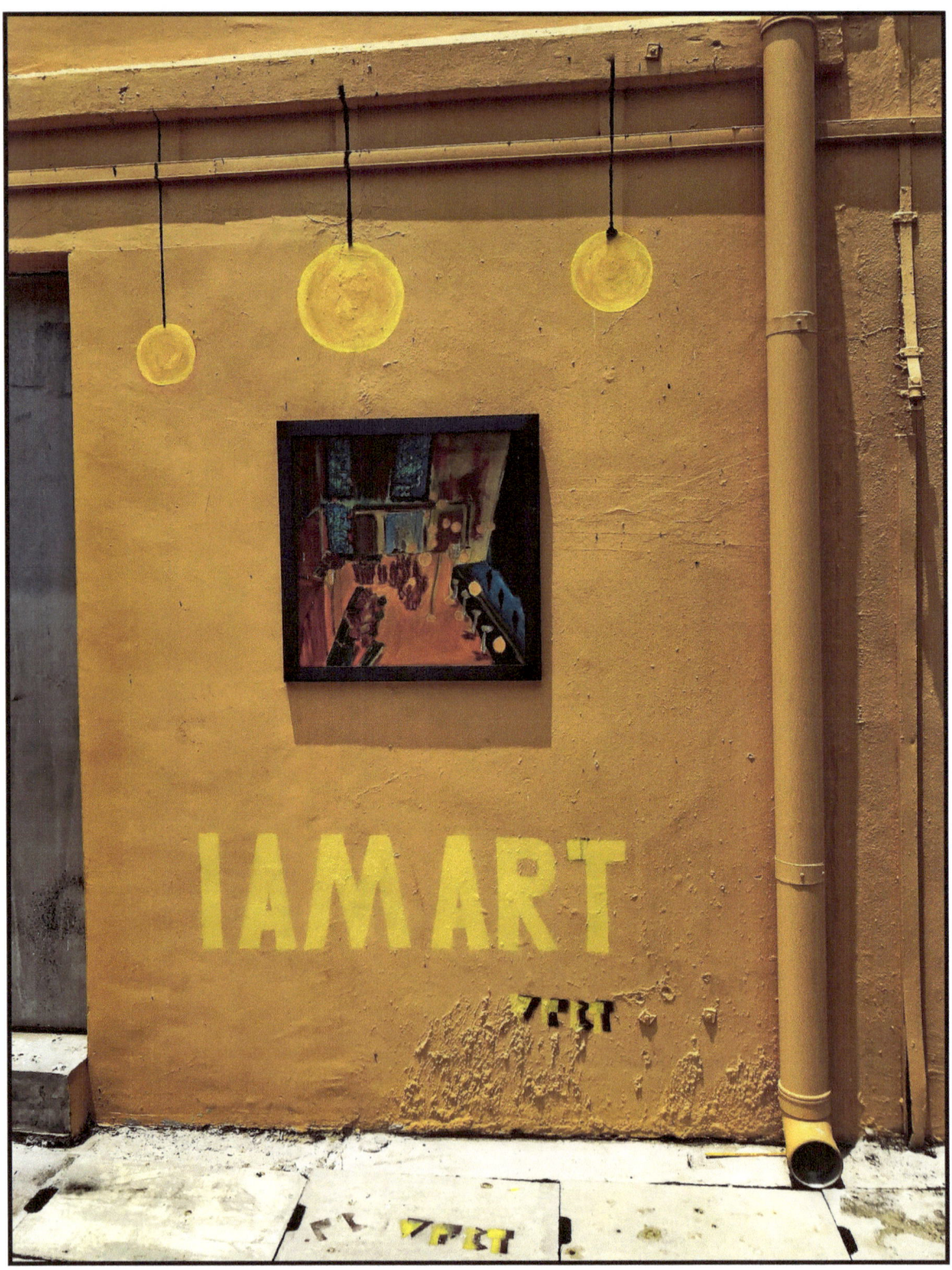

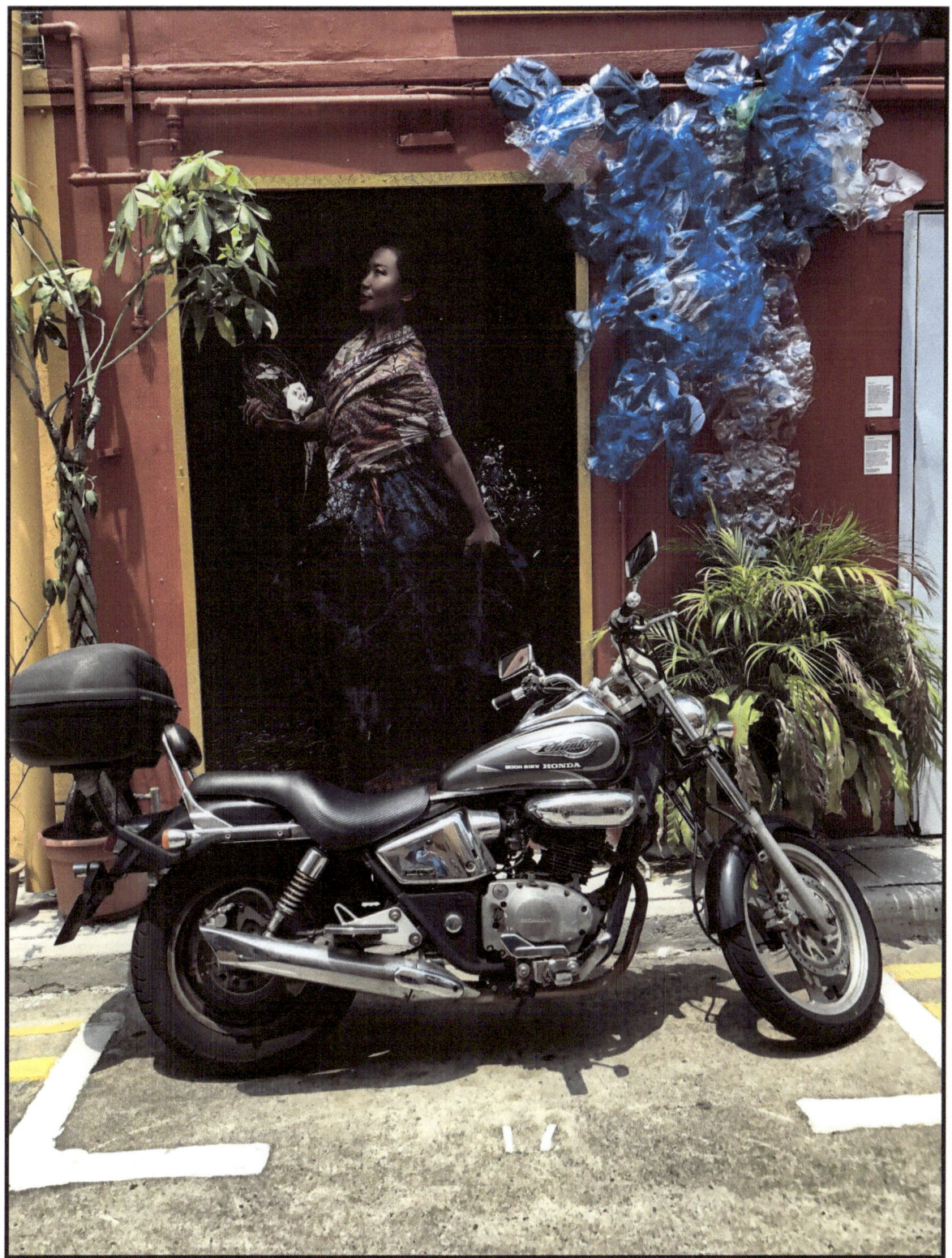

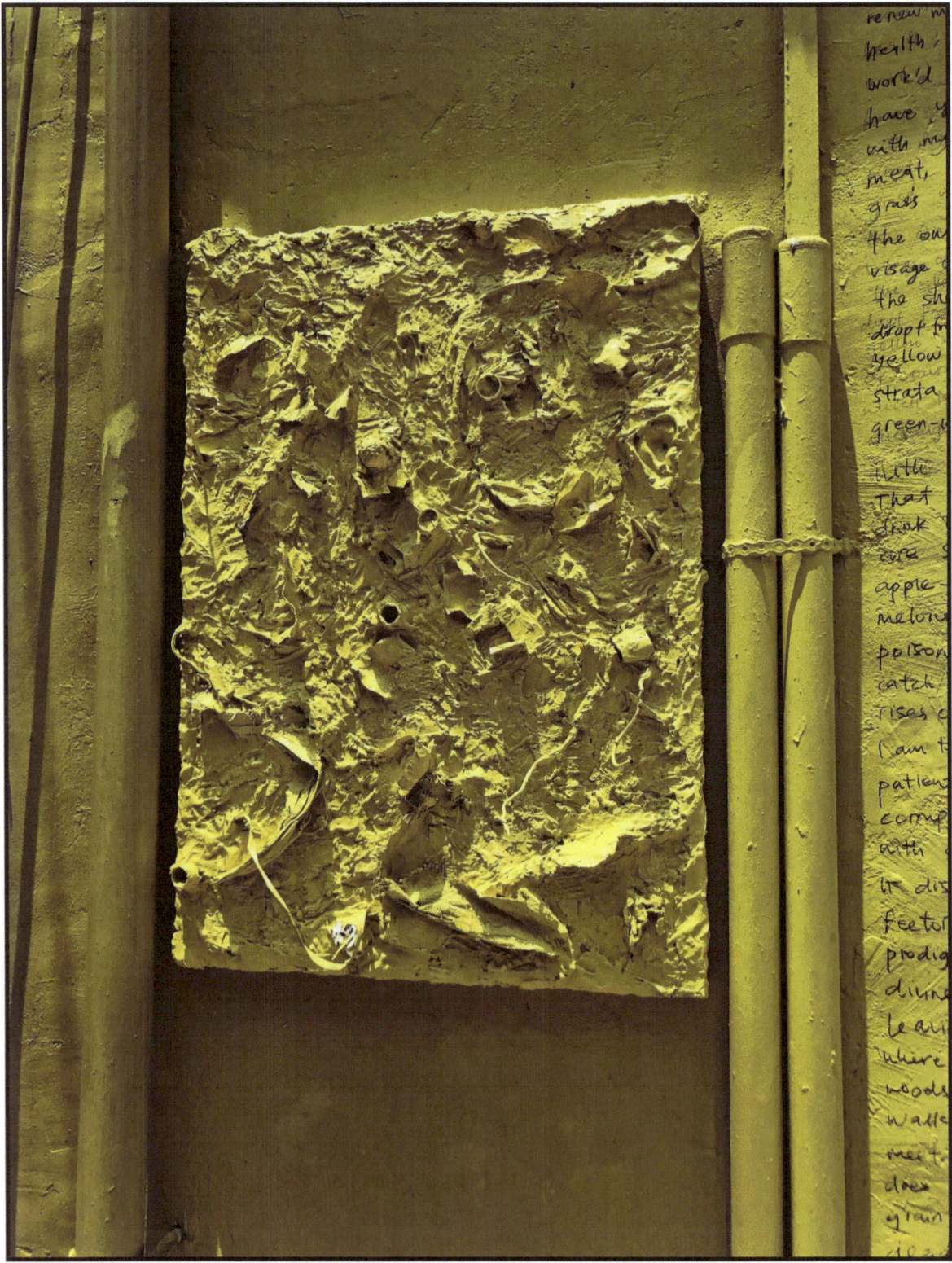

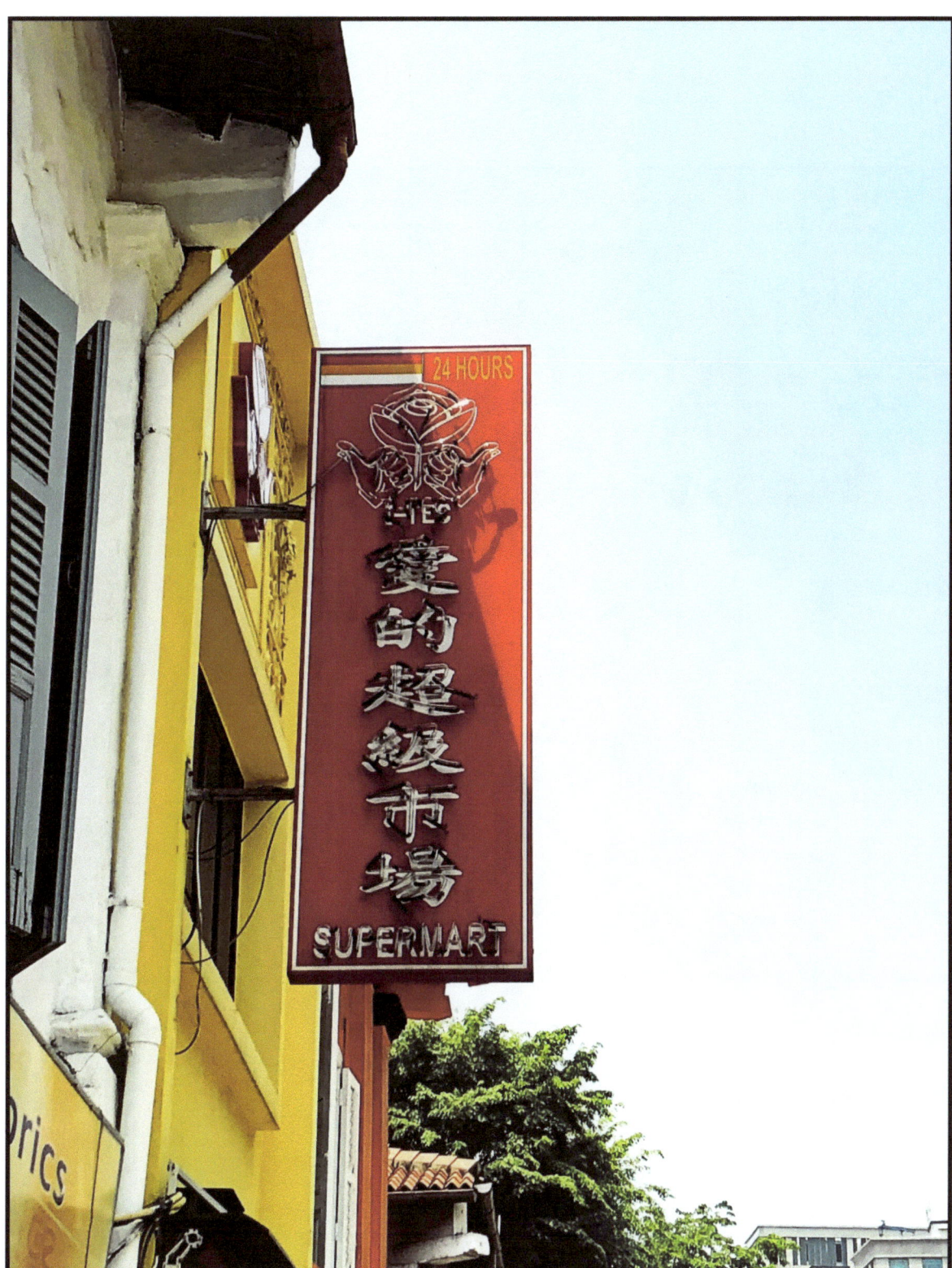

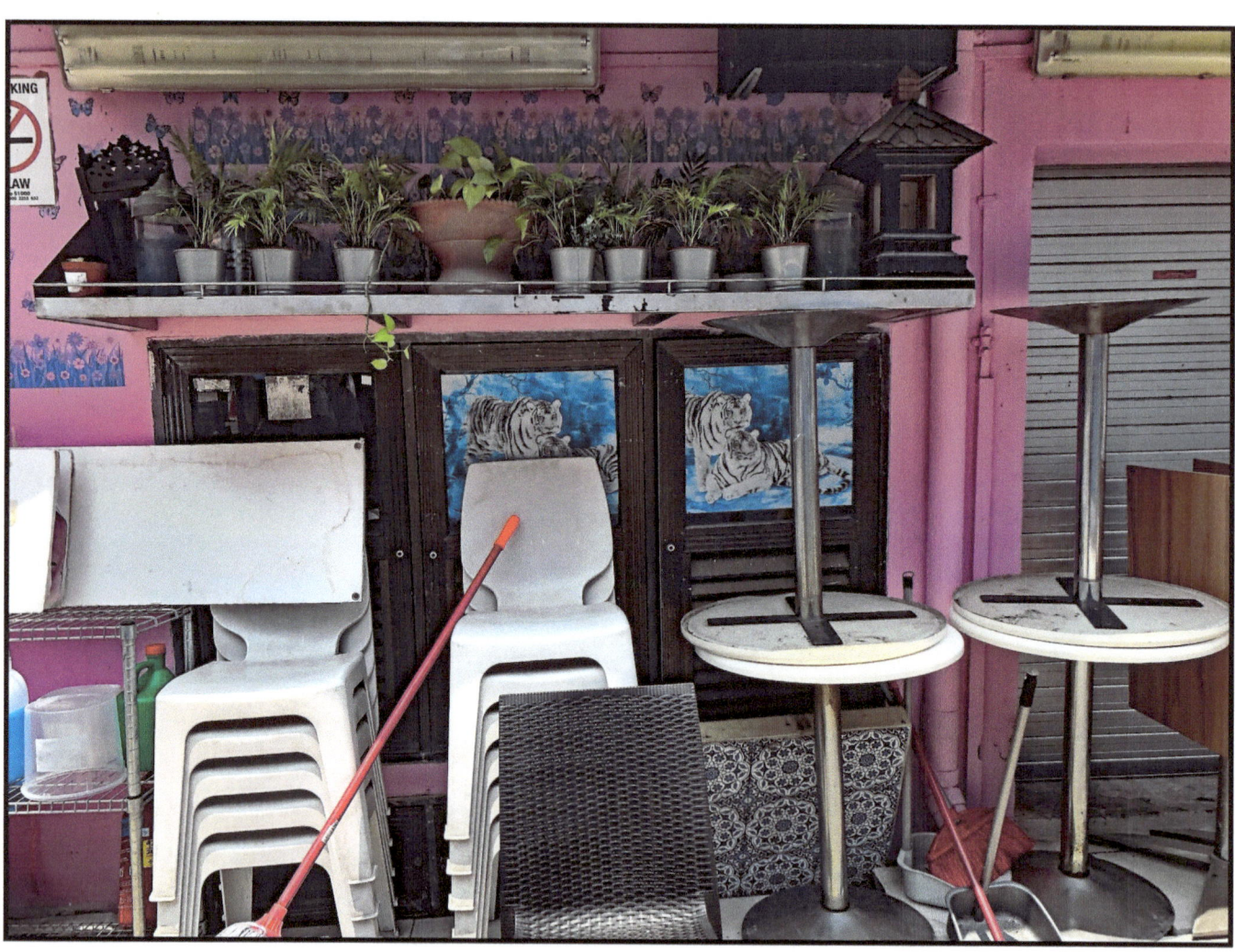

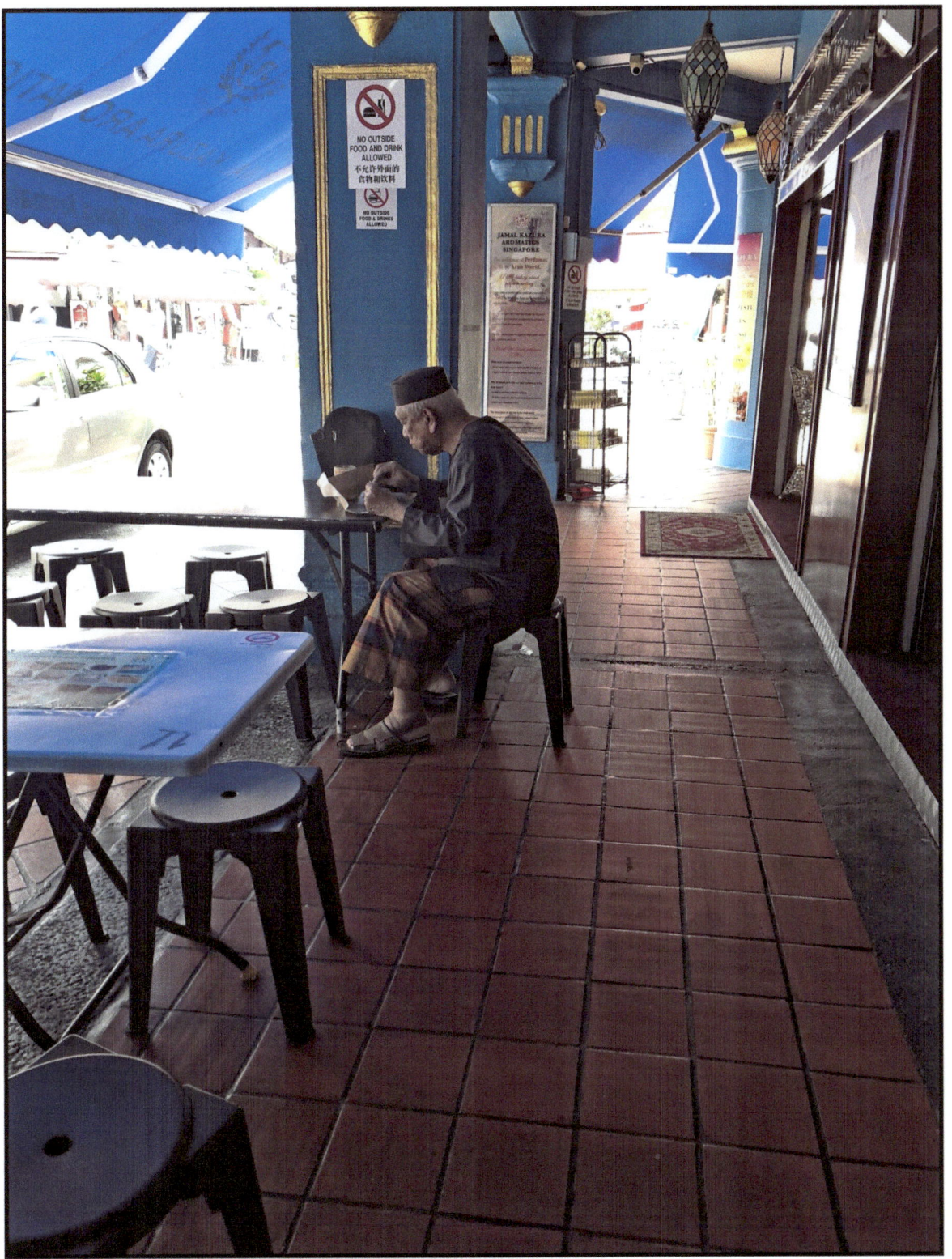

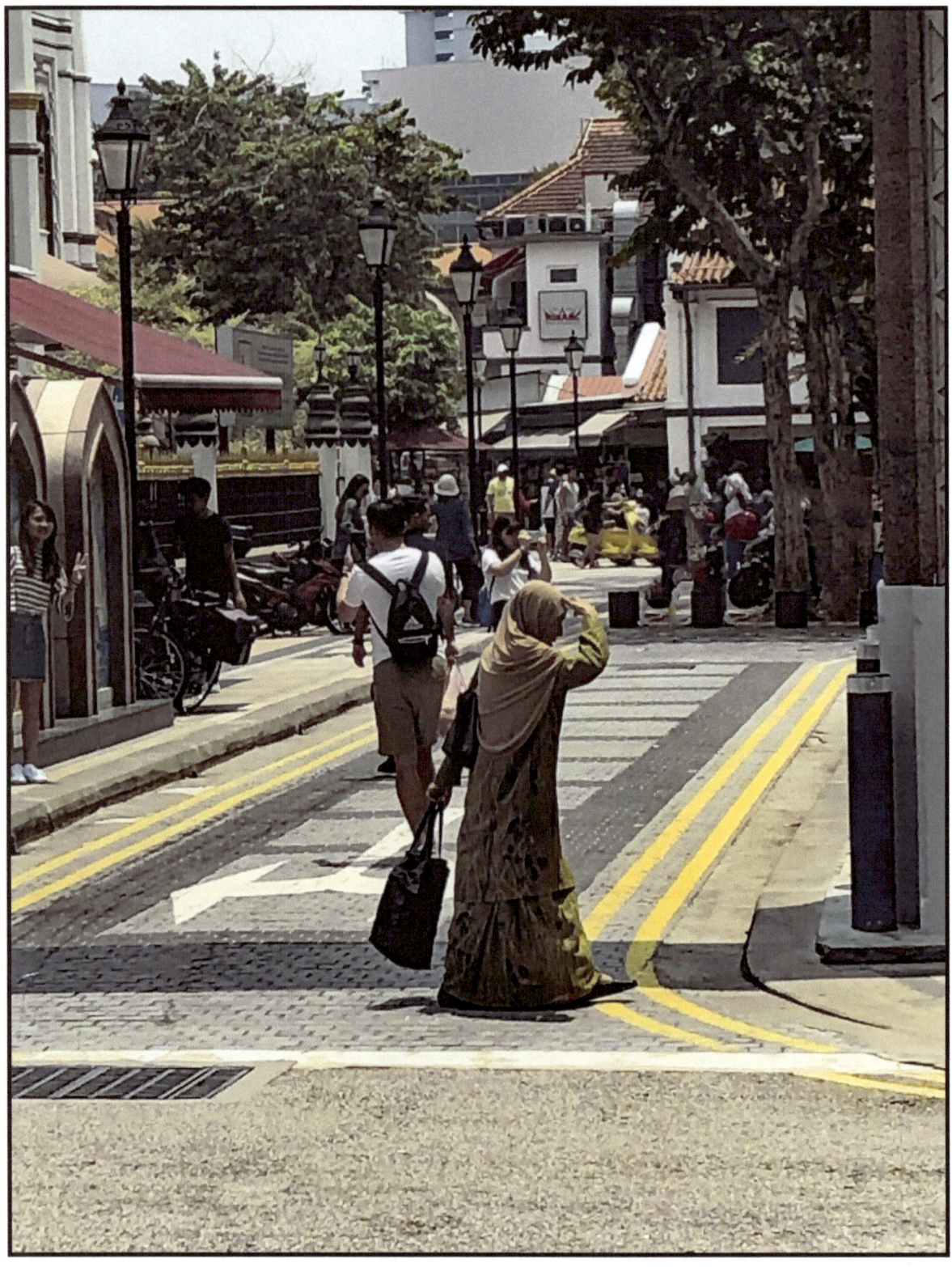

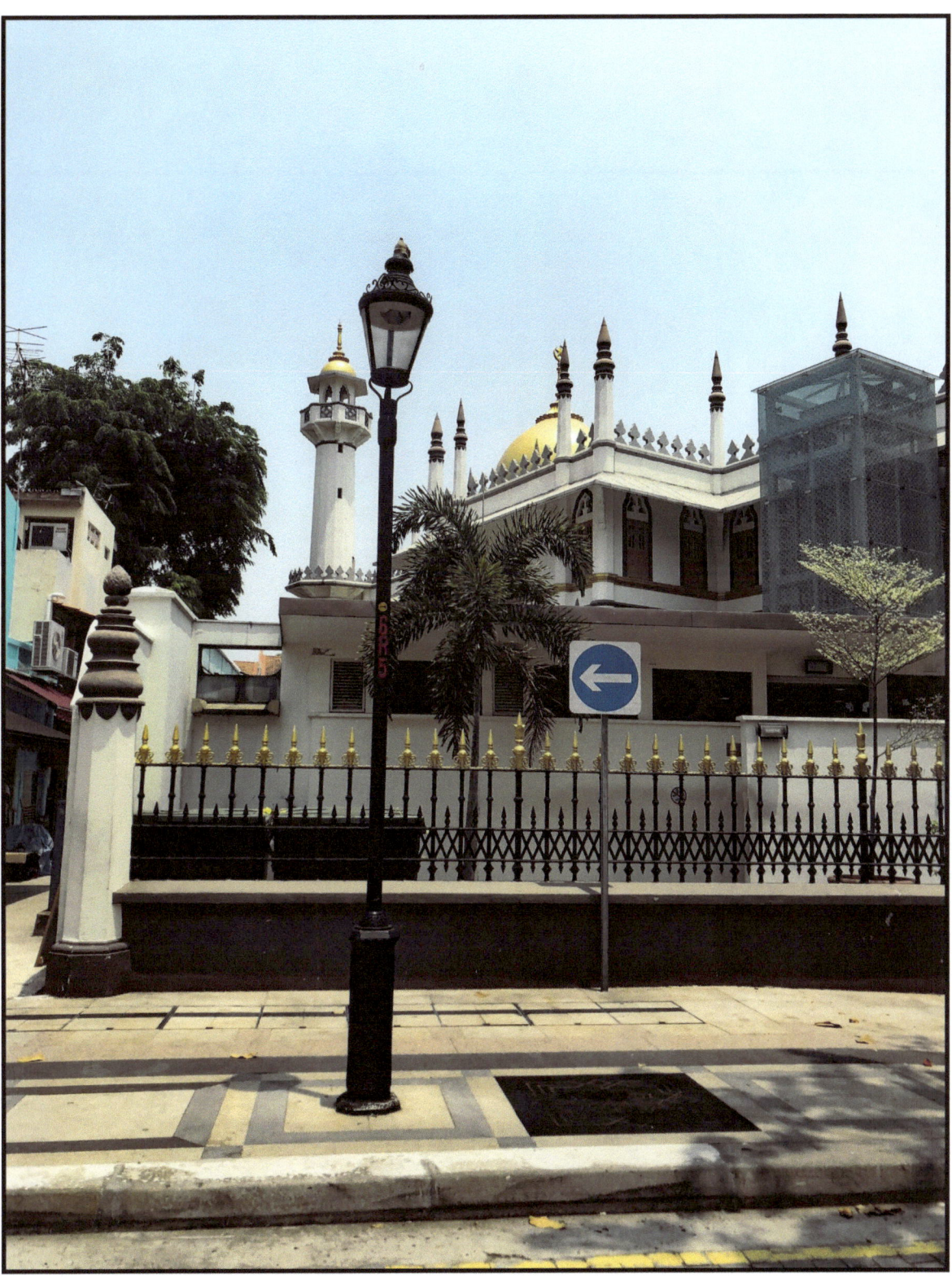

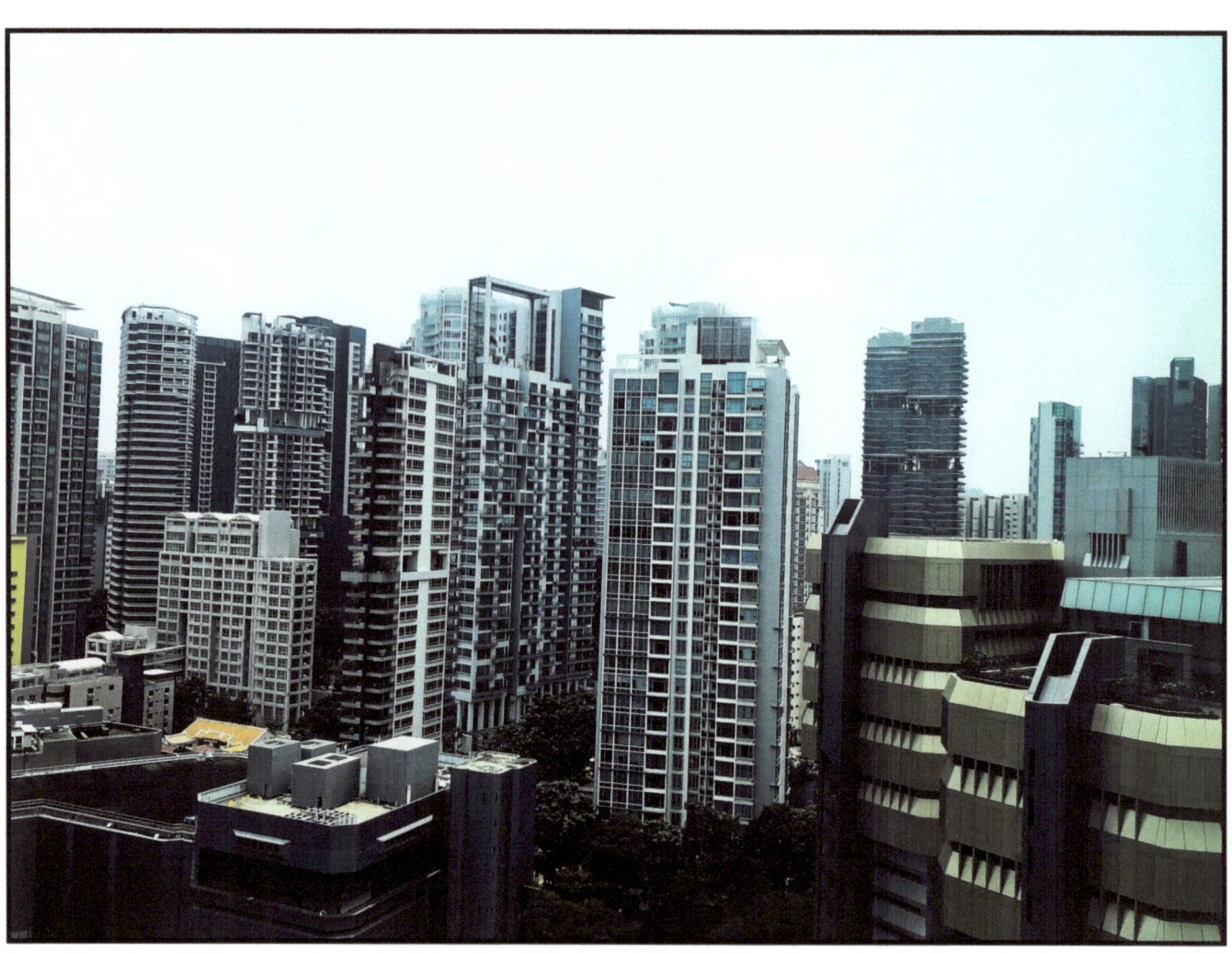

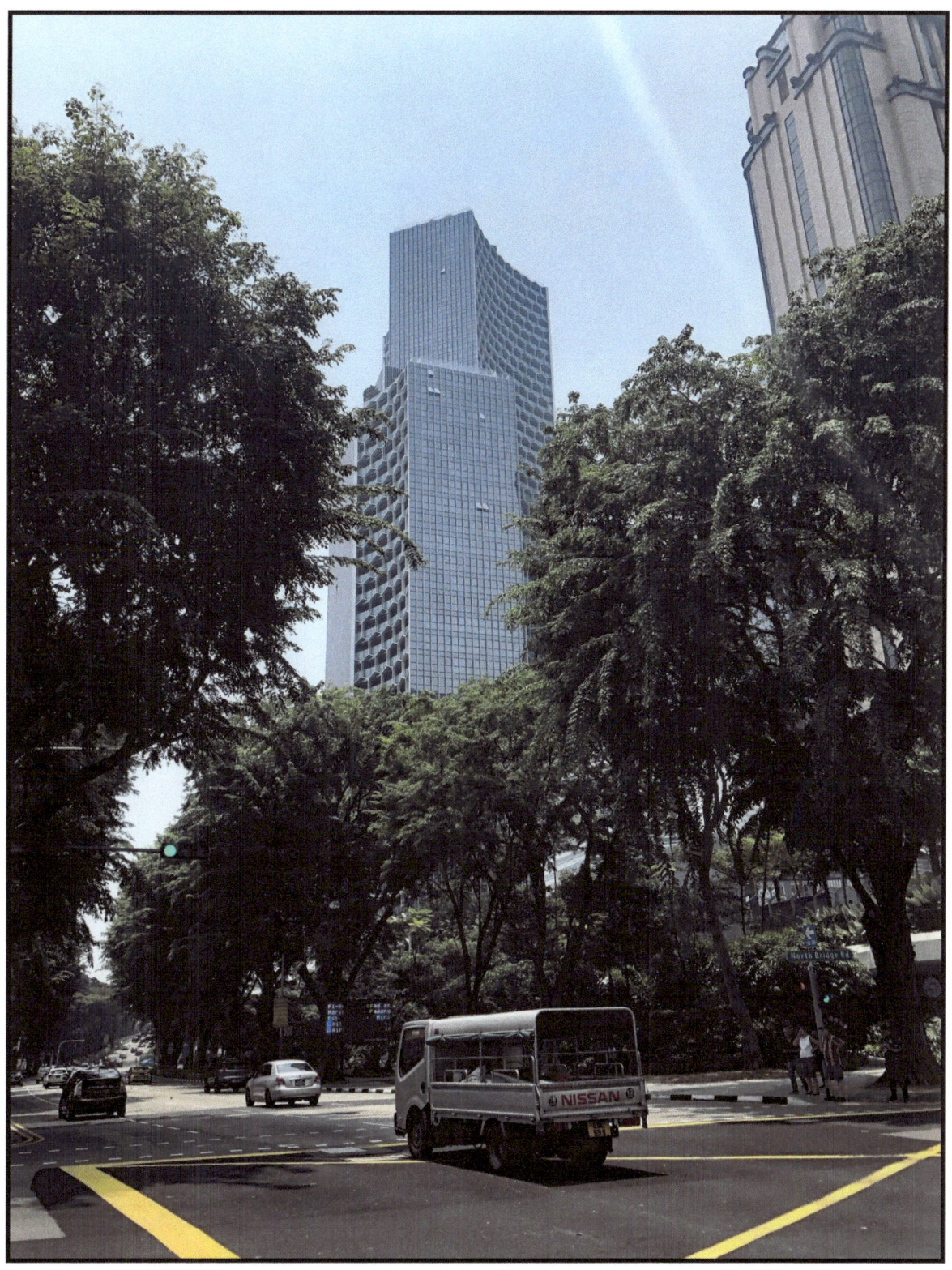

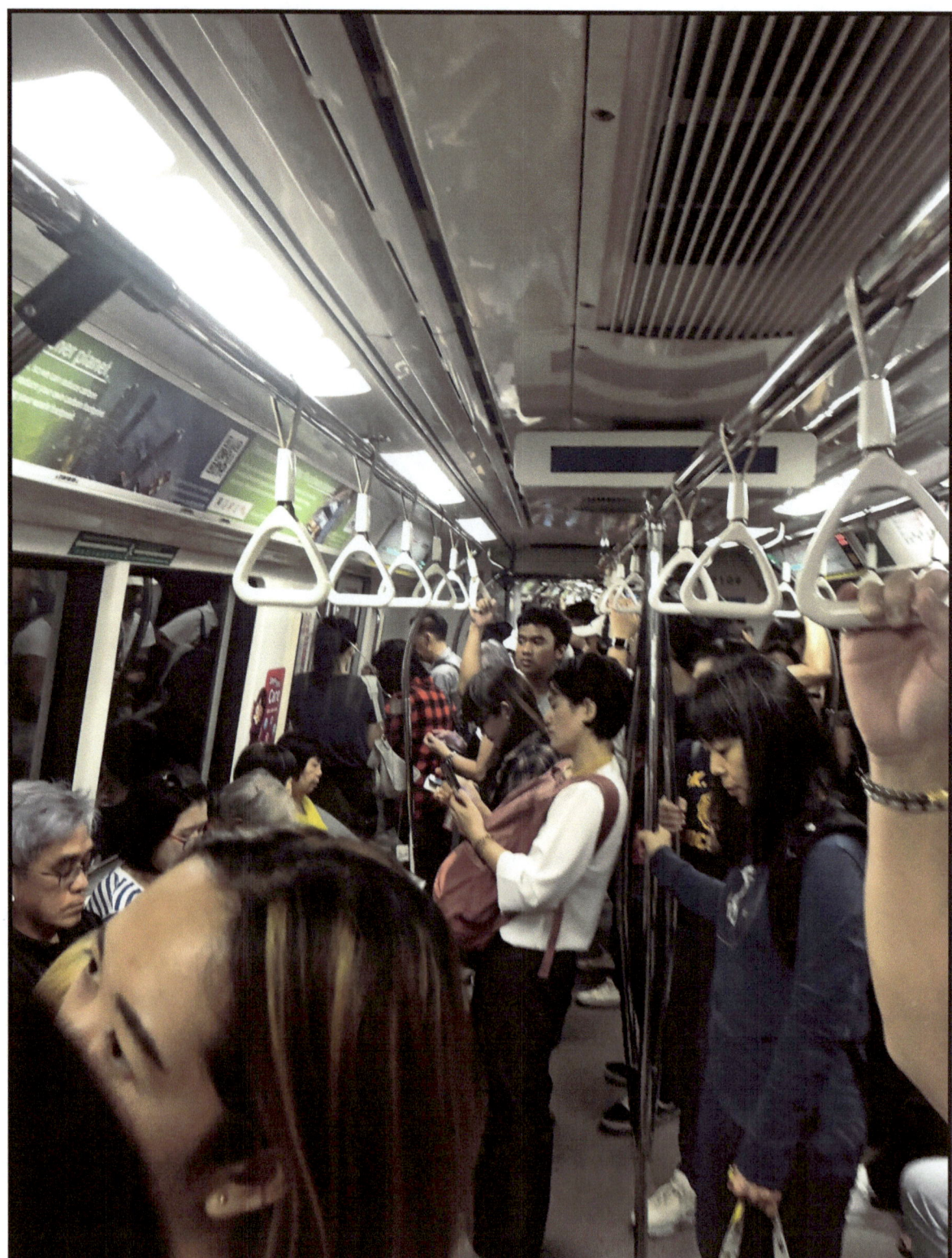

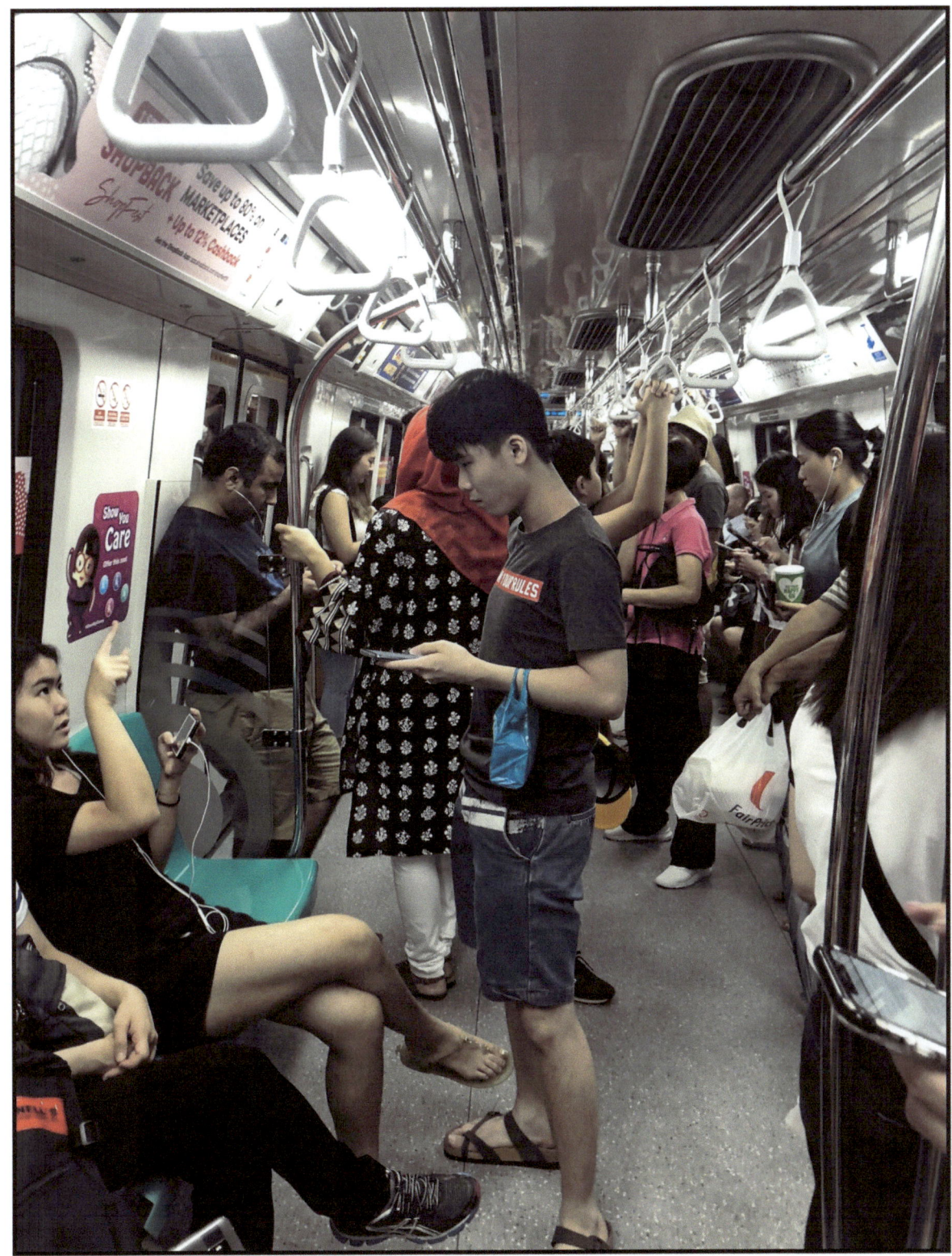

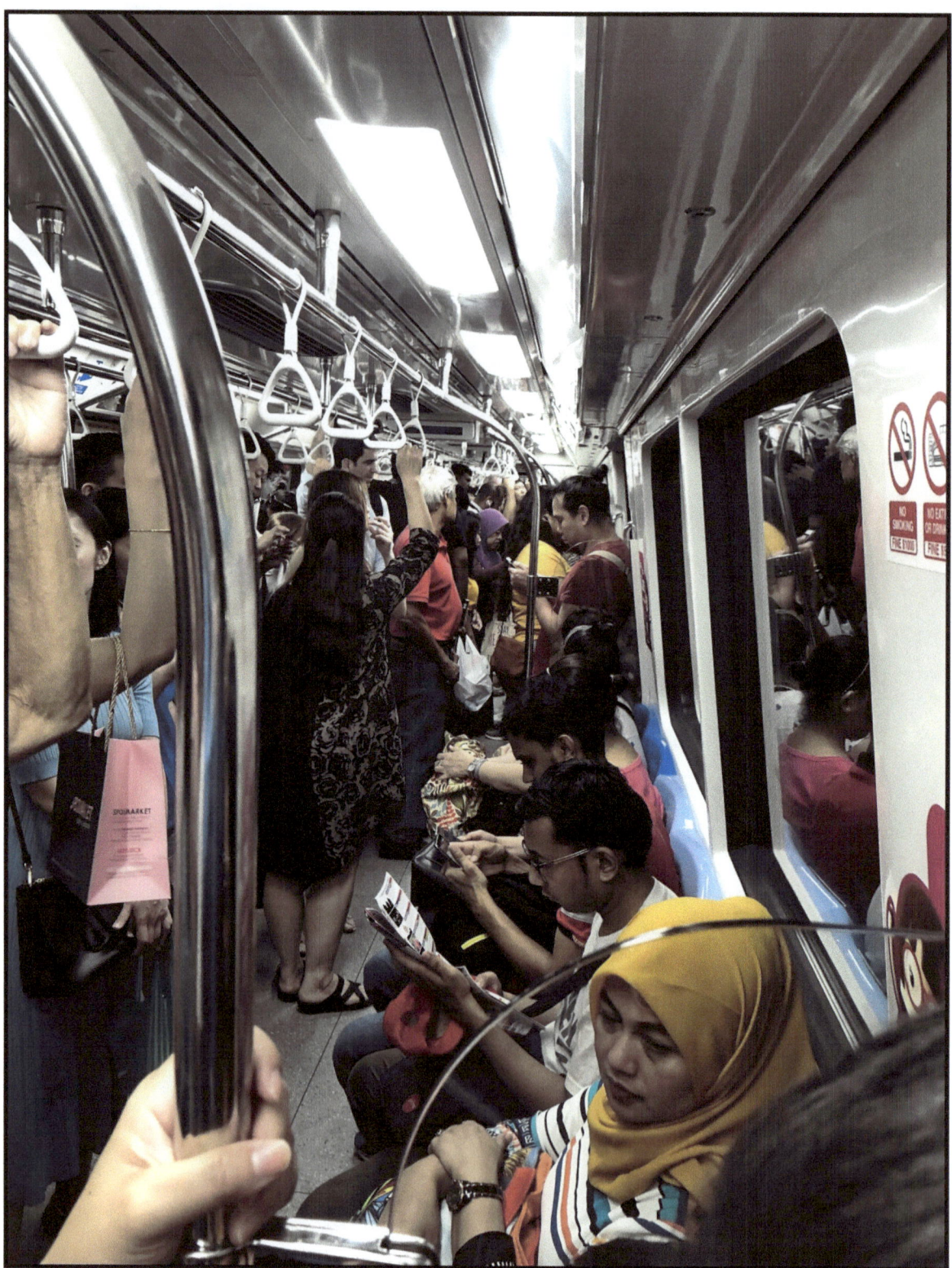

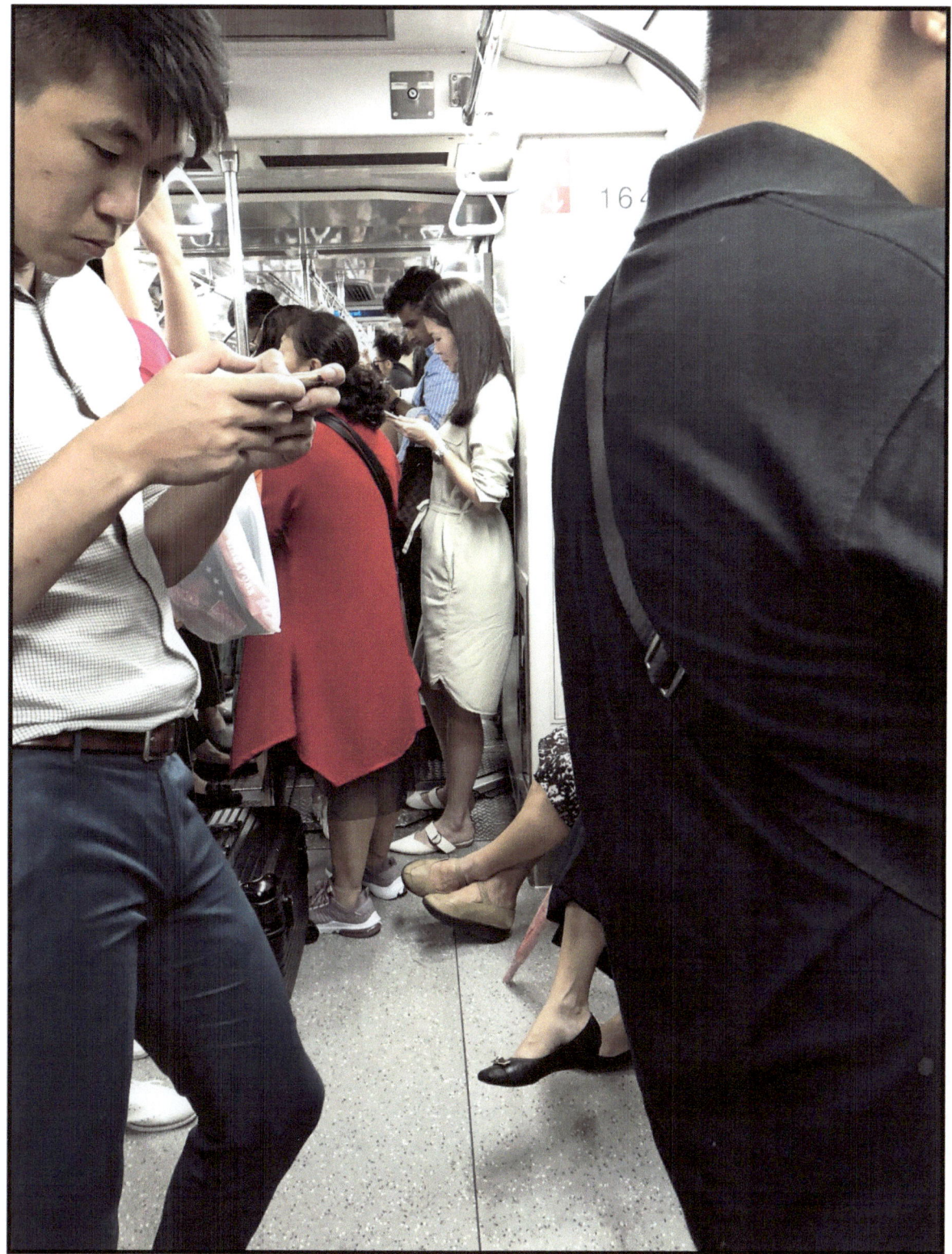

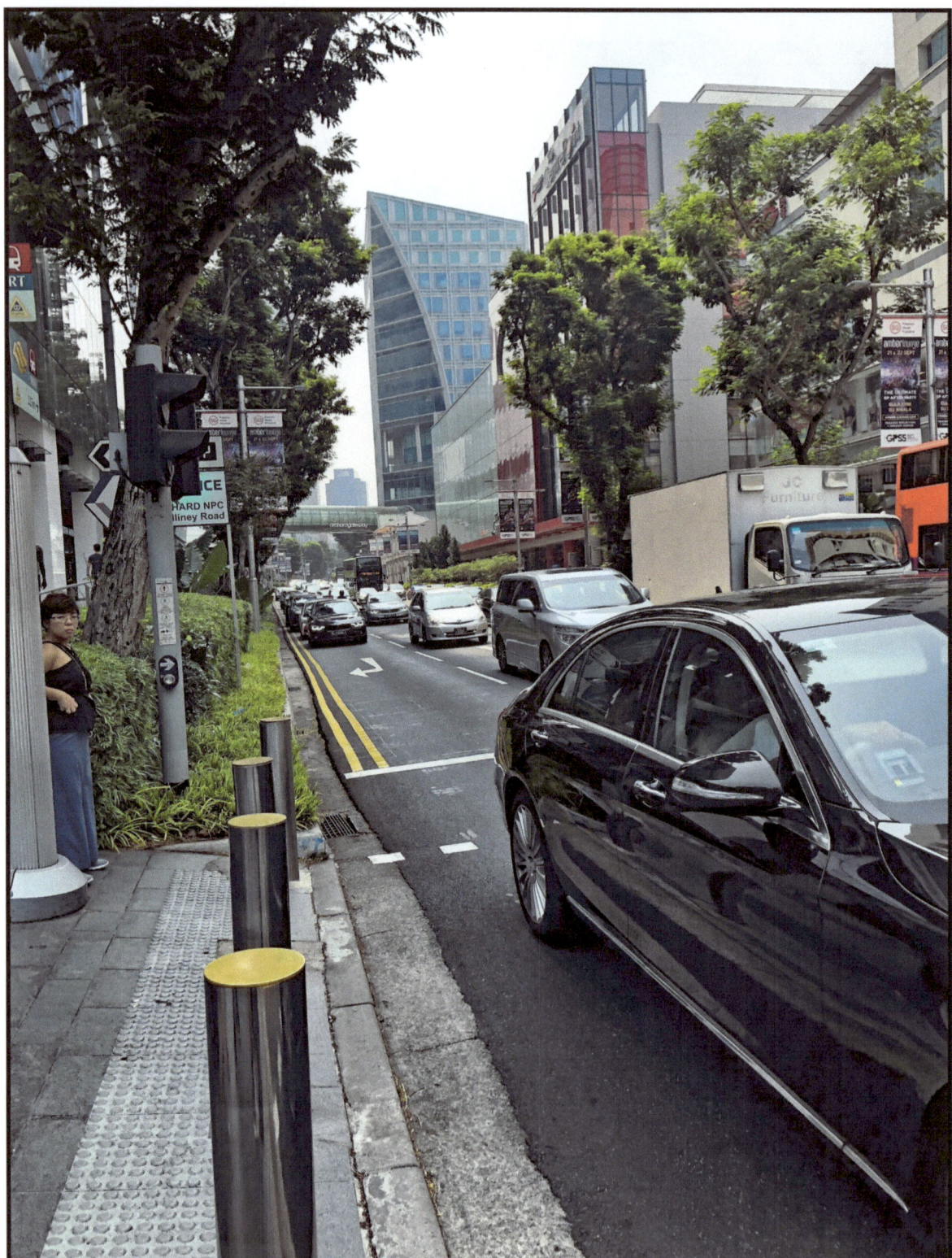

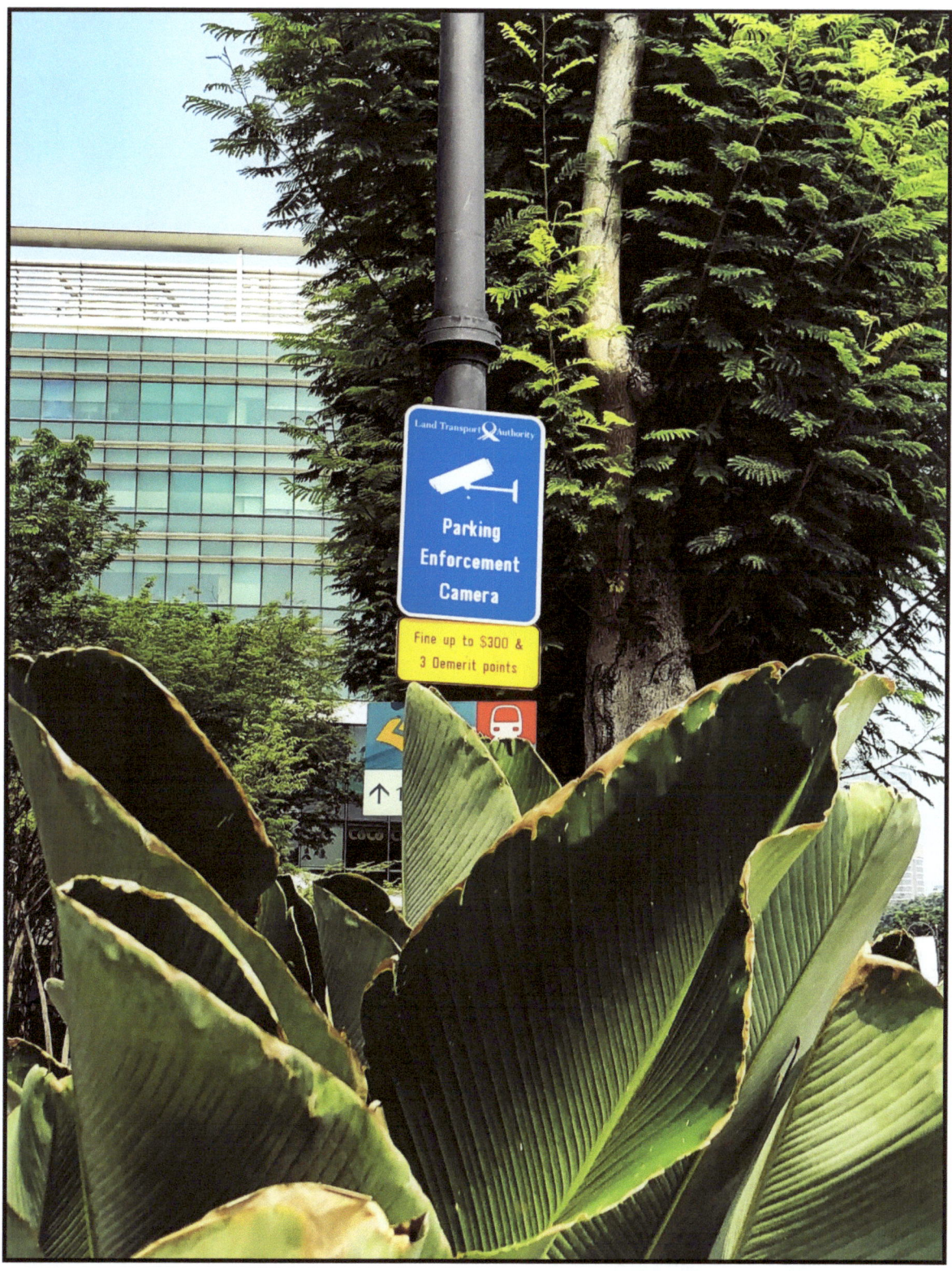

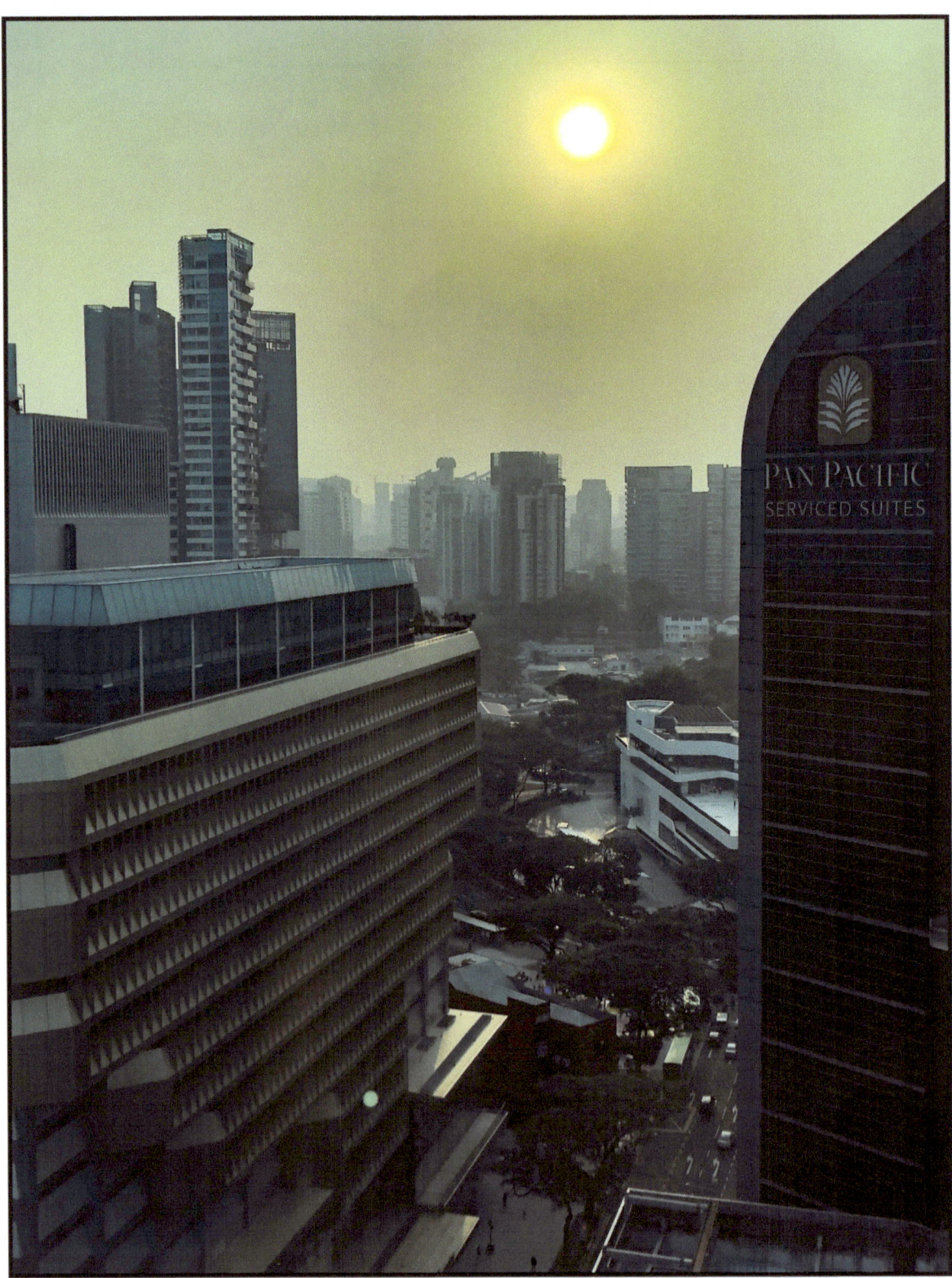

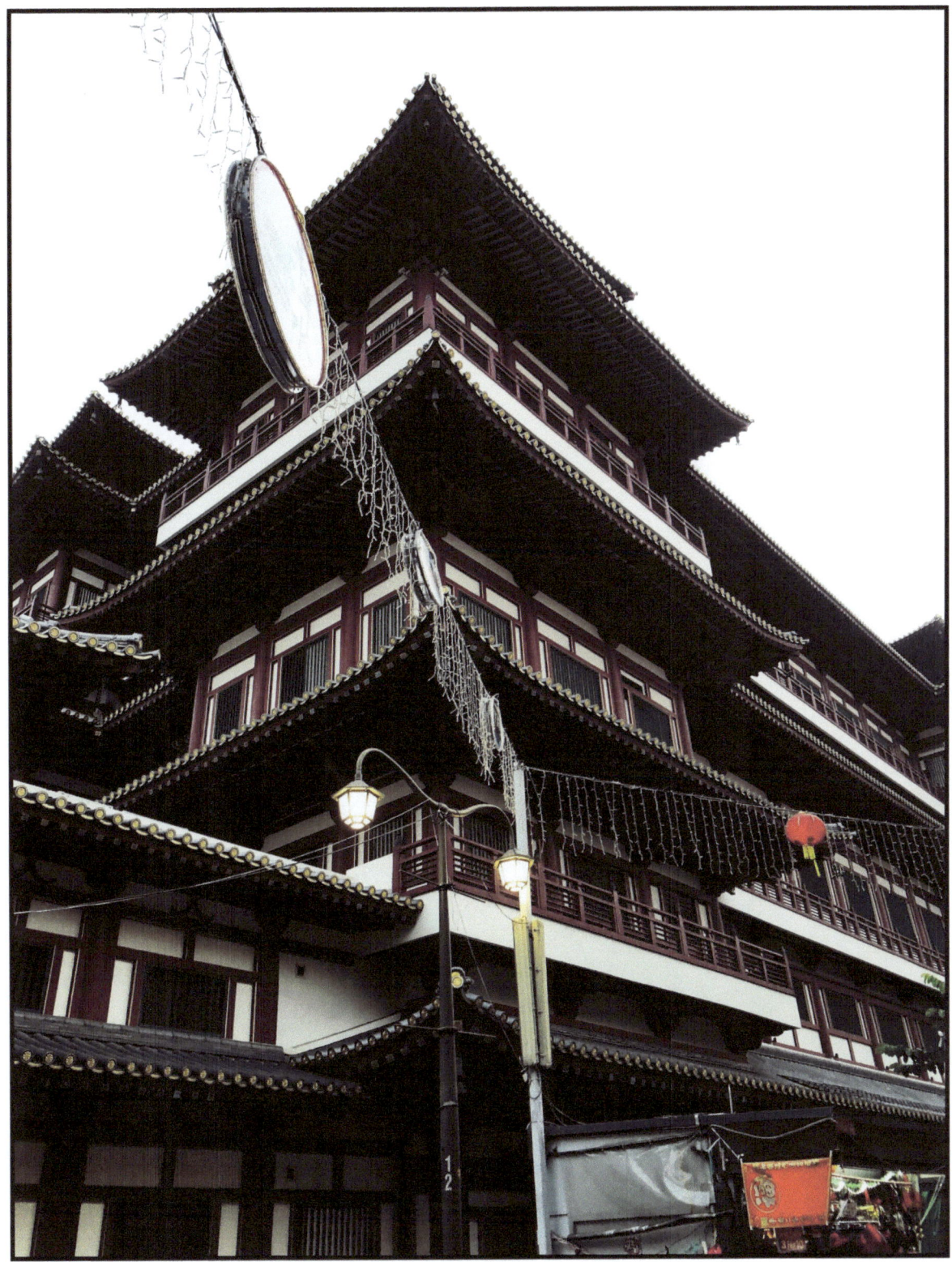

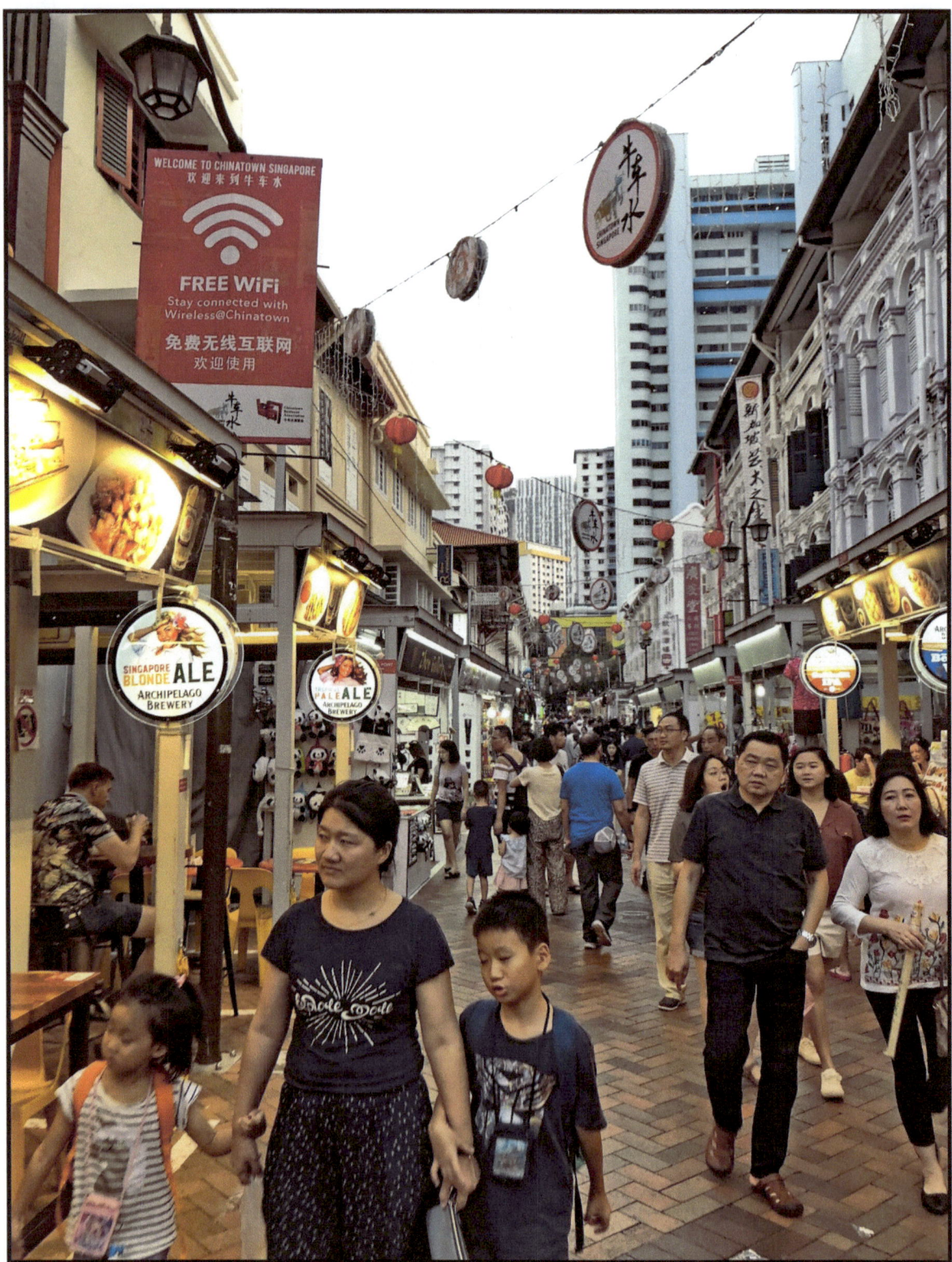

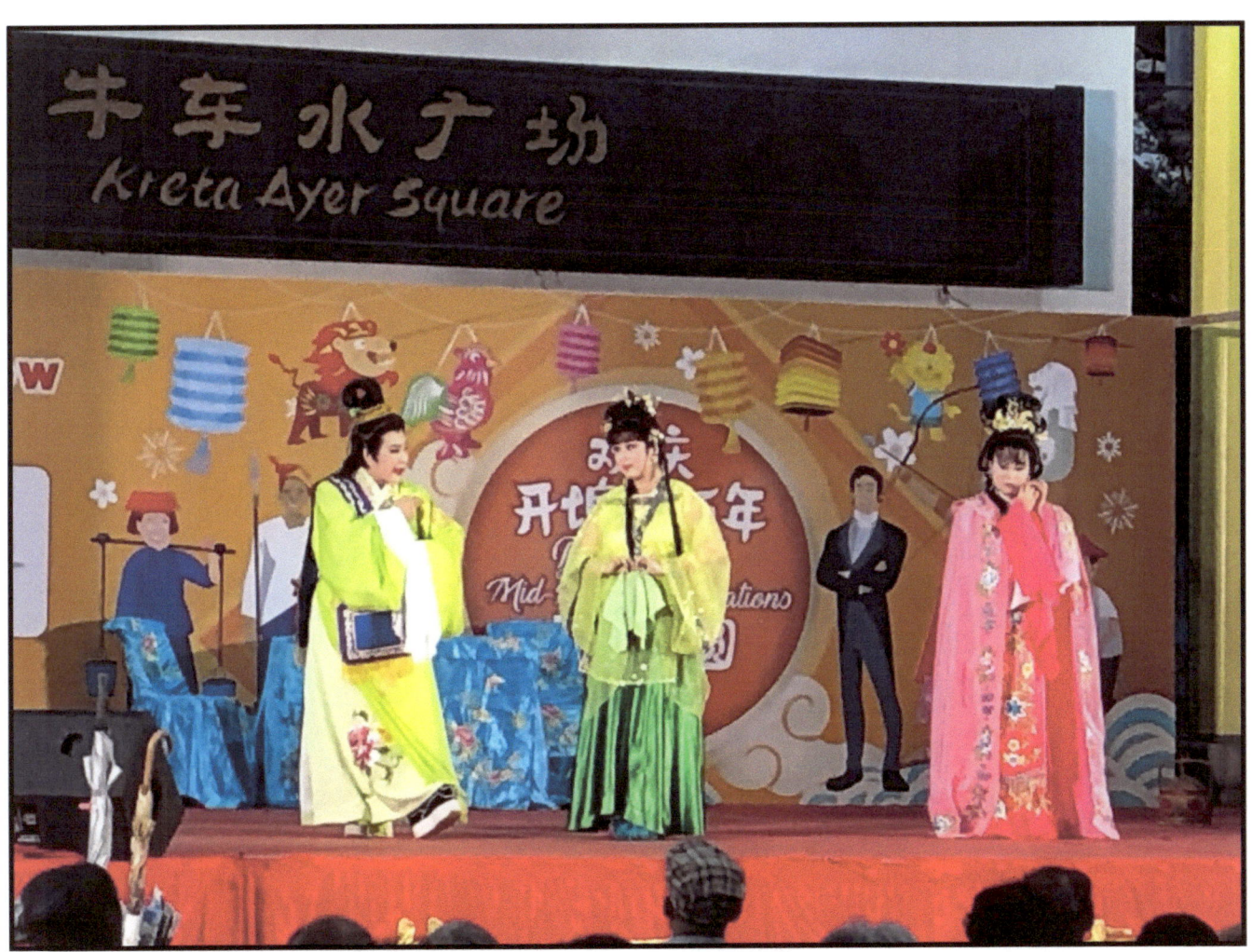

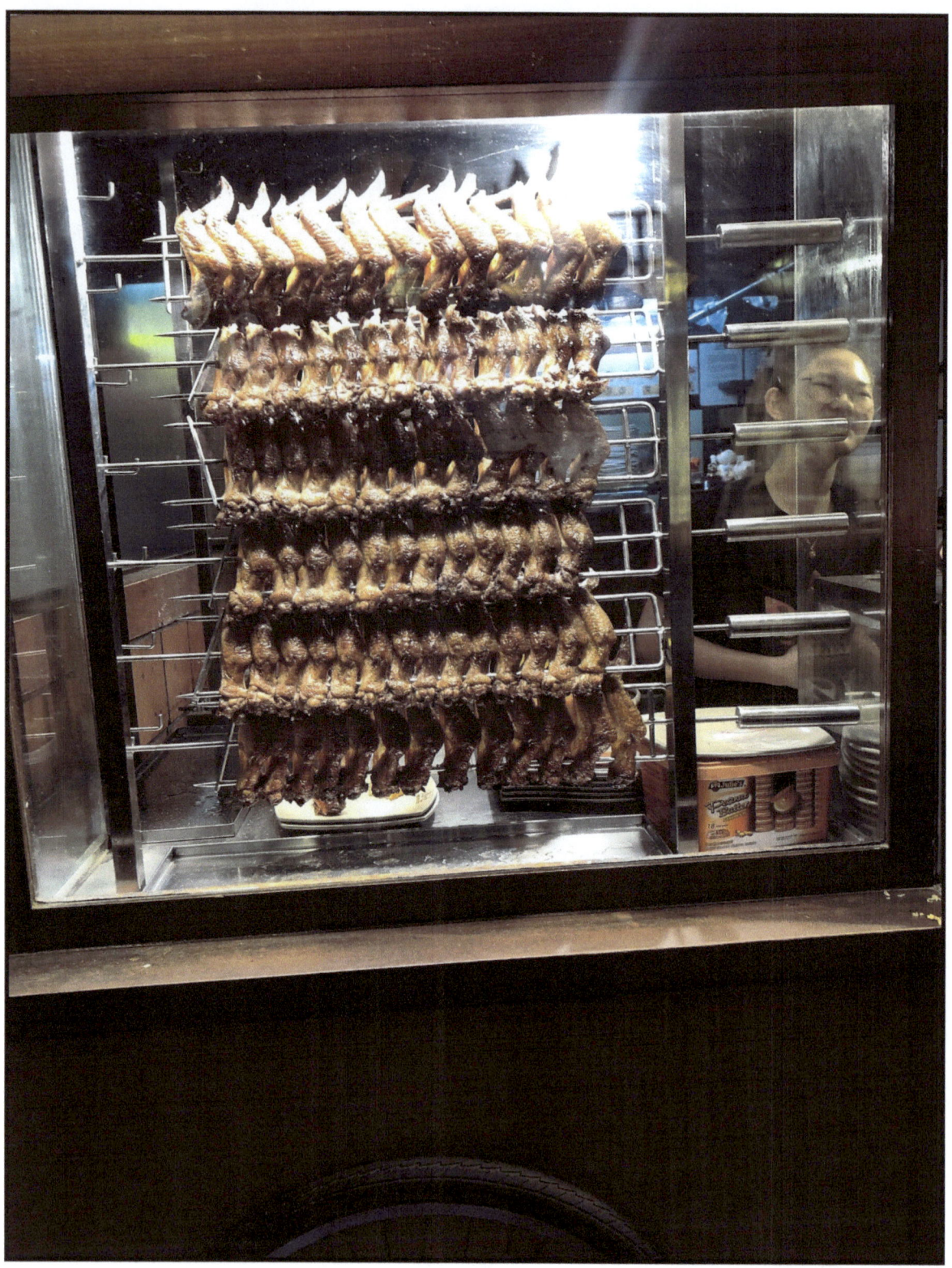

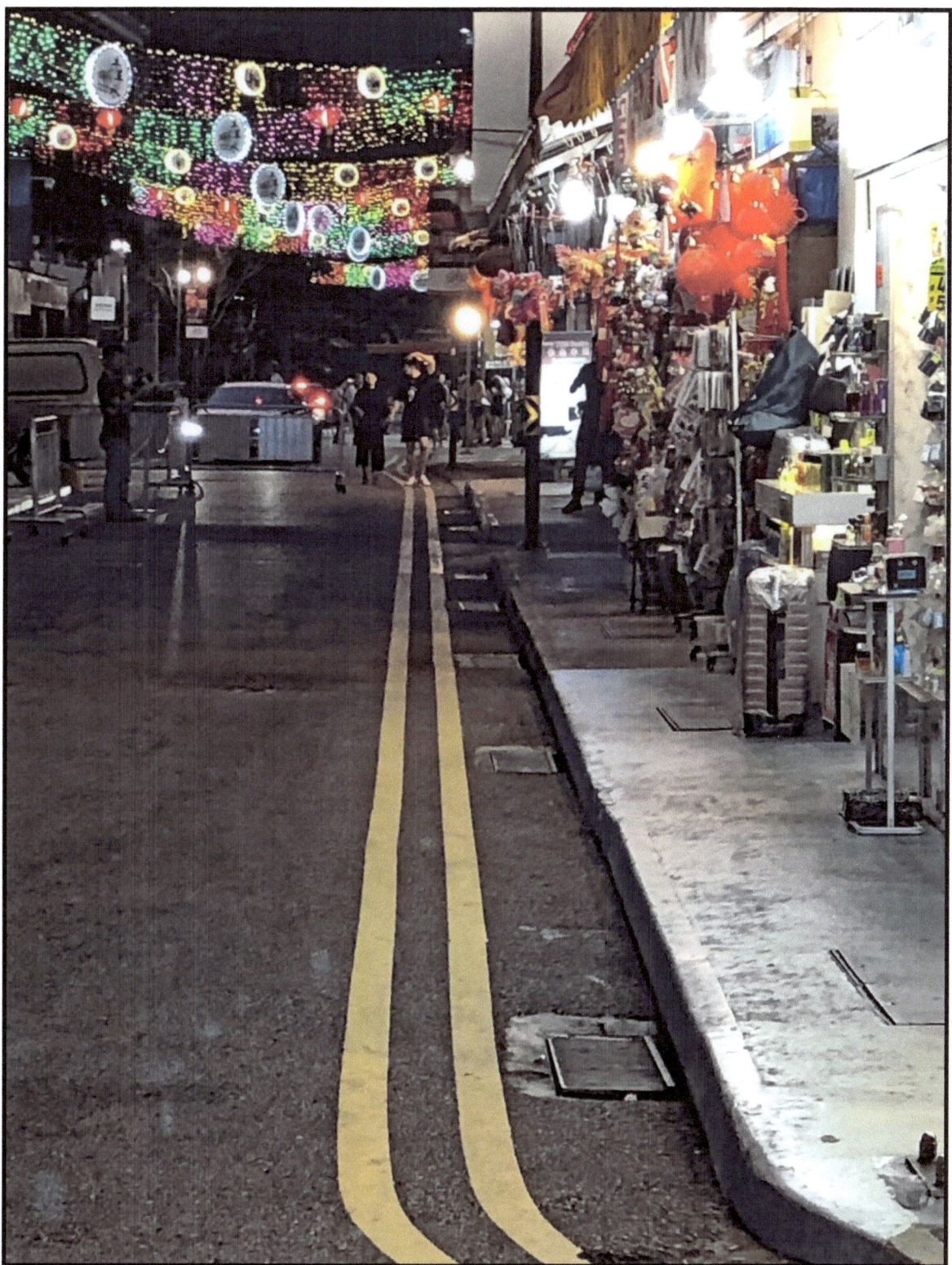

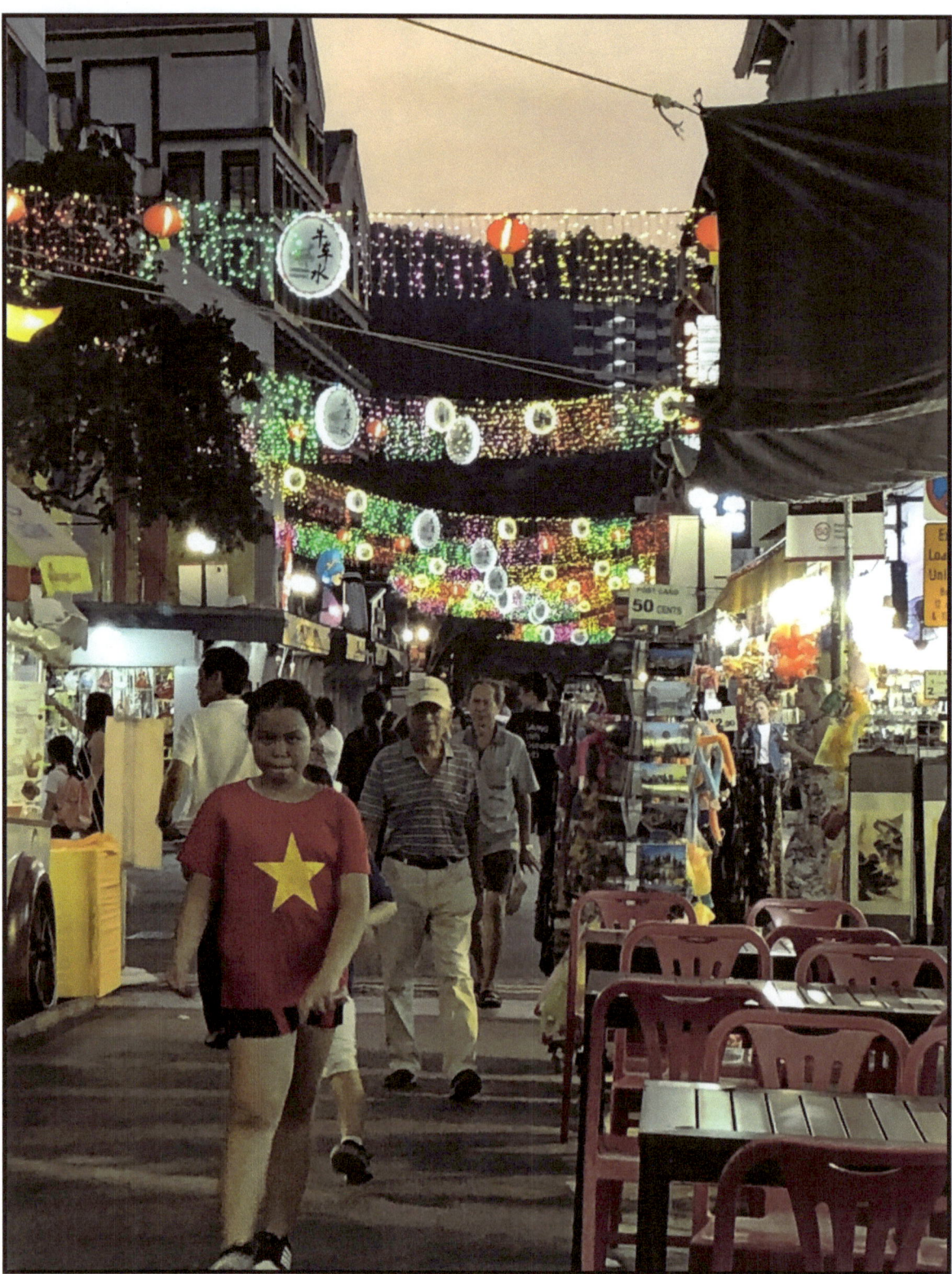

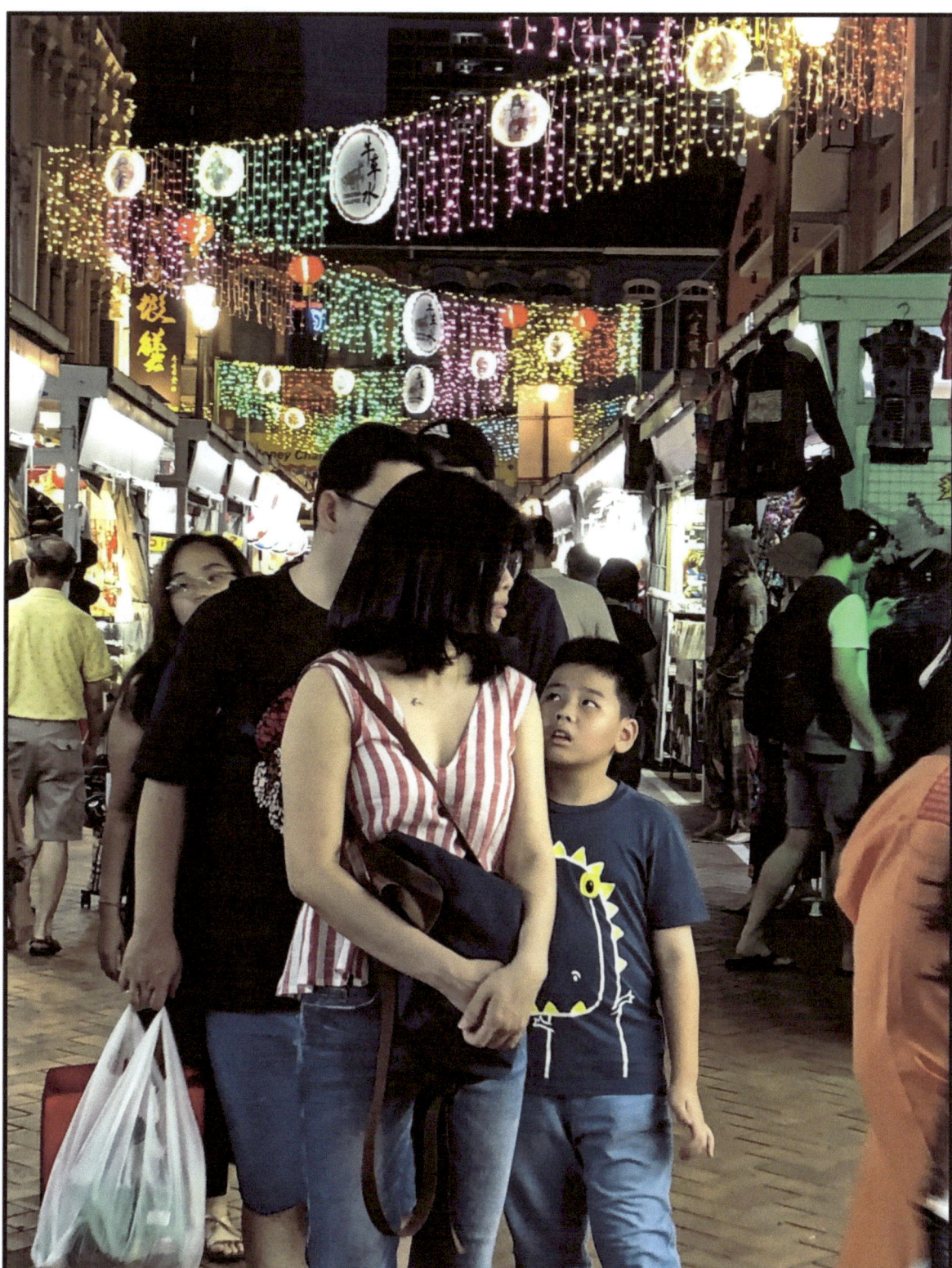

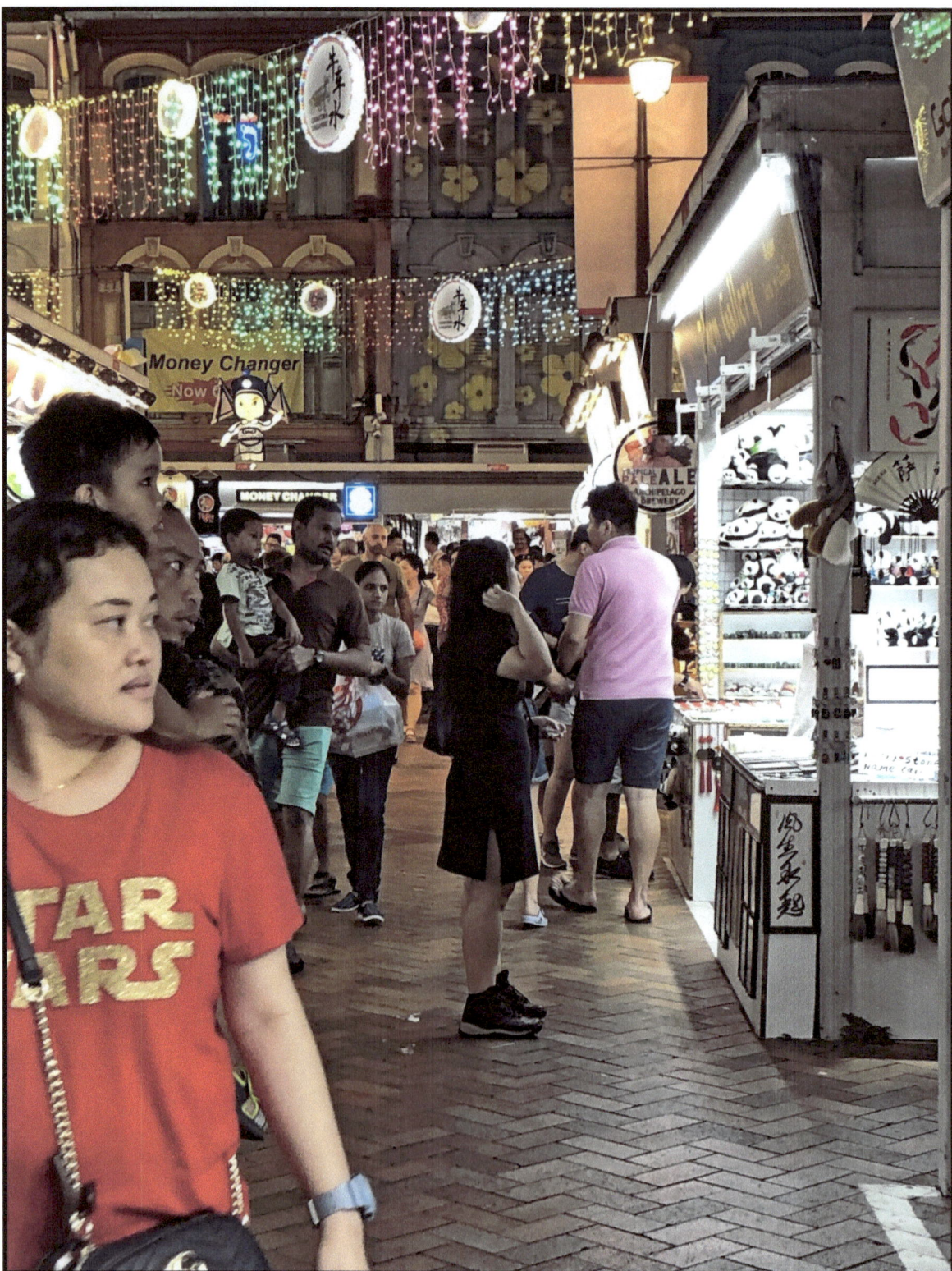

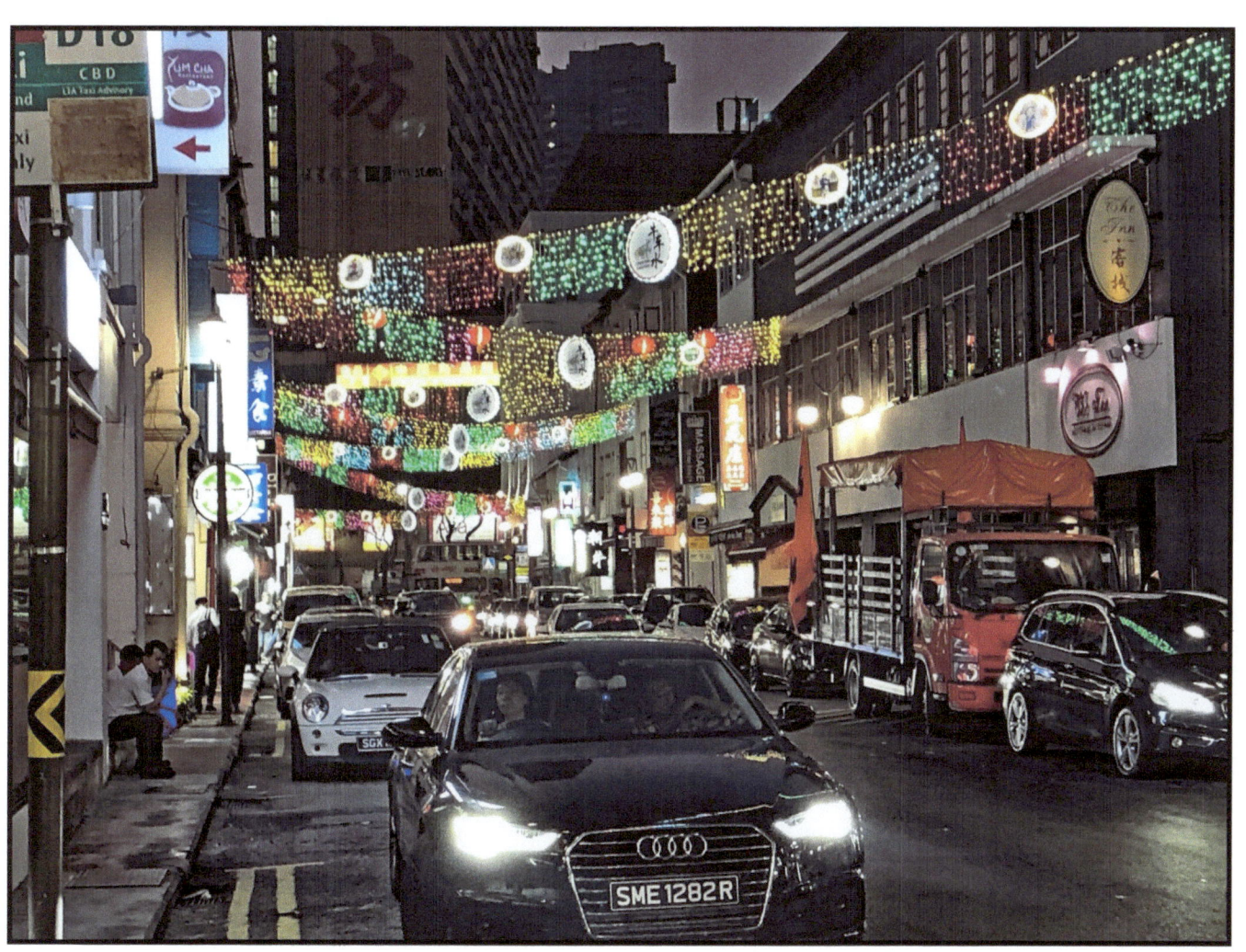

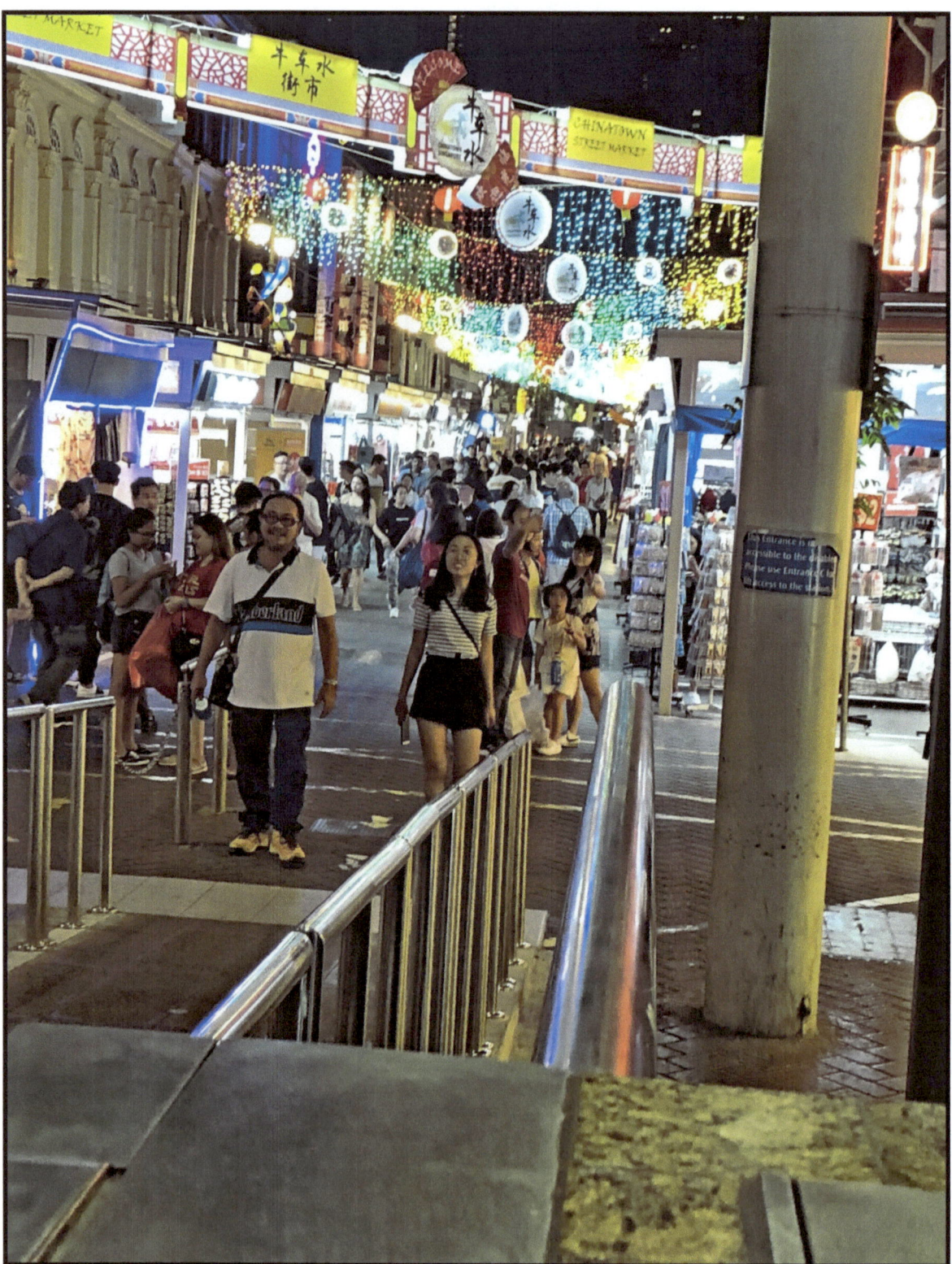

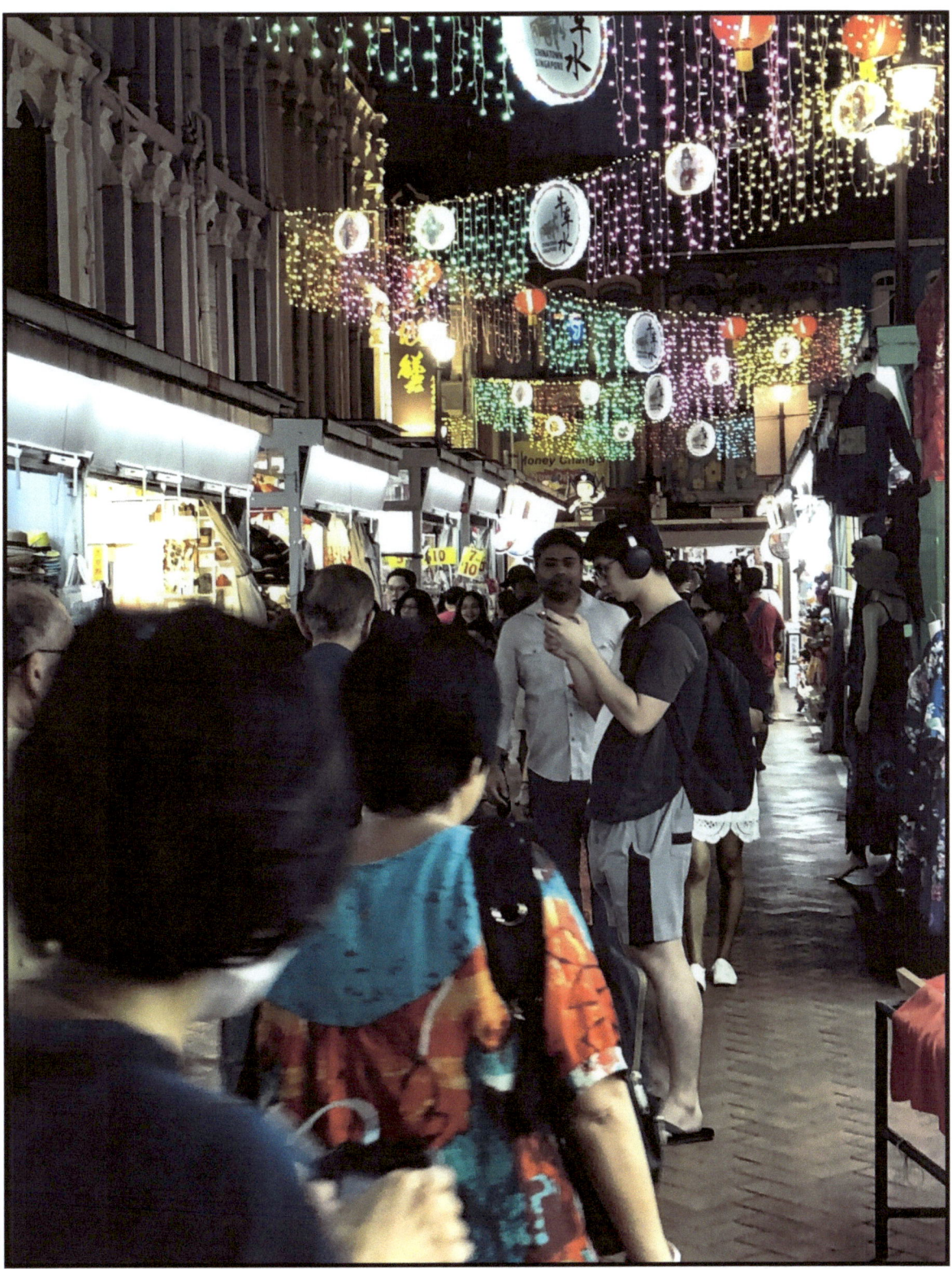

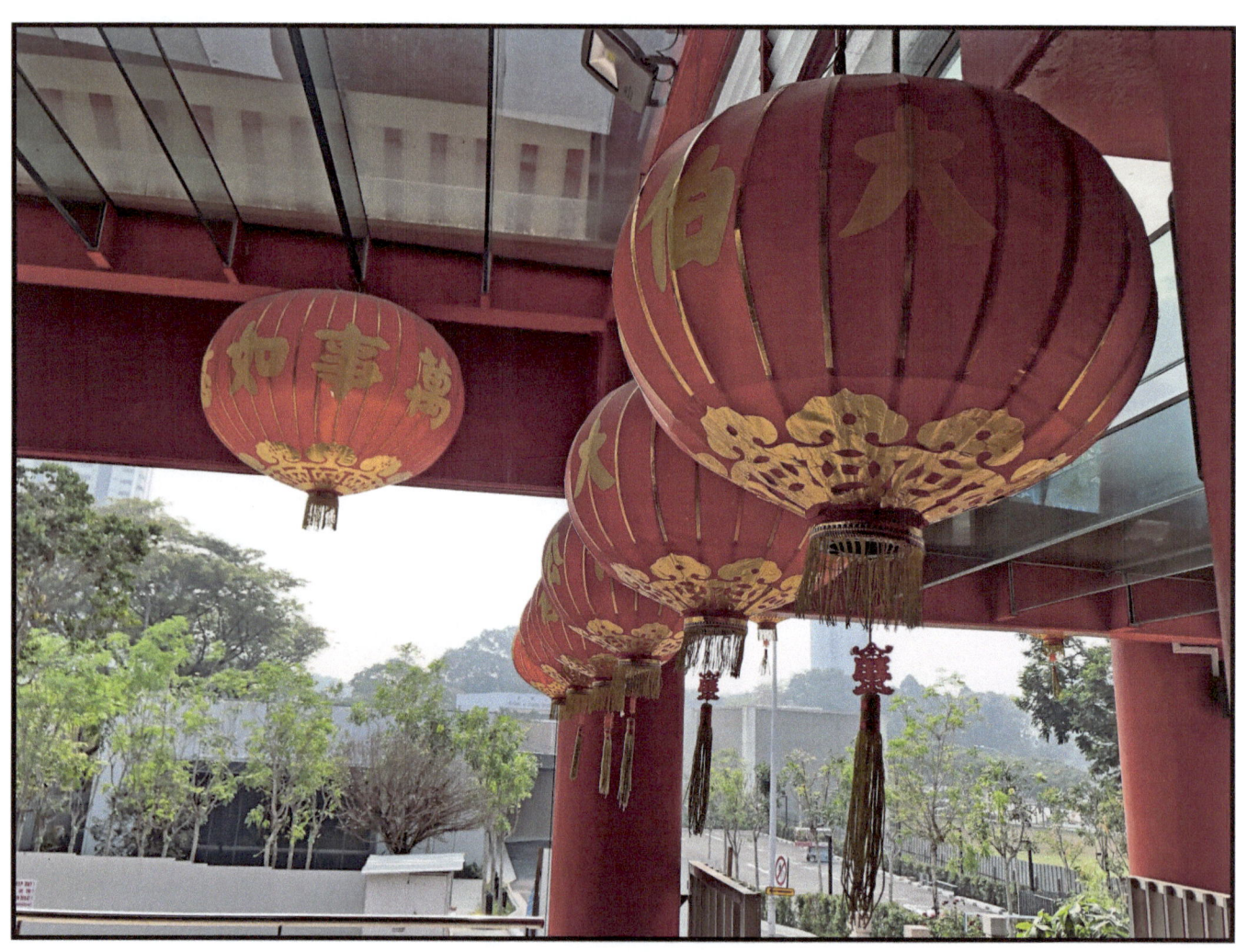

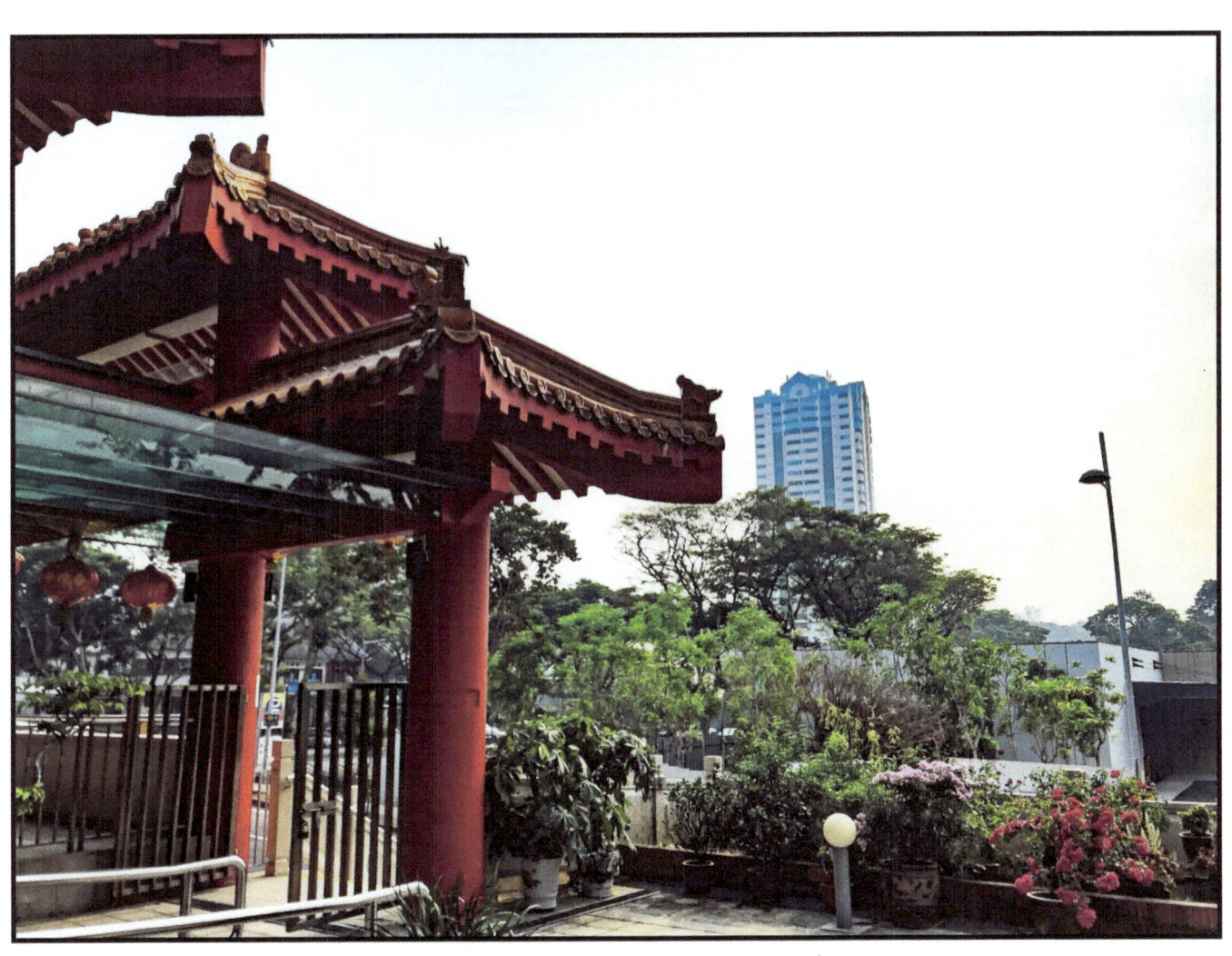

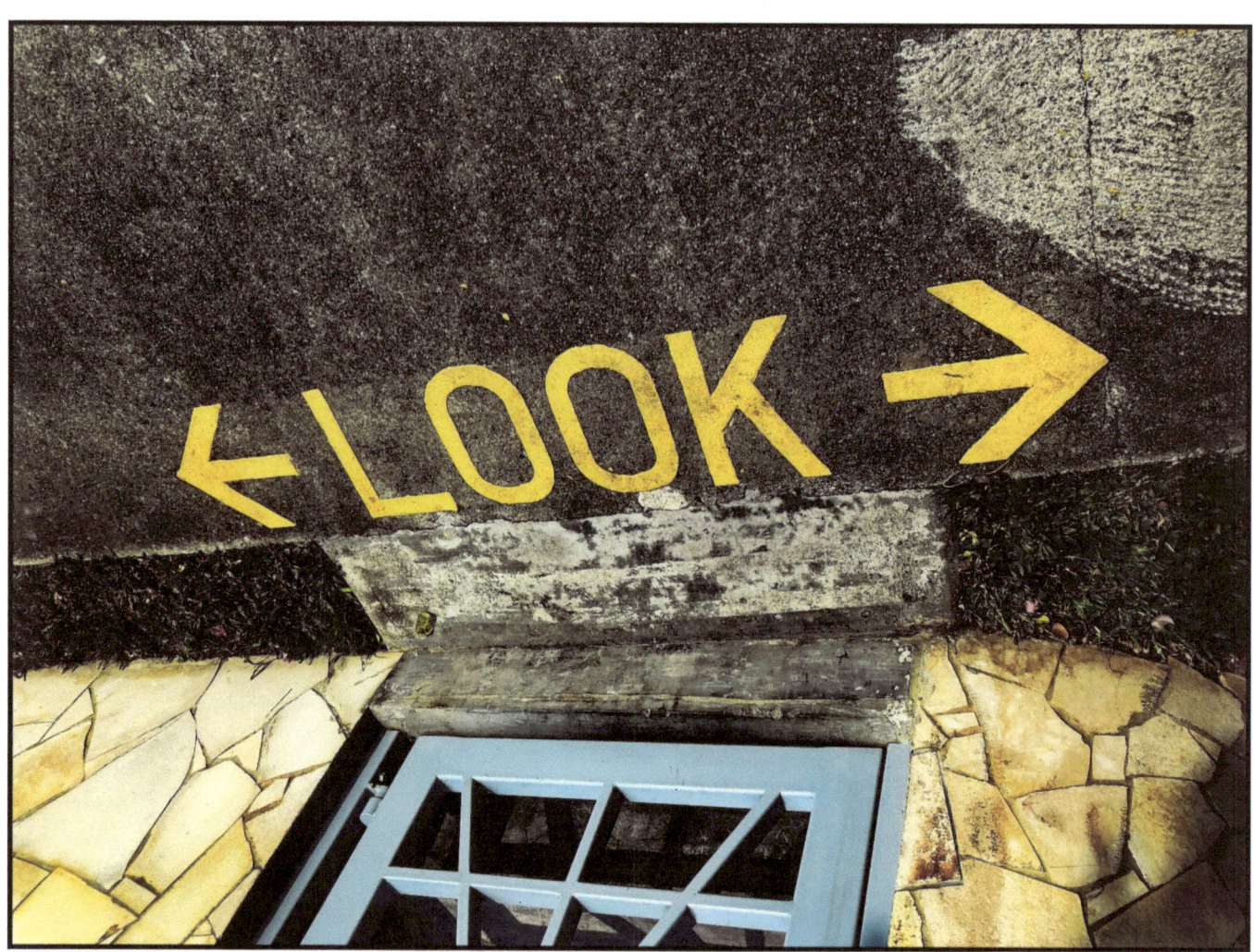

NO OPEN FIRES AND NO BARBECUING	**NO SMOKING**	**NO FEEDING OF WILD ANIMALS**
NO LITTERING	**NO PETS**	**NO FISHING OR POACHING**
NO RELEASING OF ANIMALS	**NO PLAYING OF MUSIC**	**NO PLUCKING OF PLANTS**
NO FEEDING OF MONKEYS FINE UP TO $50,000 AND/OR JAIL	**NO BICYCLE**	**NO FLYING OF MODEL AIRCRAFT**

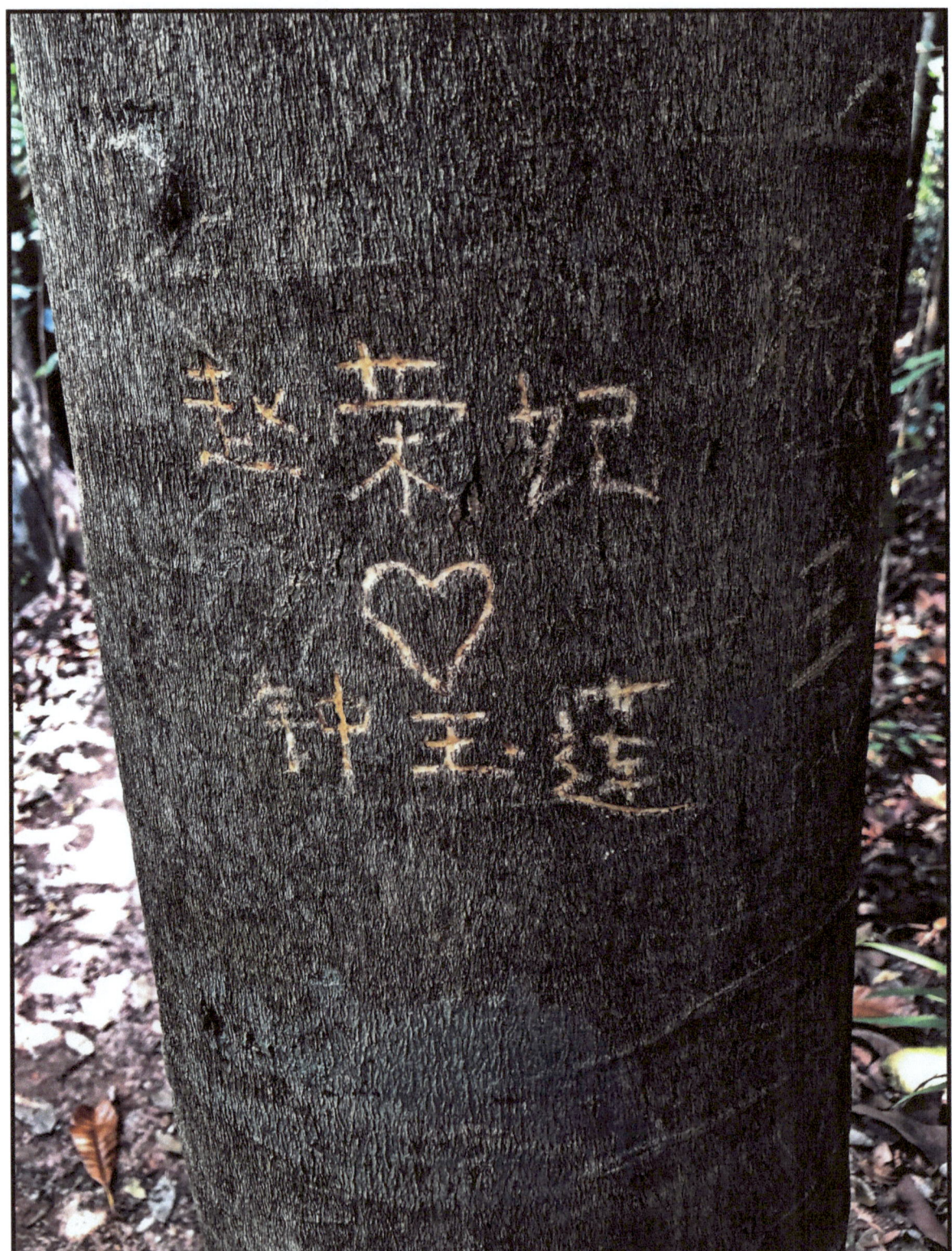

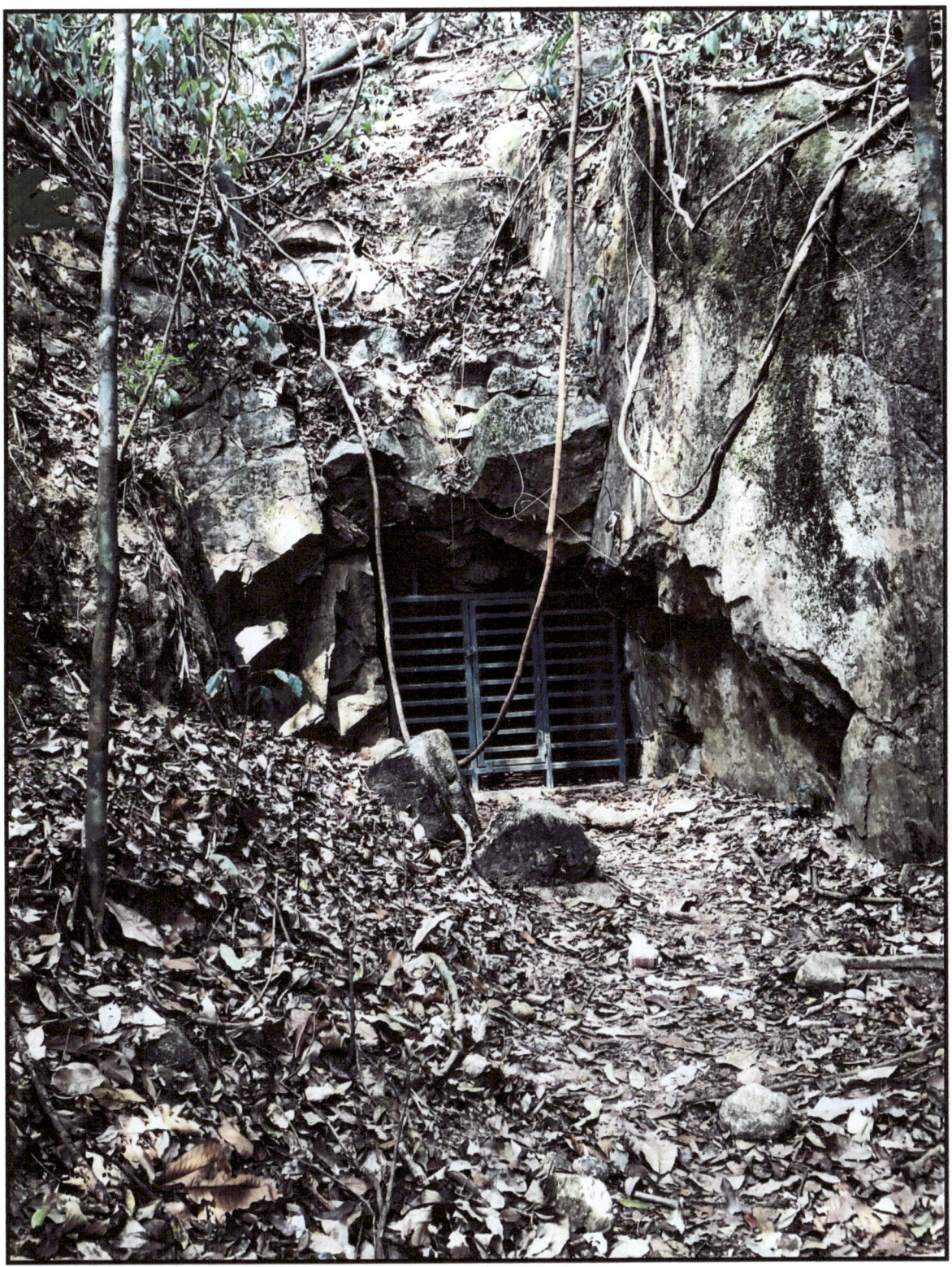

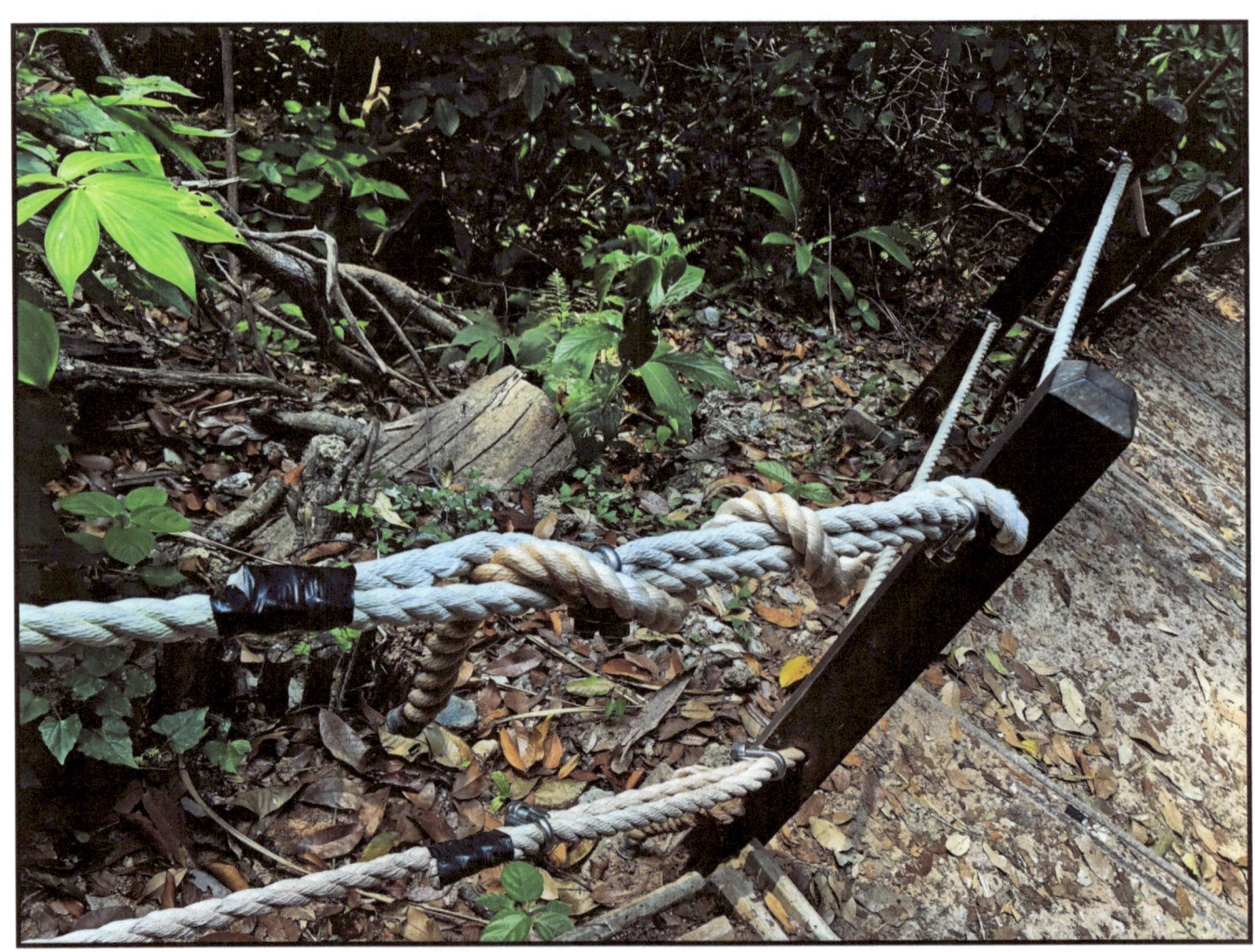

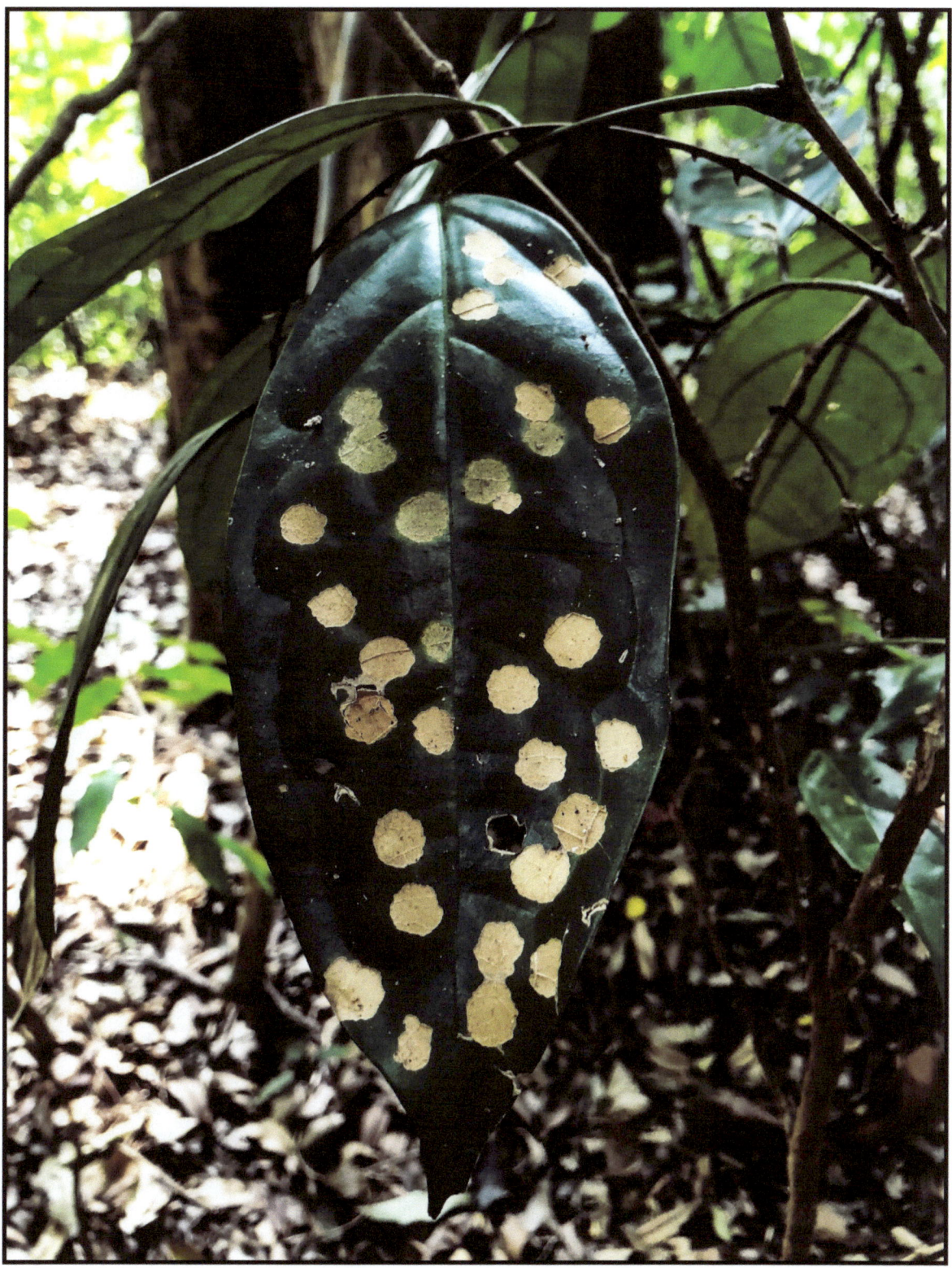

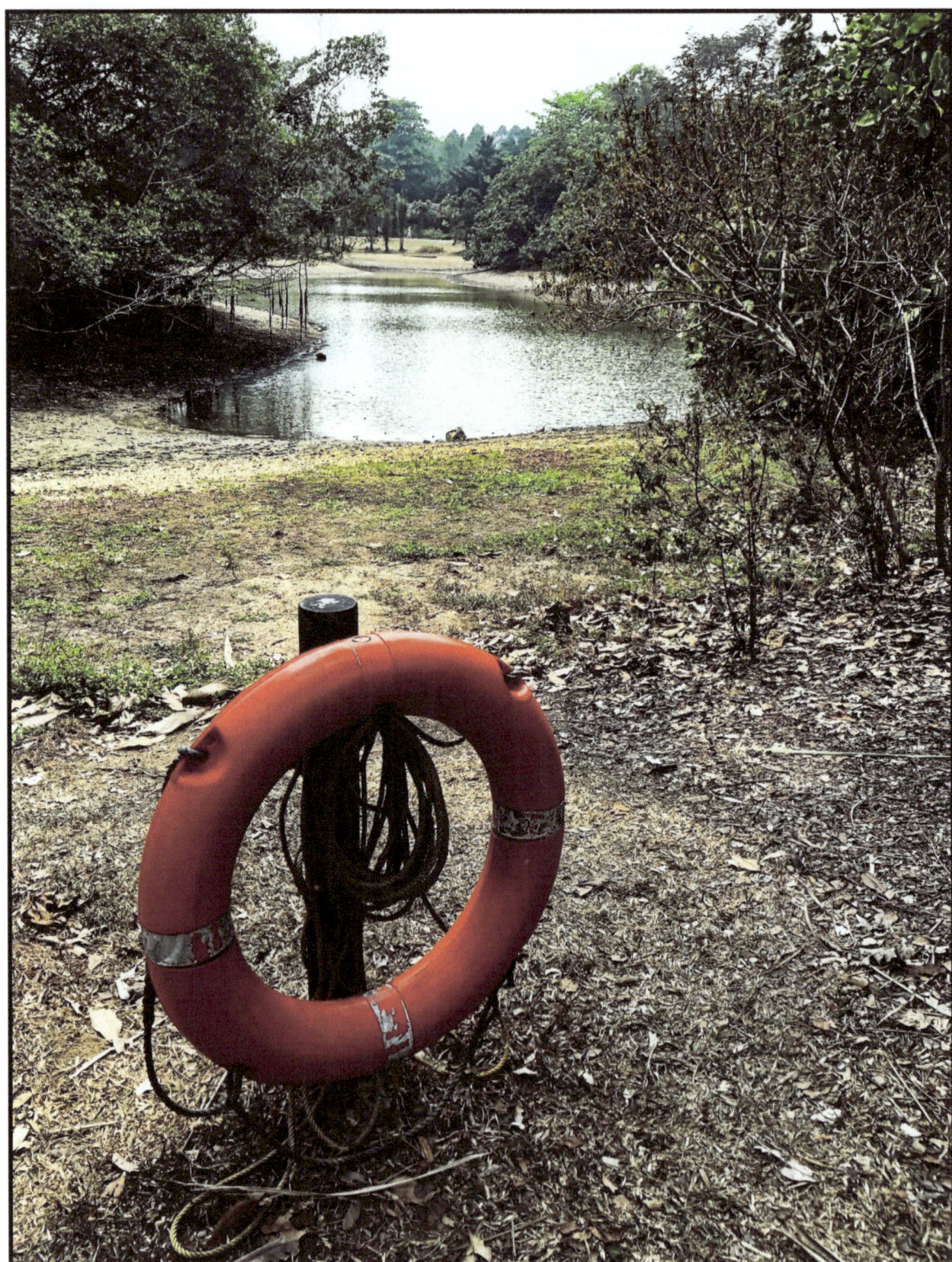

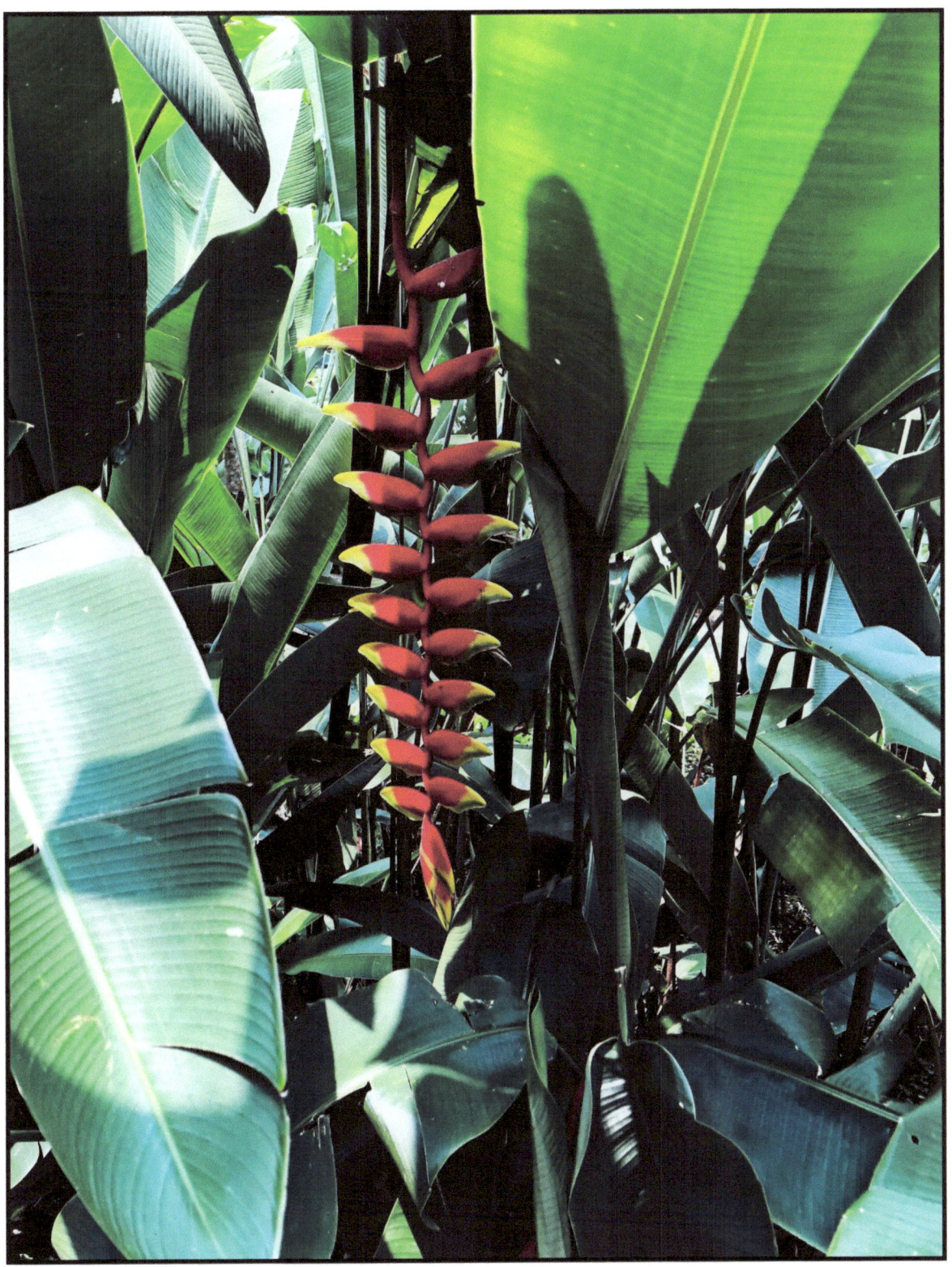

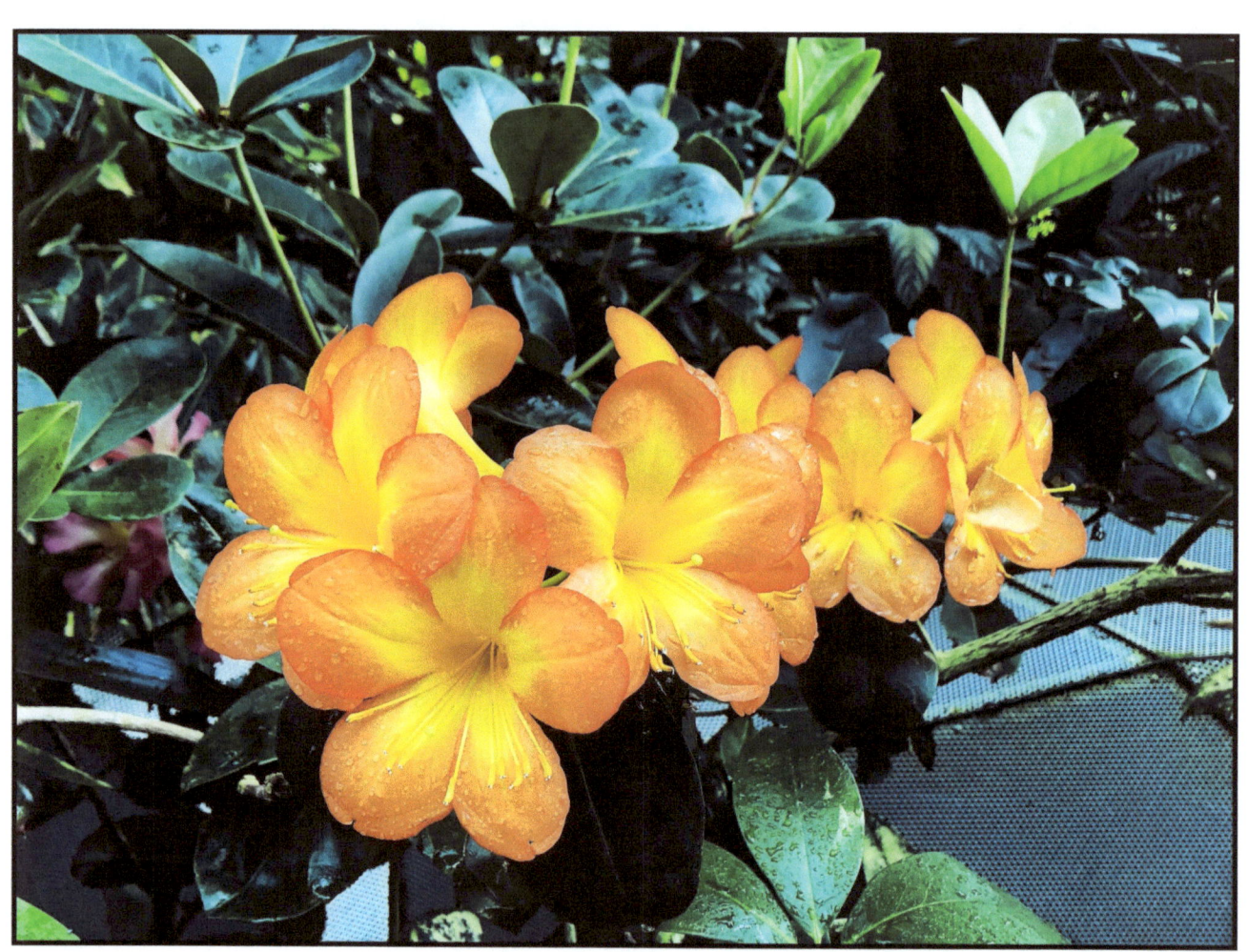

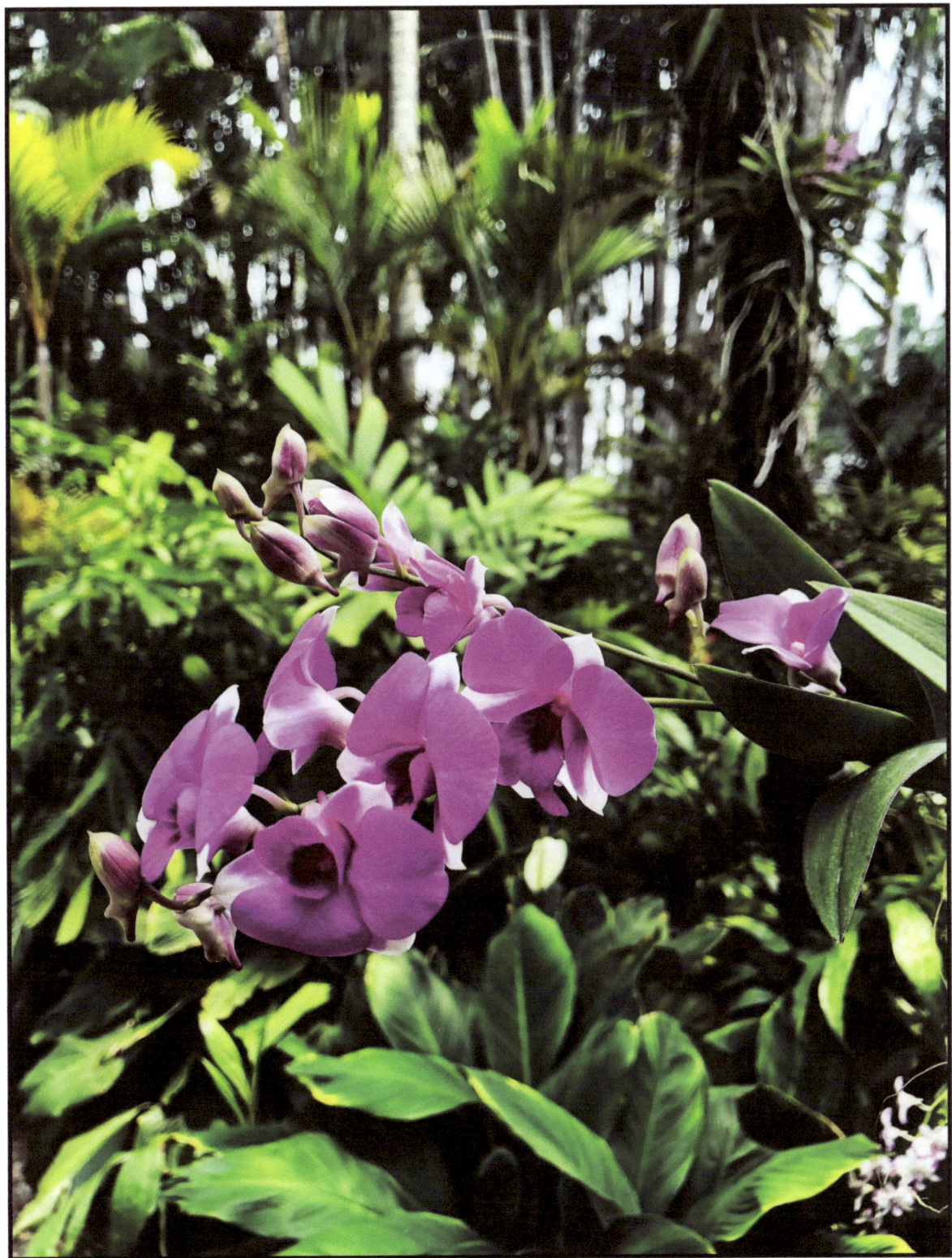

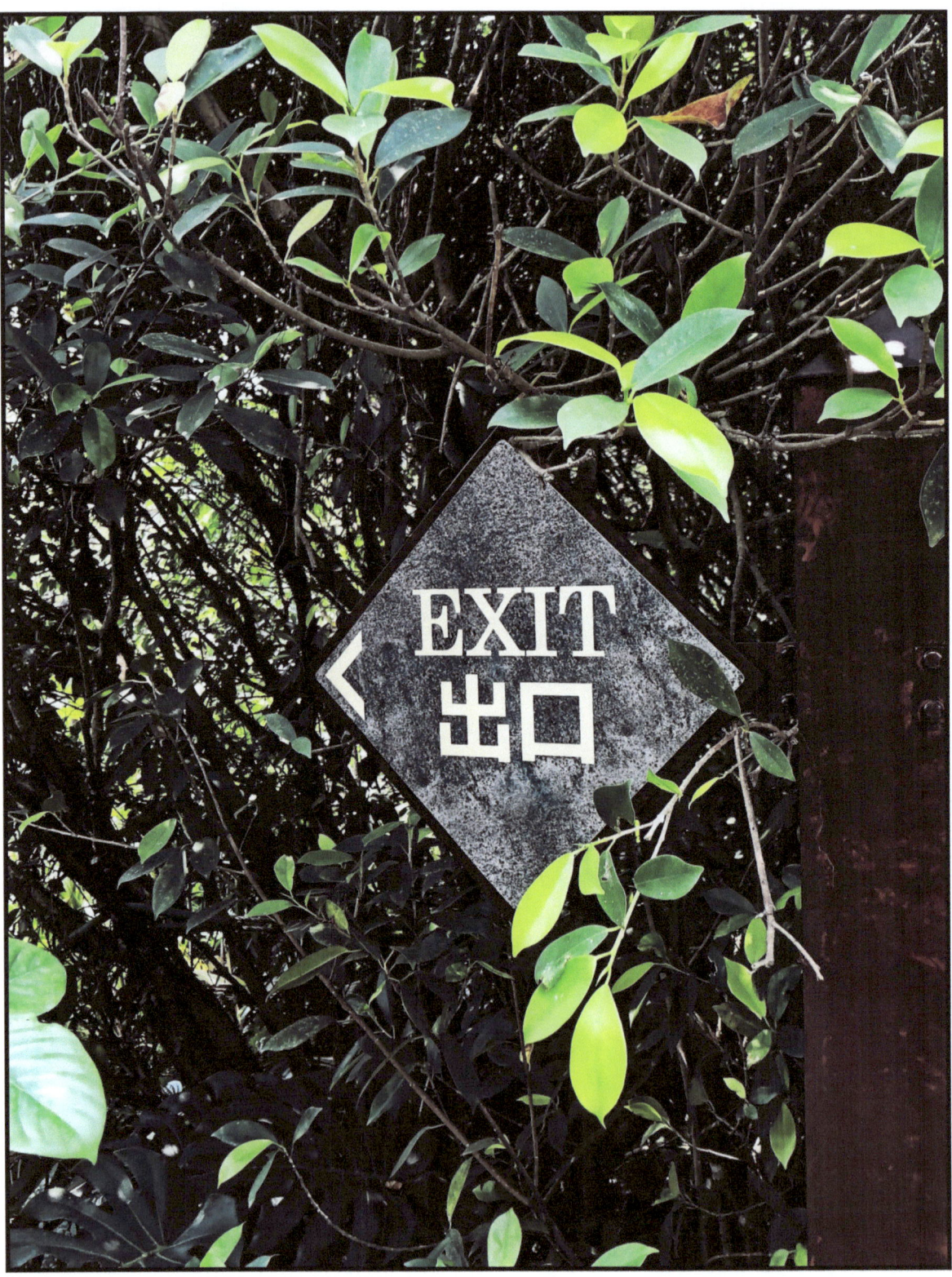

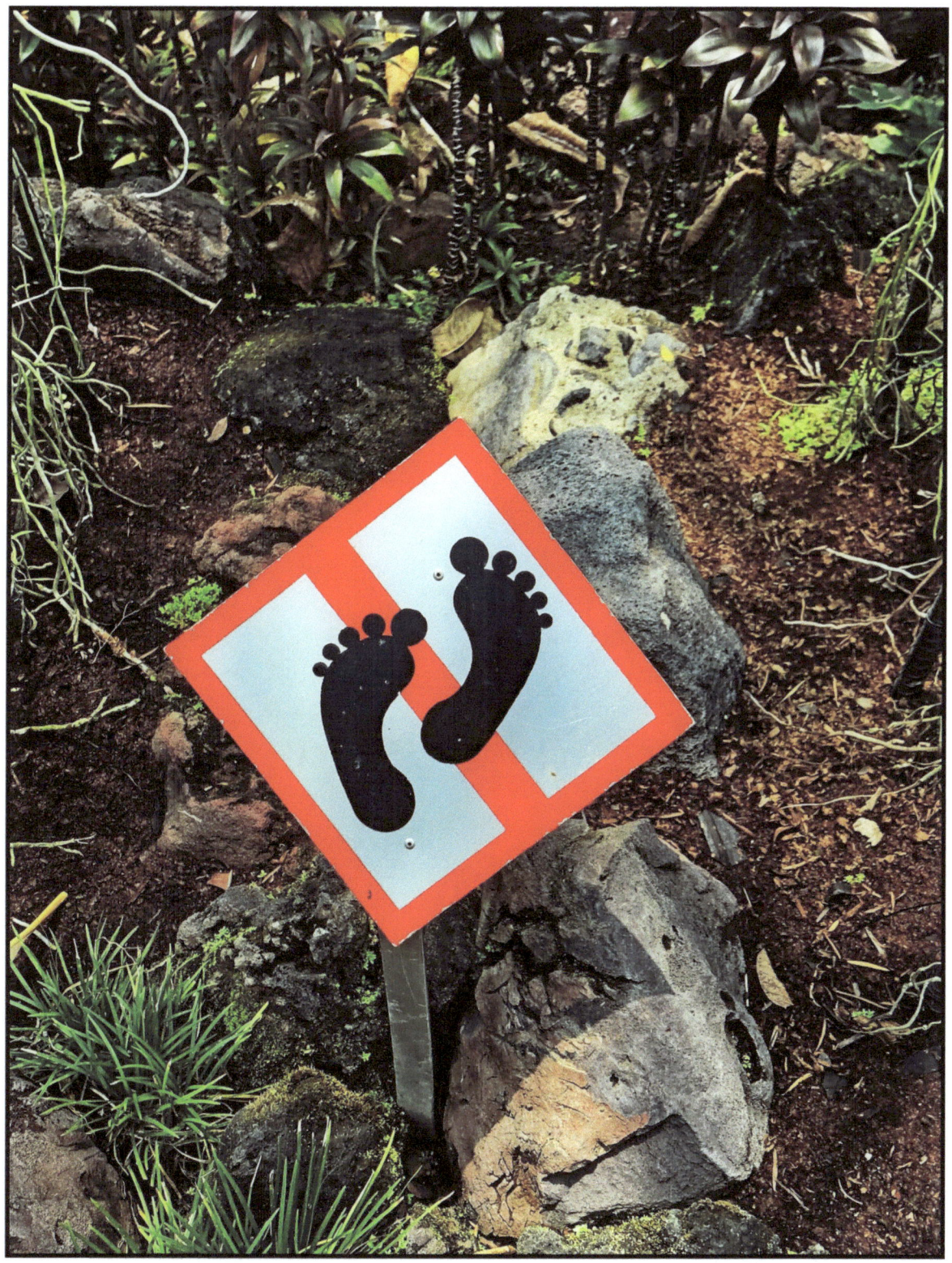

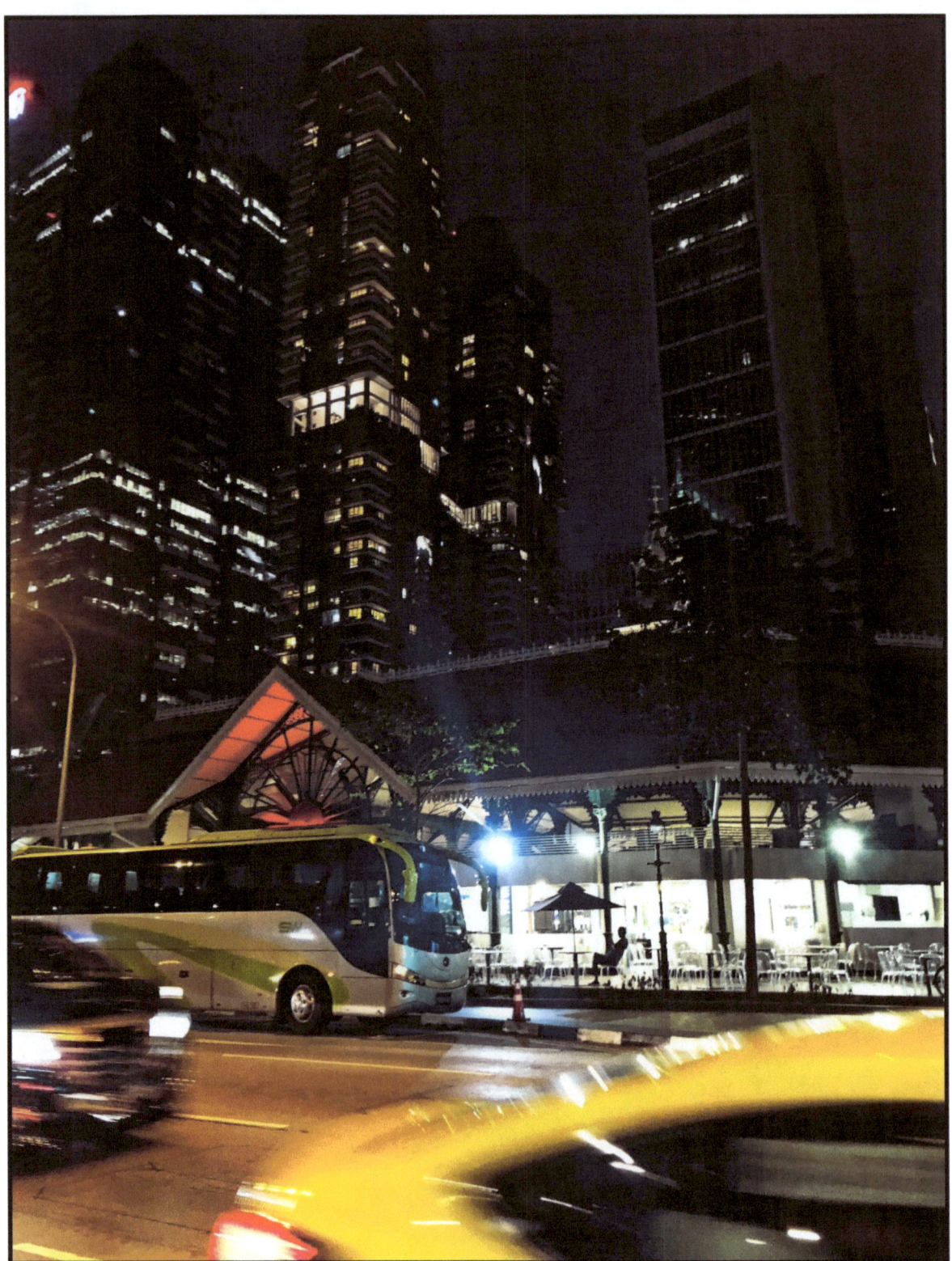

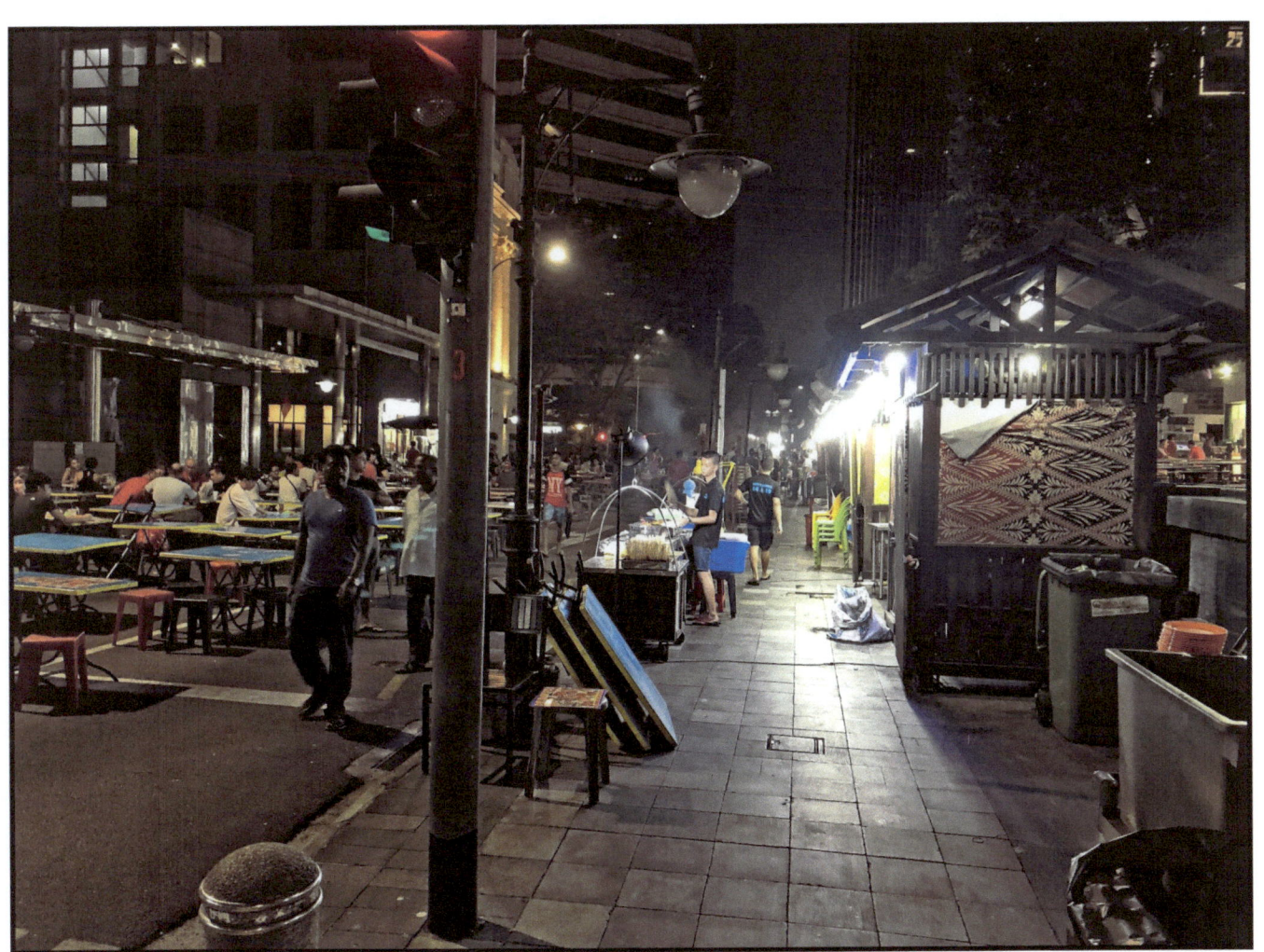

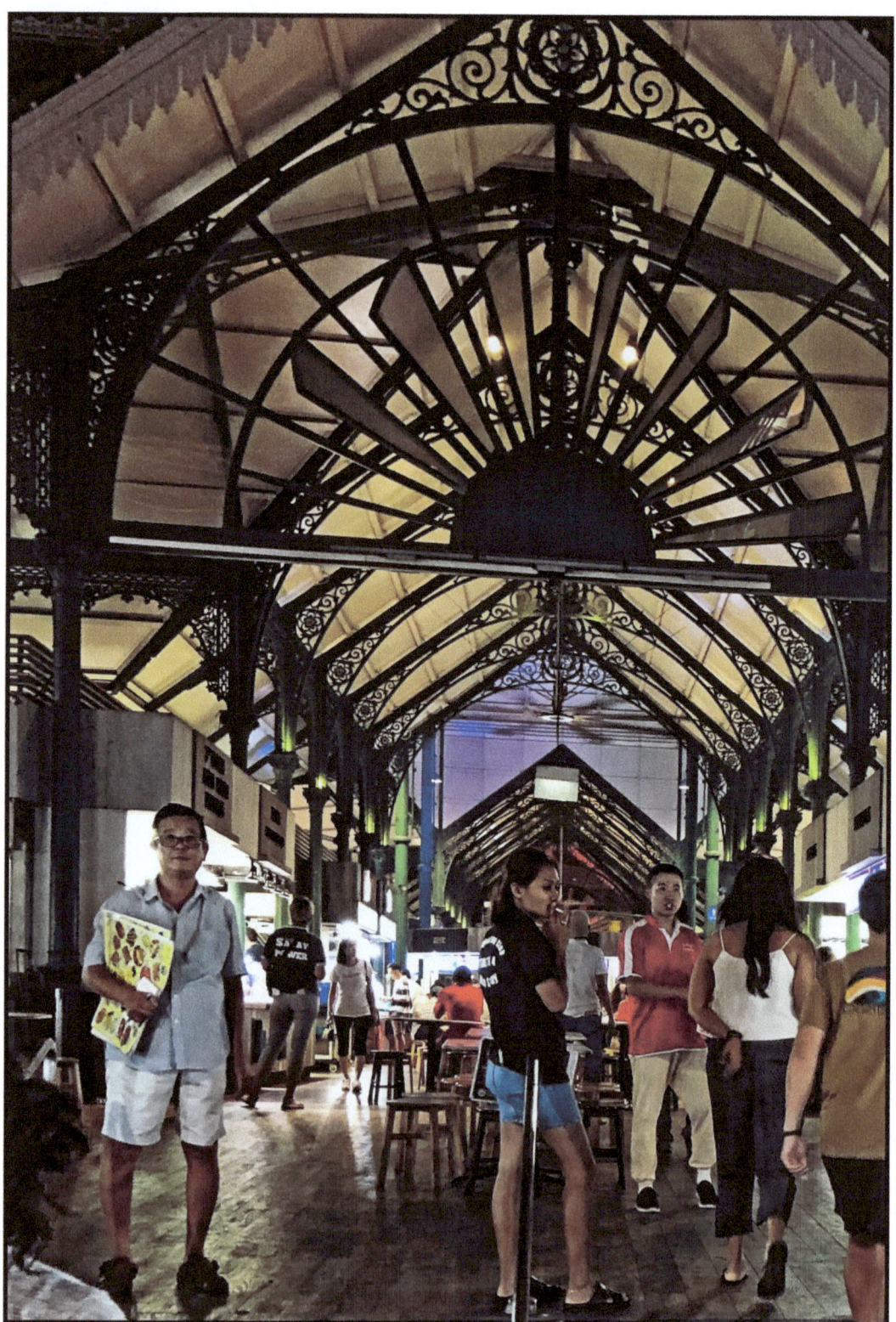

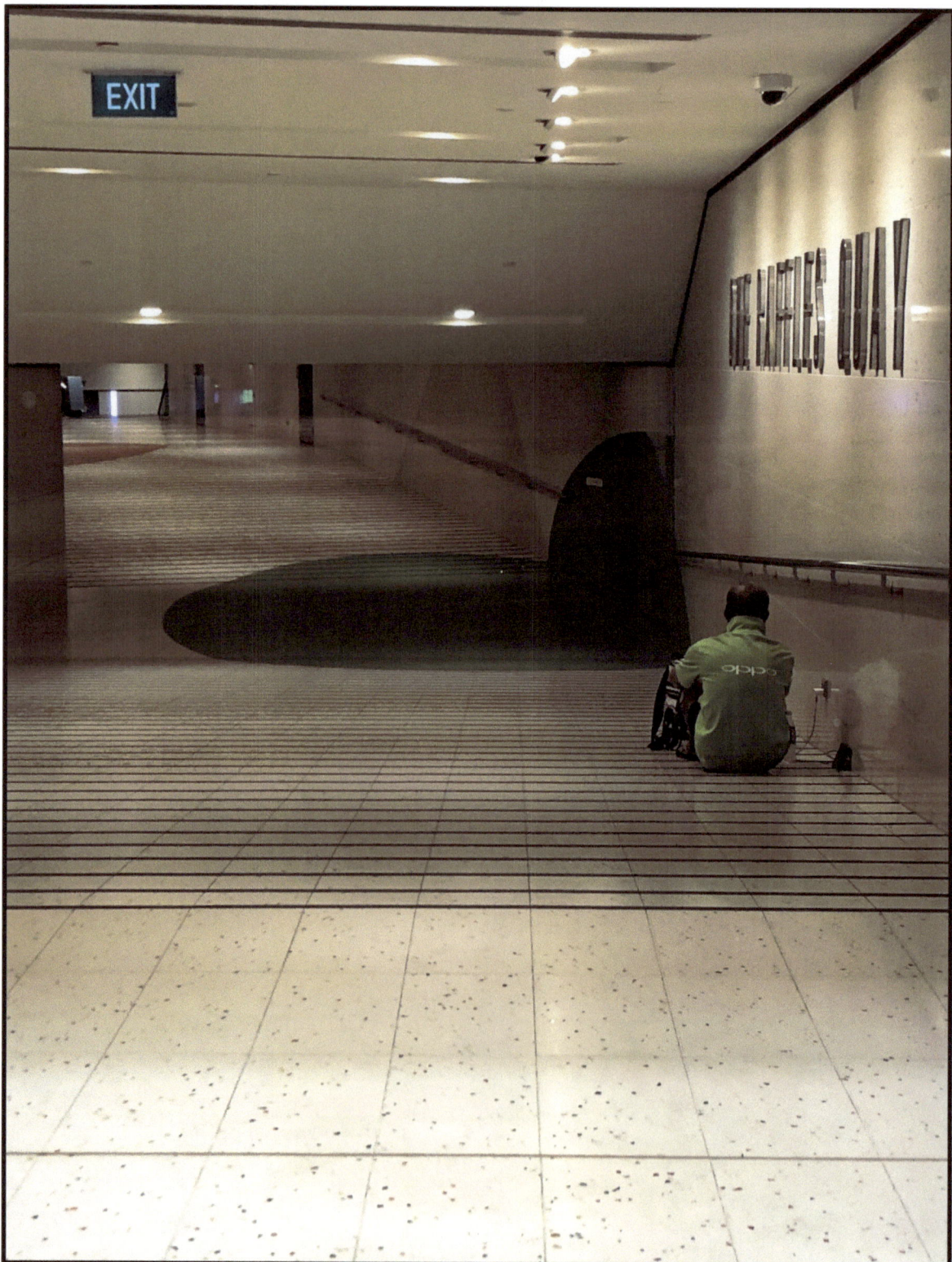

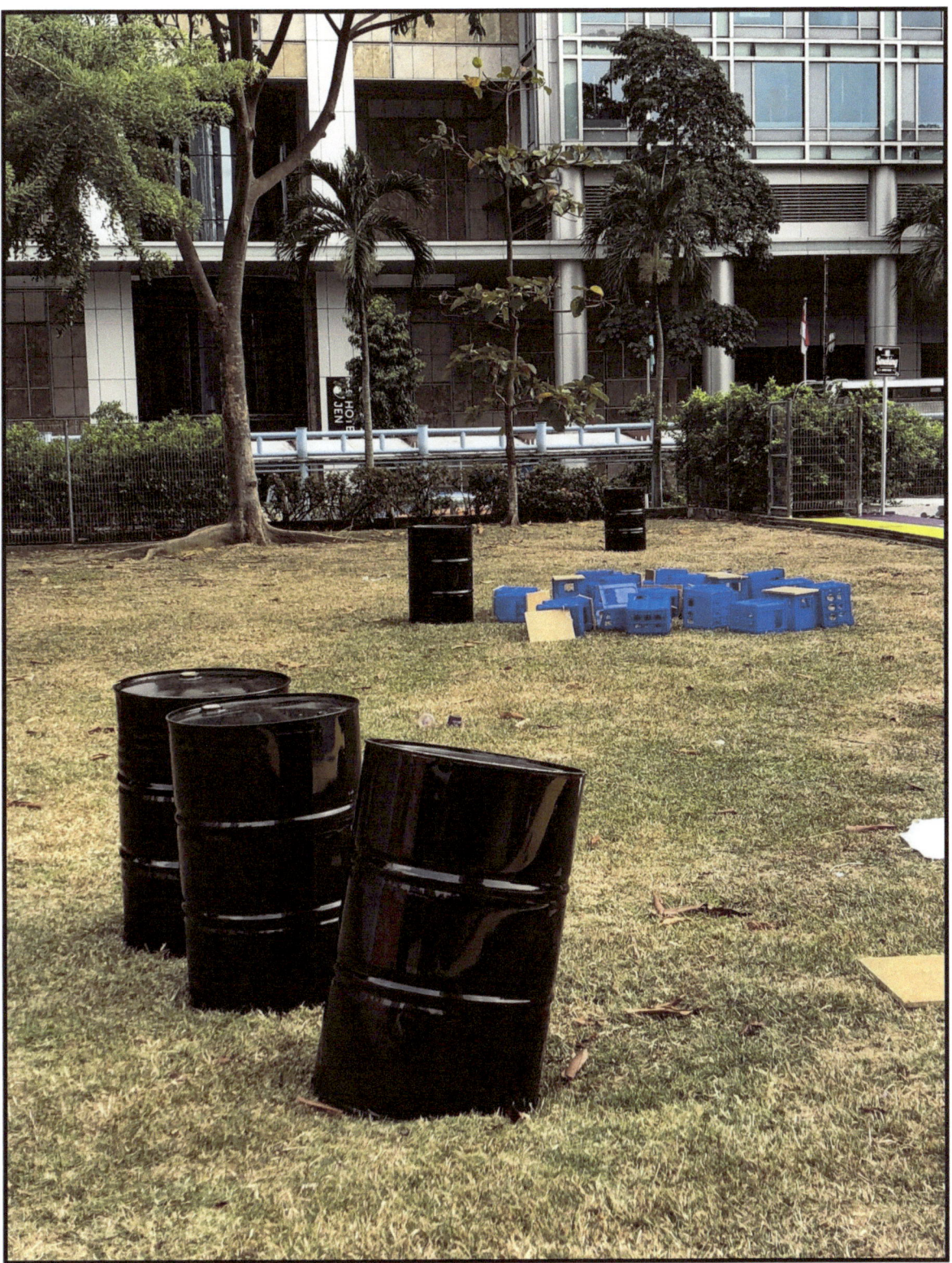

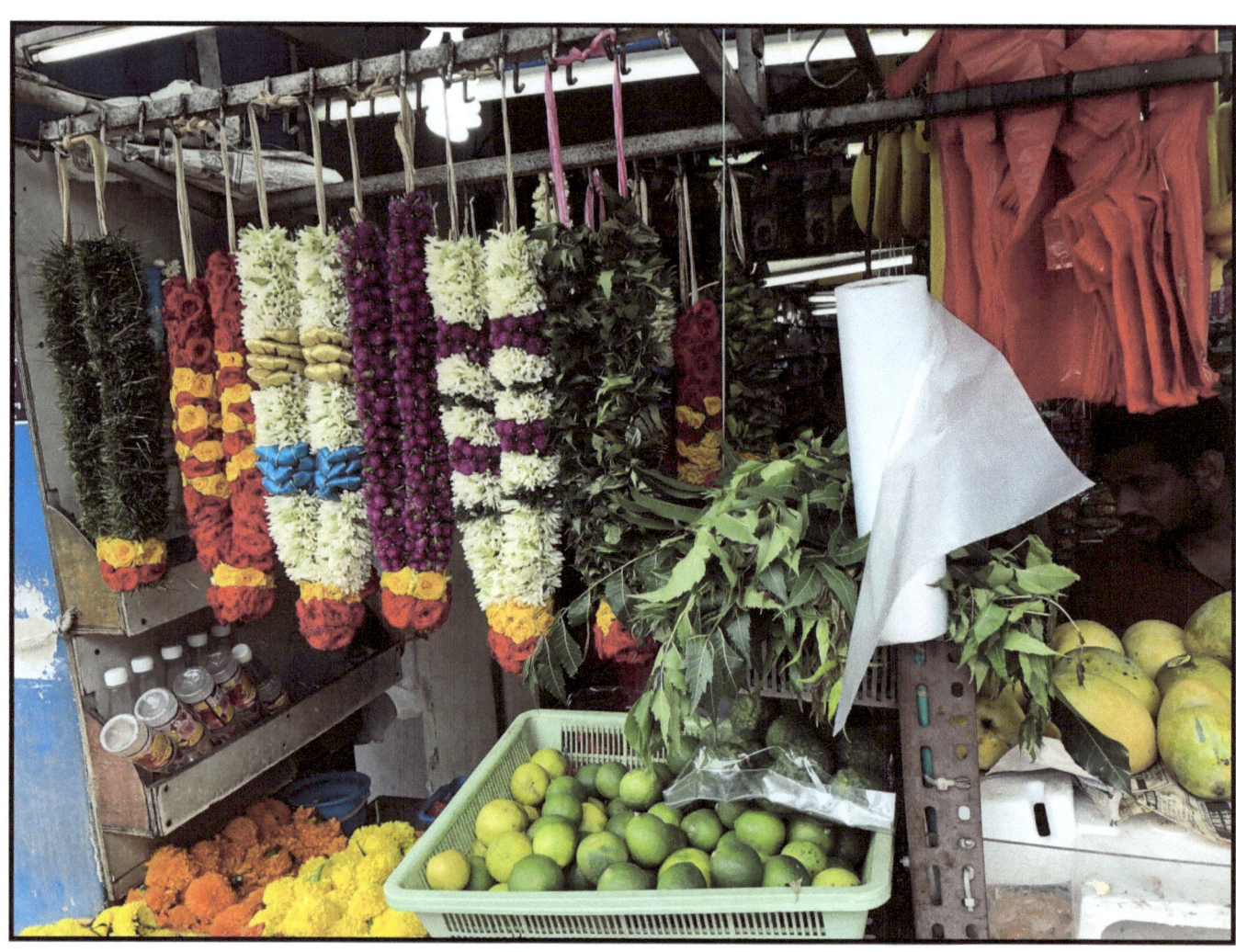

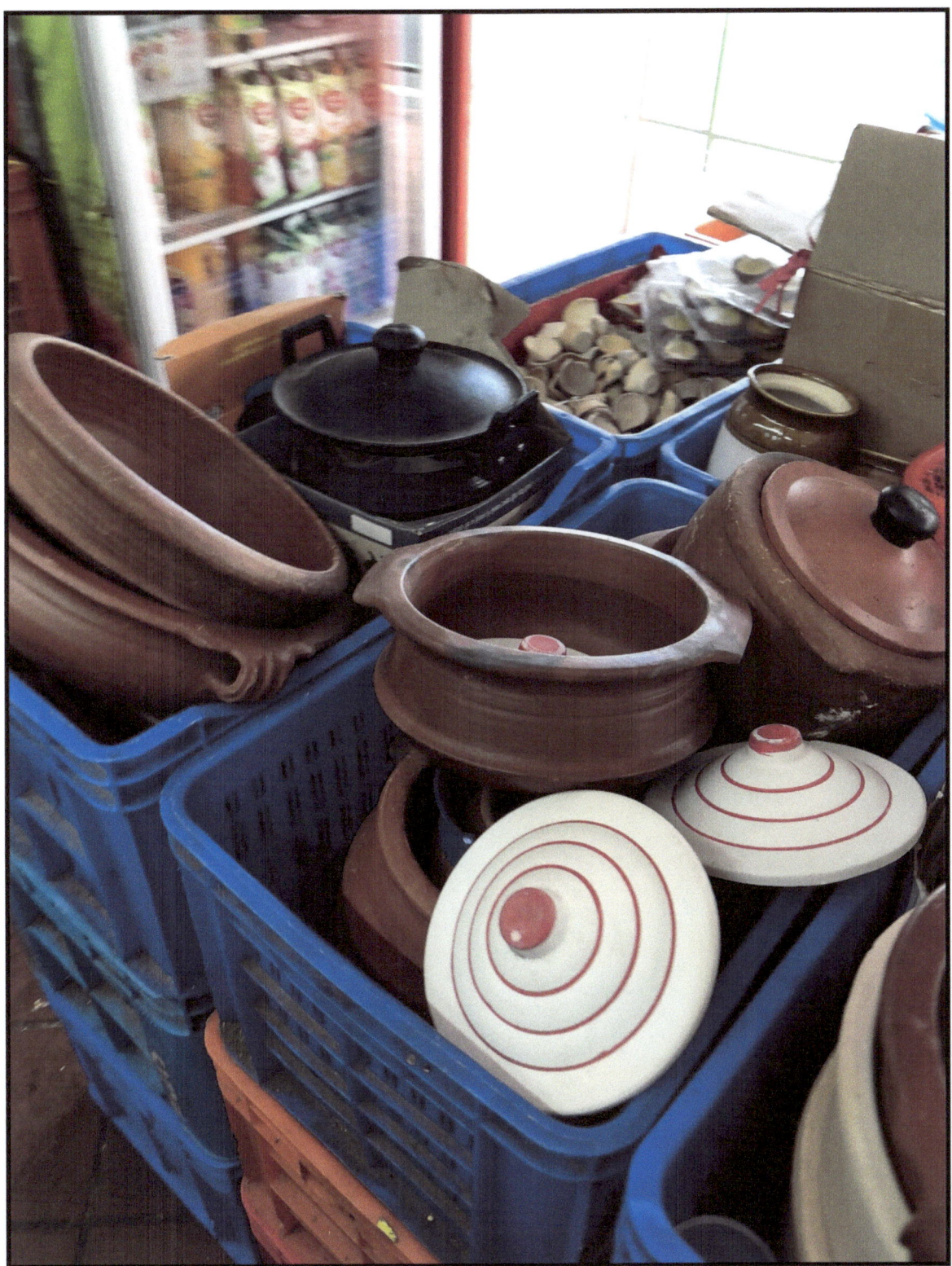

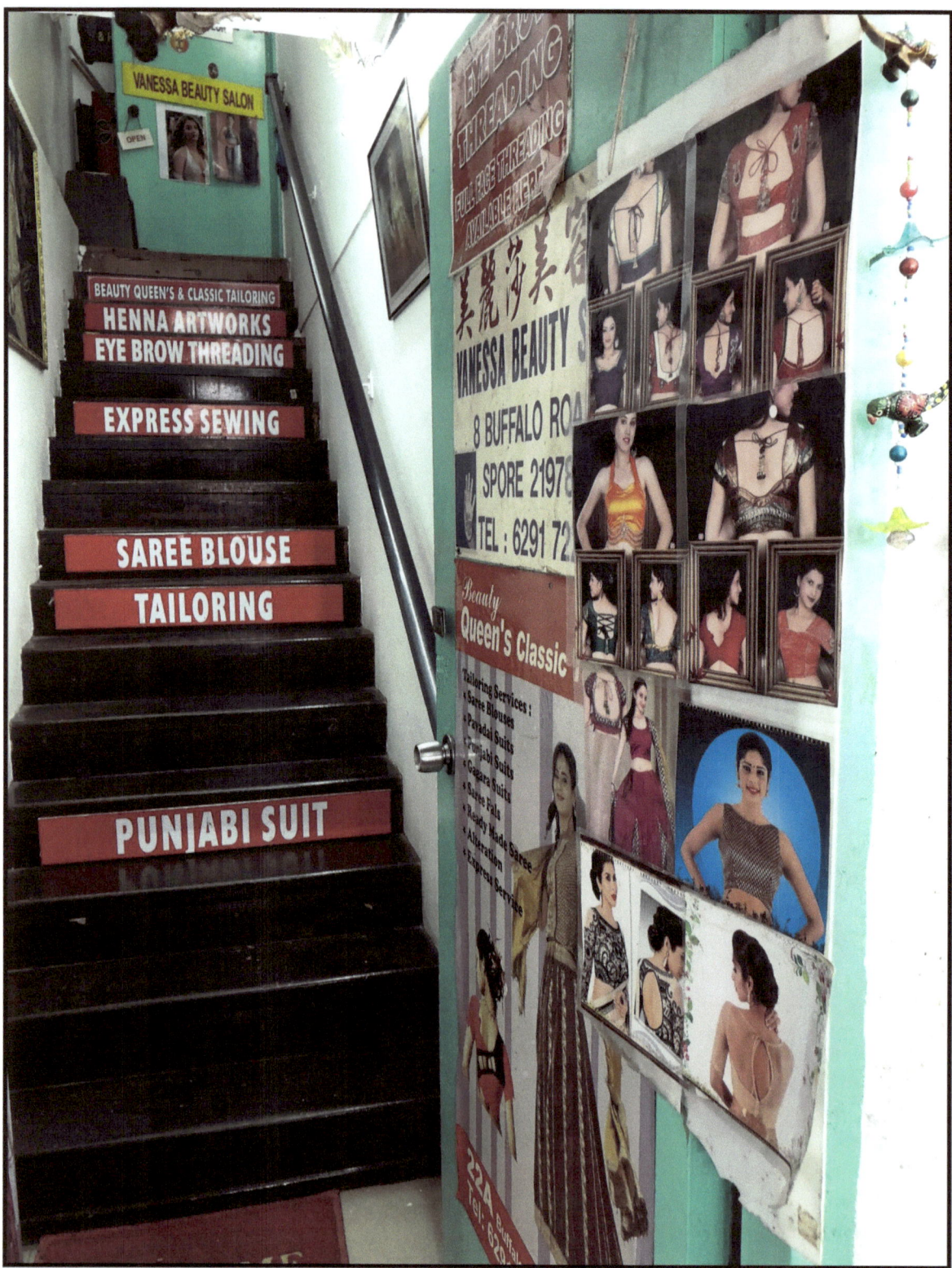

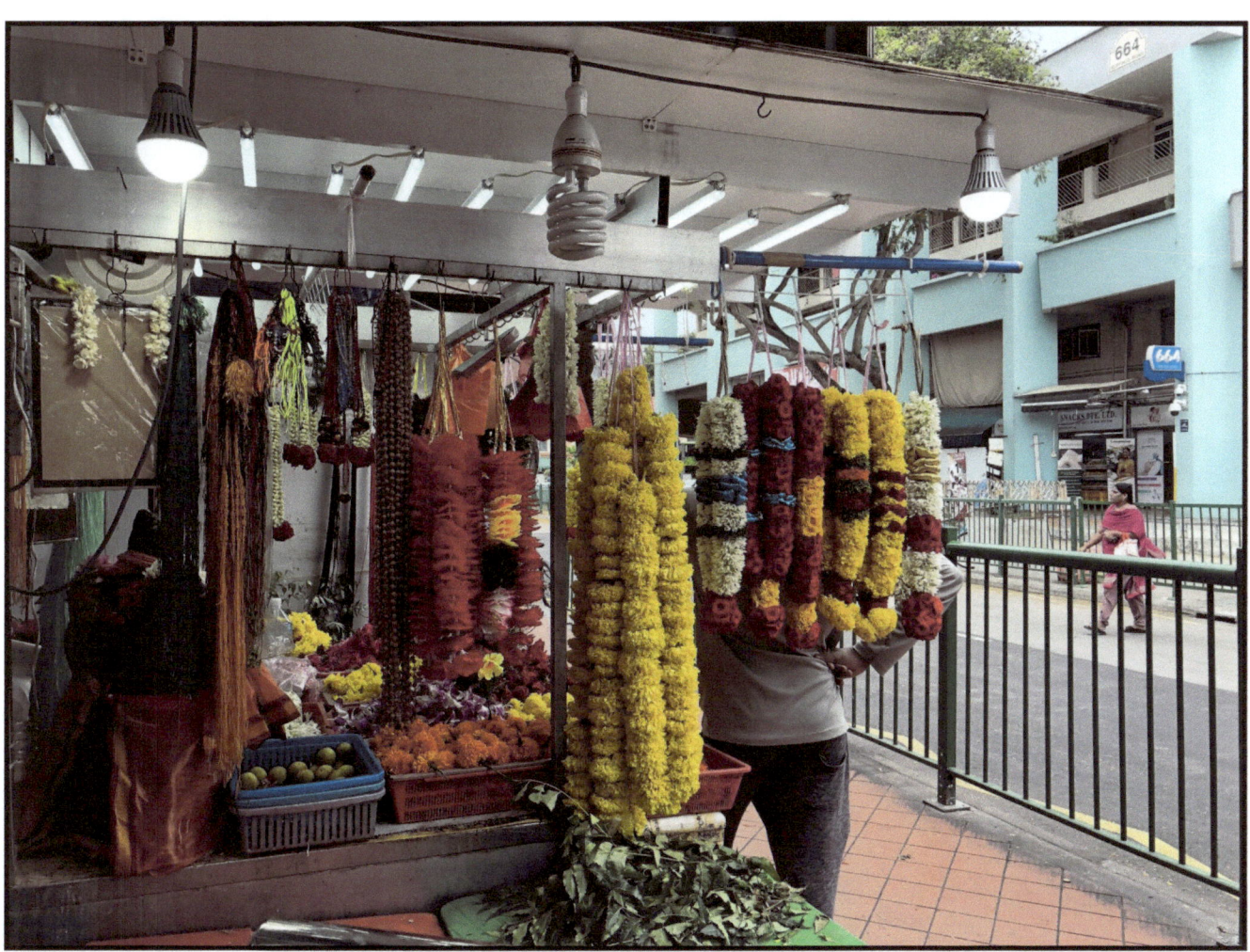

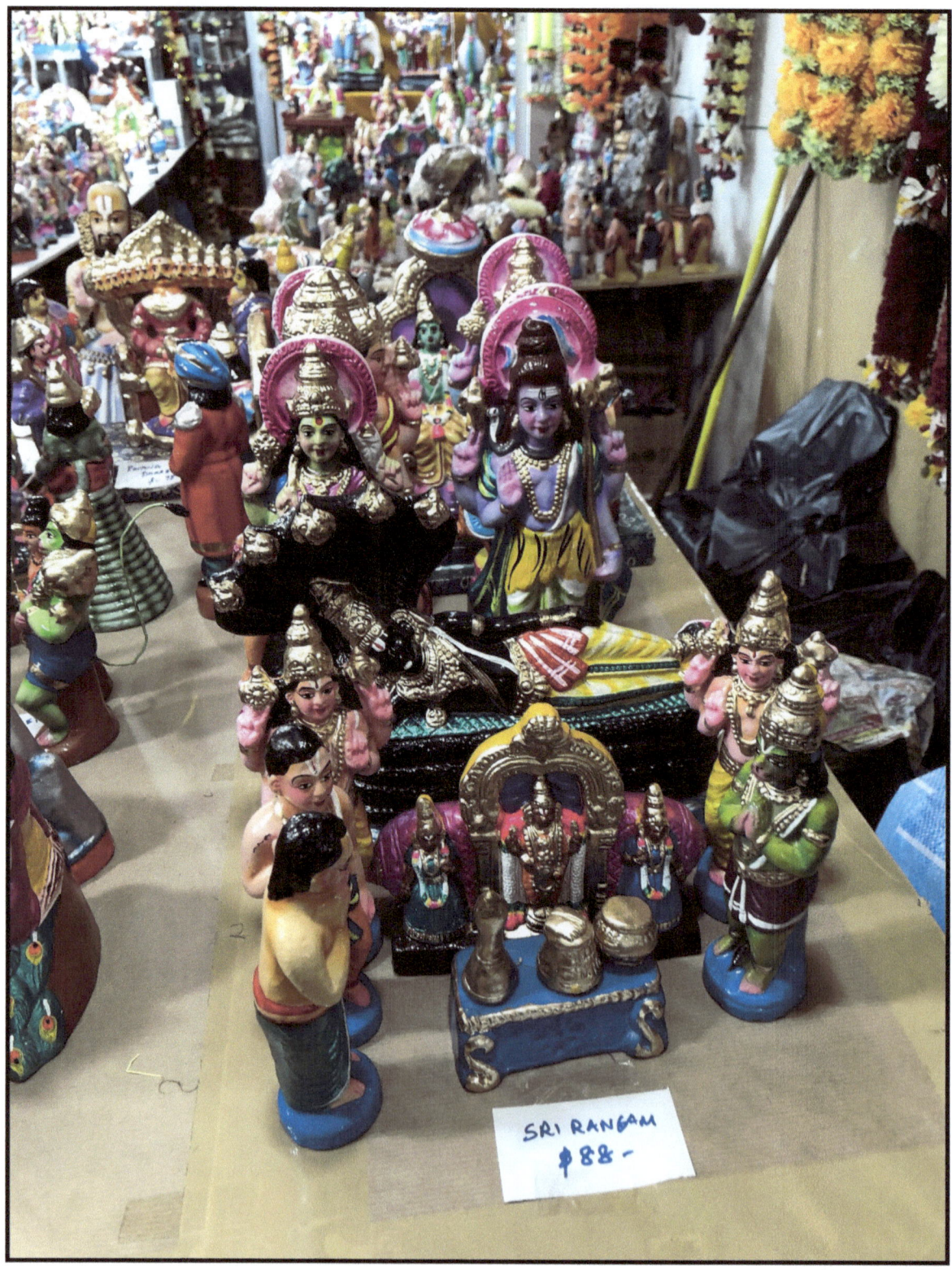

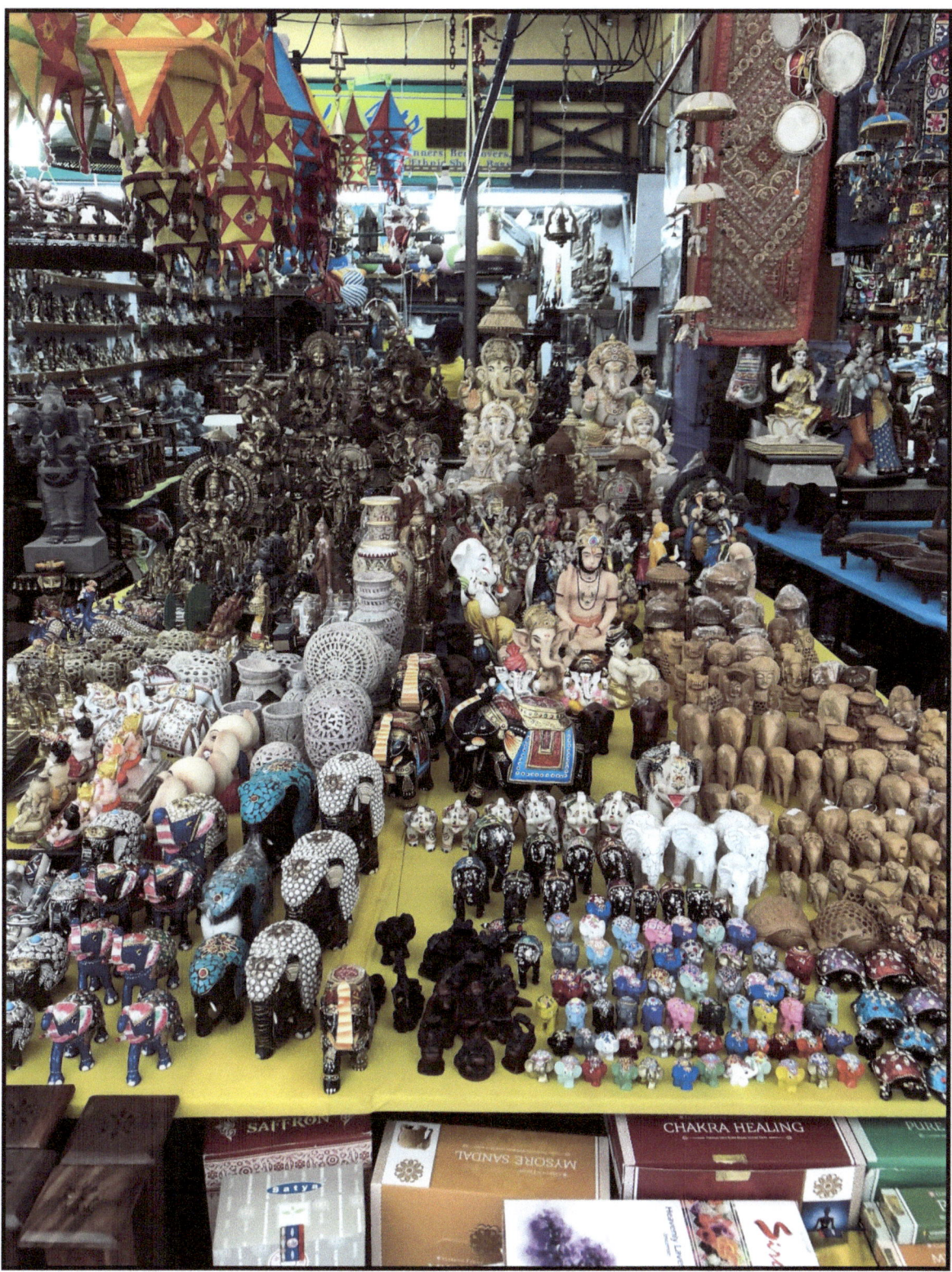

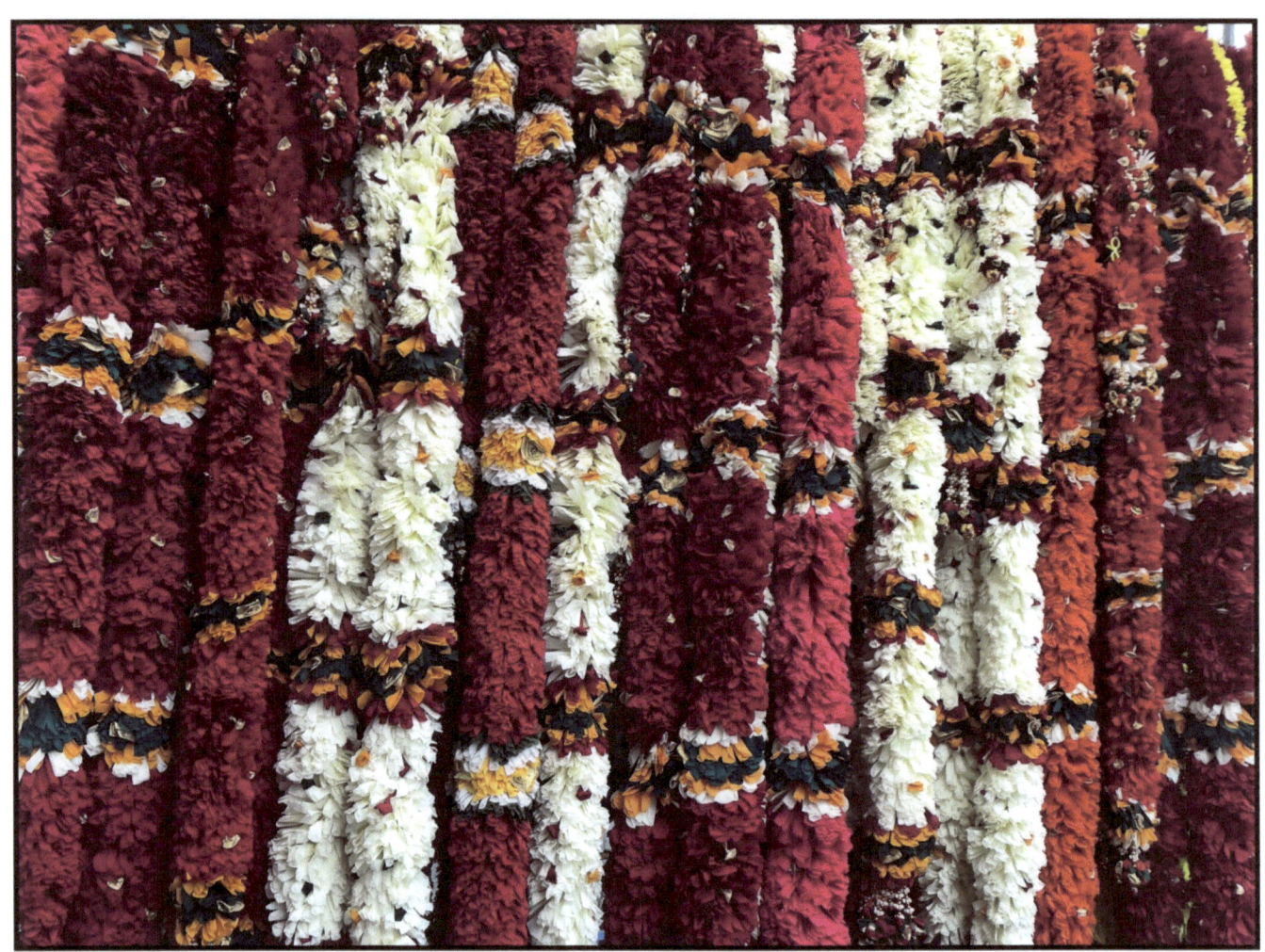

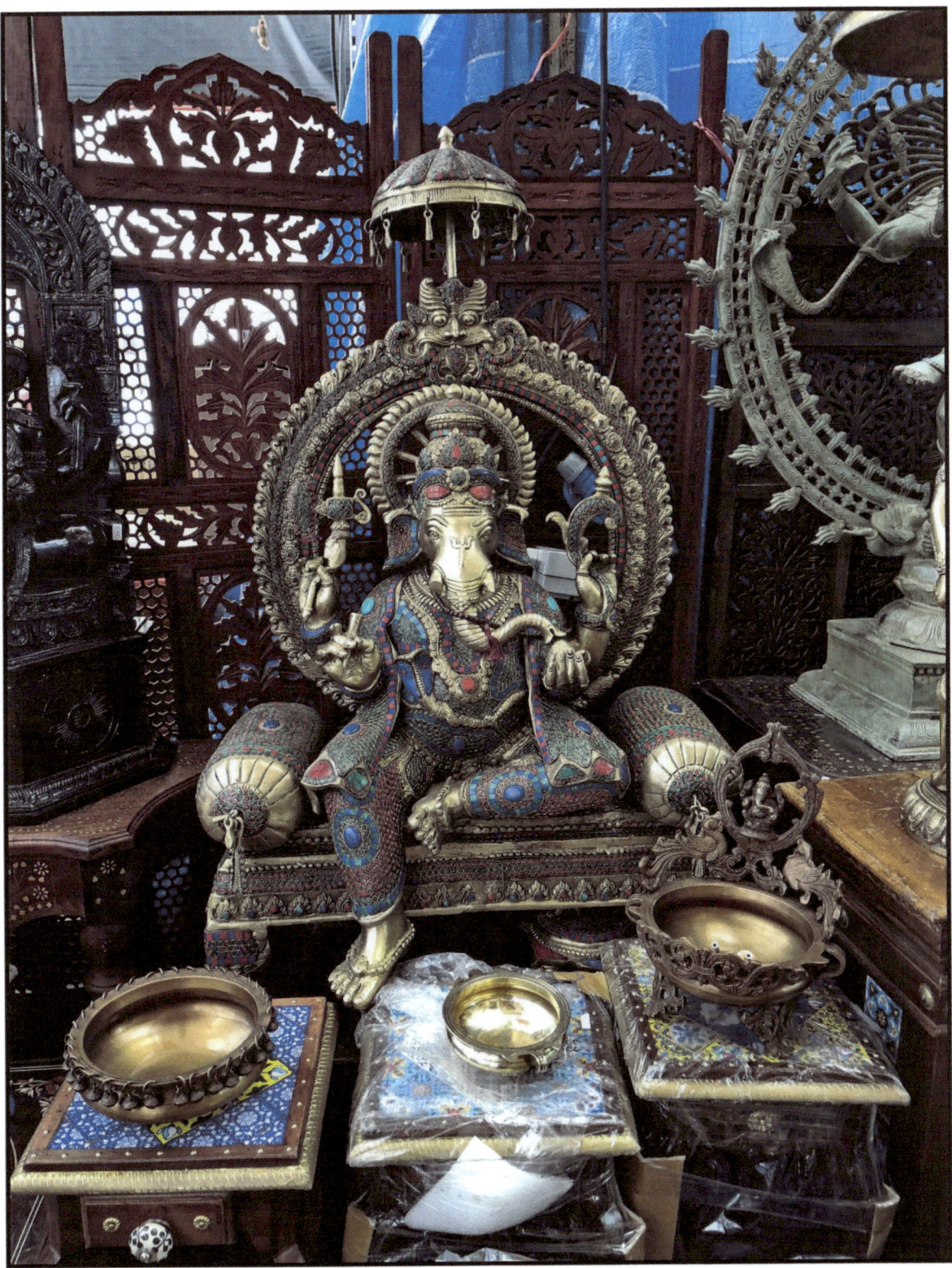

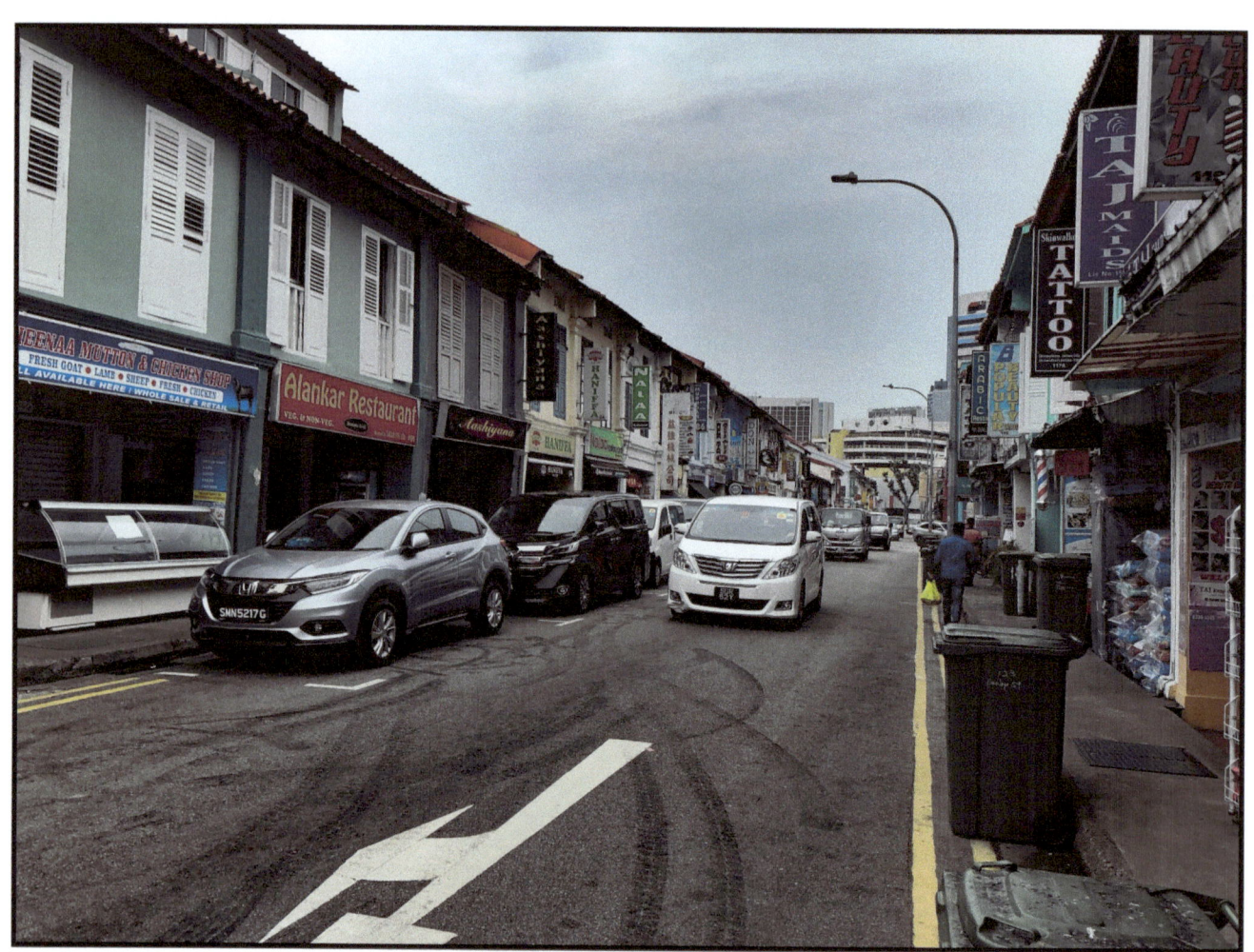

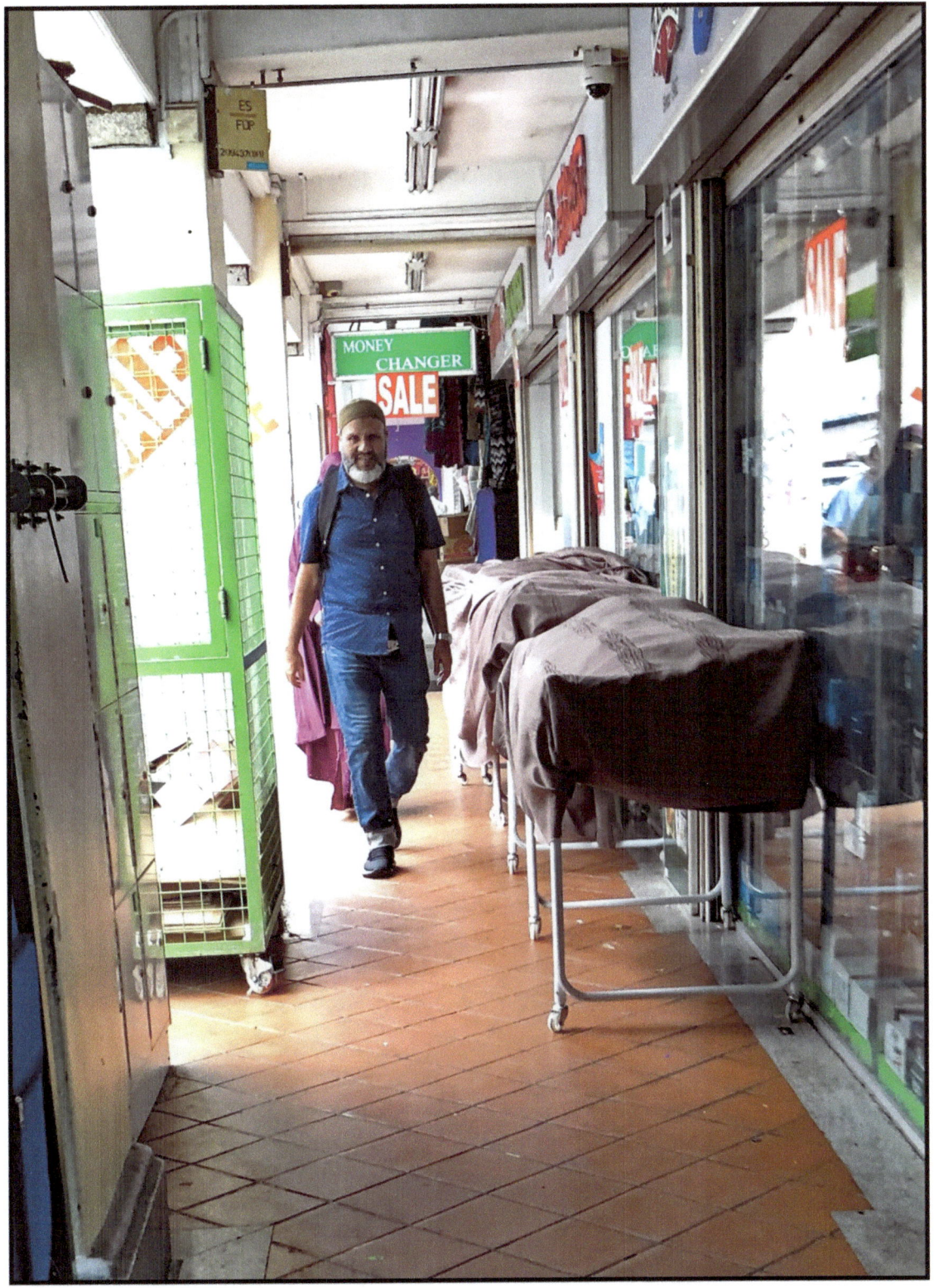

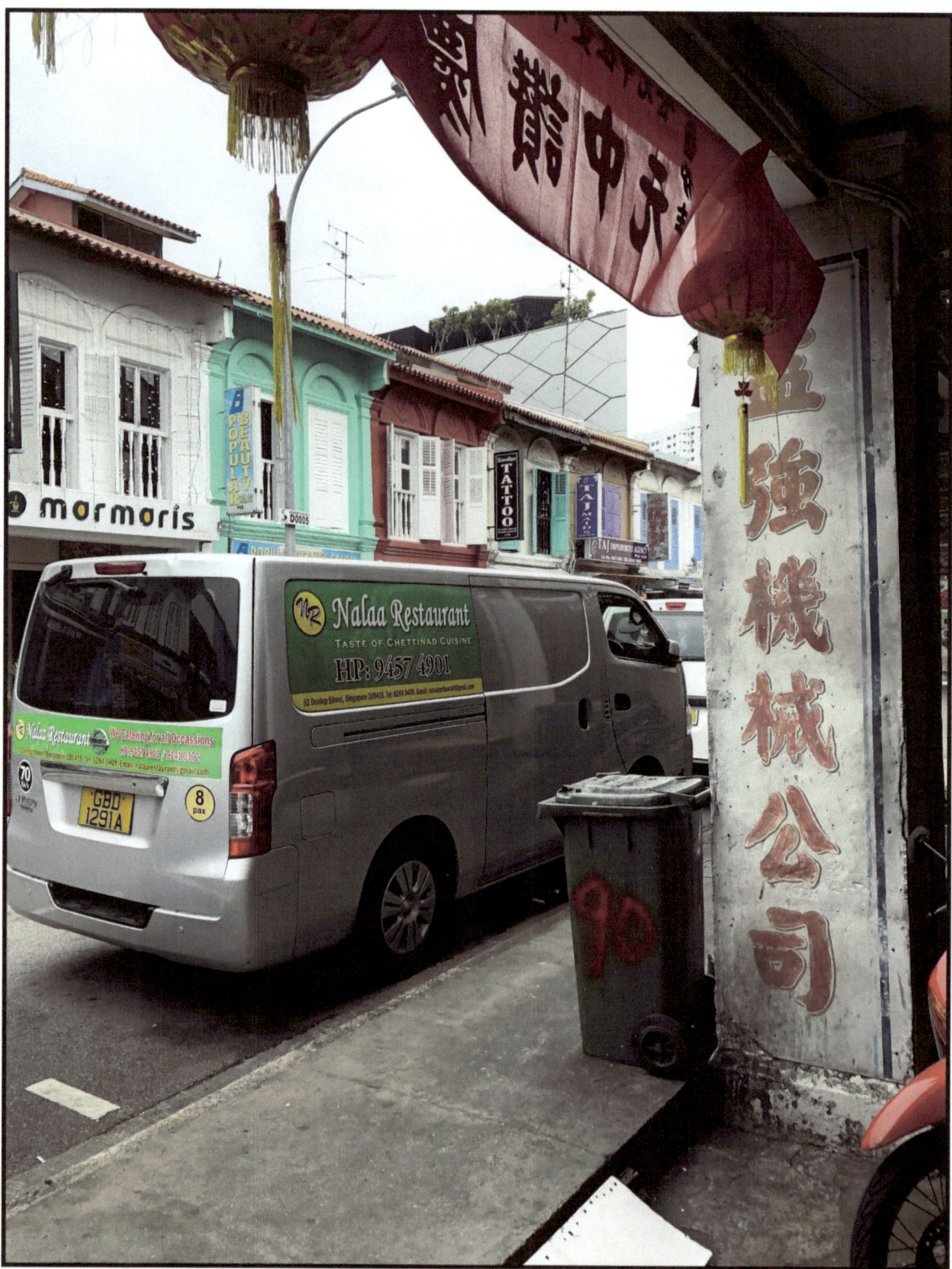

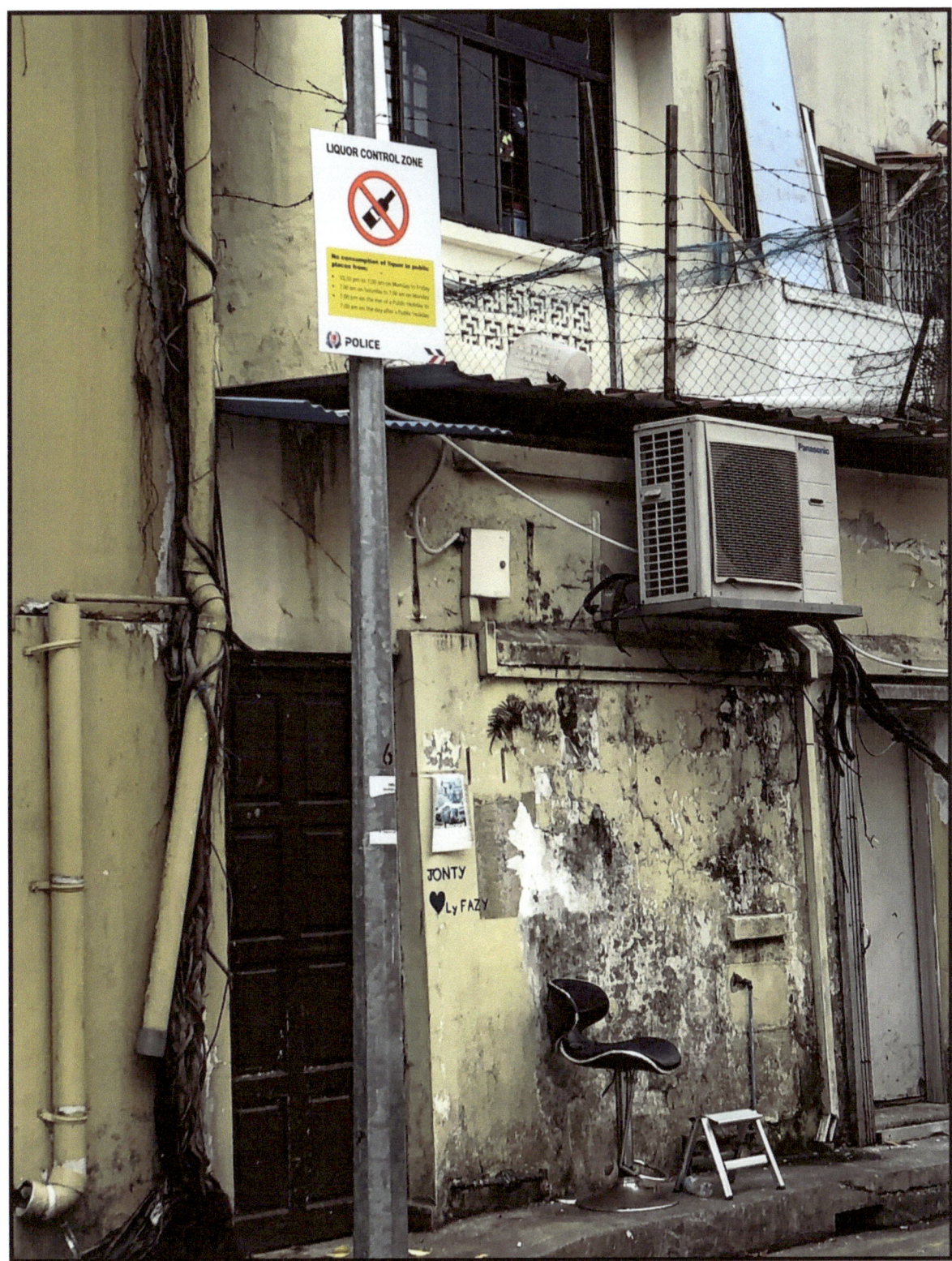

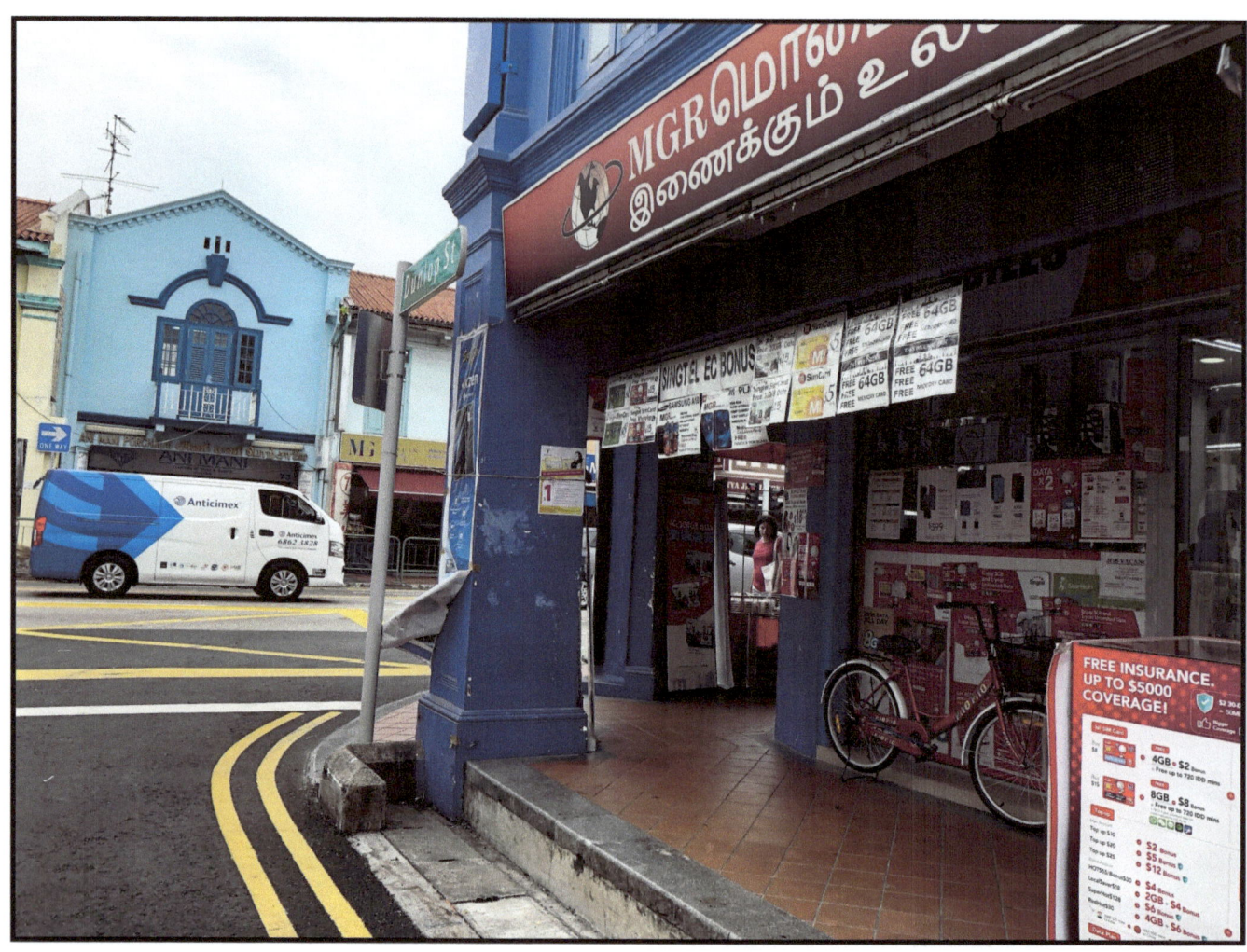

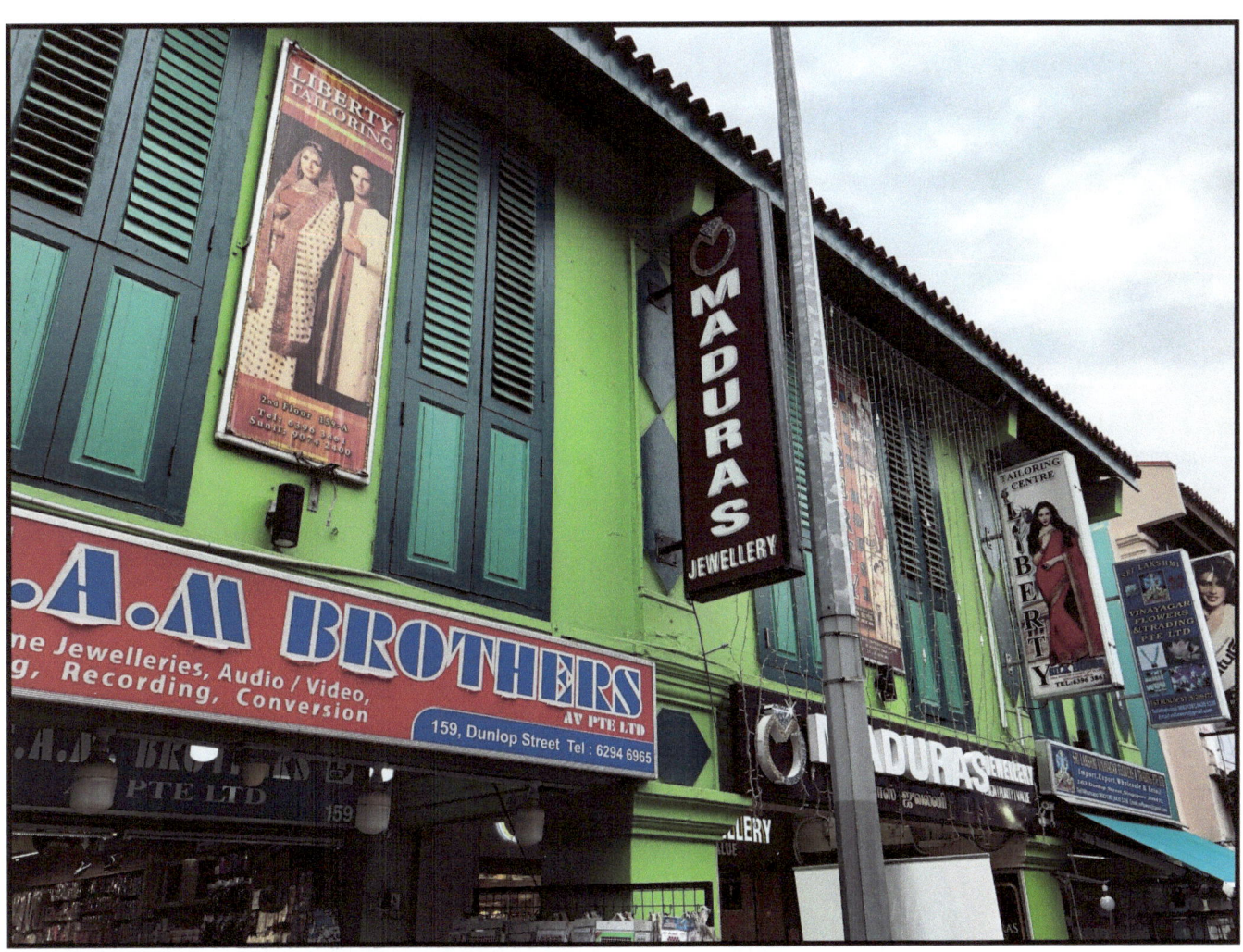

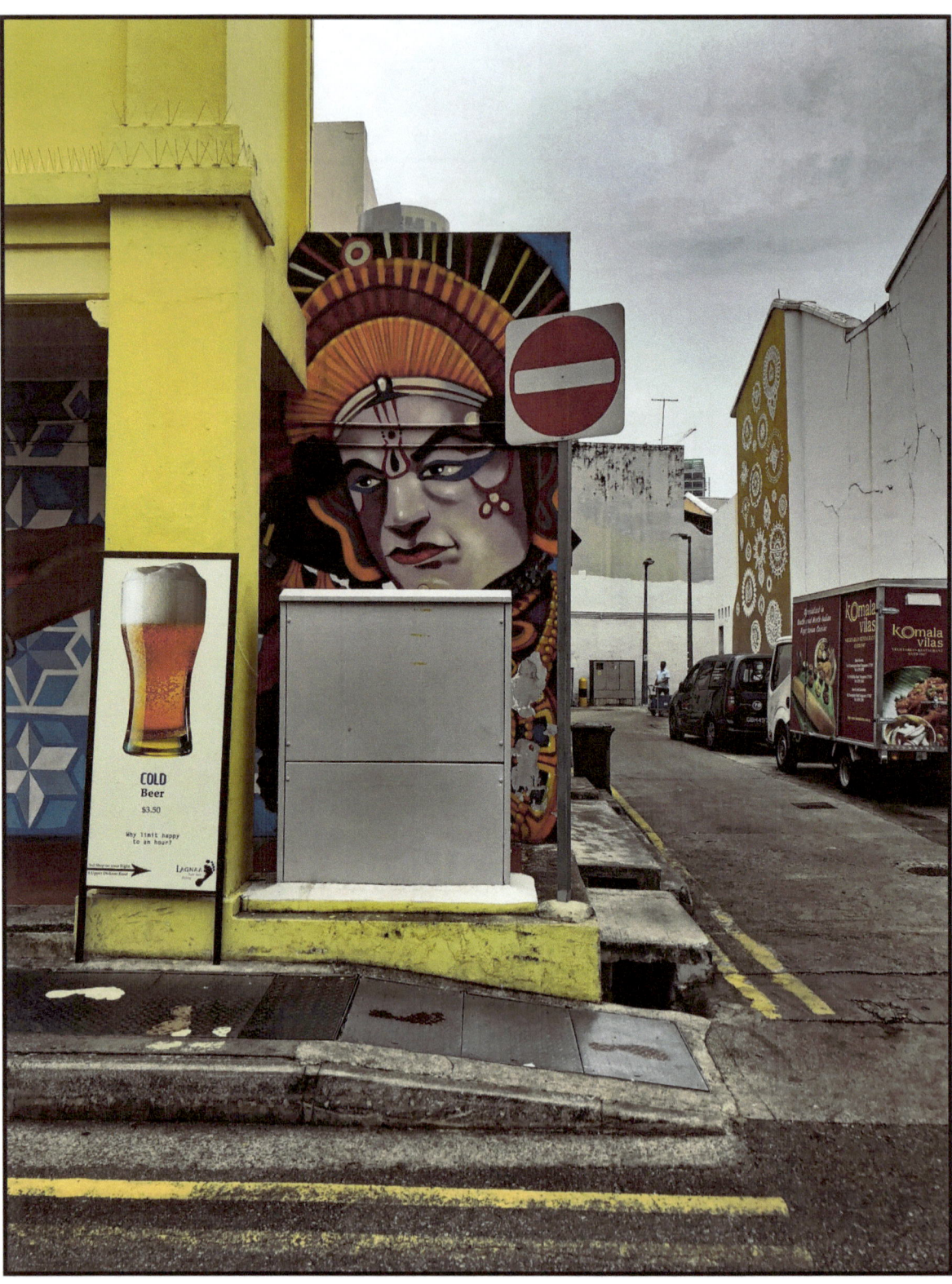

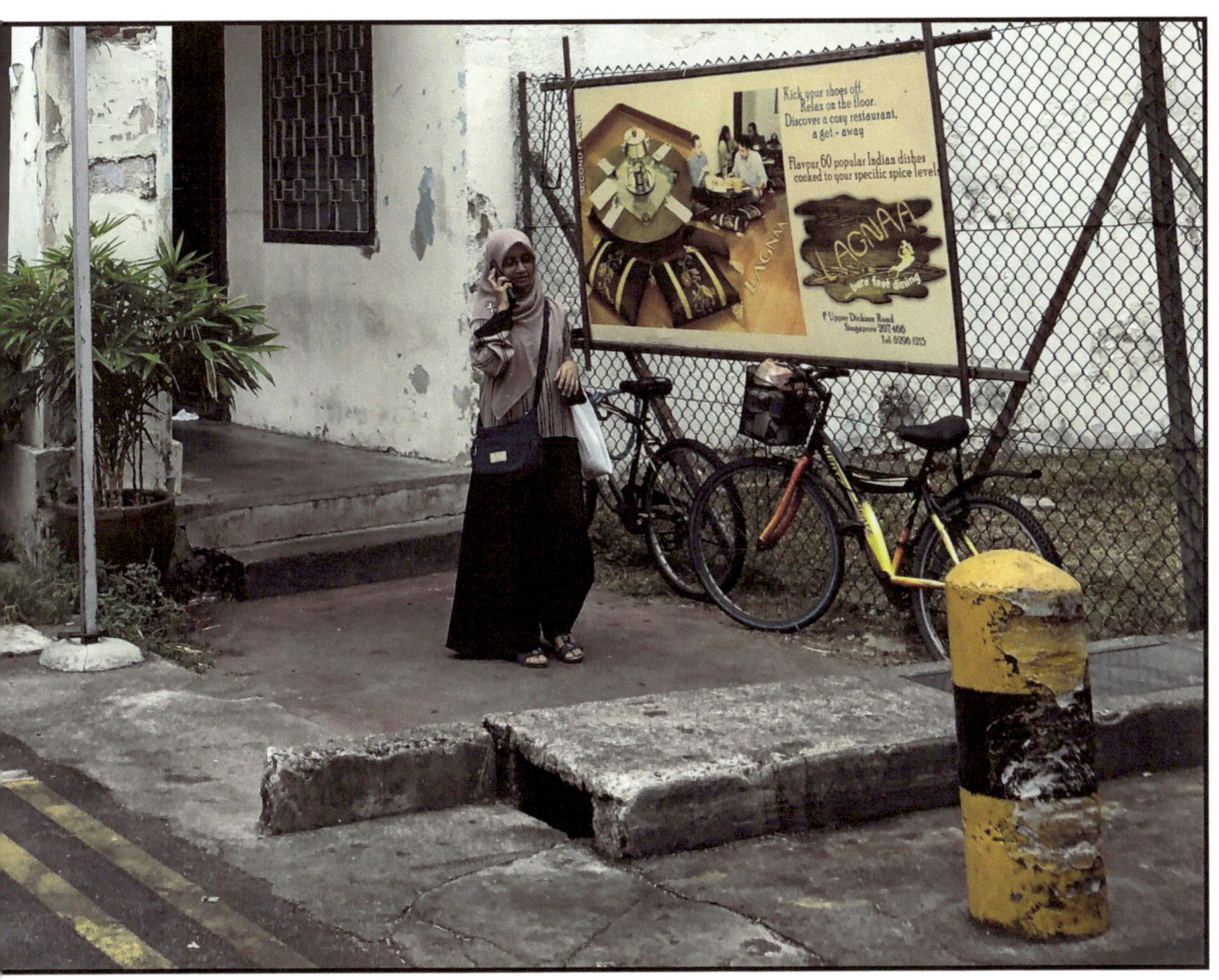

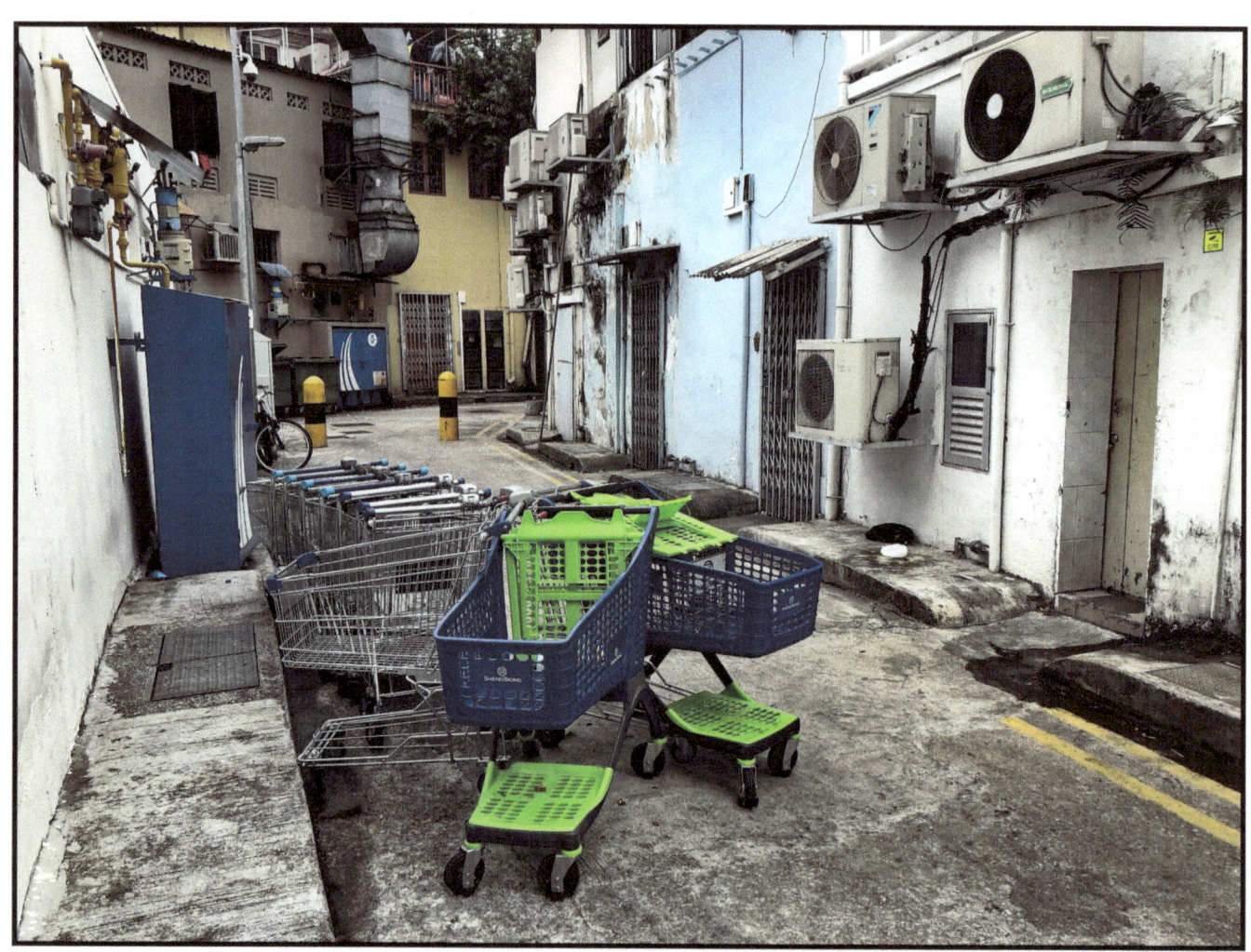

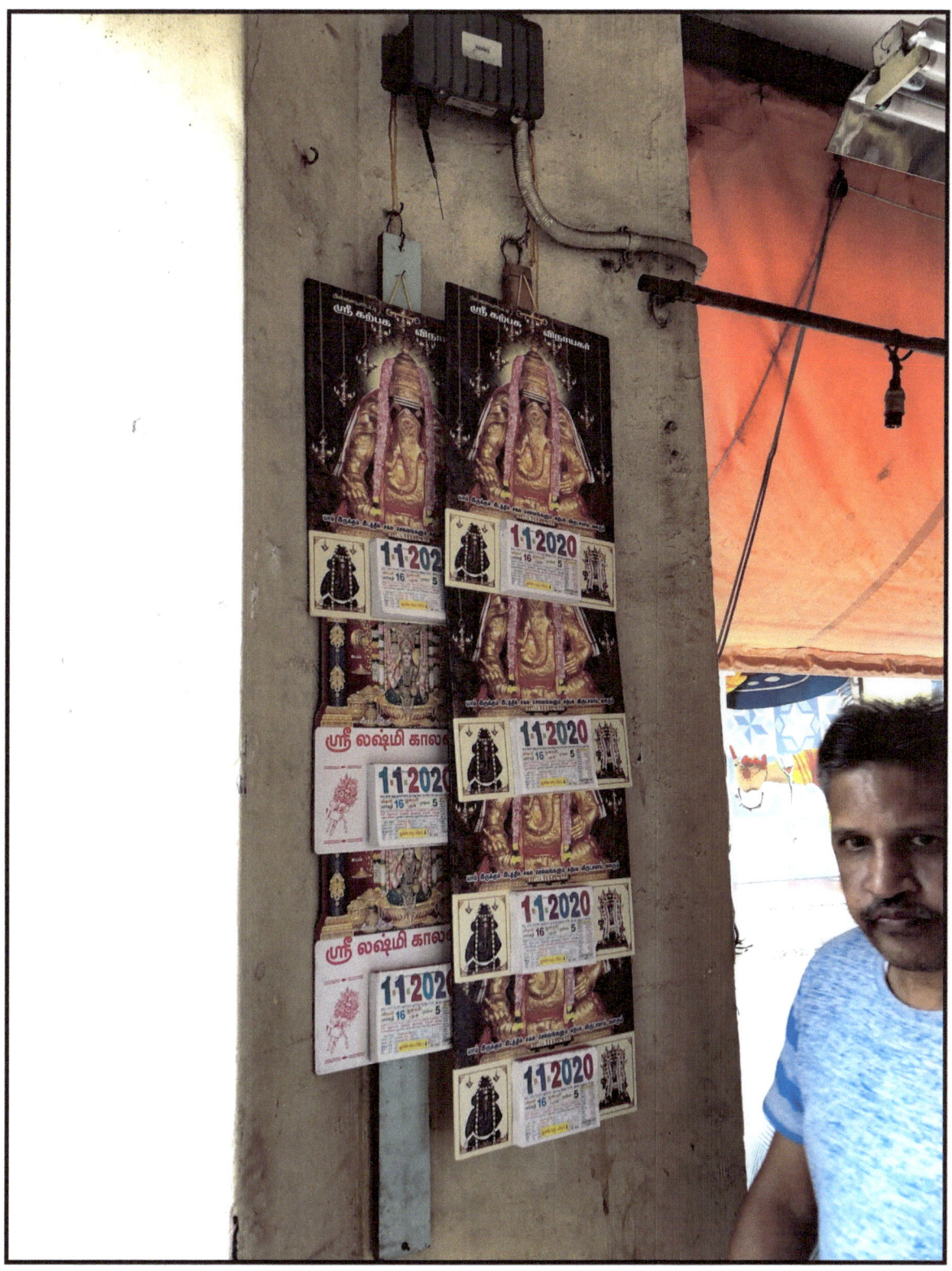

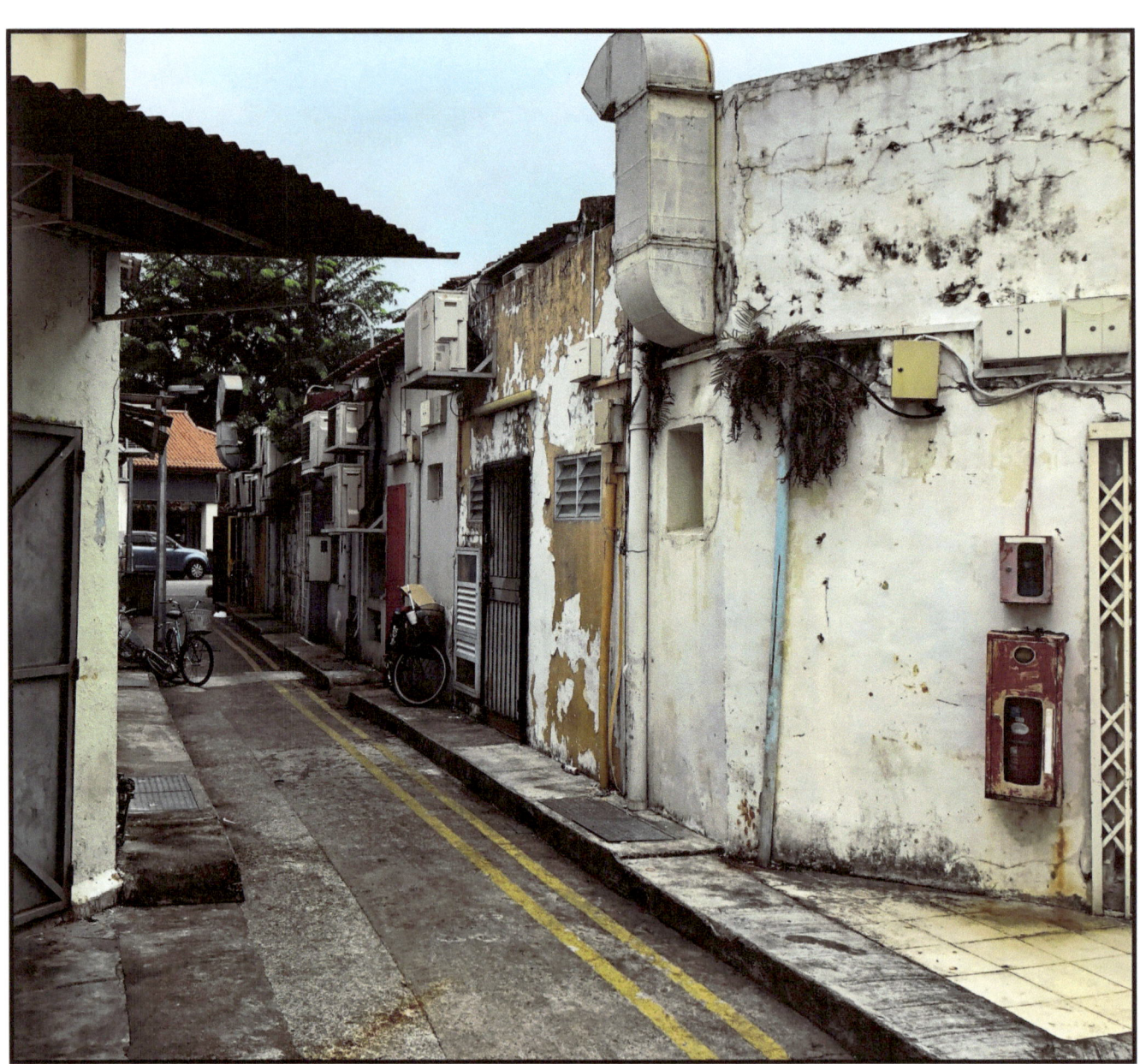

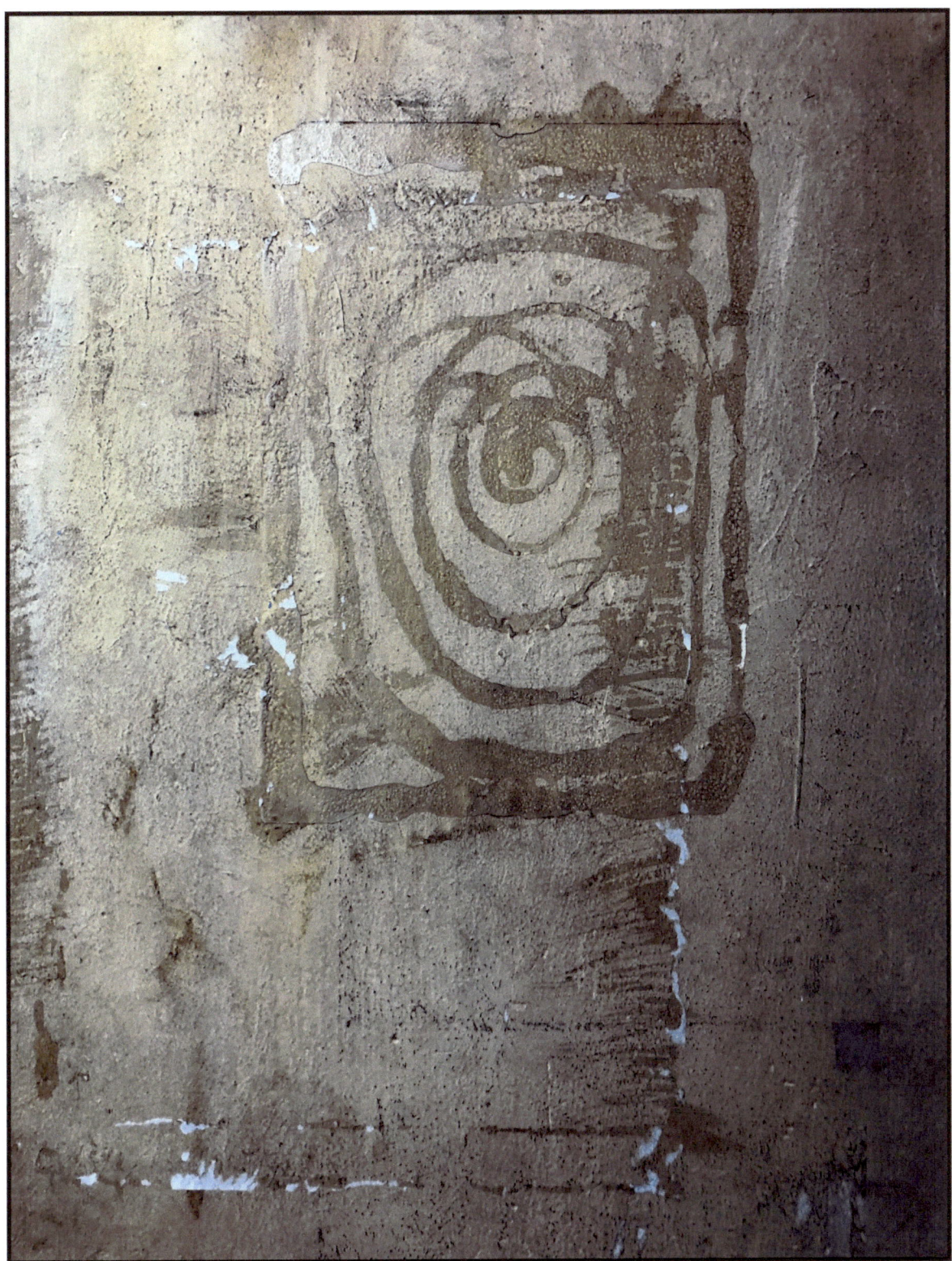

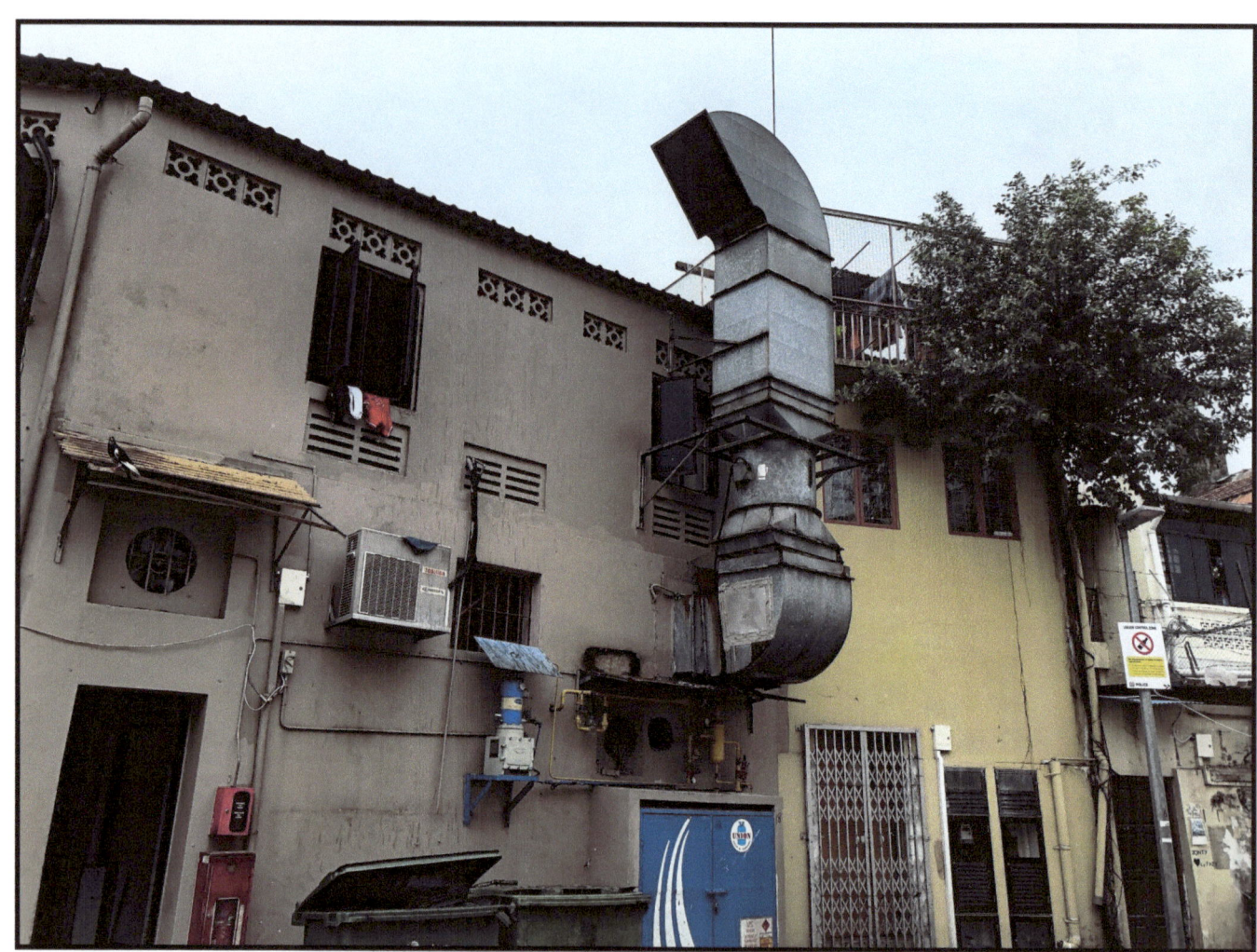

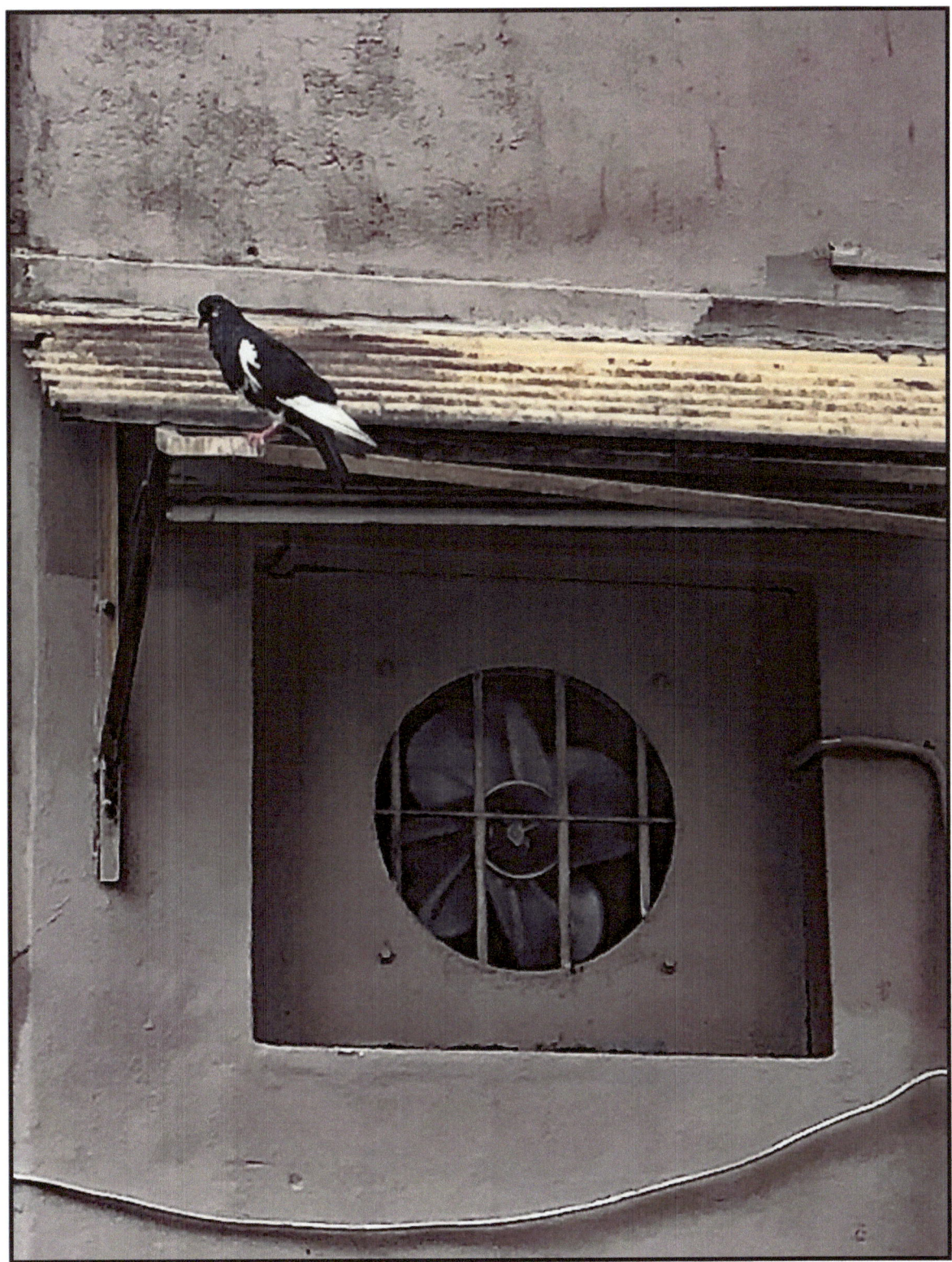

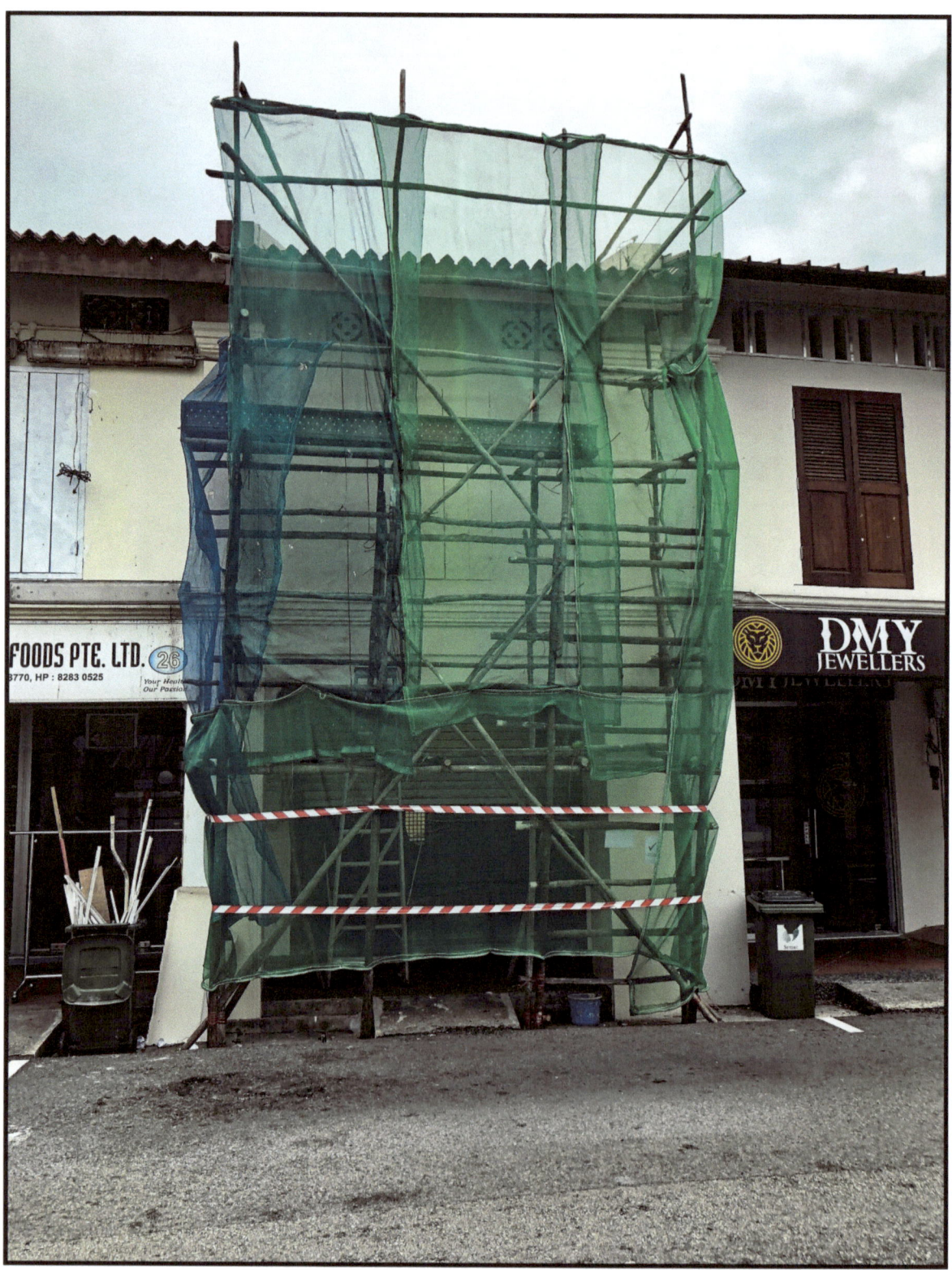

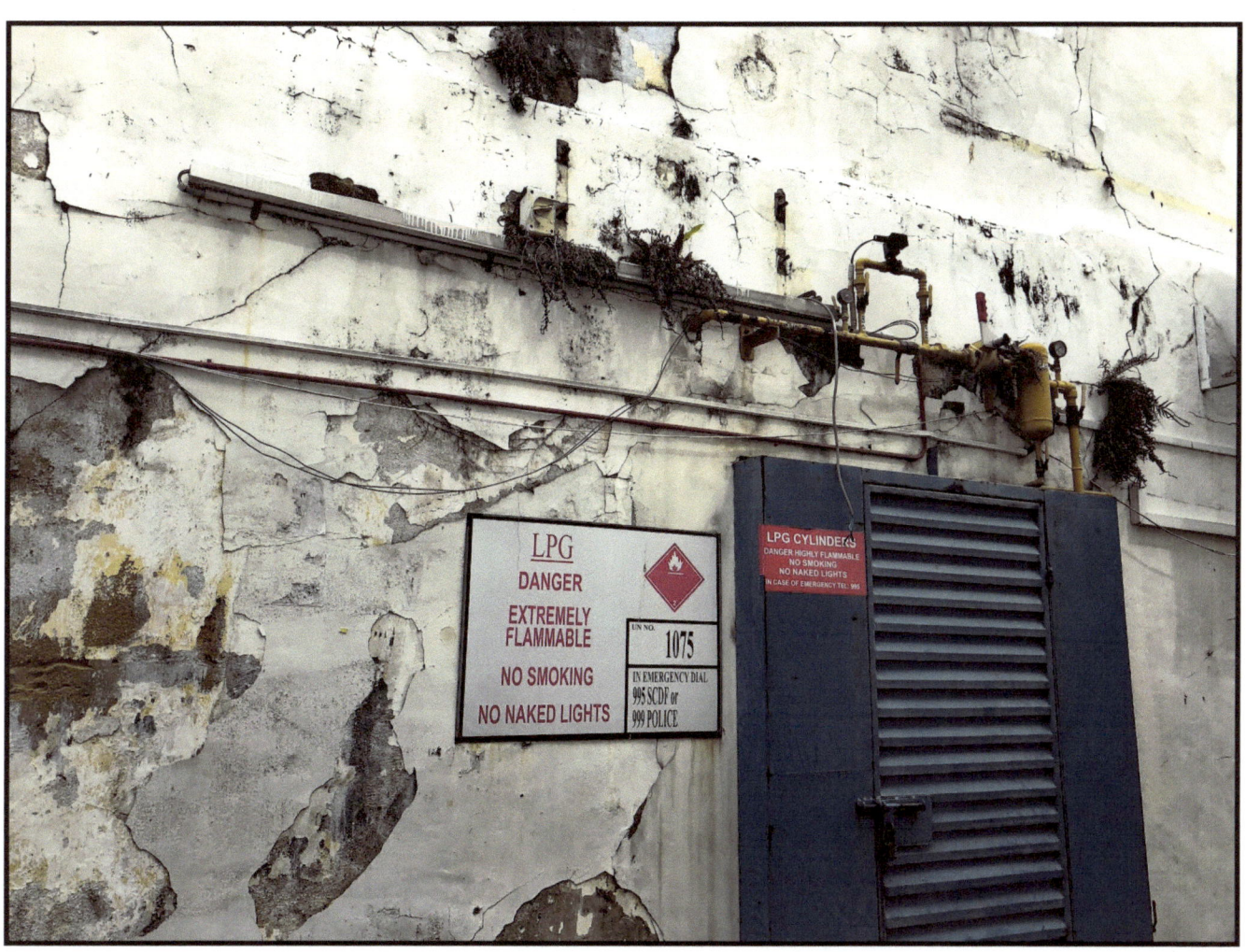

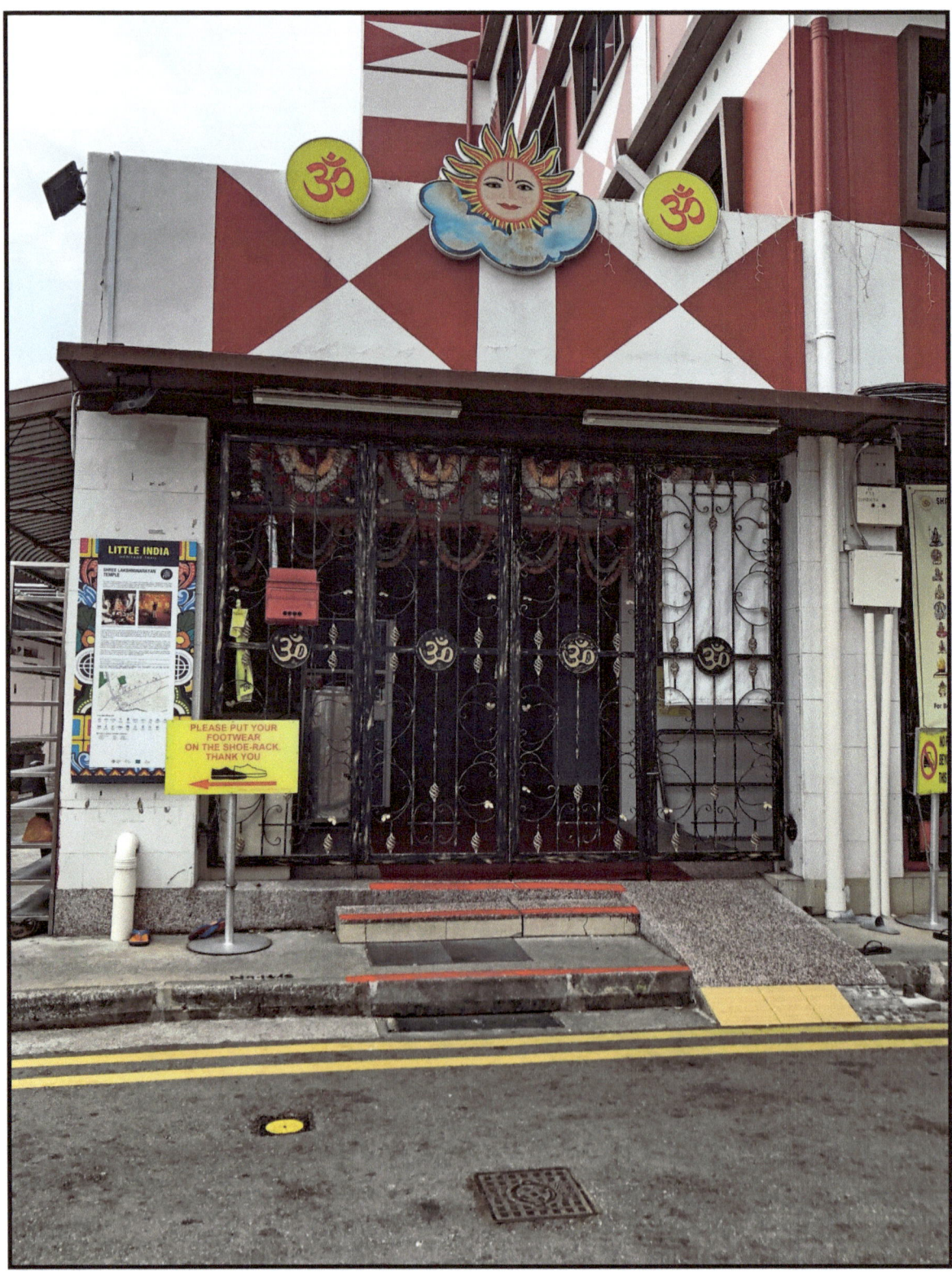

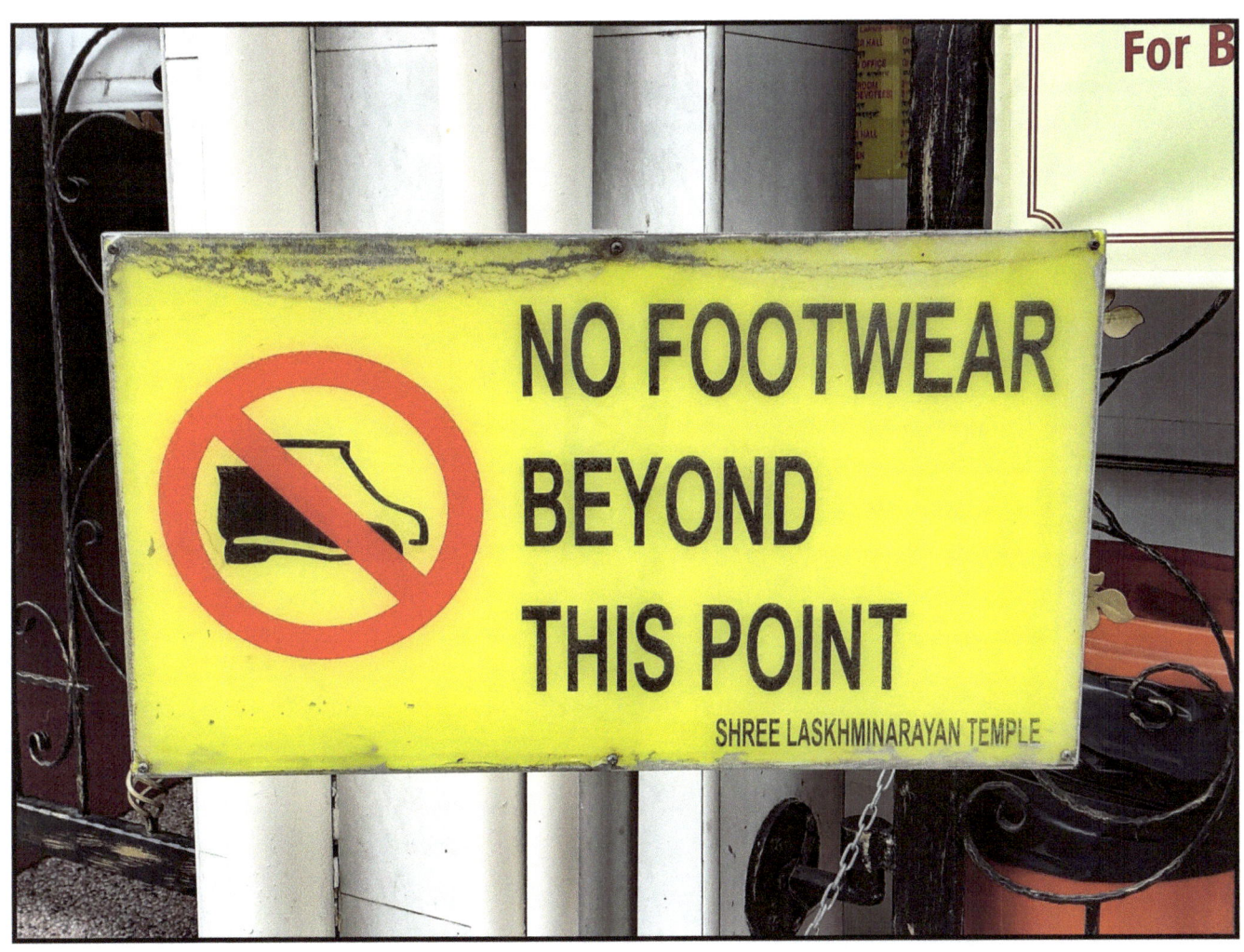

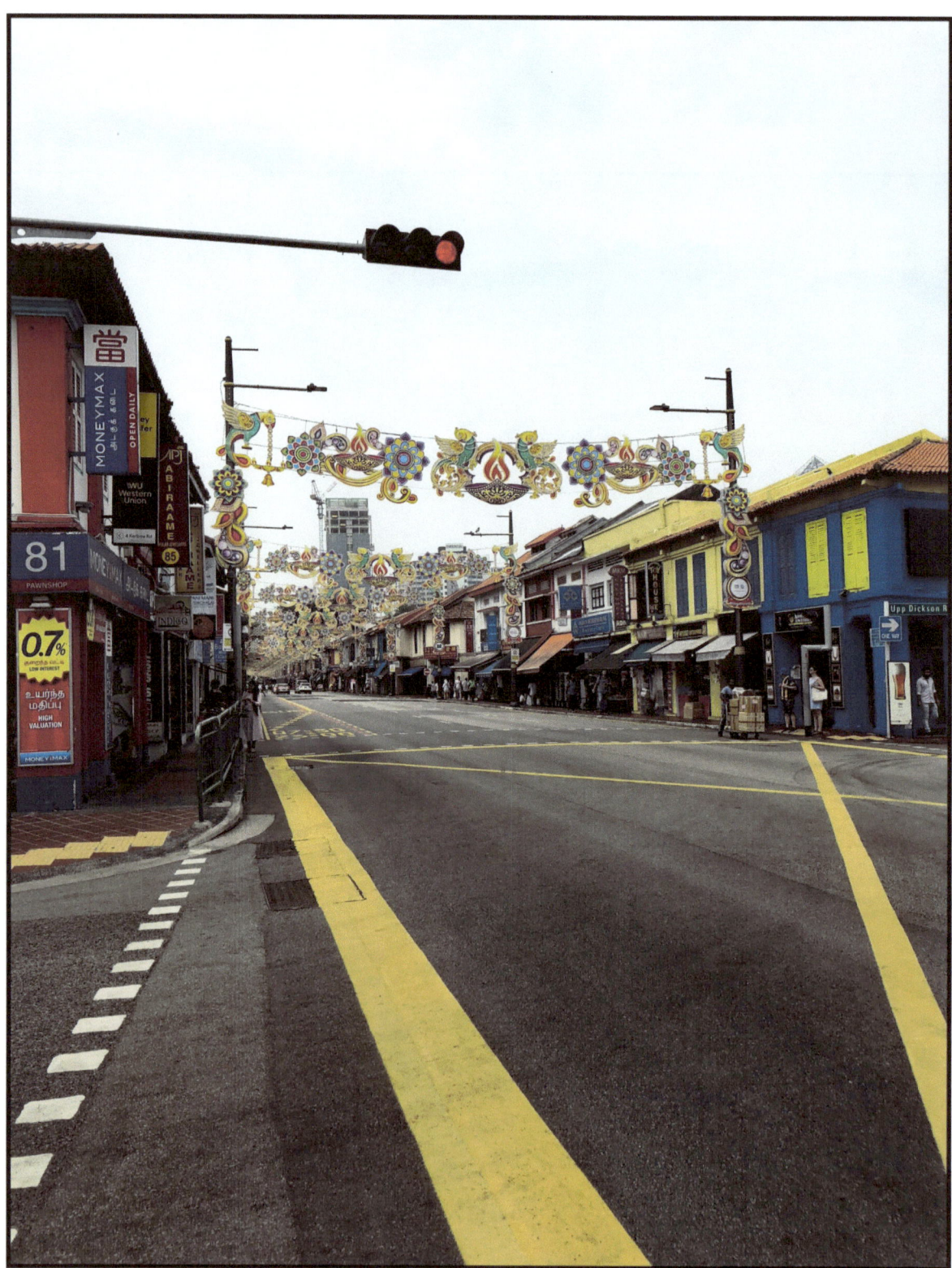

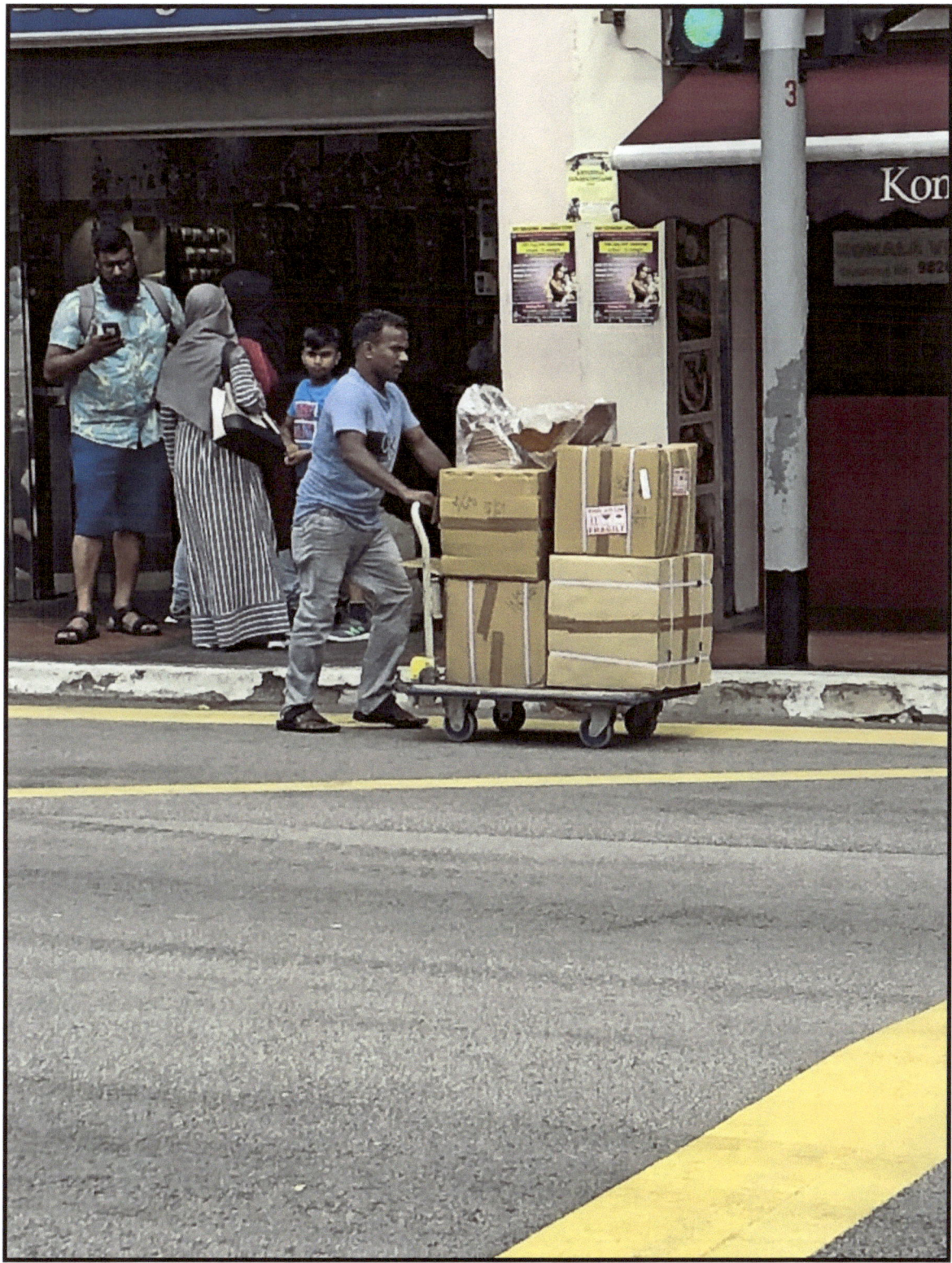

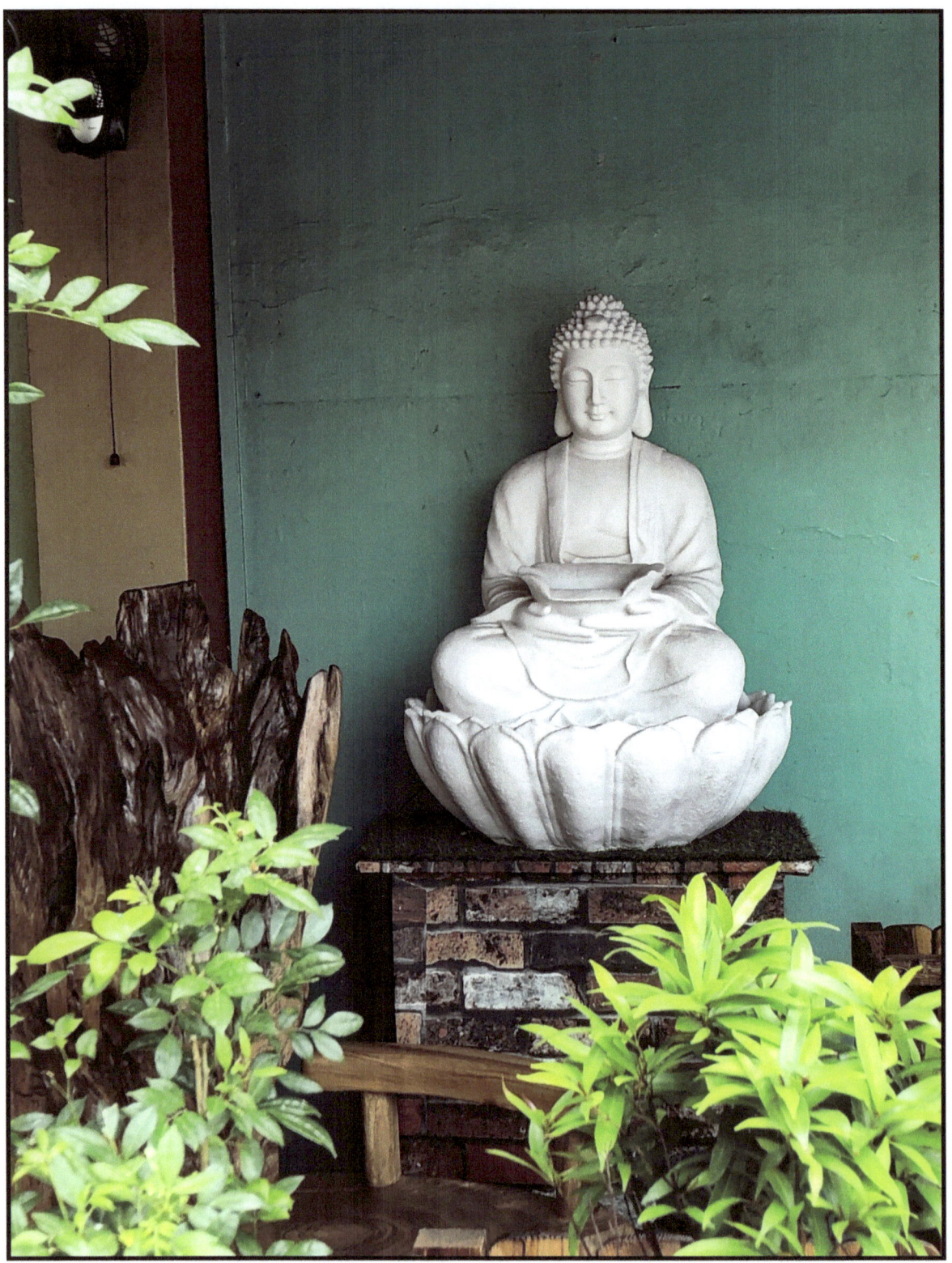

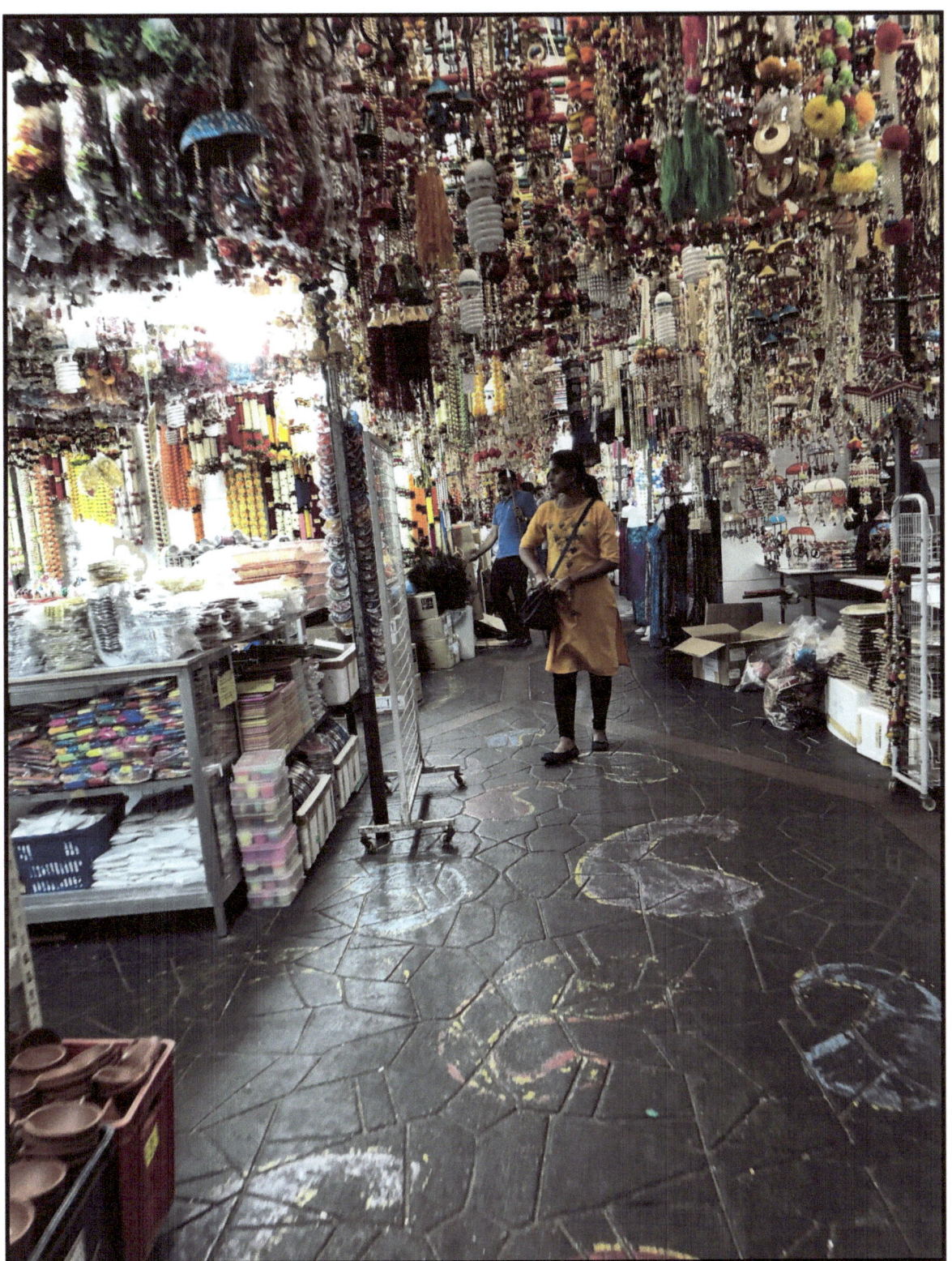

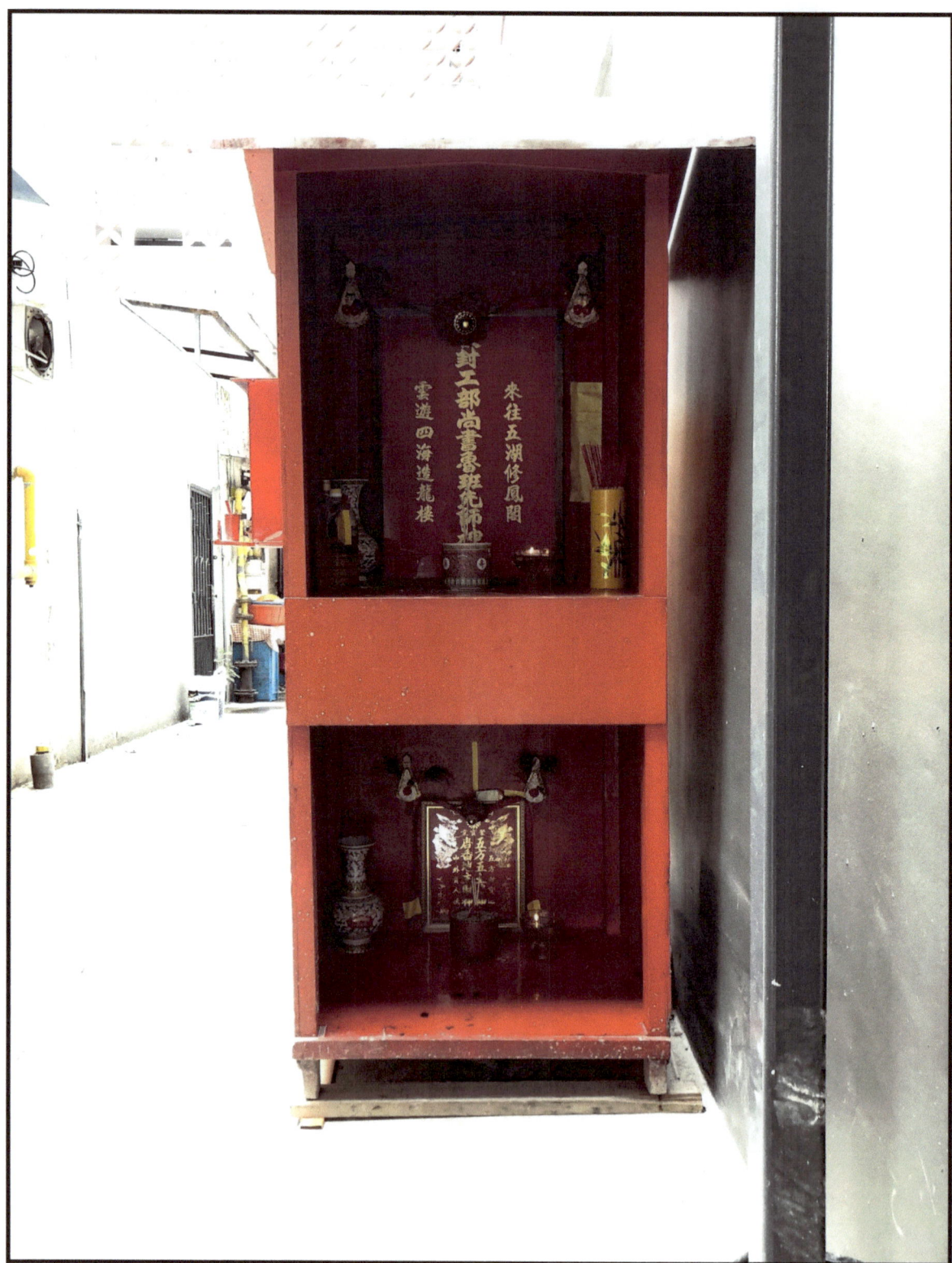

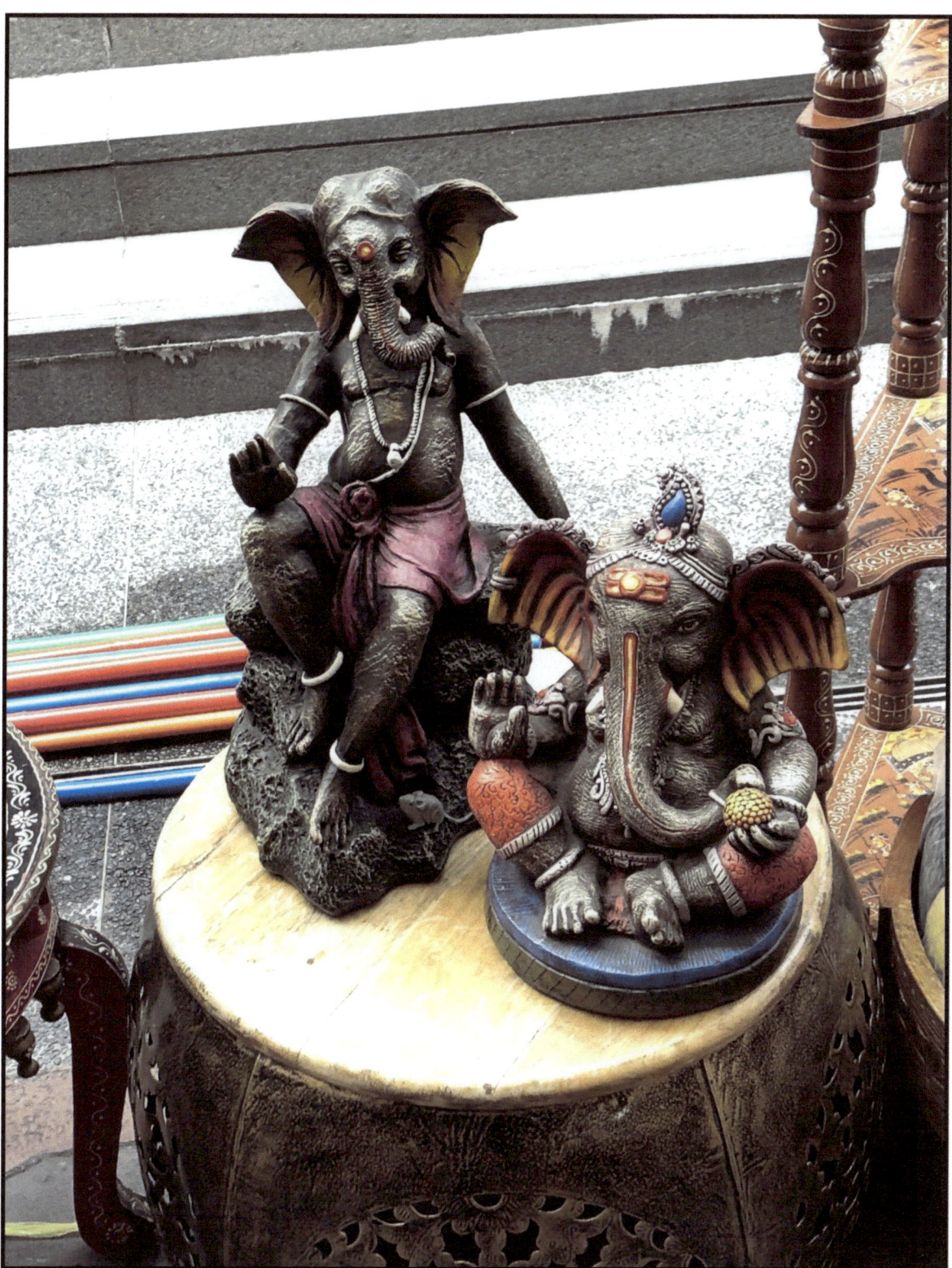

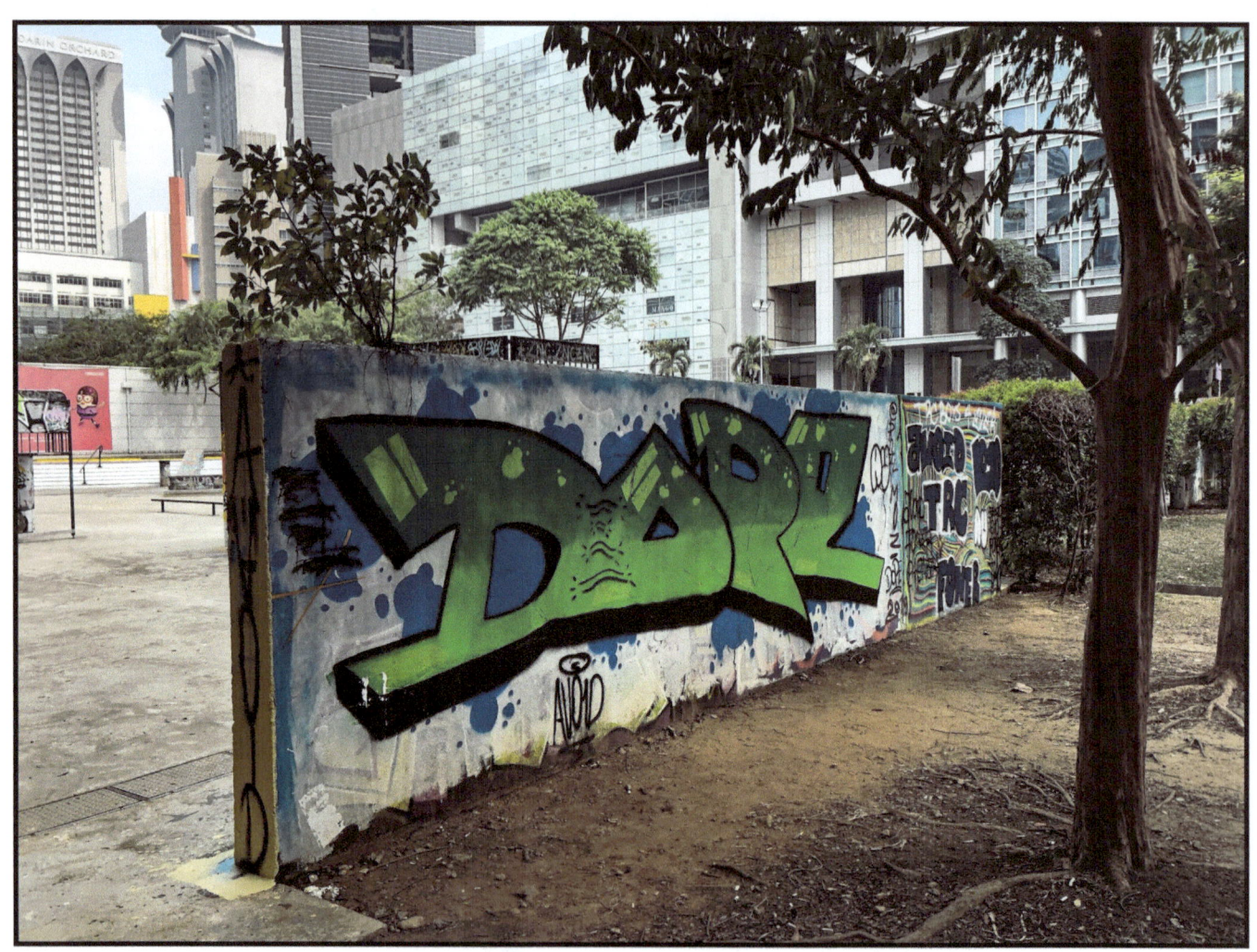

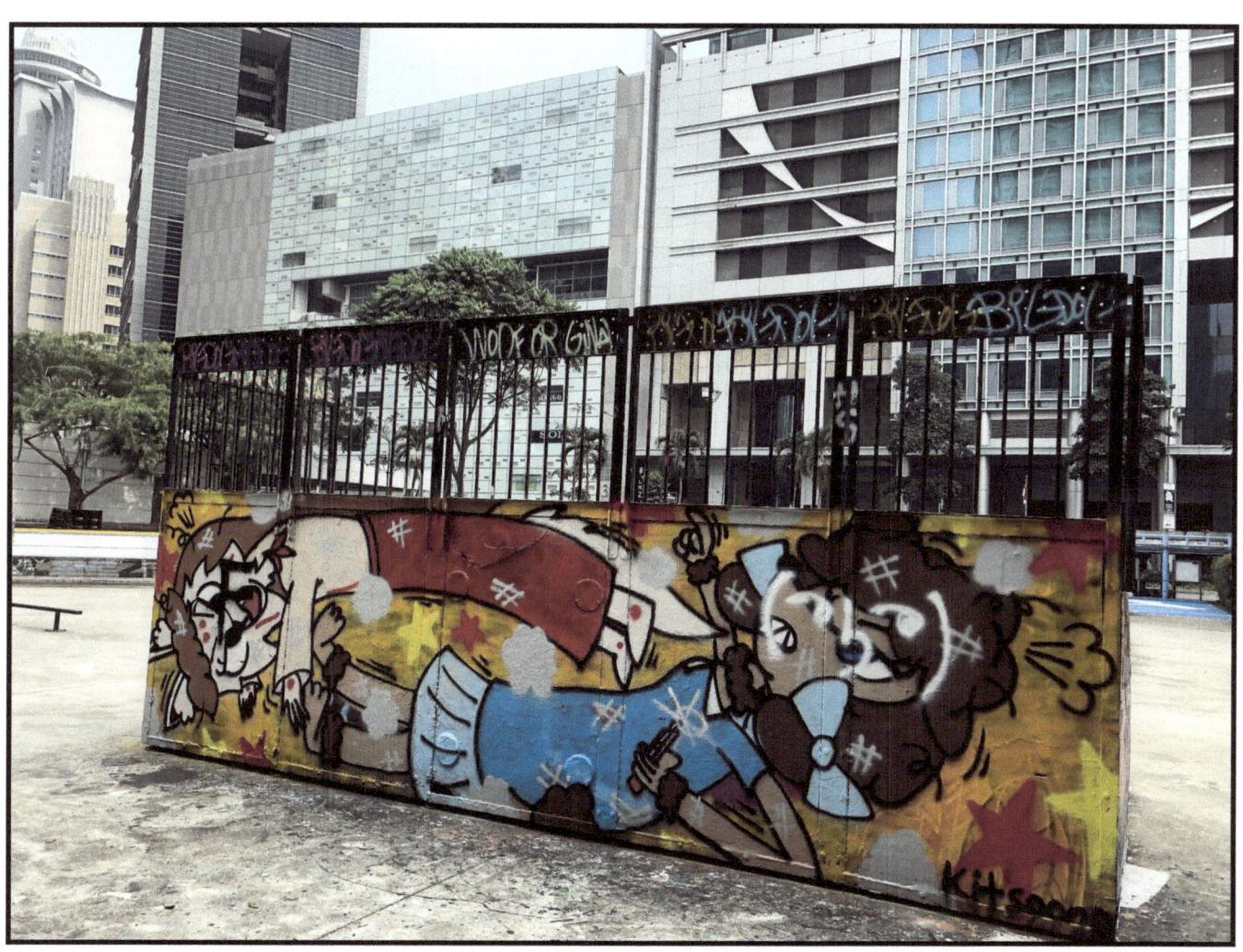

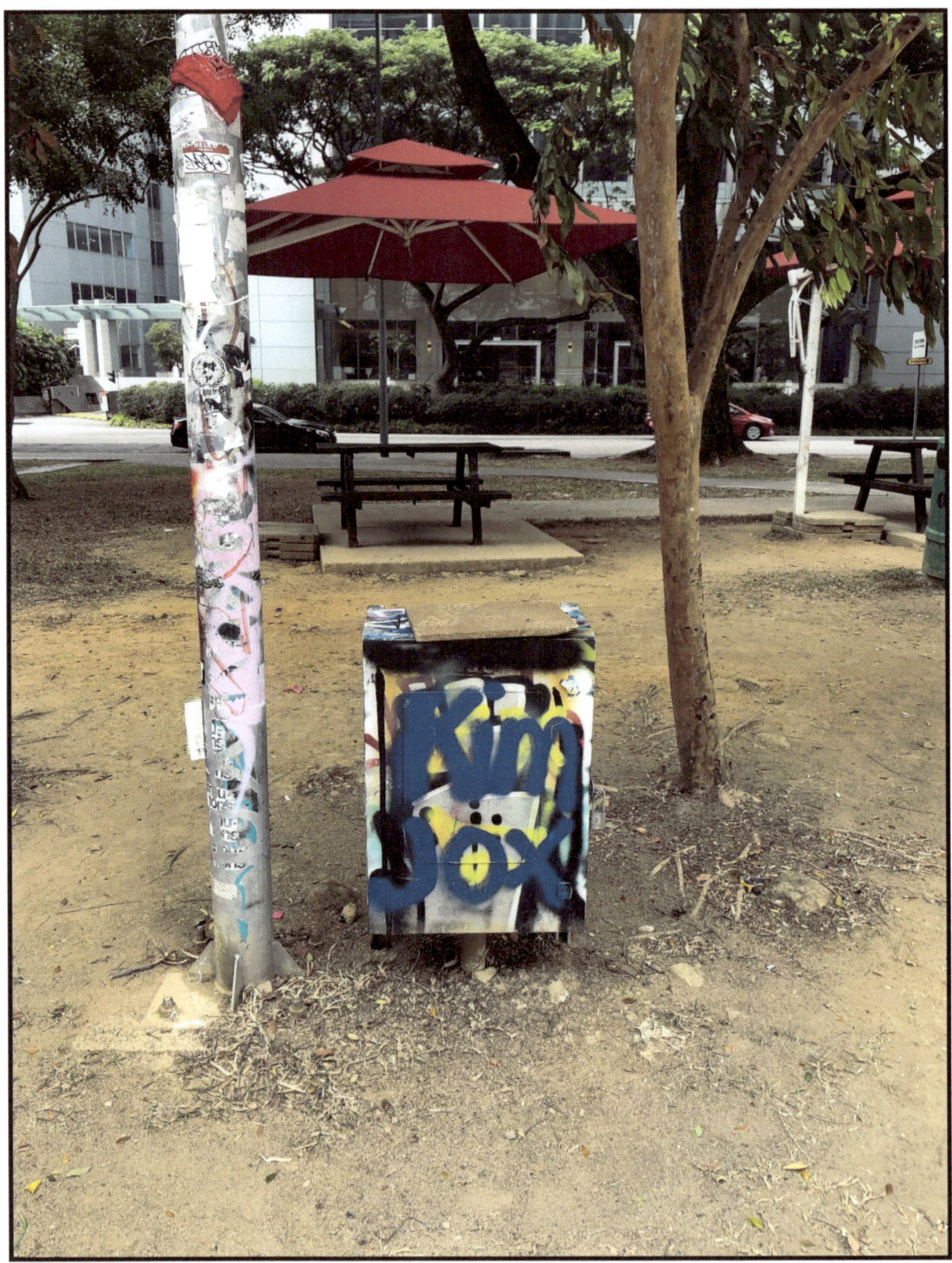

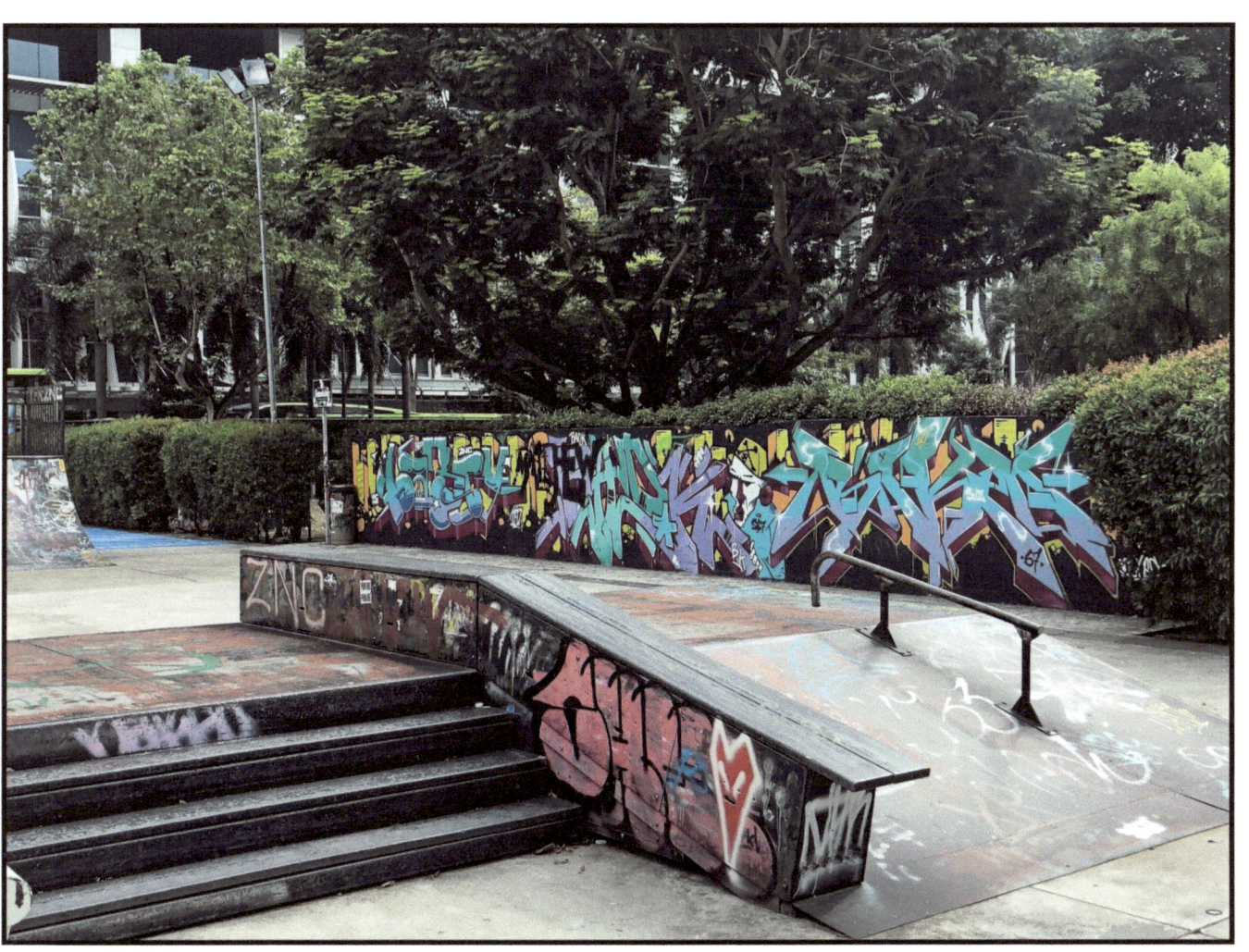

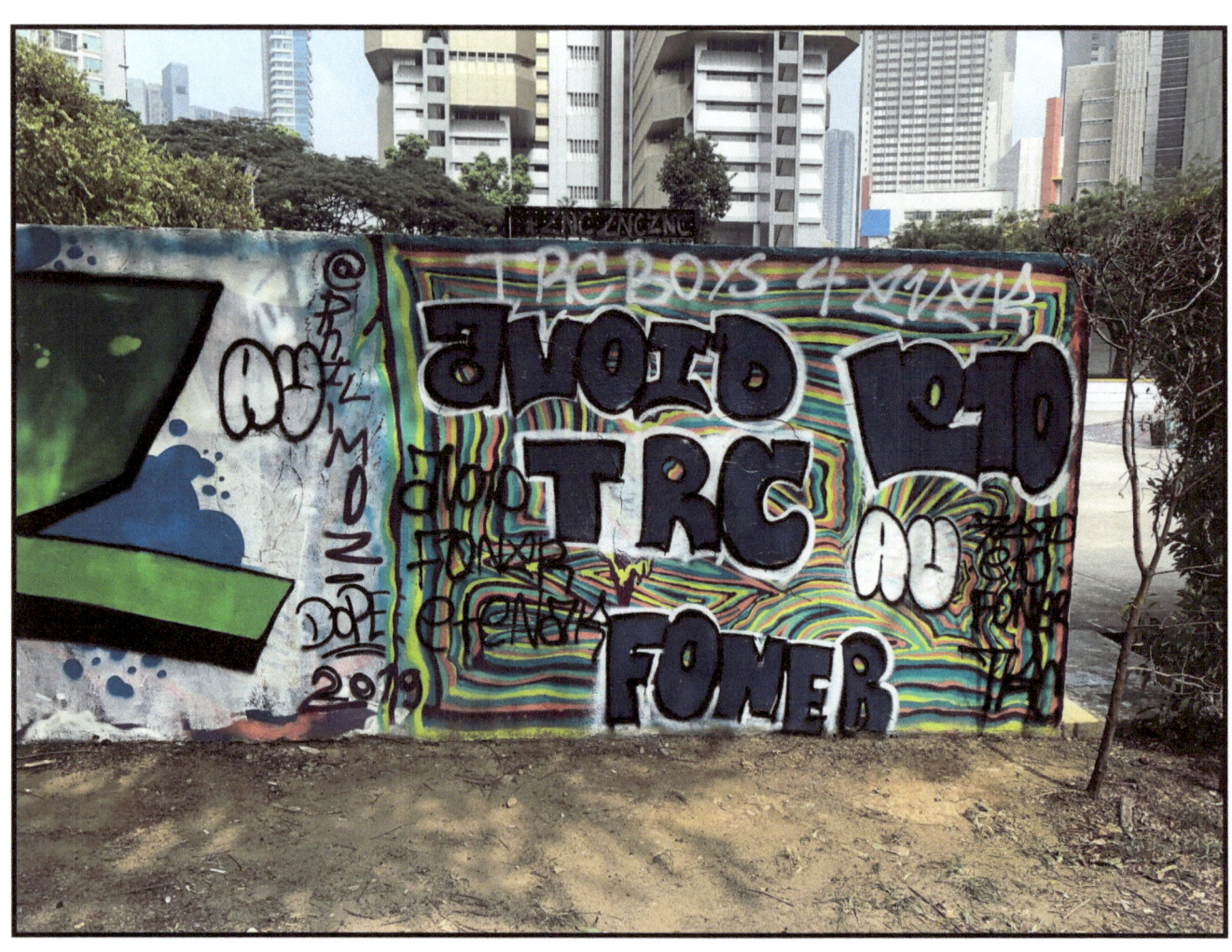

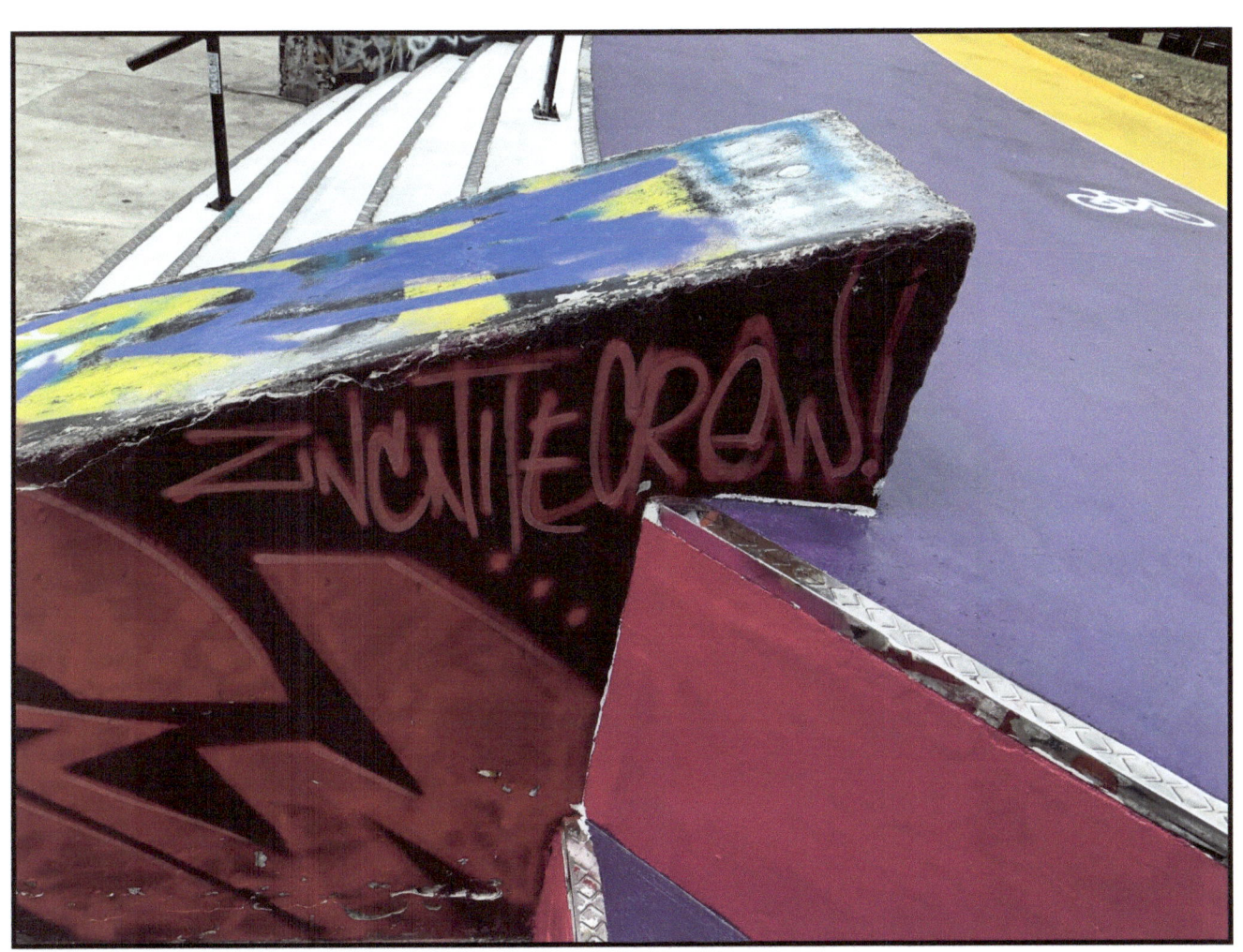

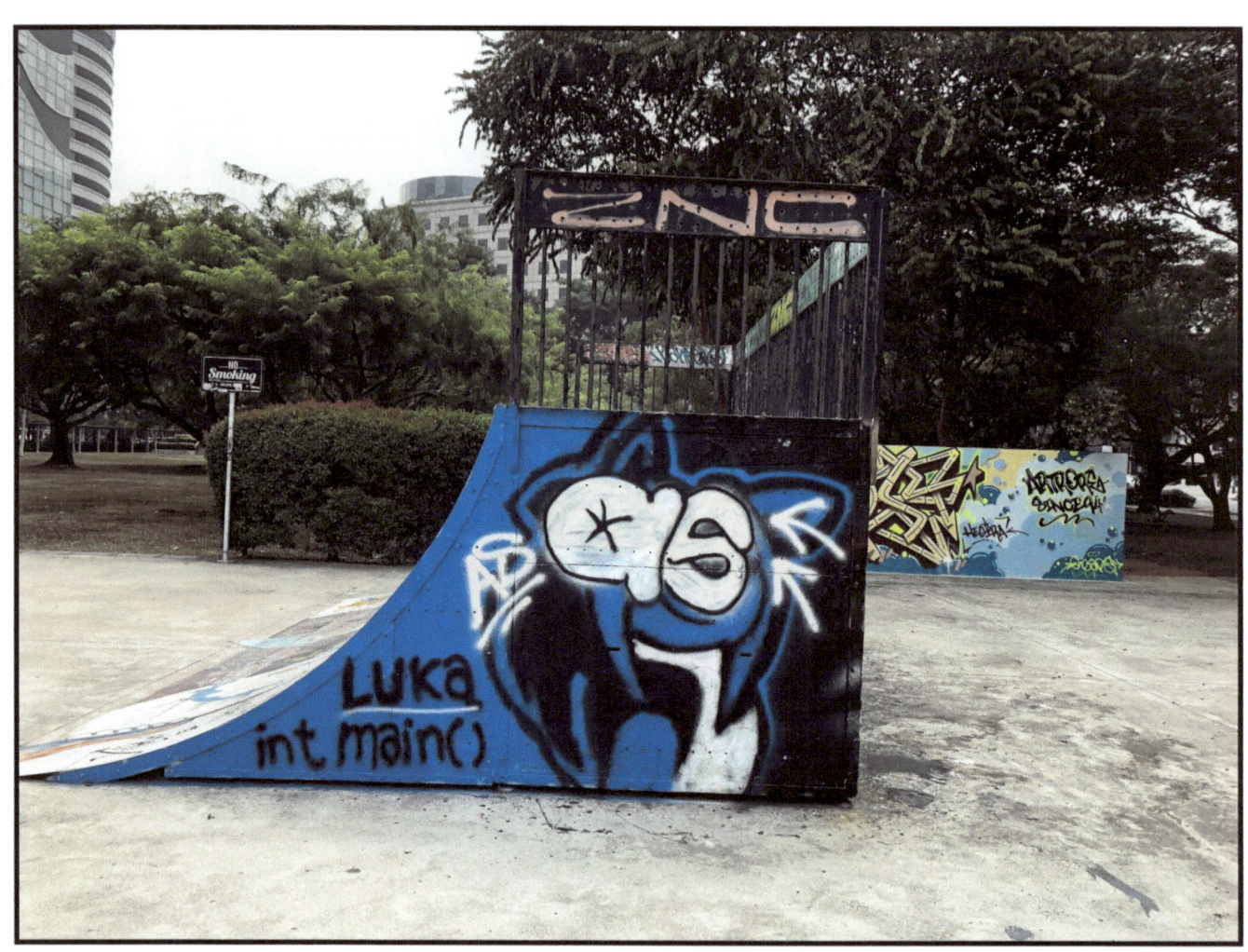

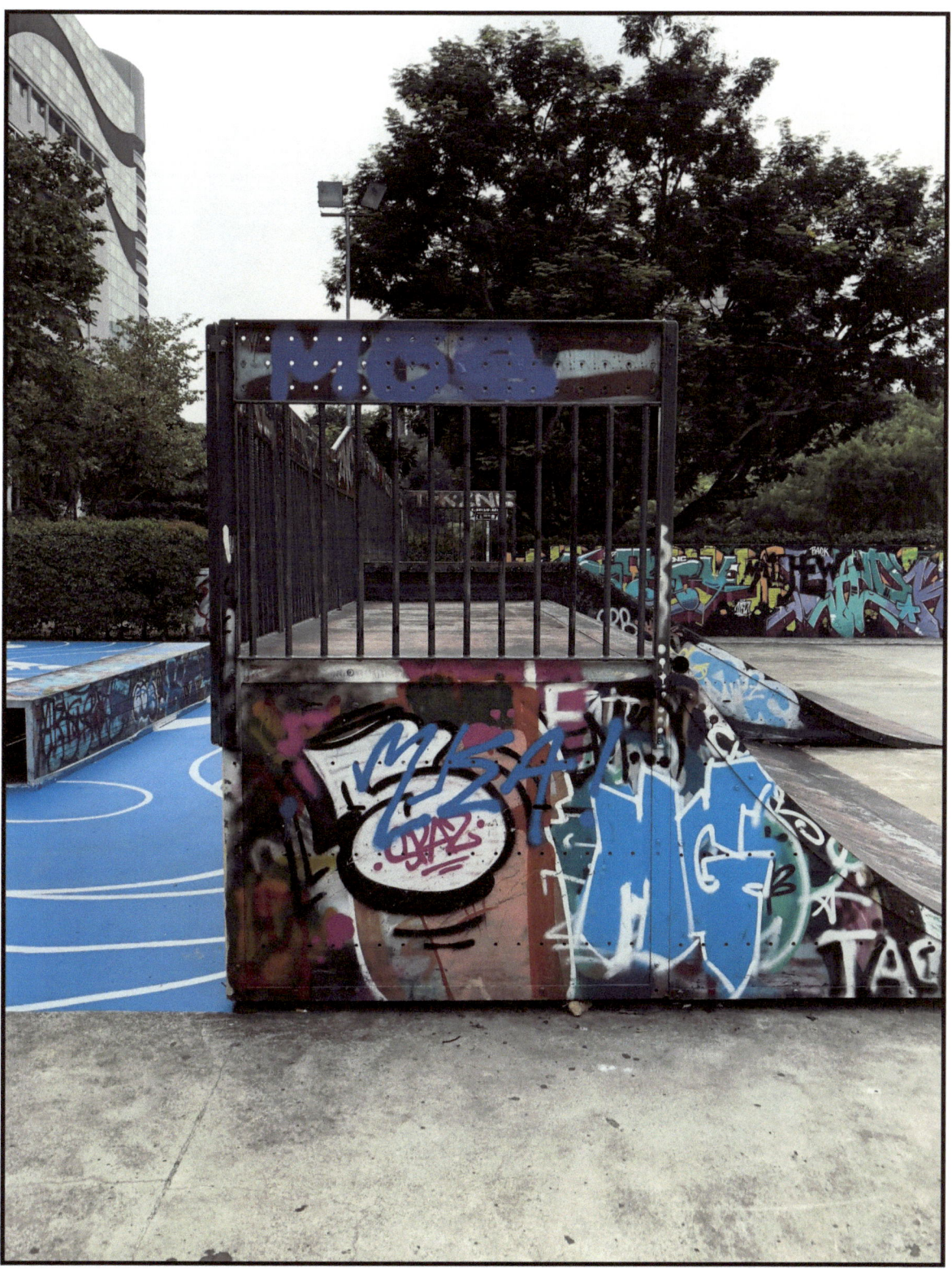

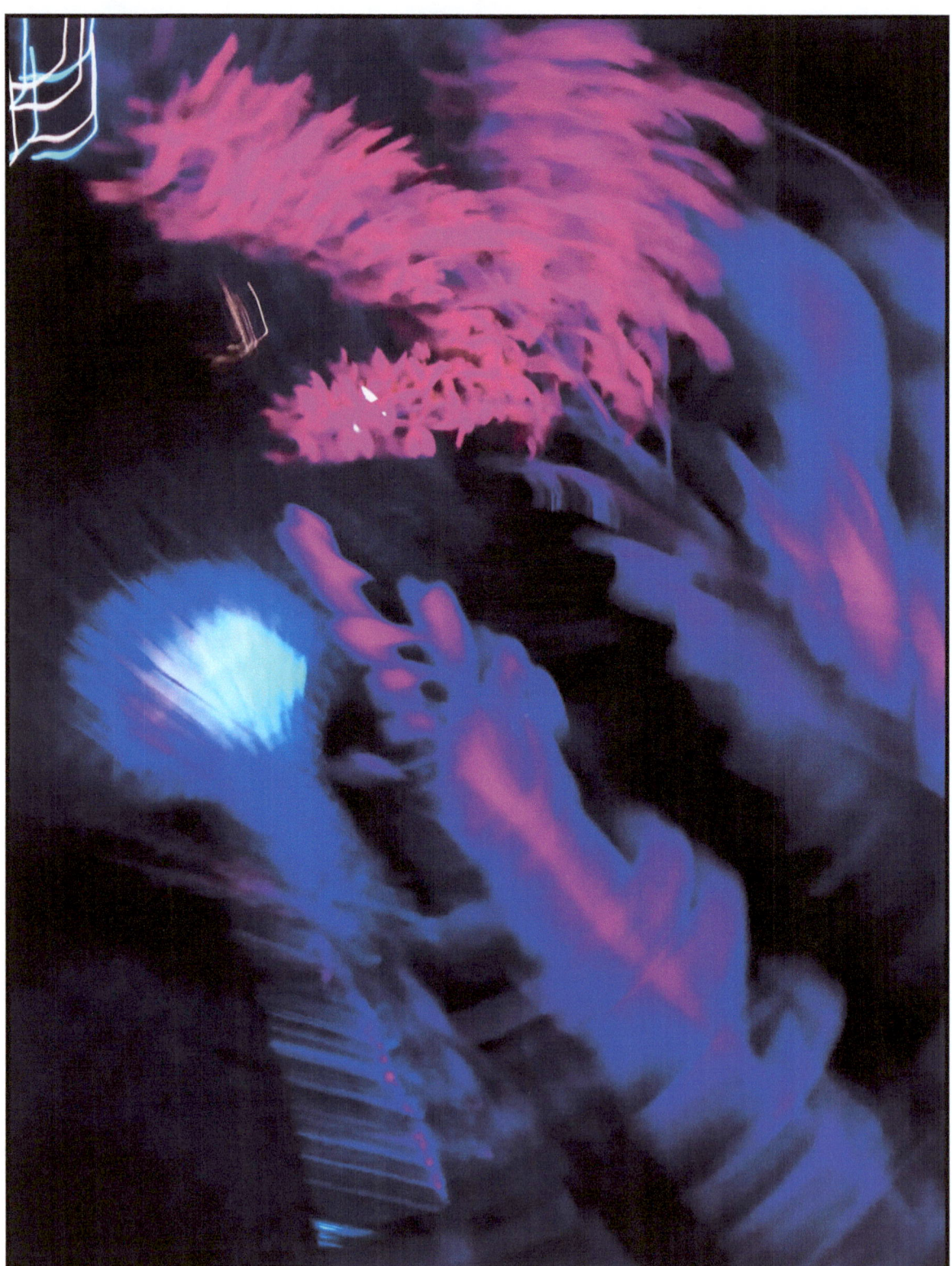

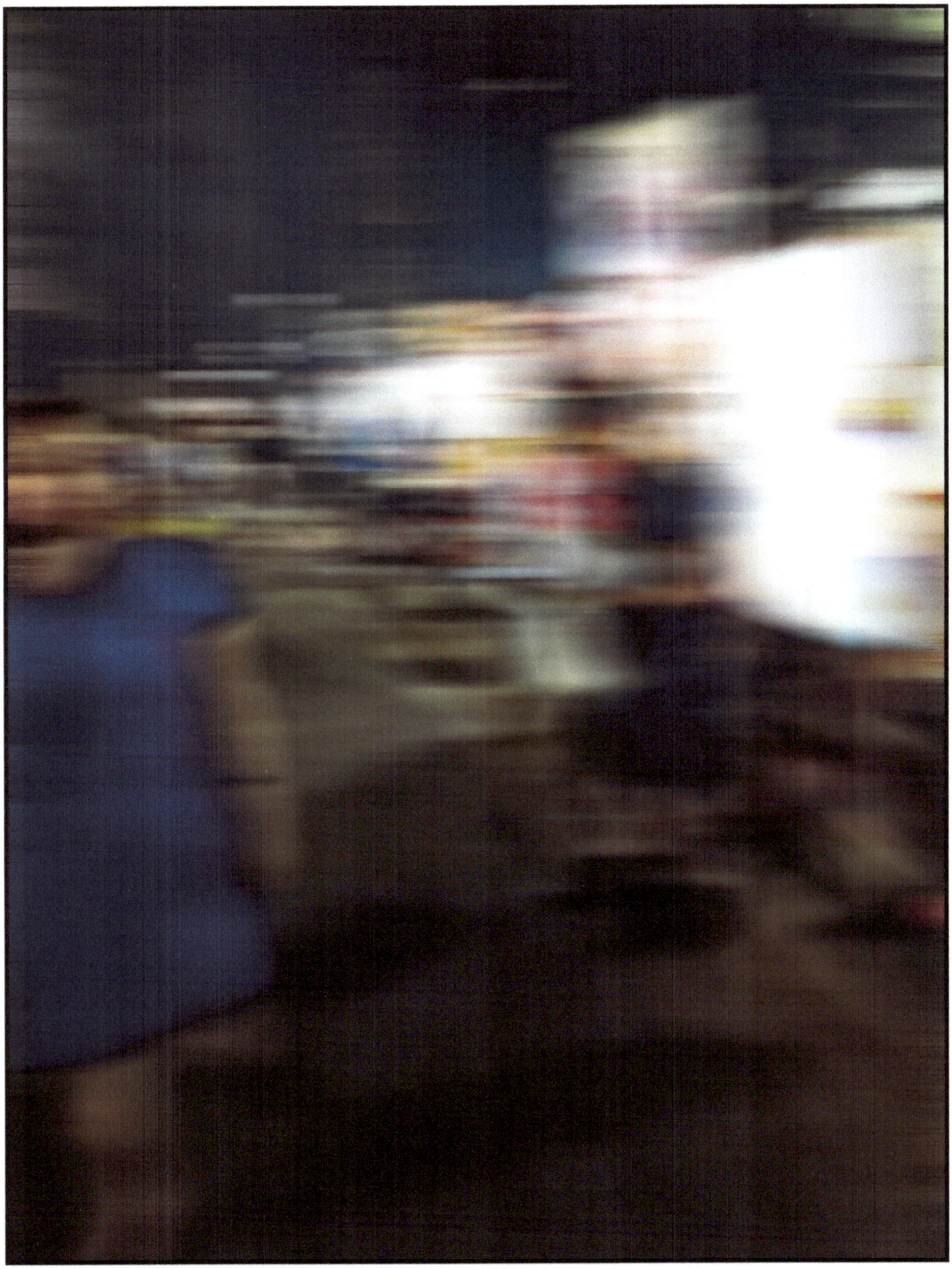

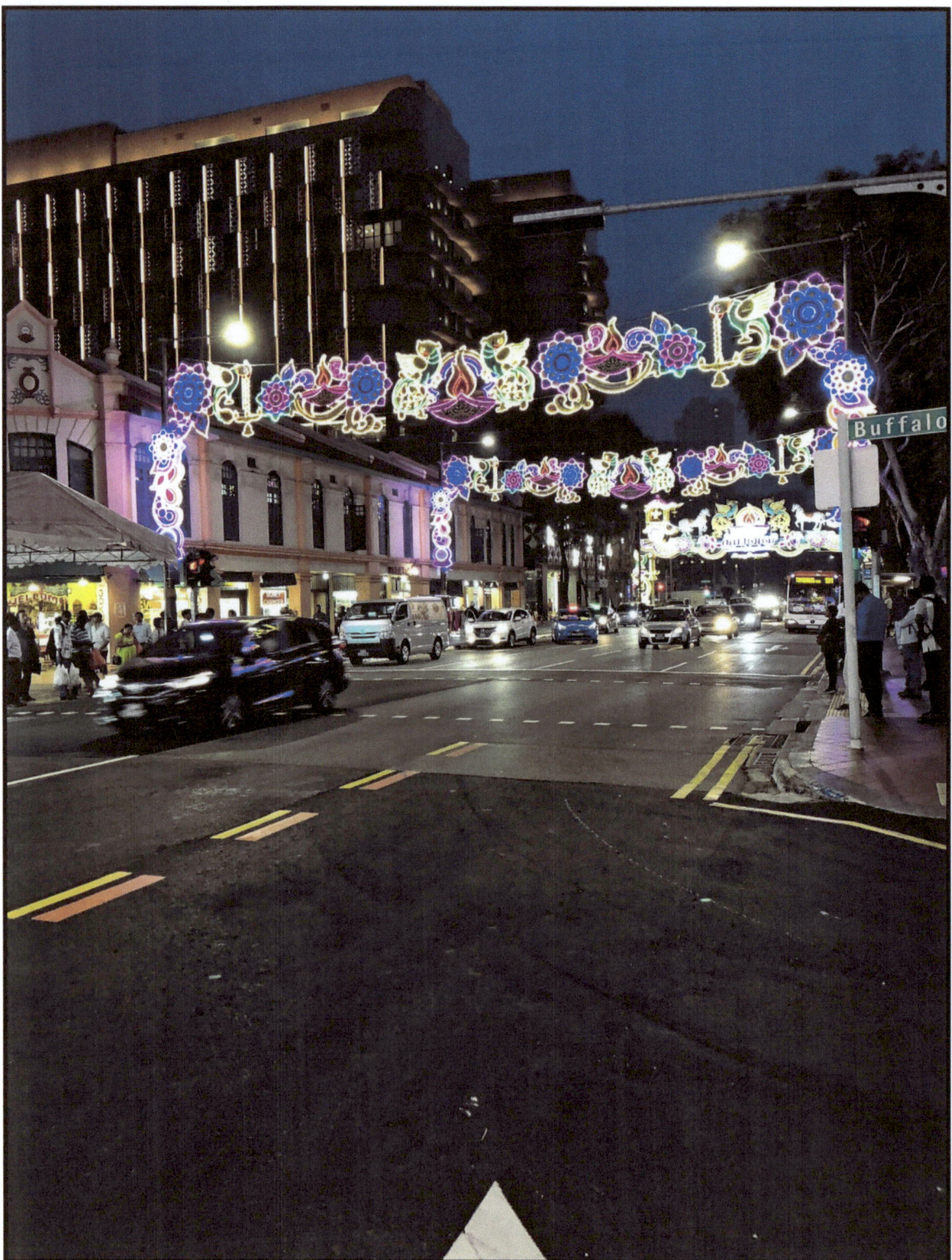

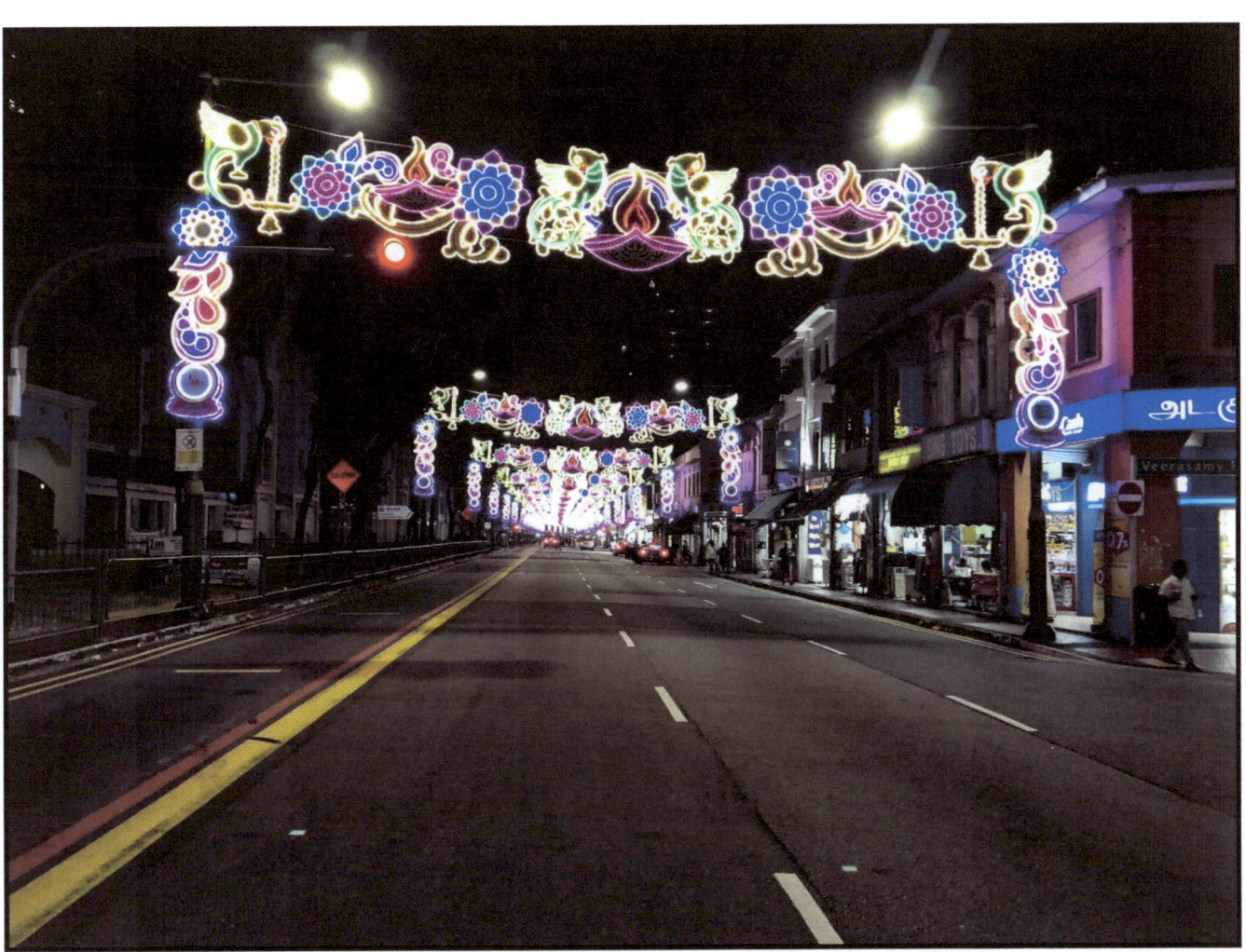

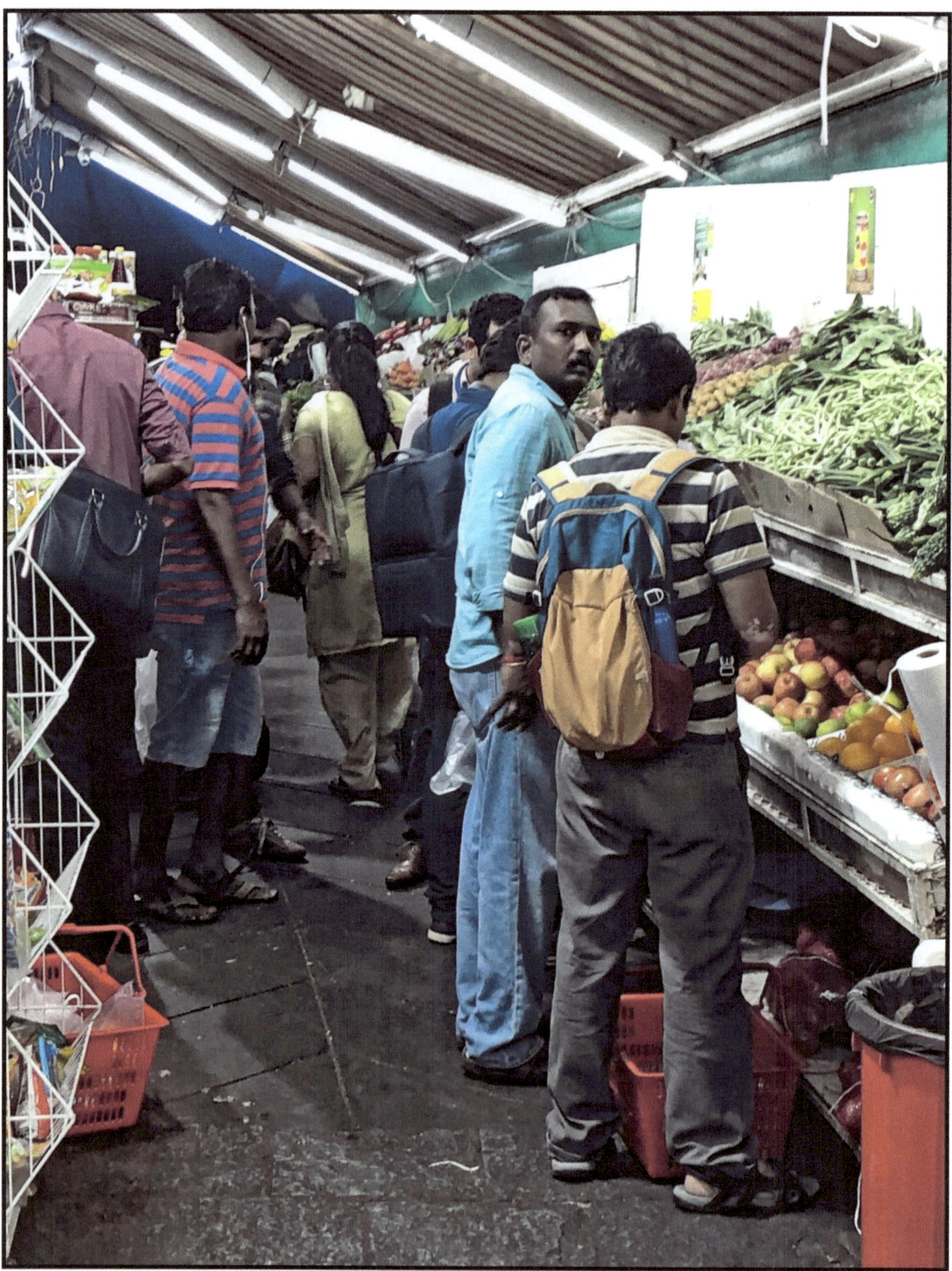

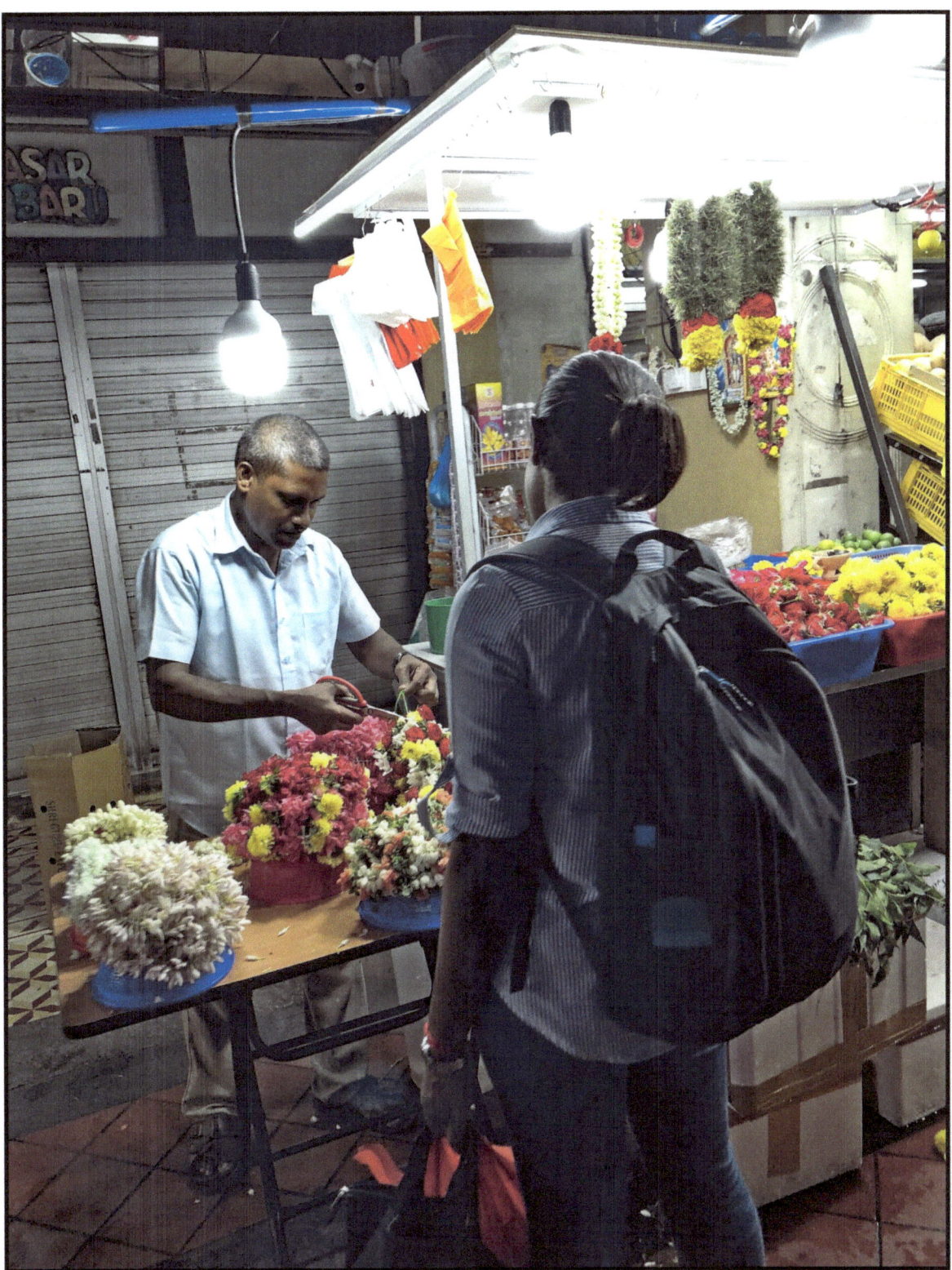

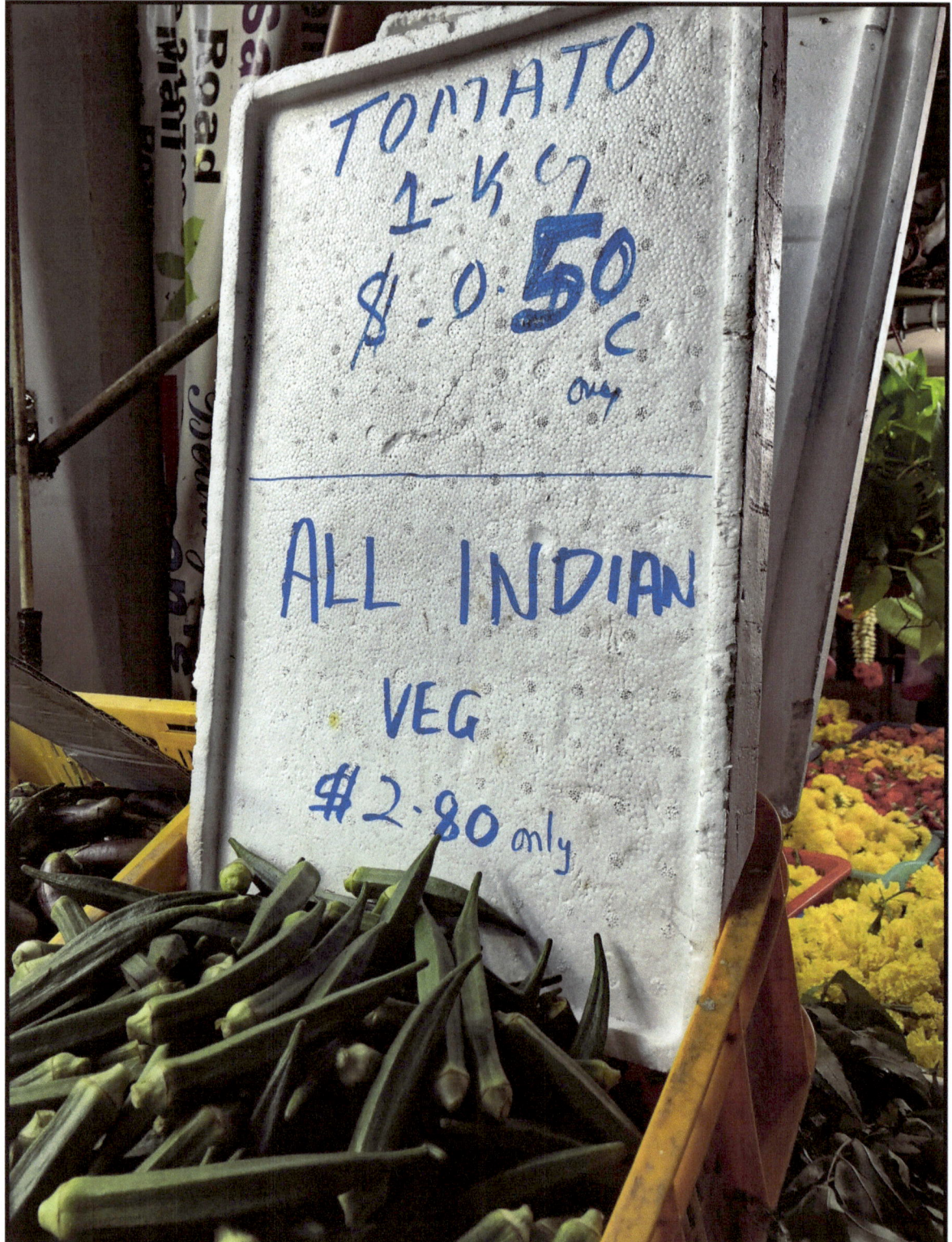

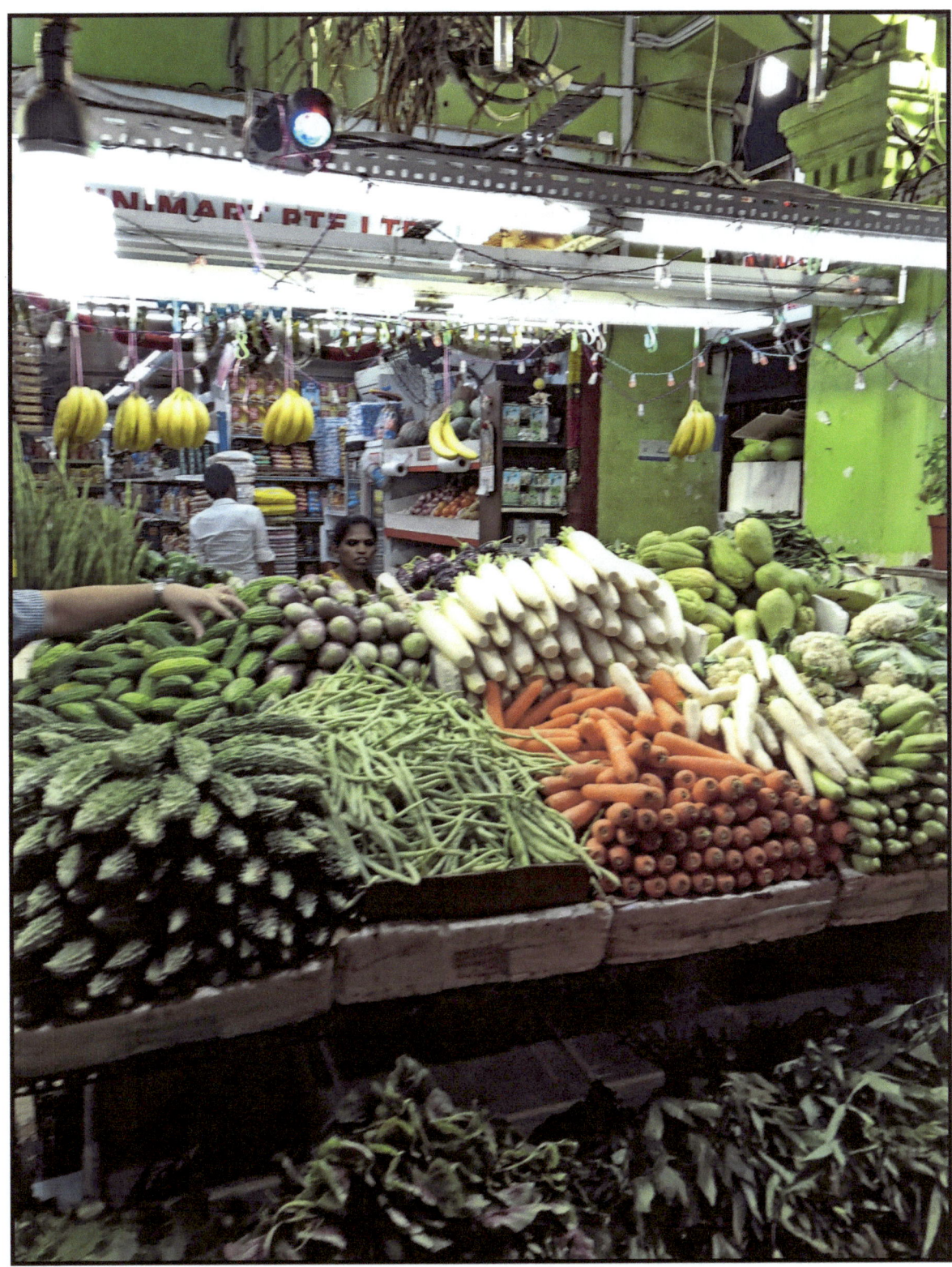

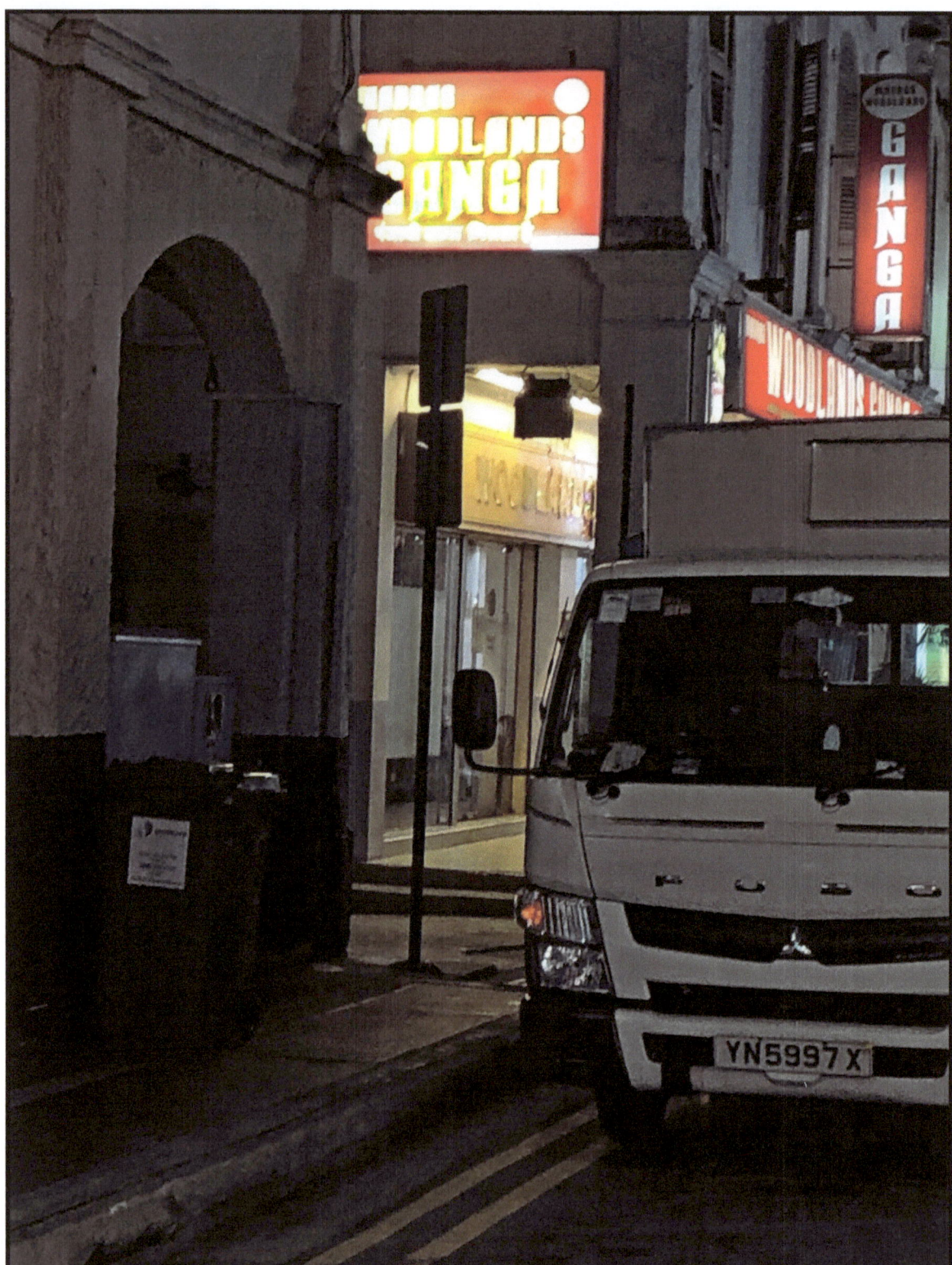

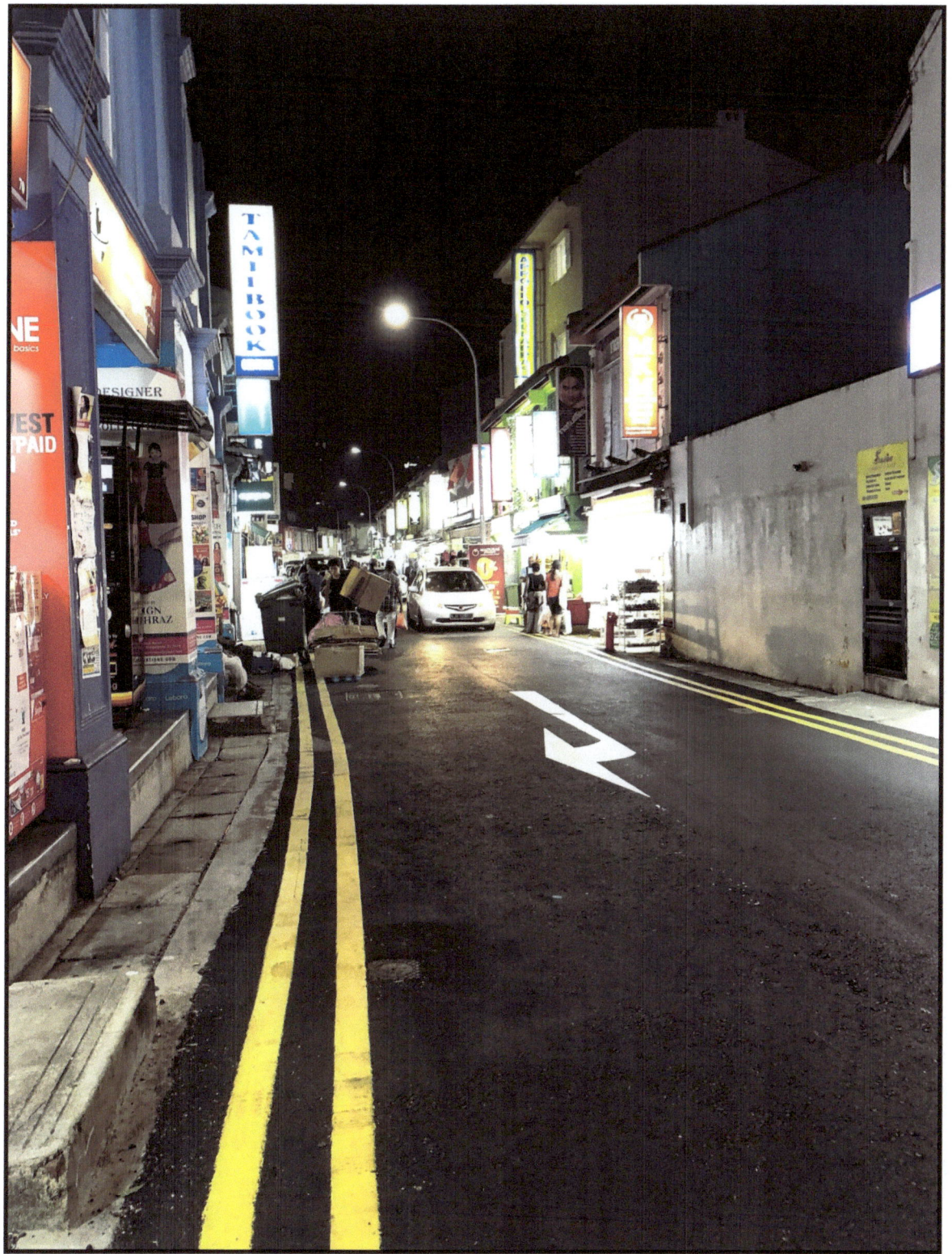

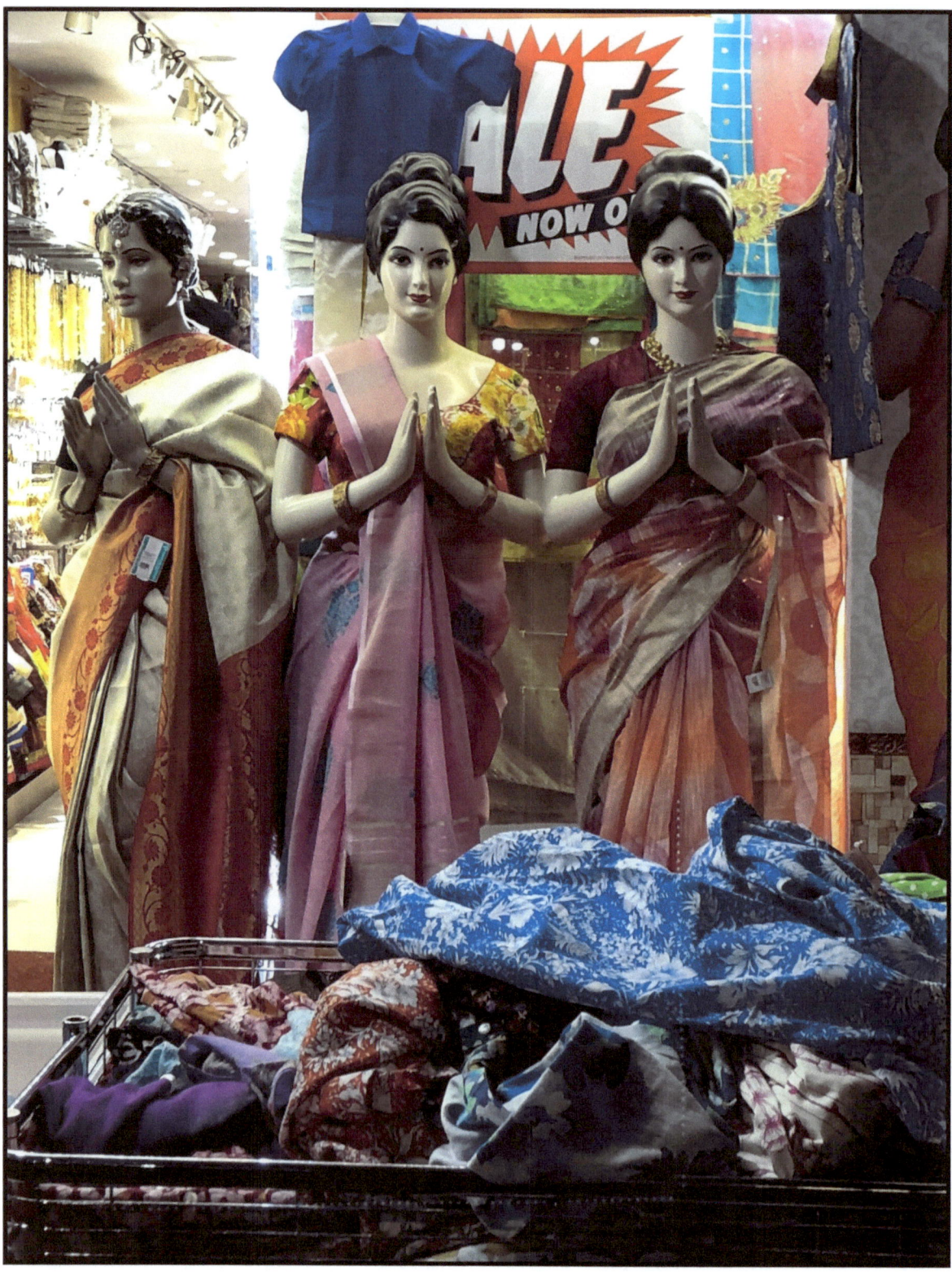

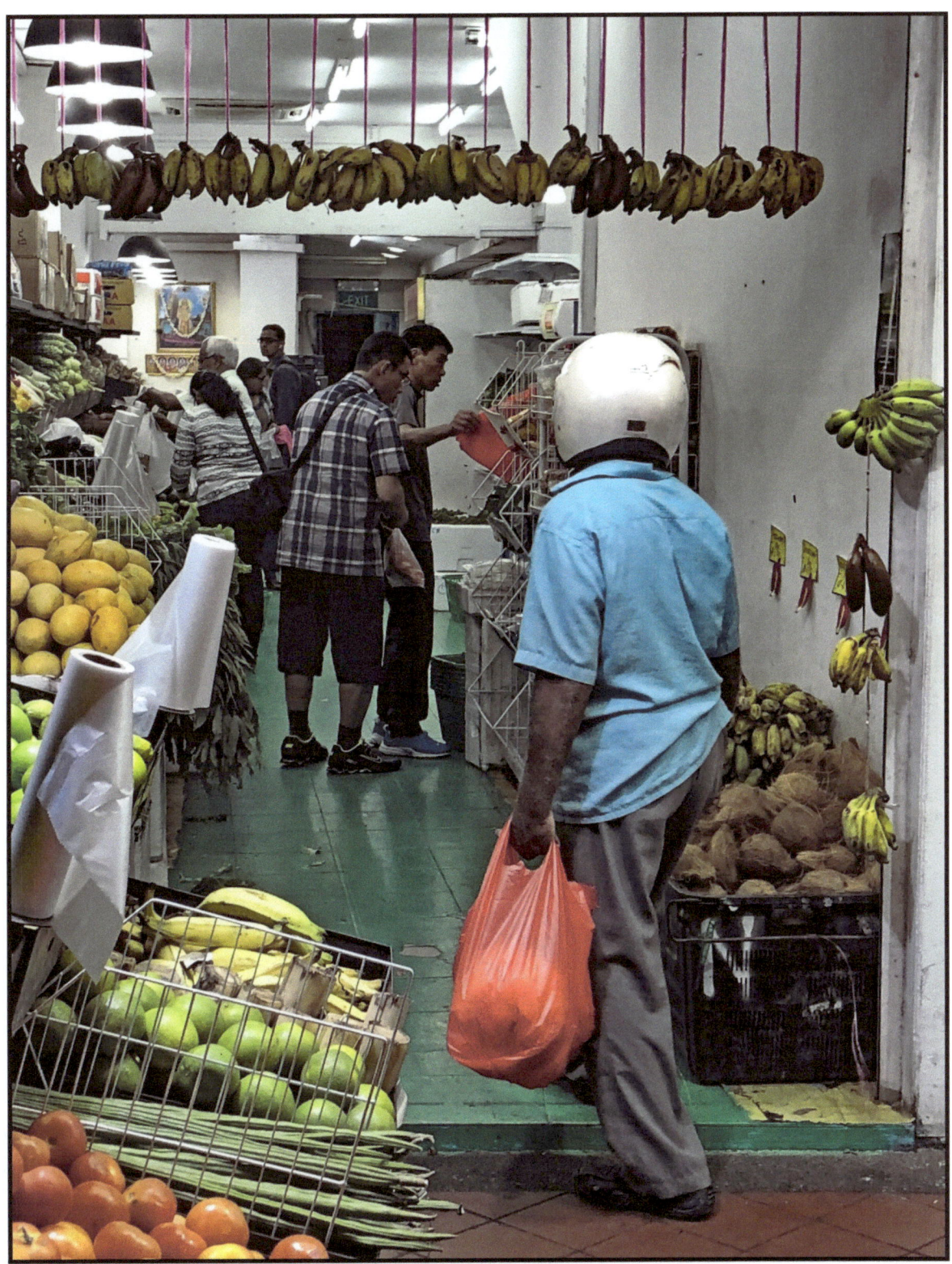

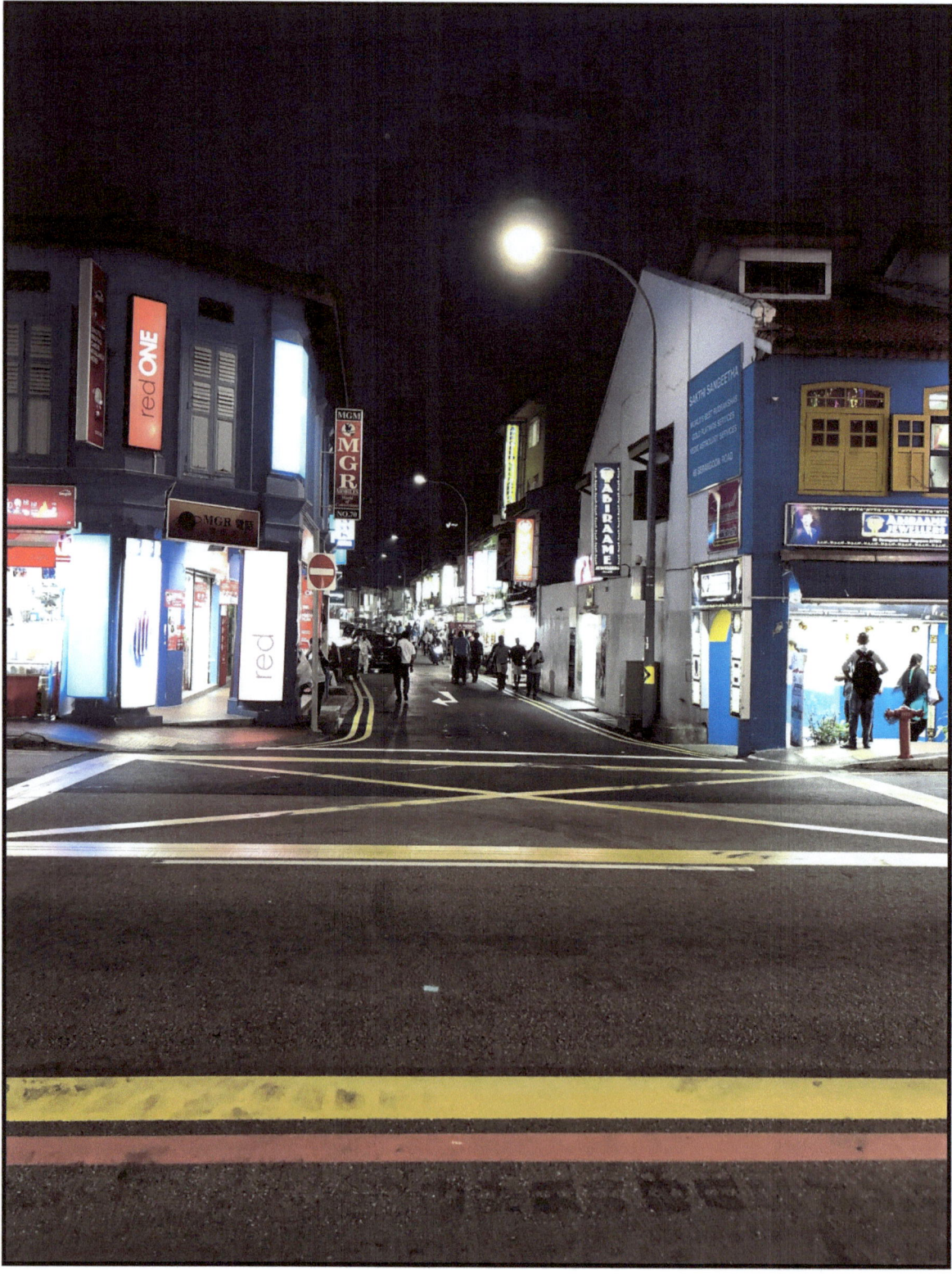

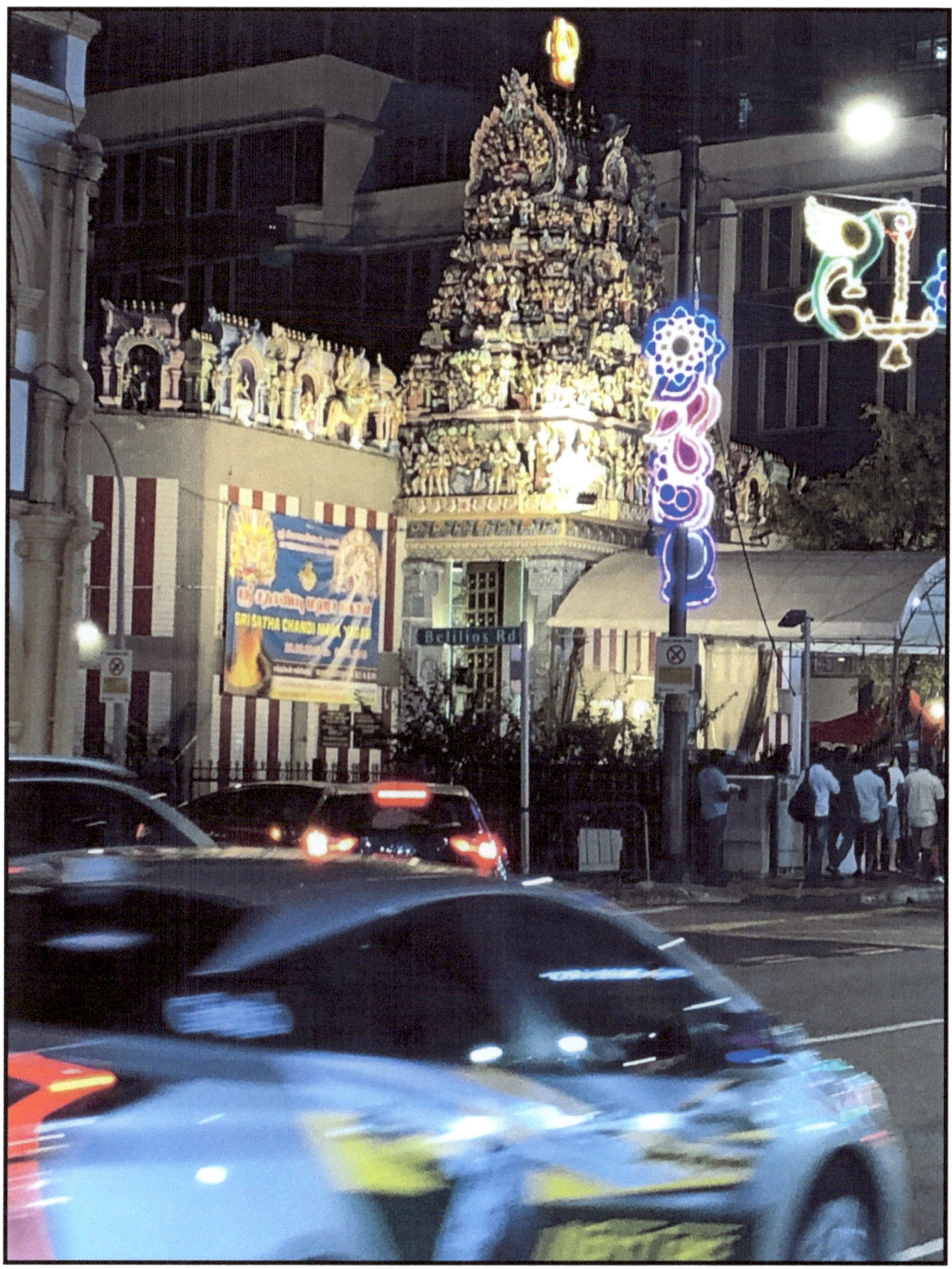

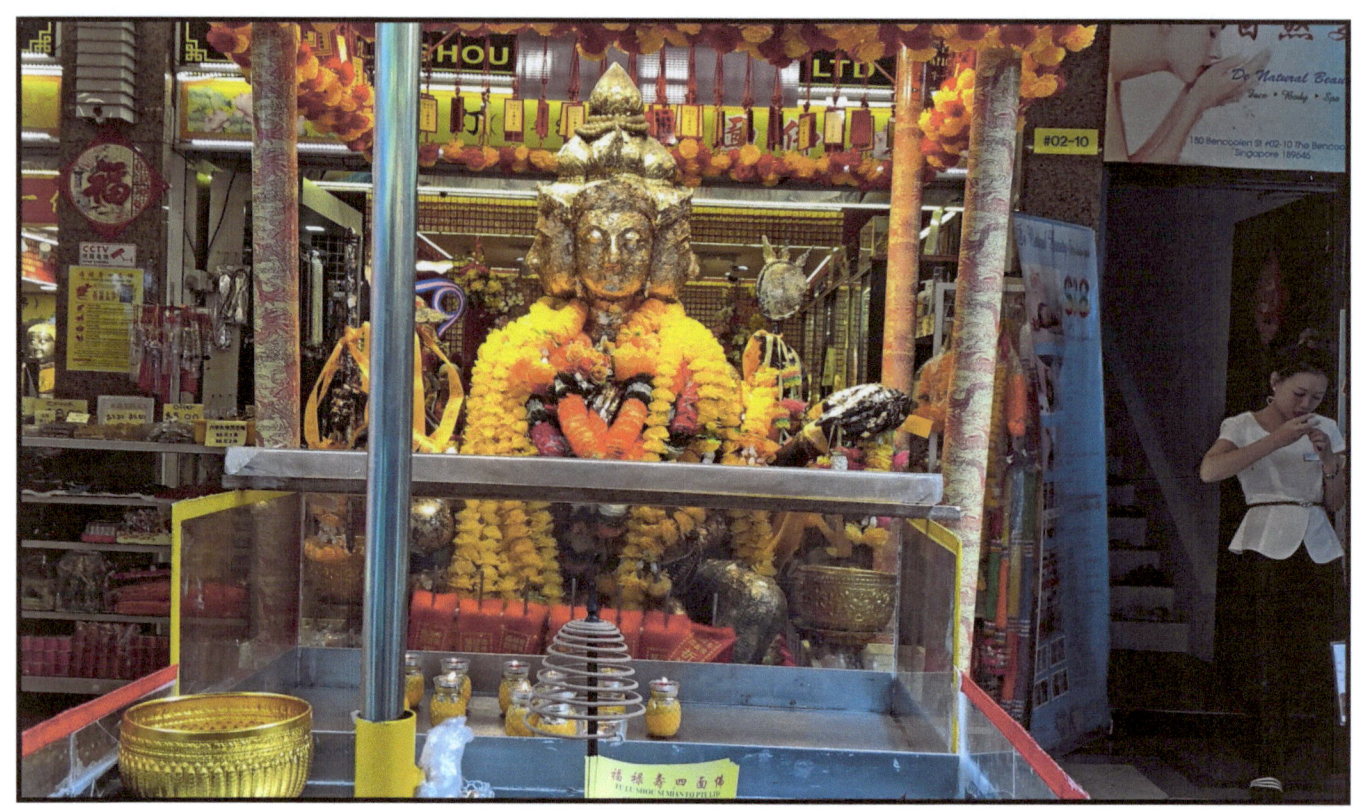

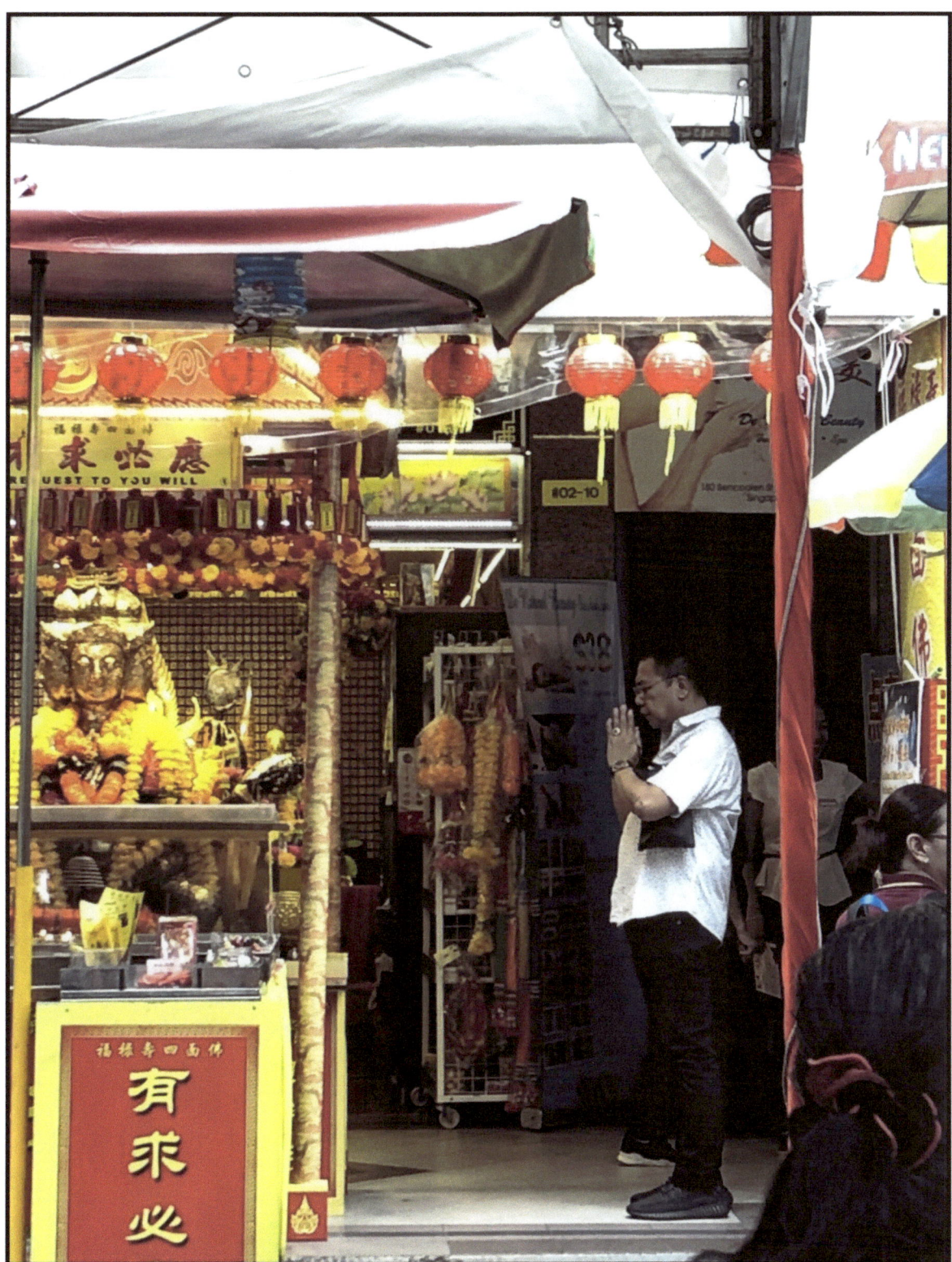

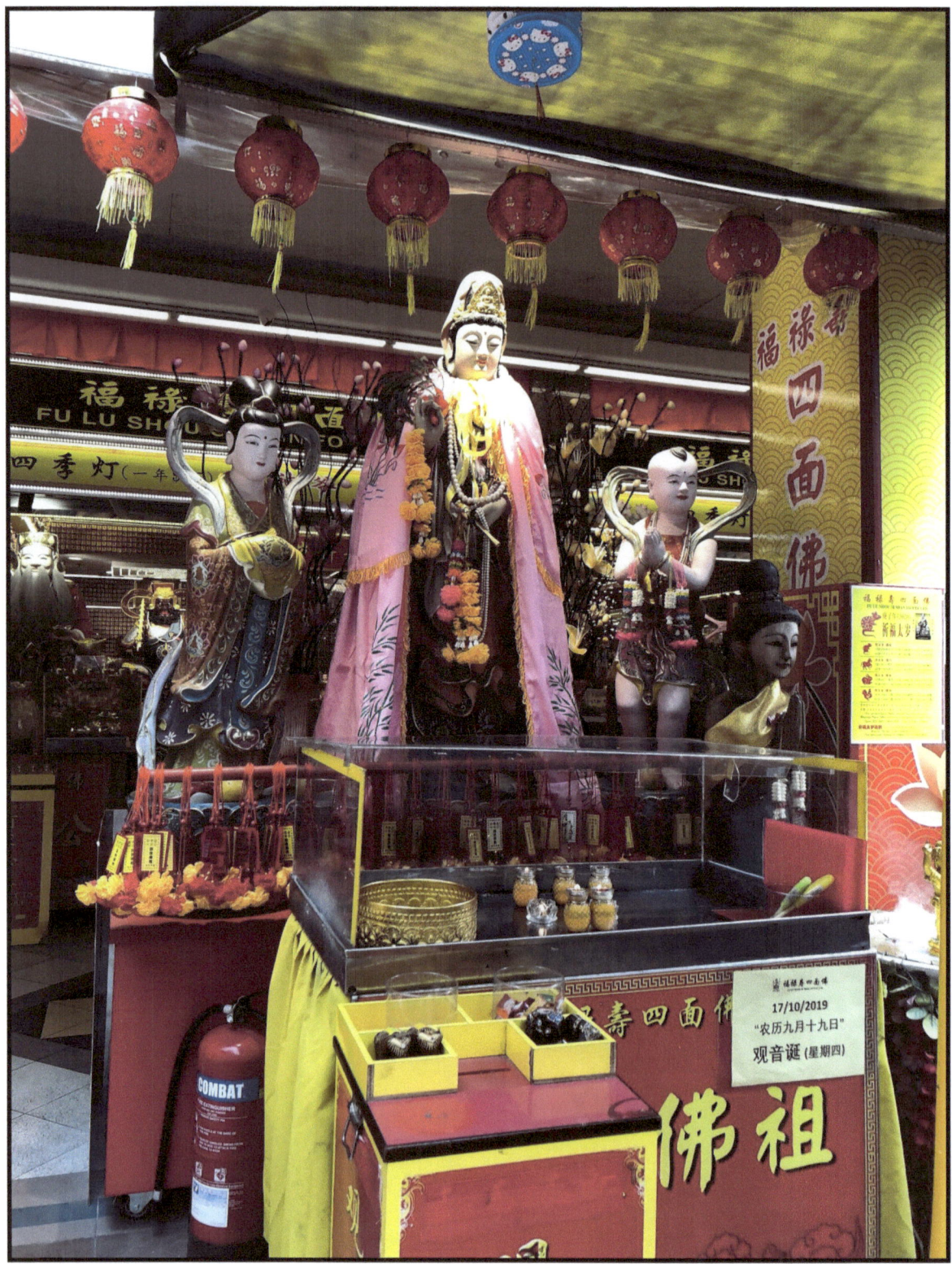

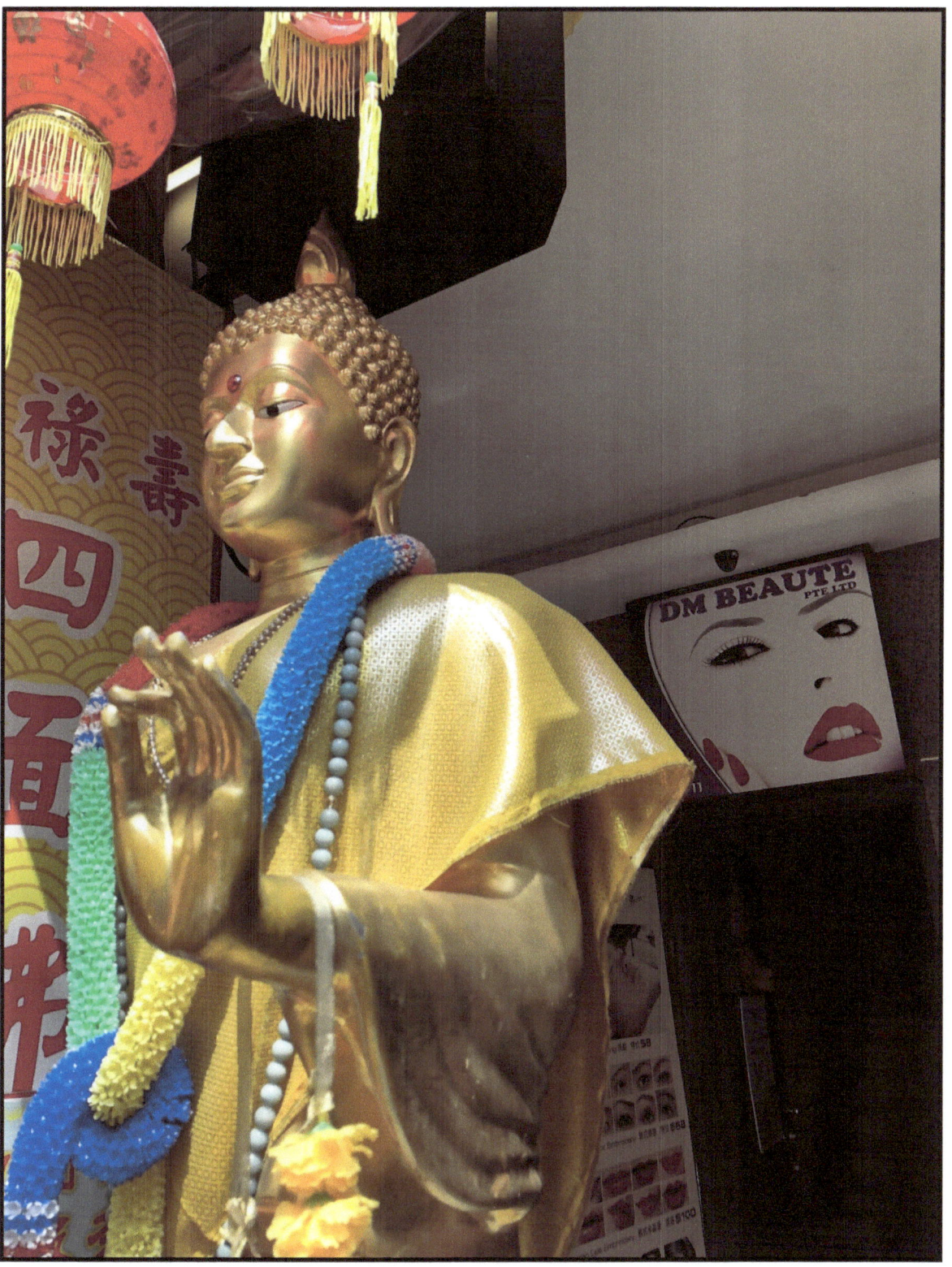

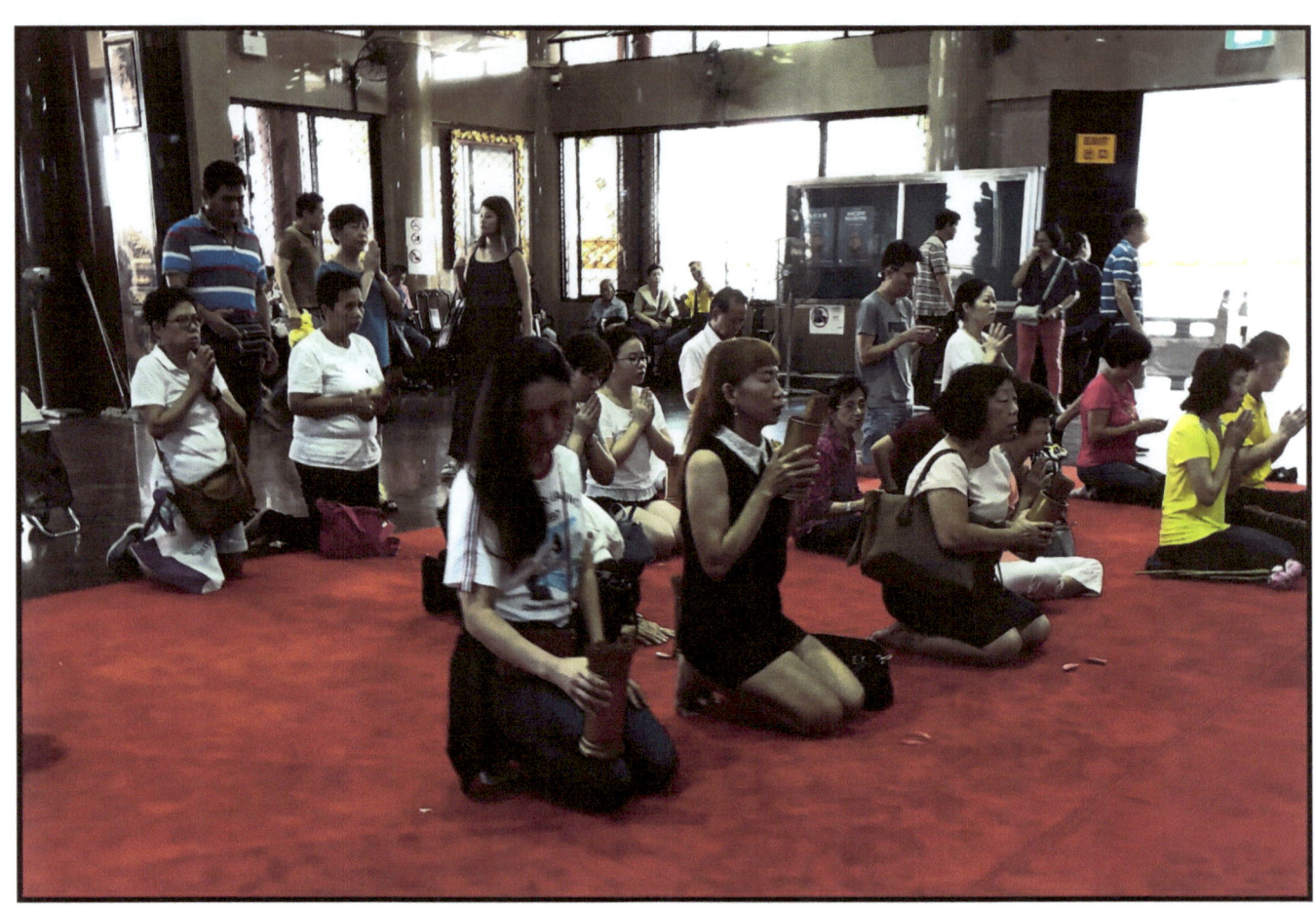

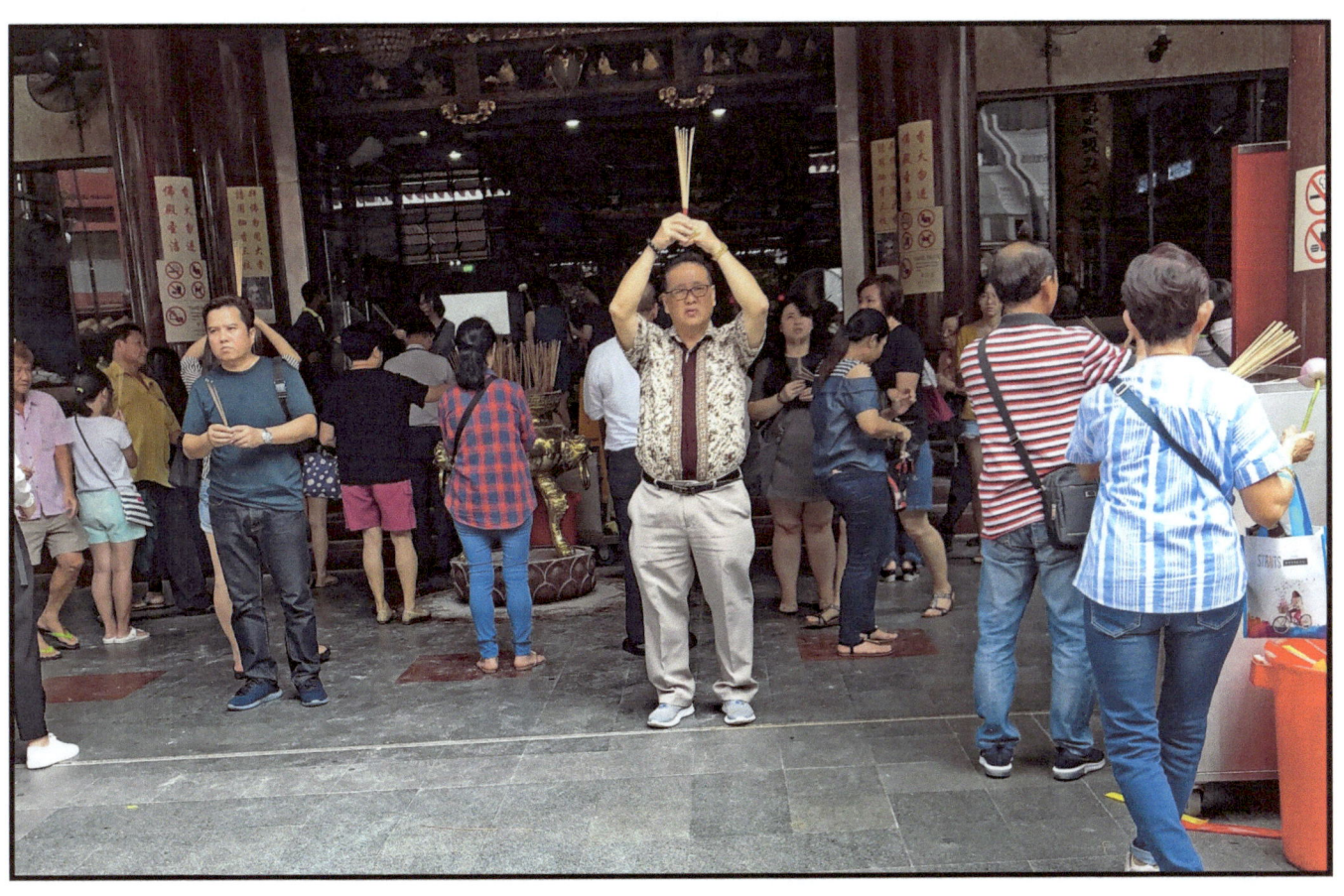

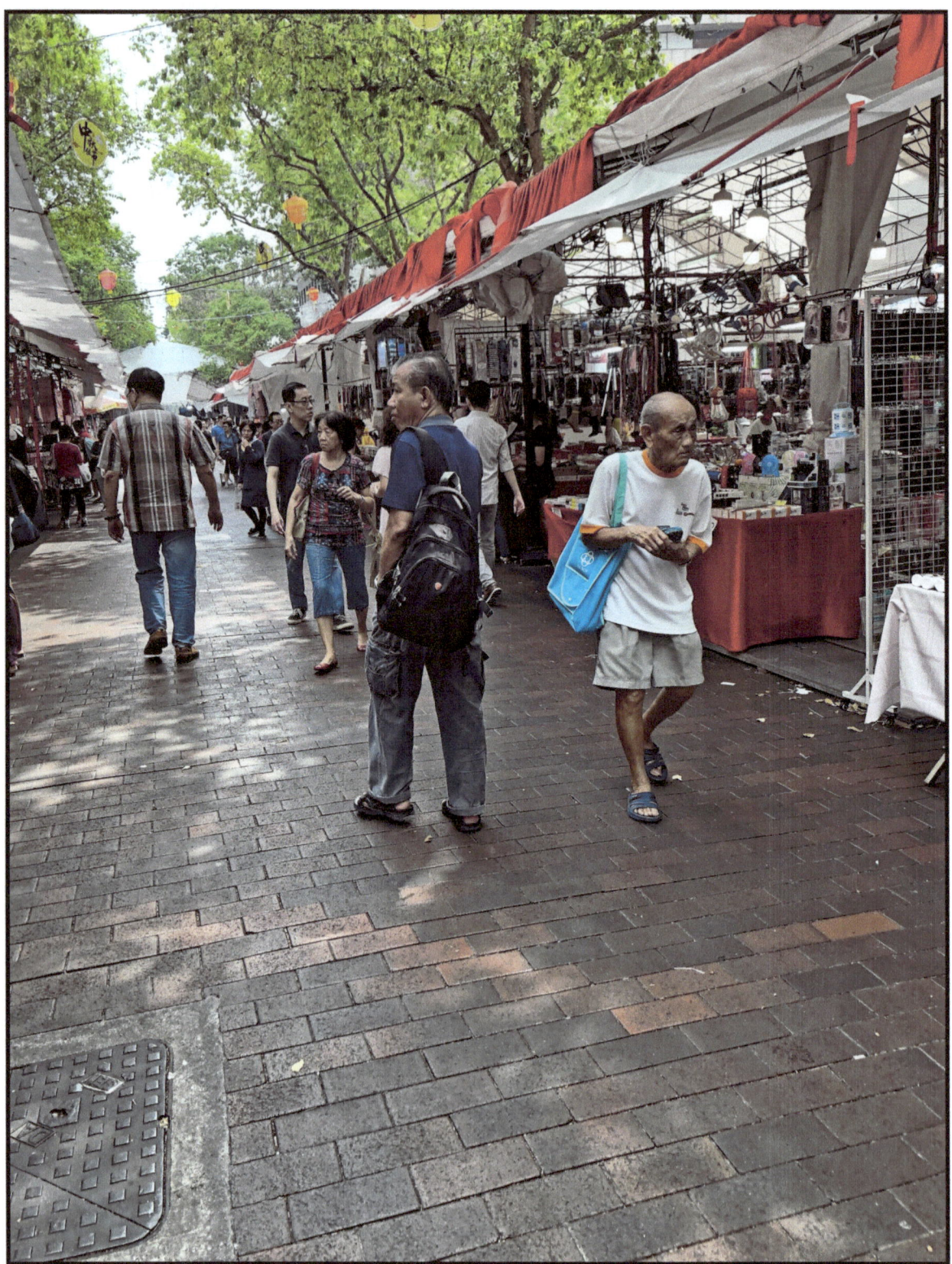

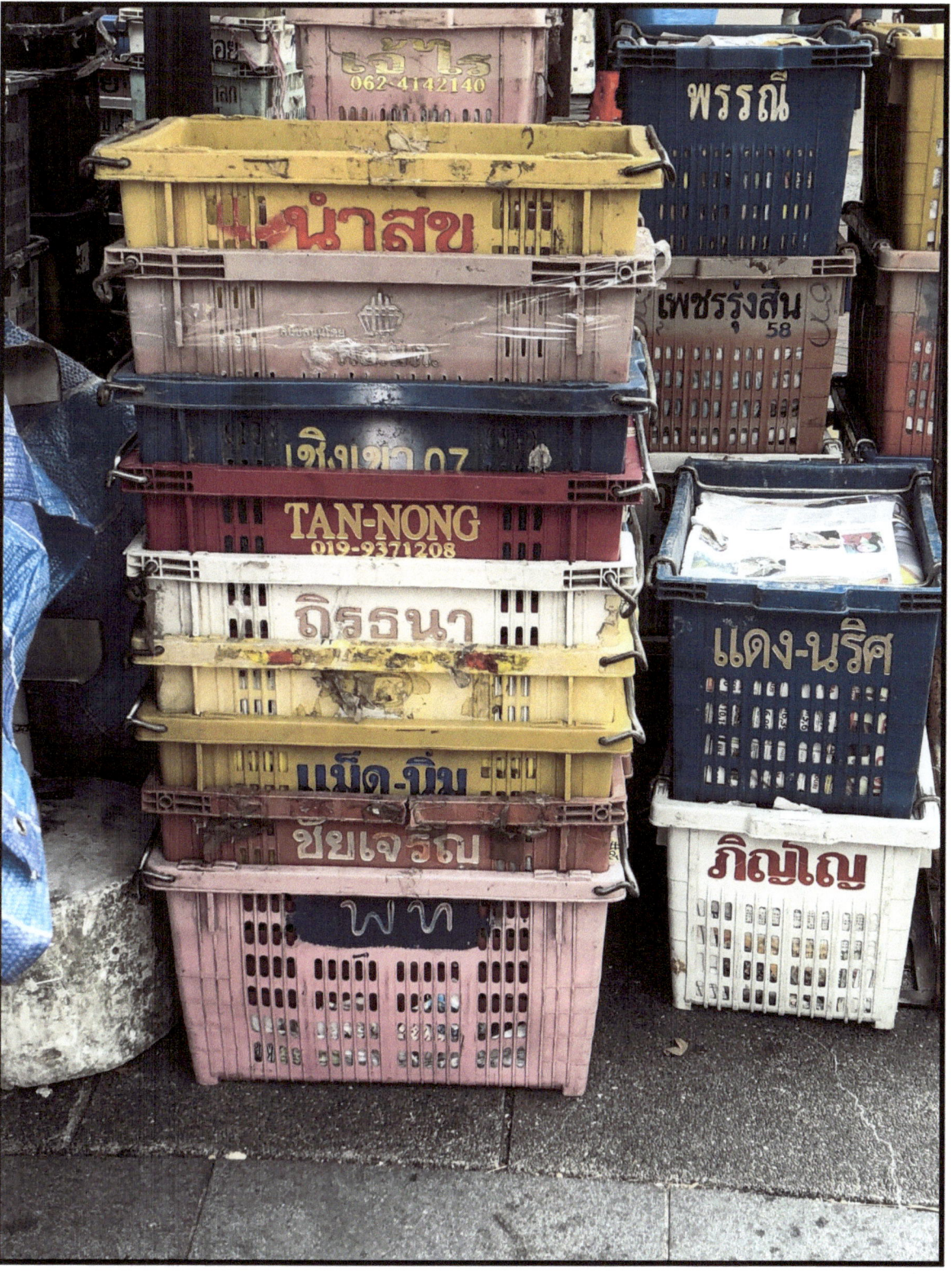

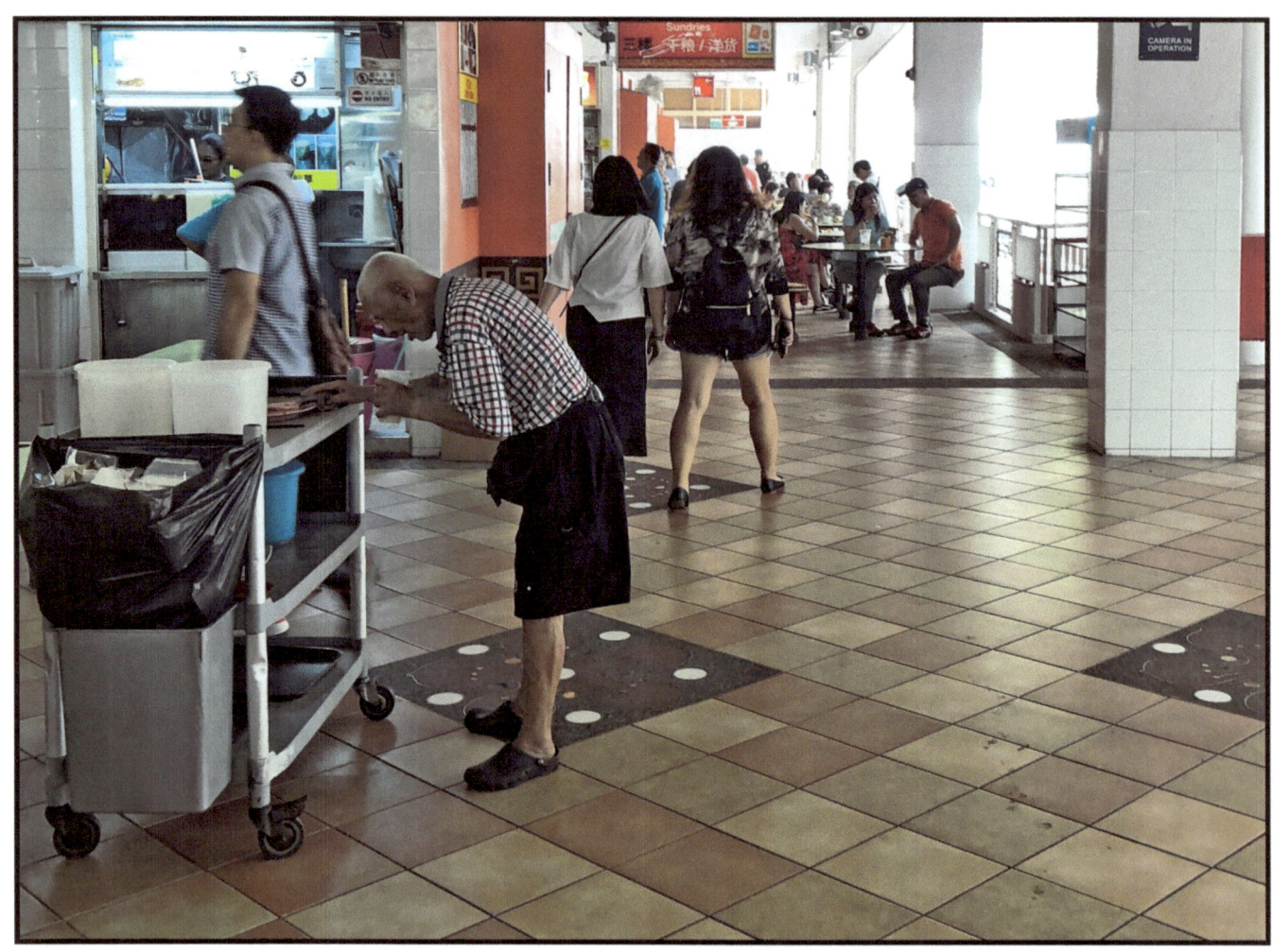

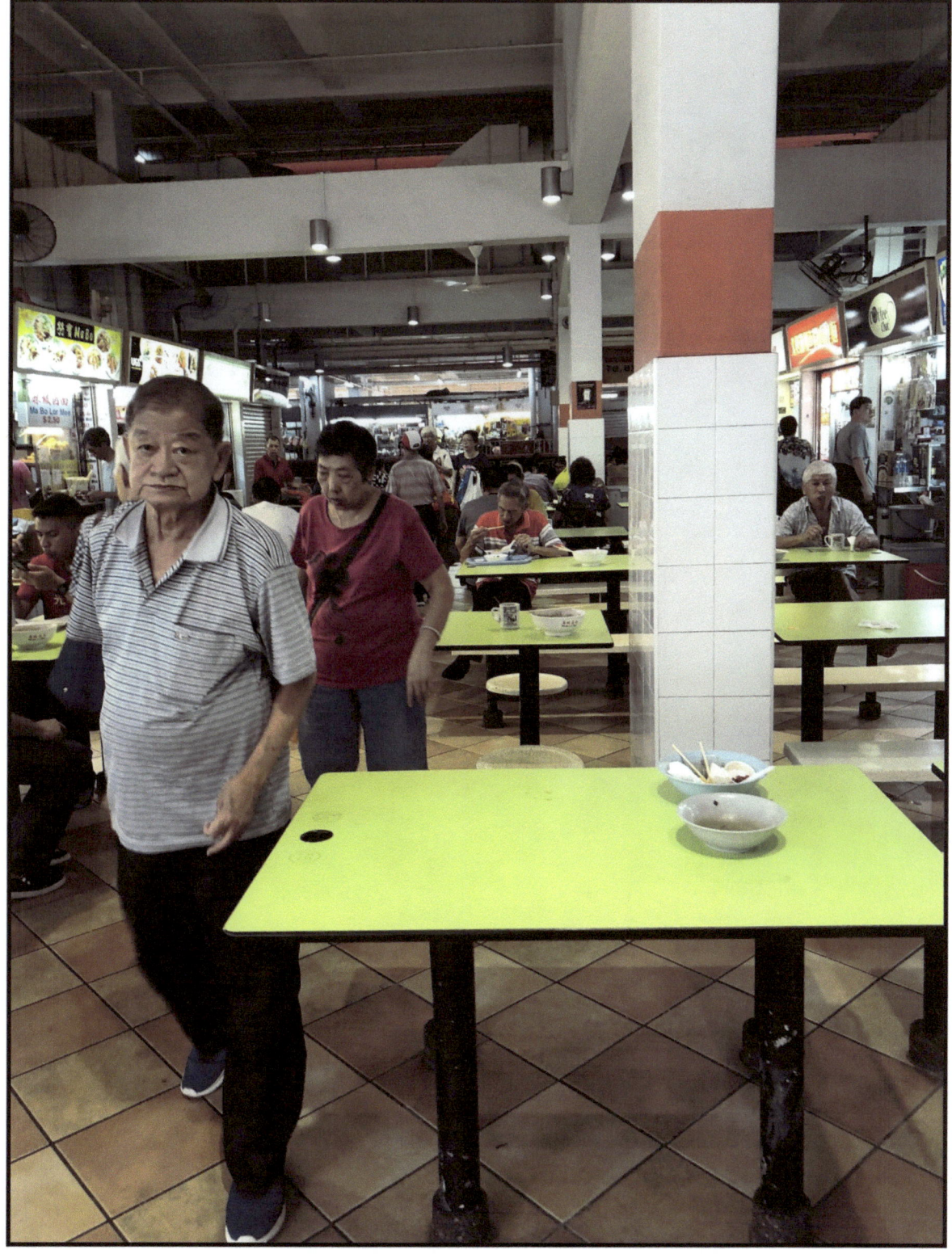

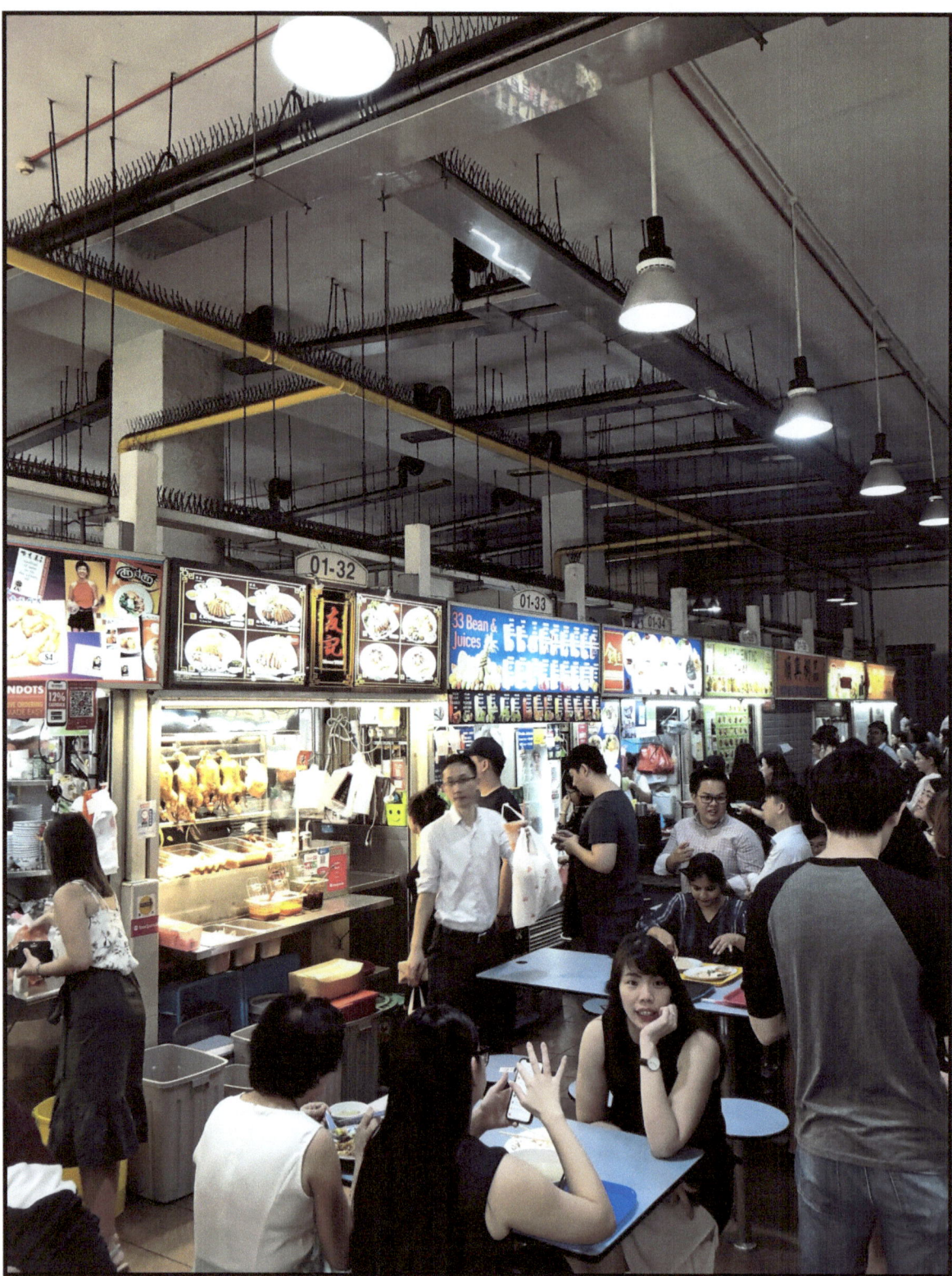

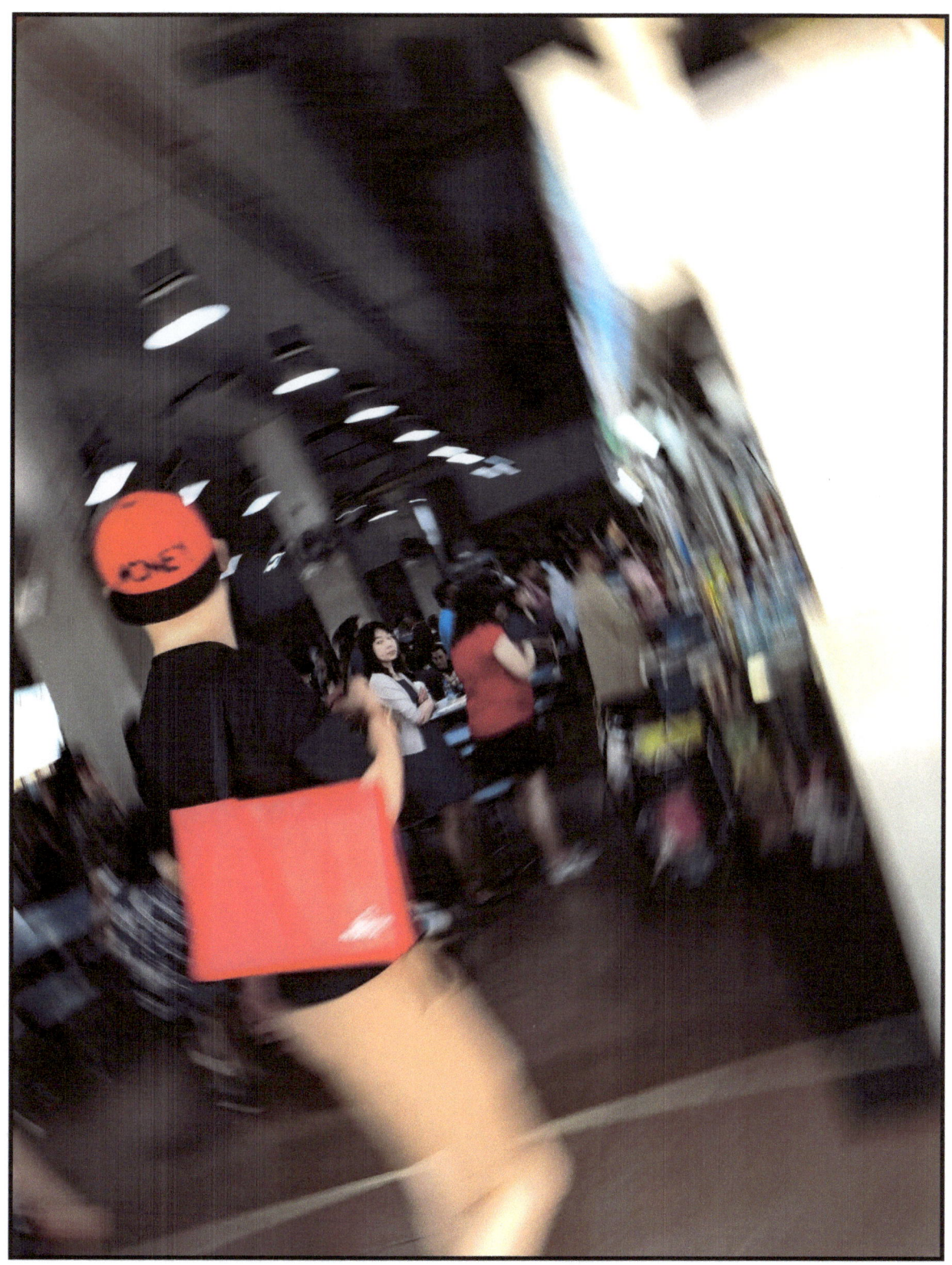

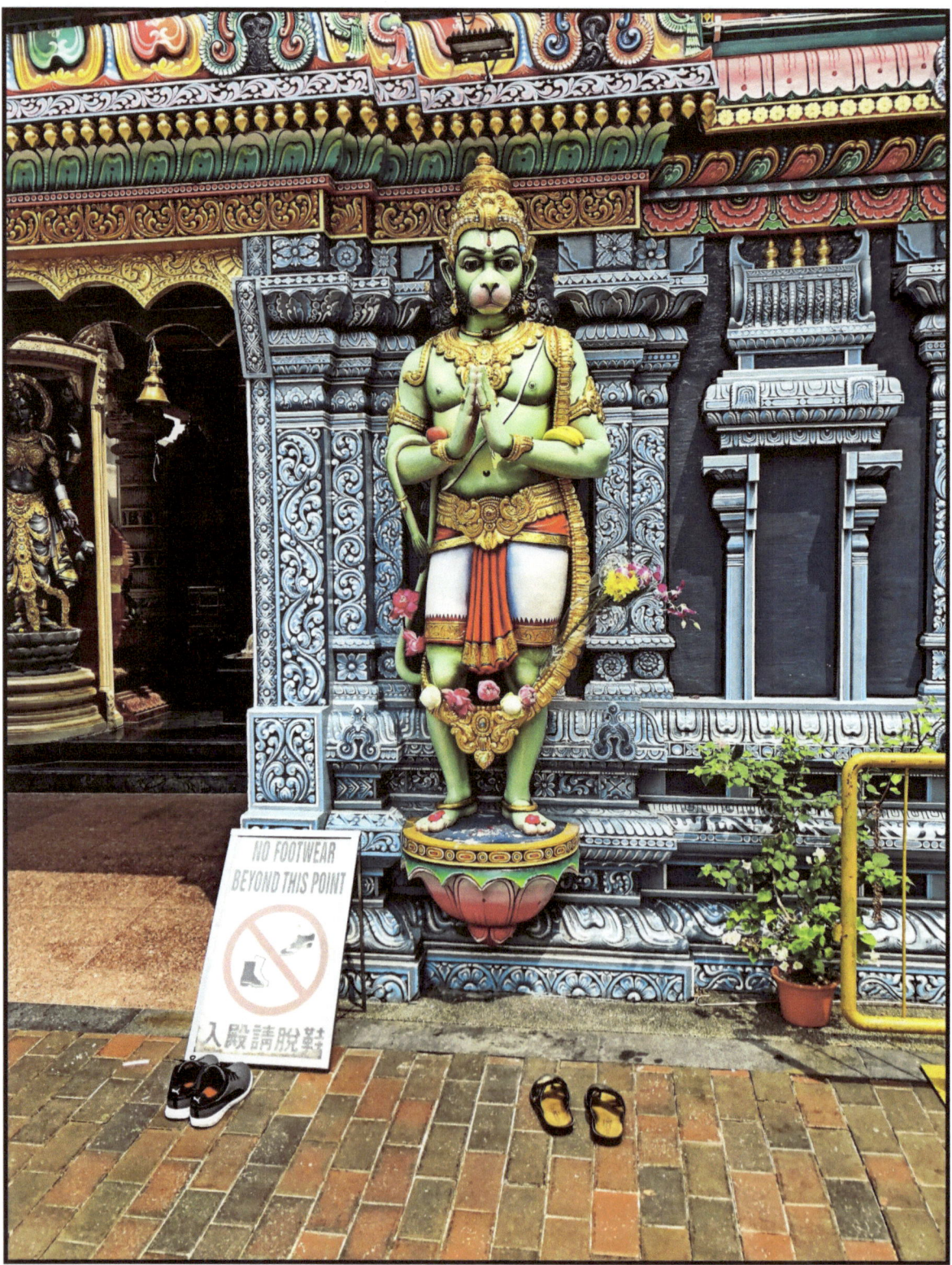

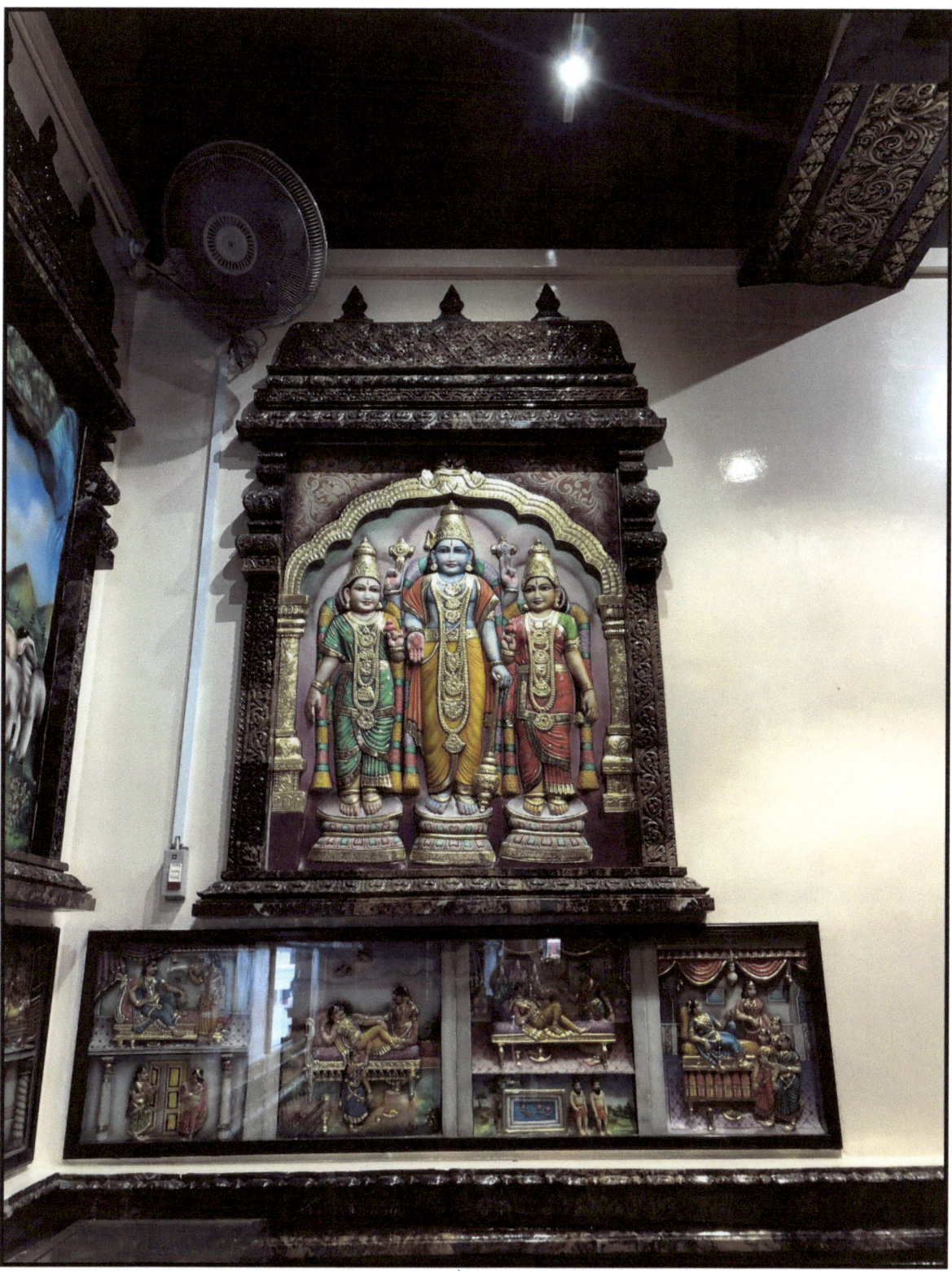

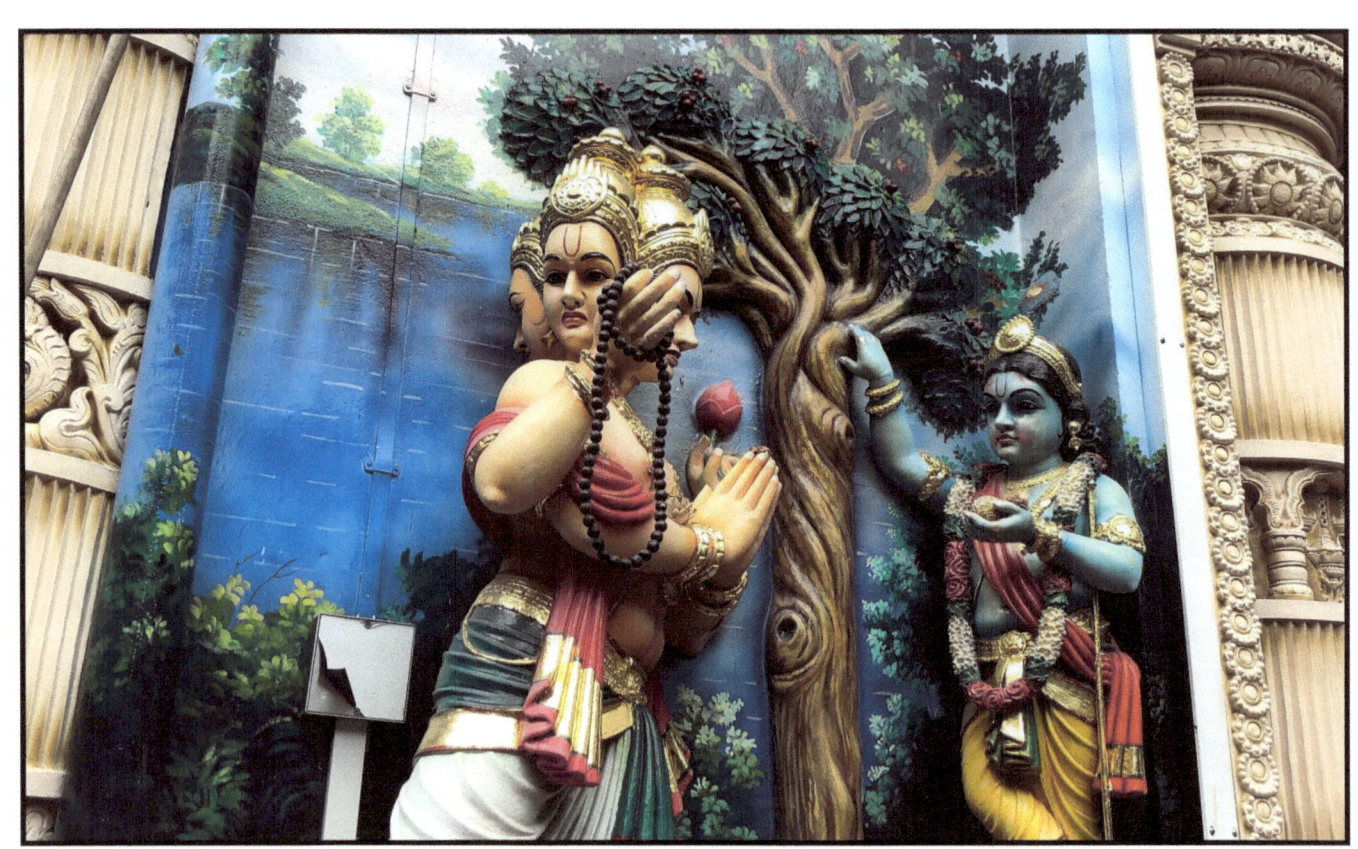

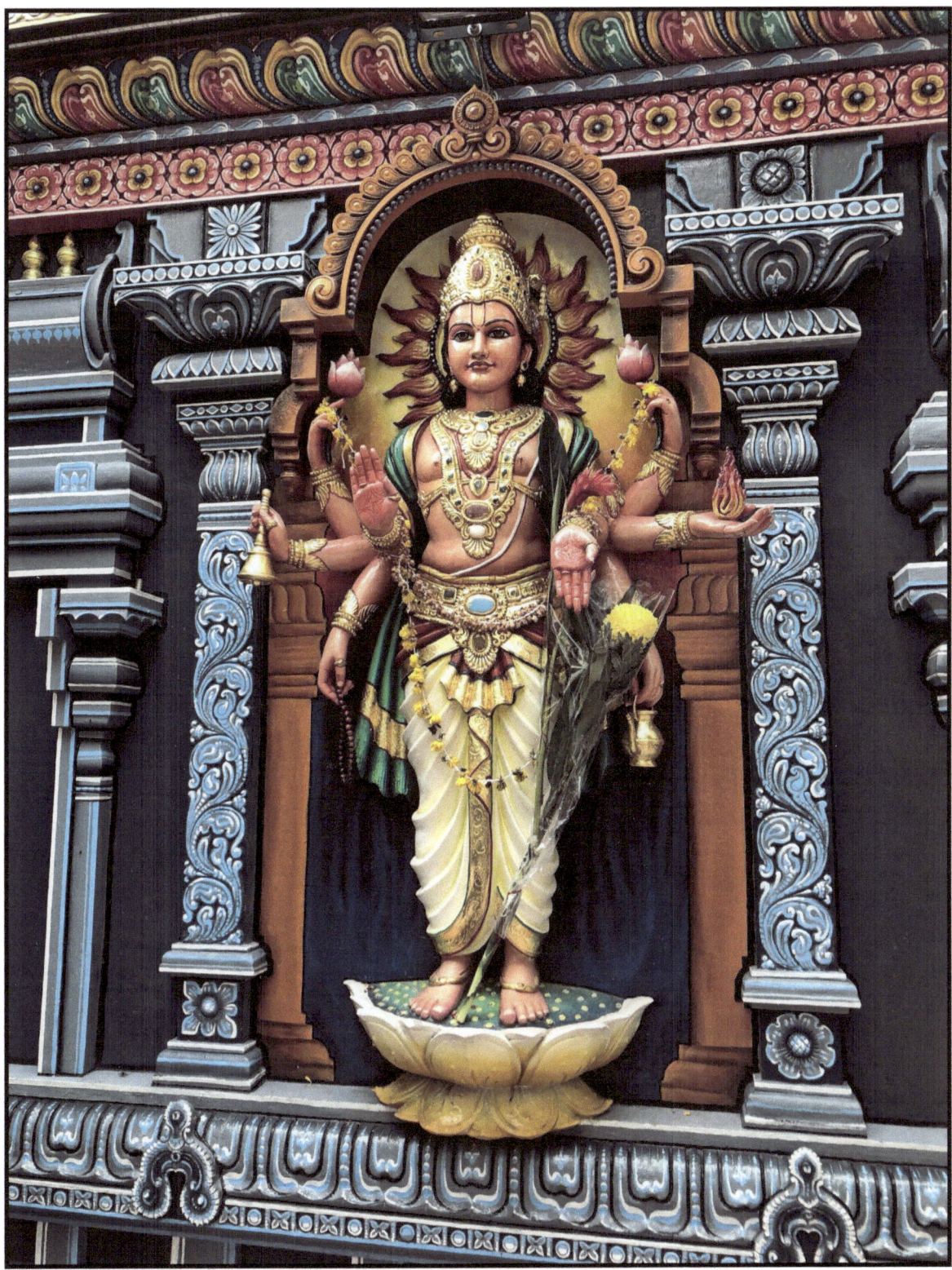

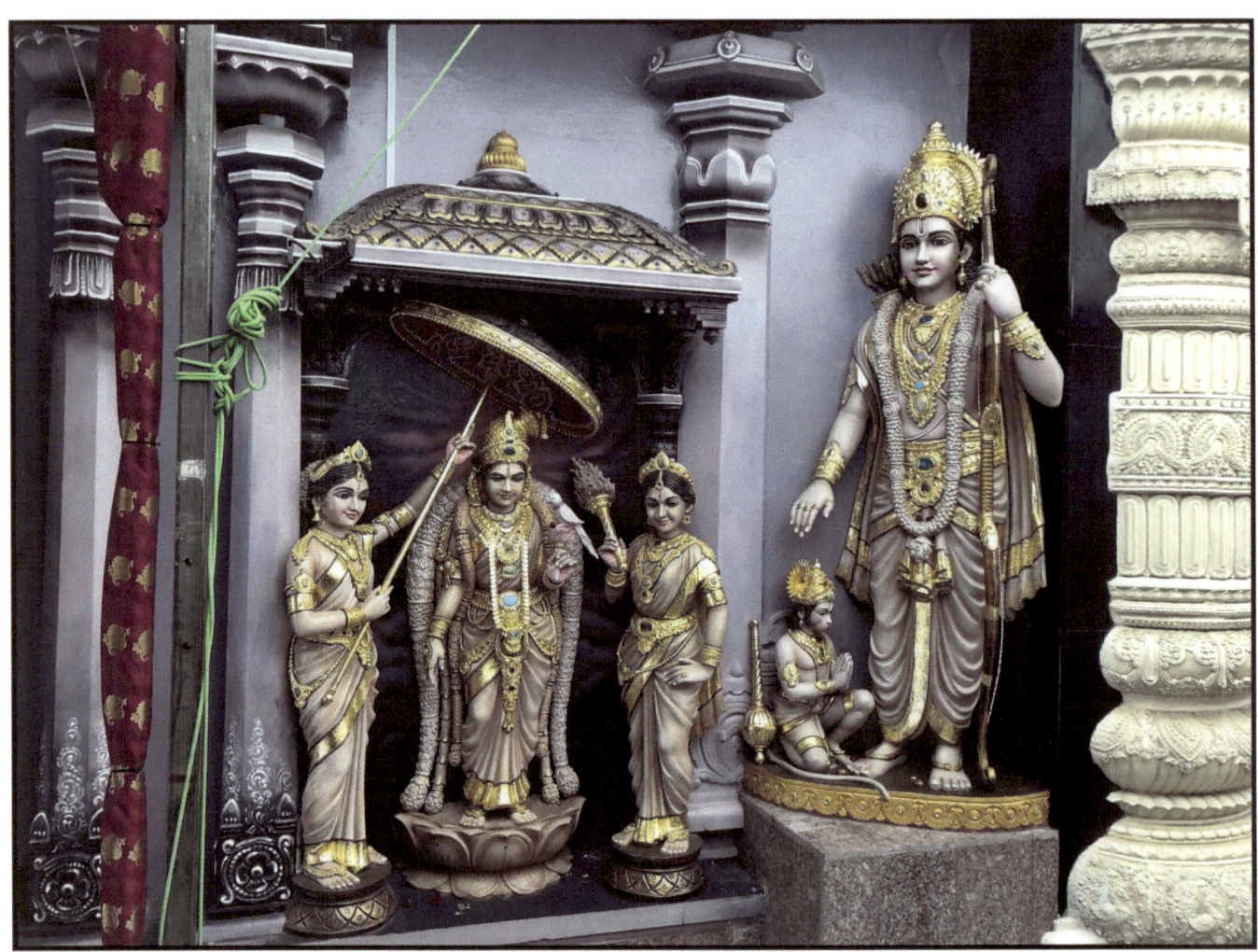

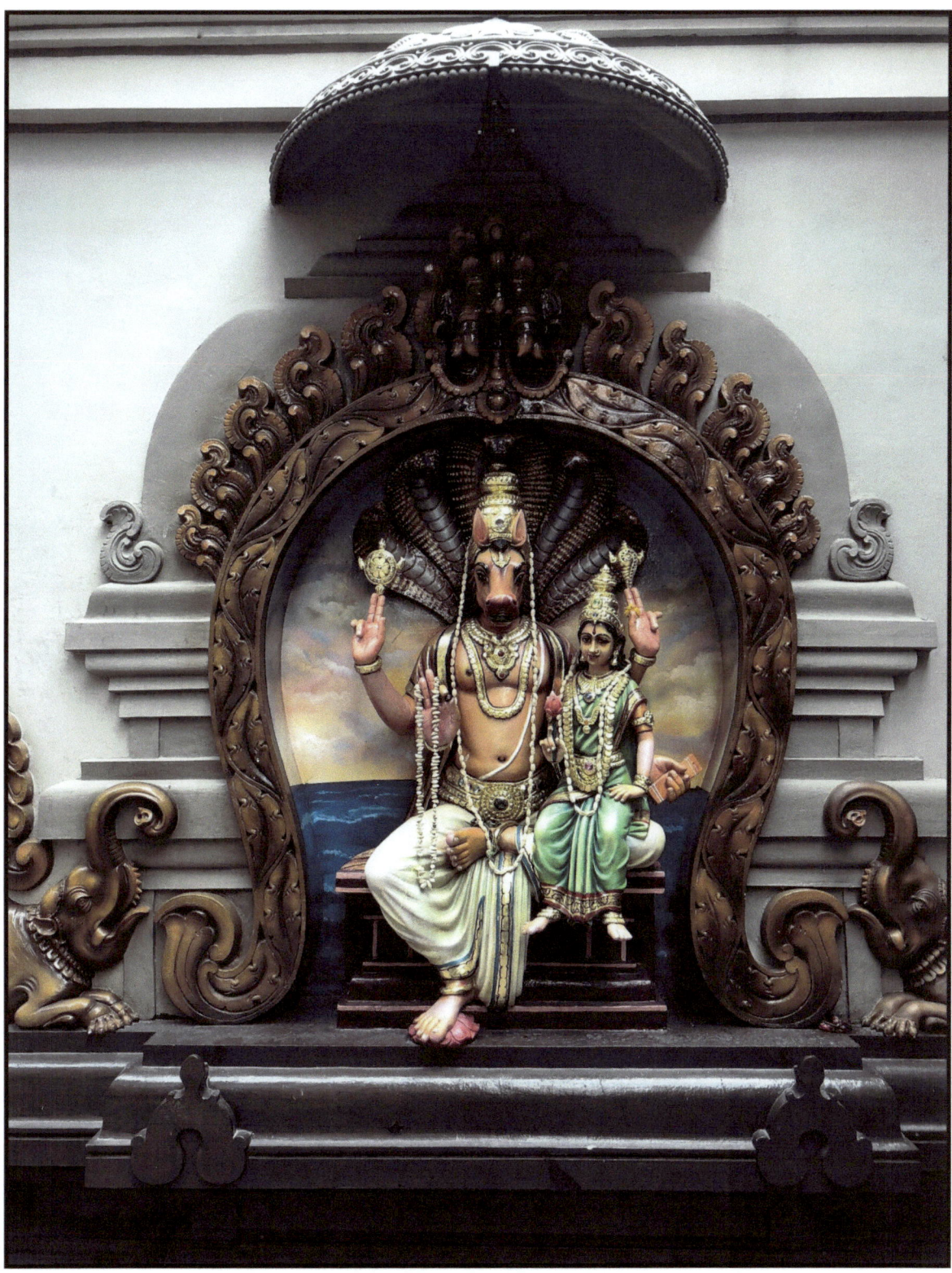

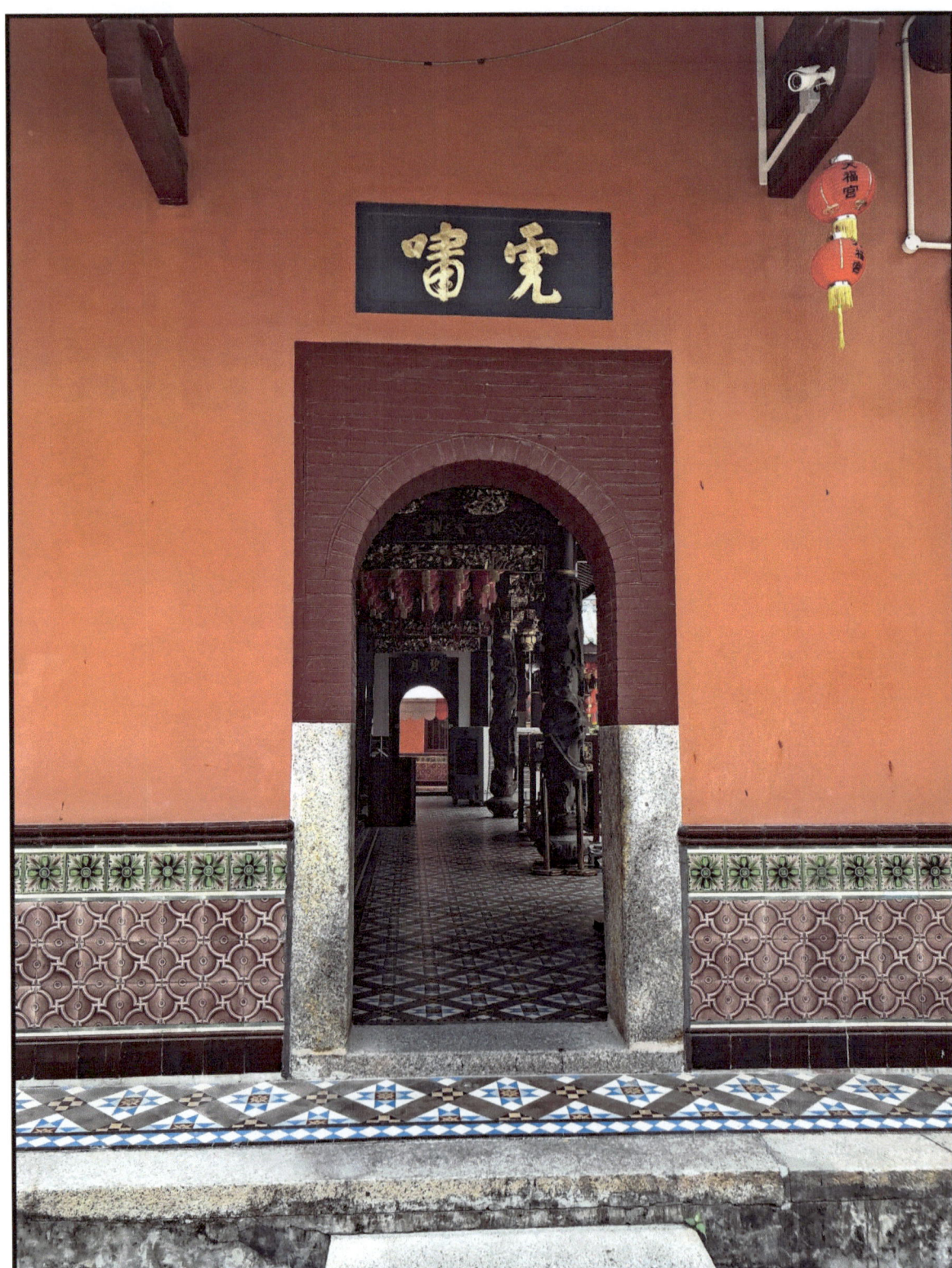

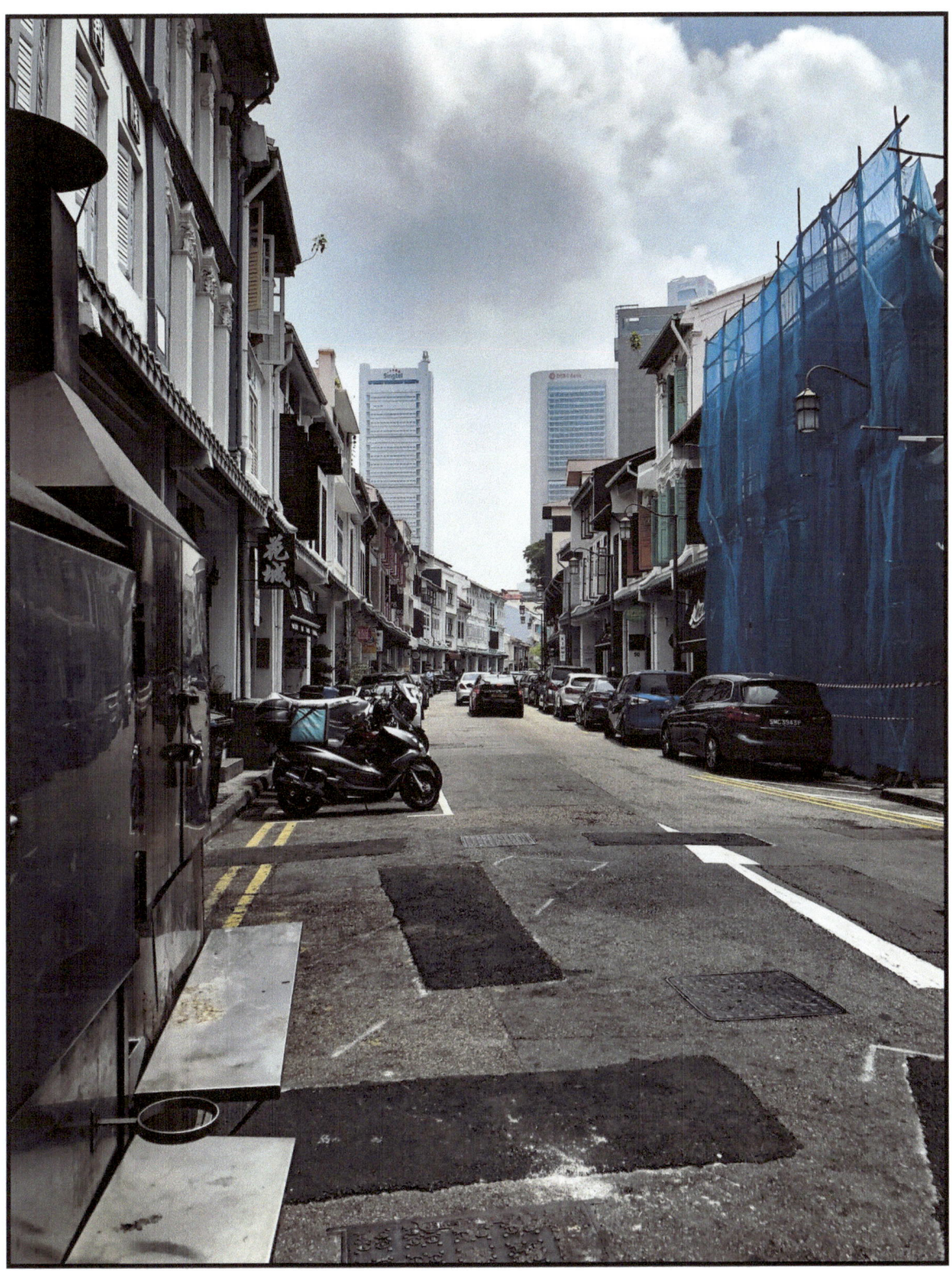

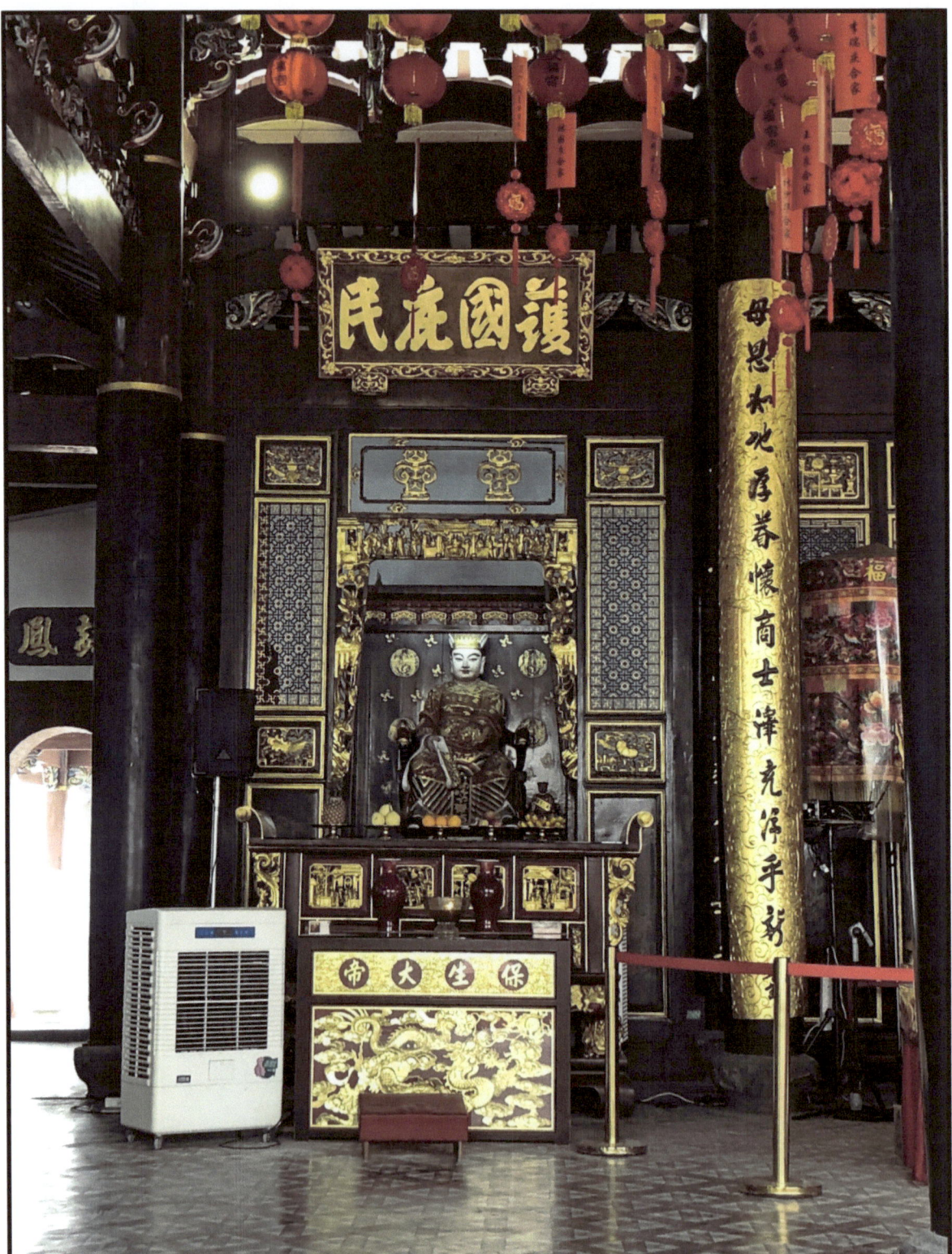

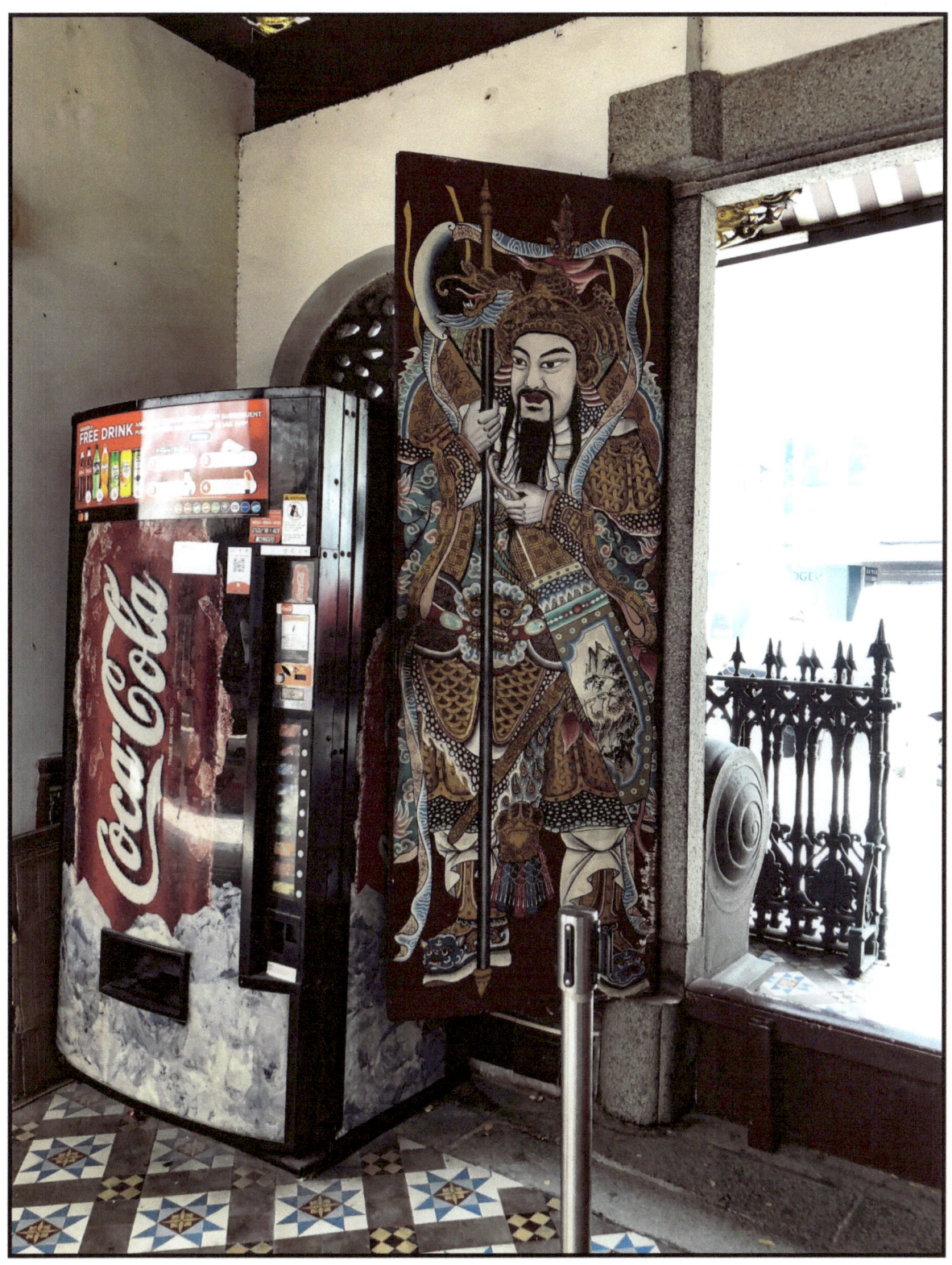

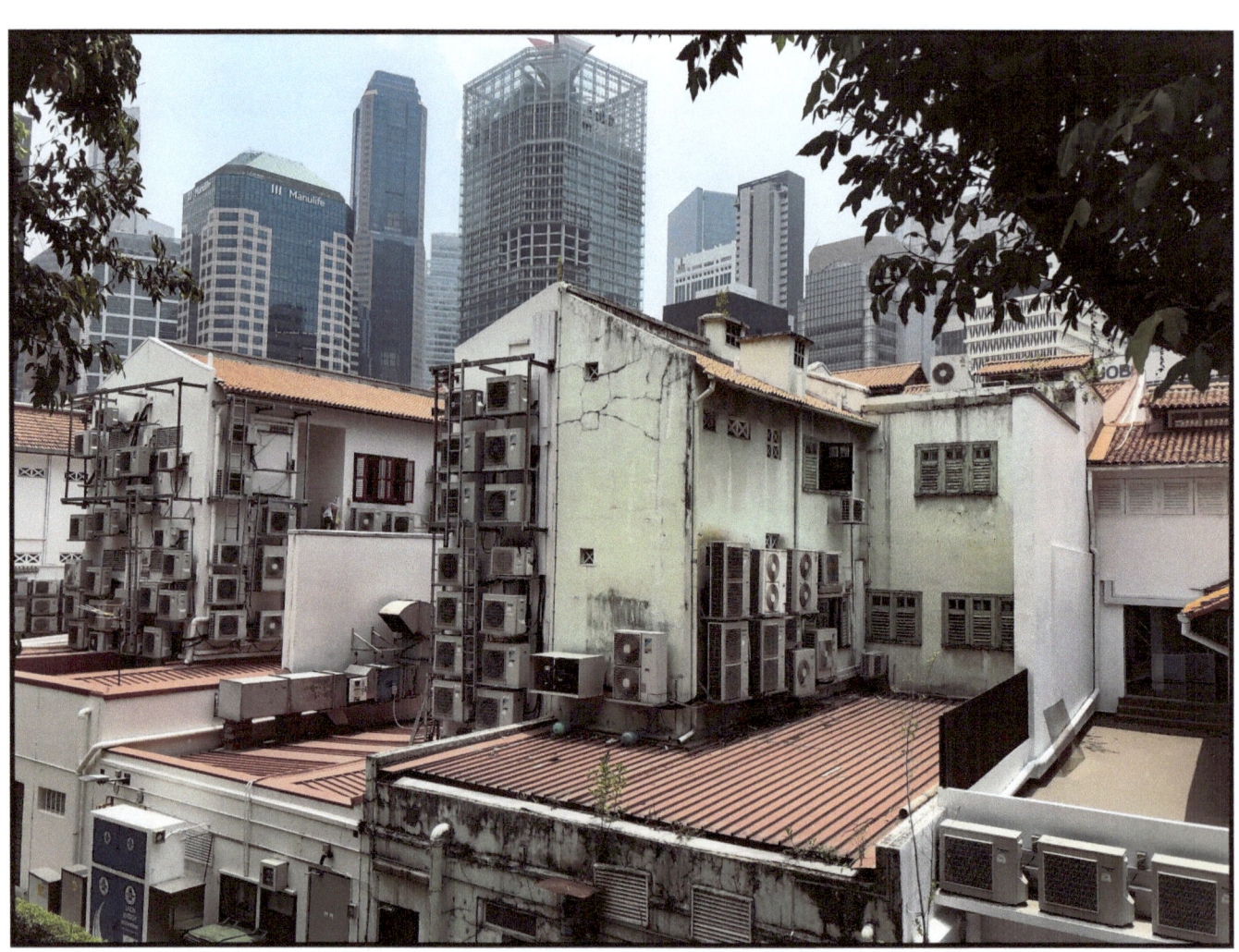

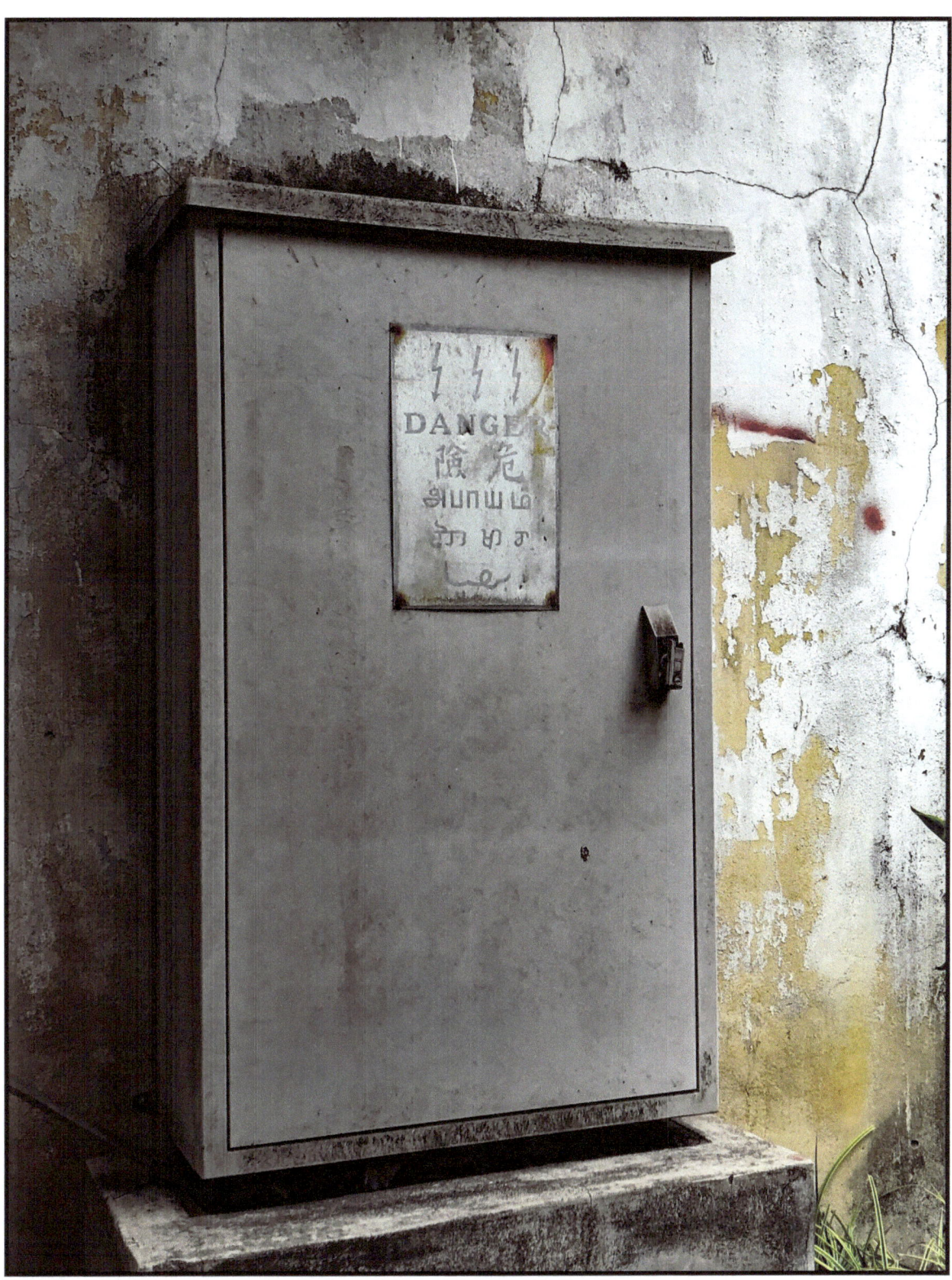

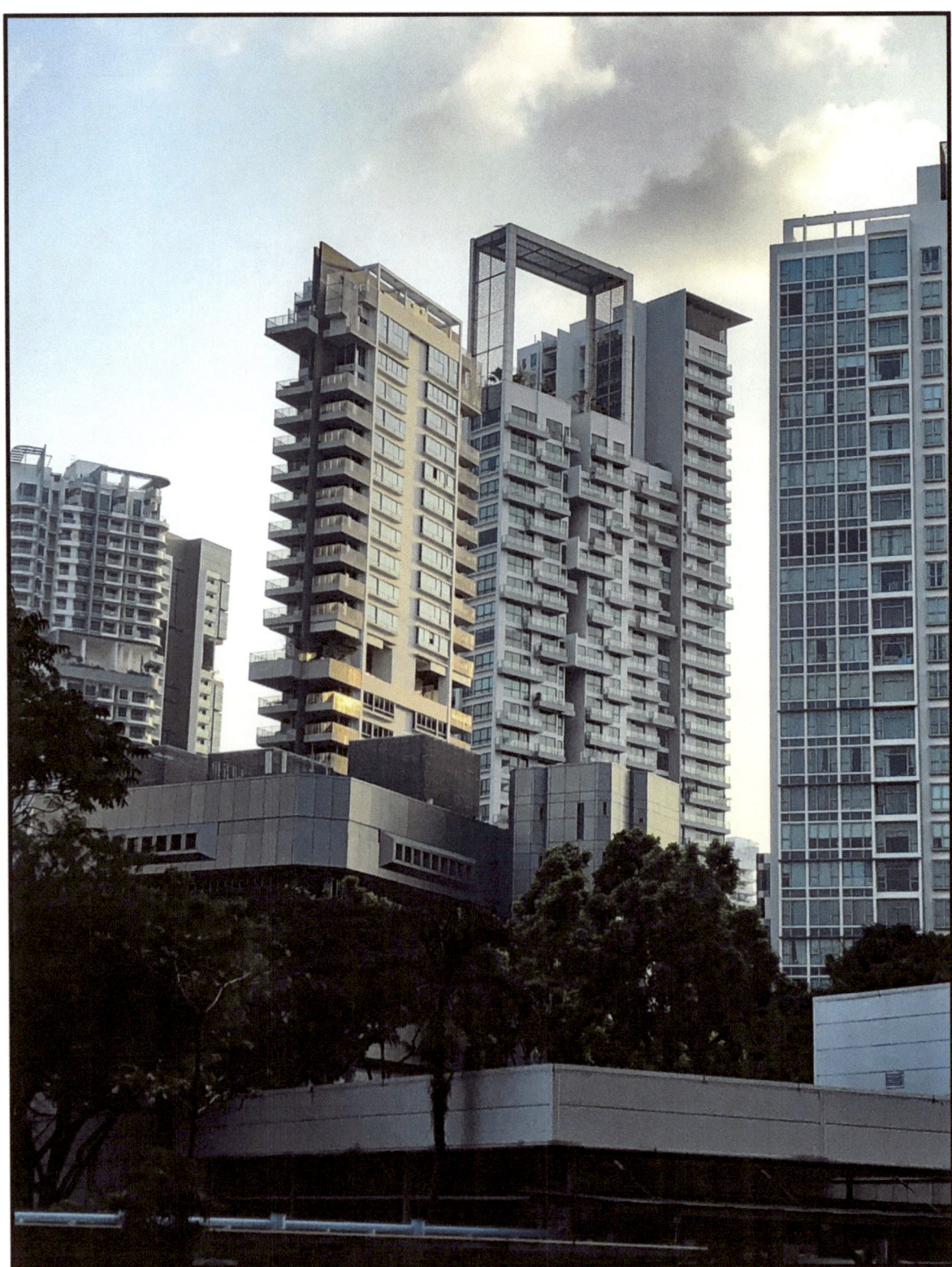

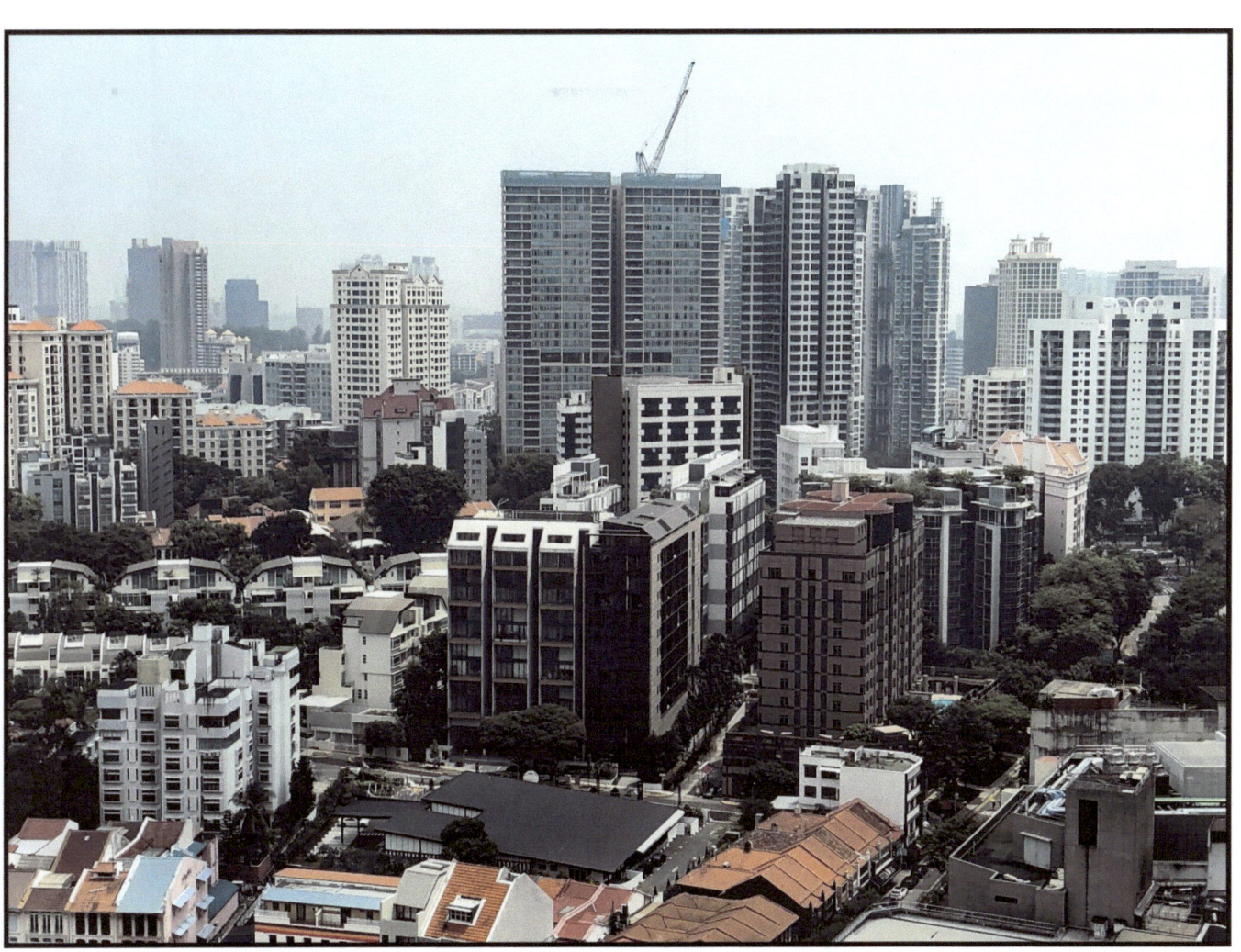

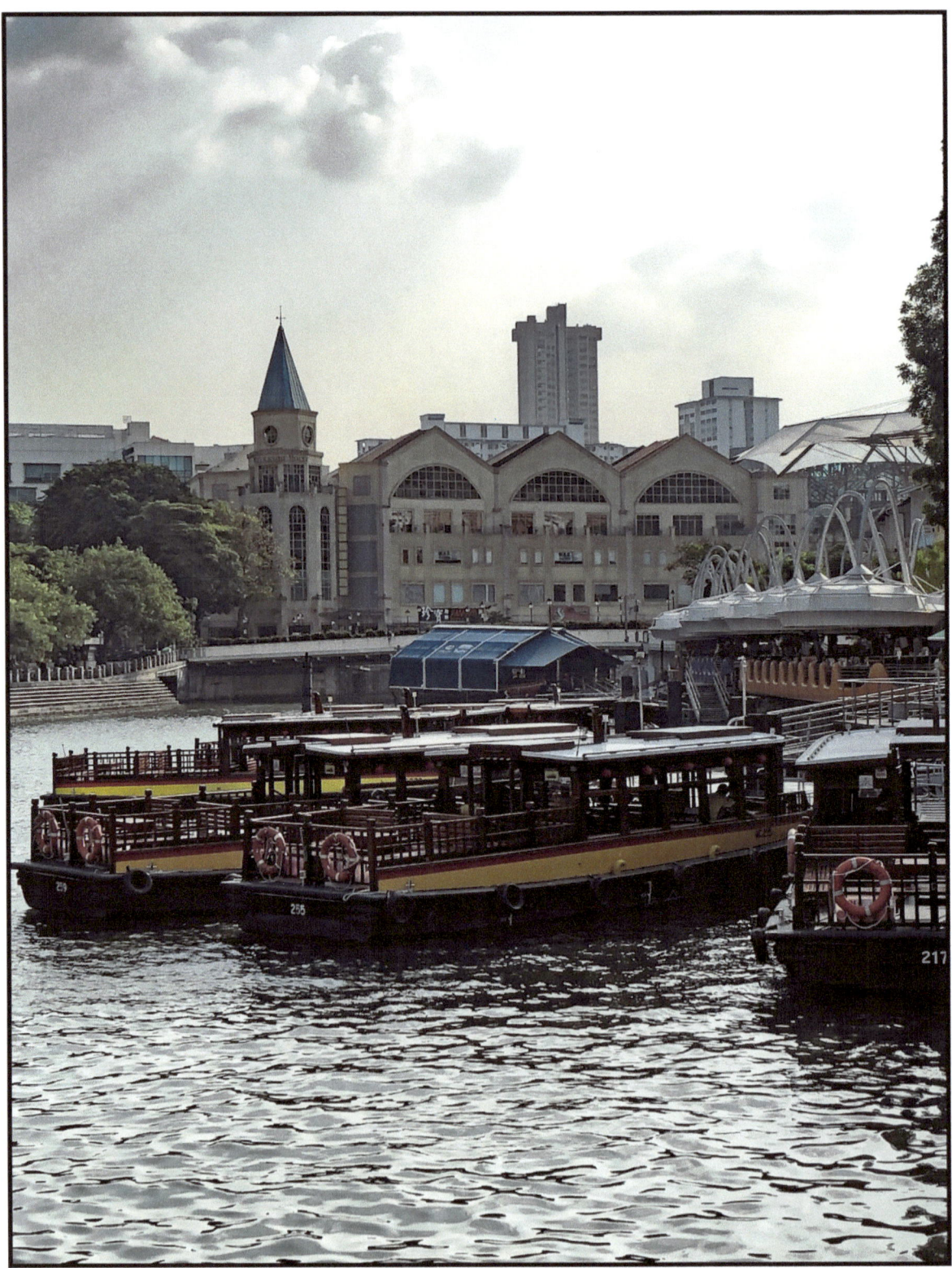

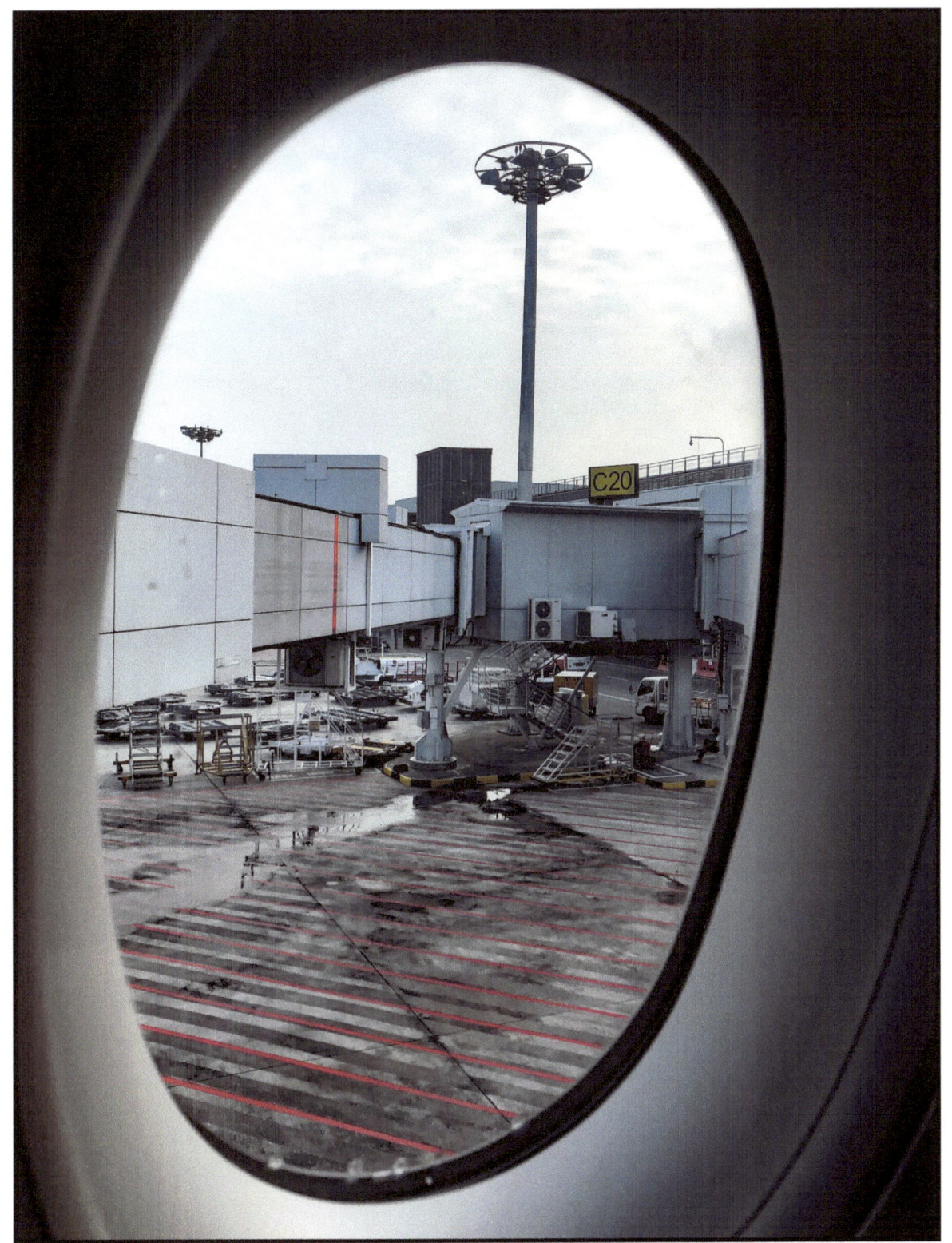

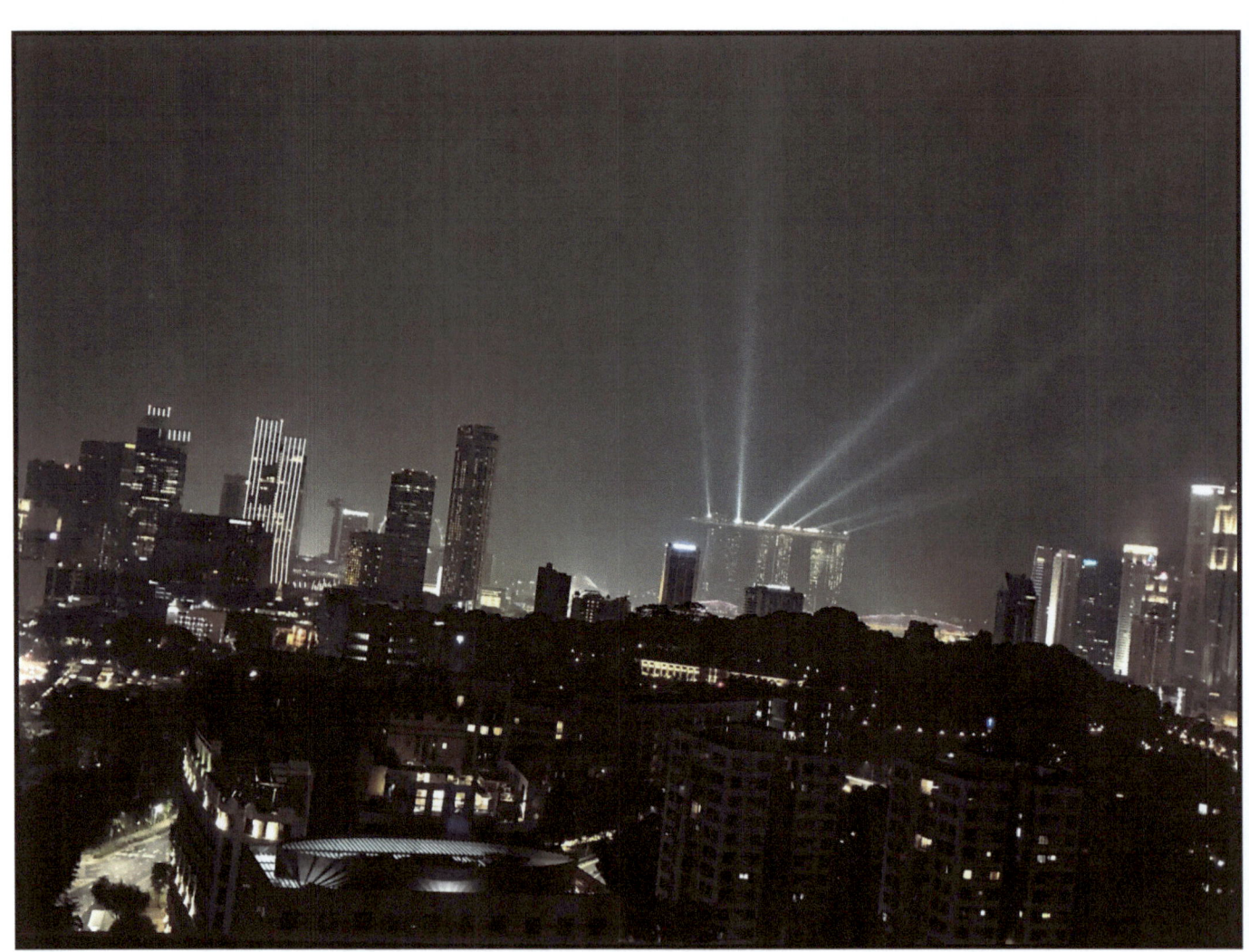

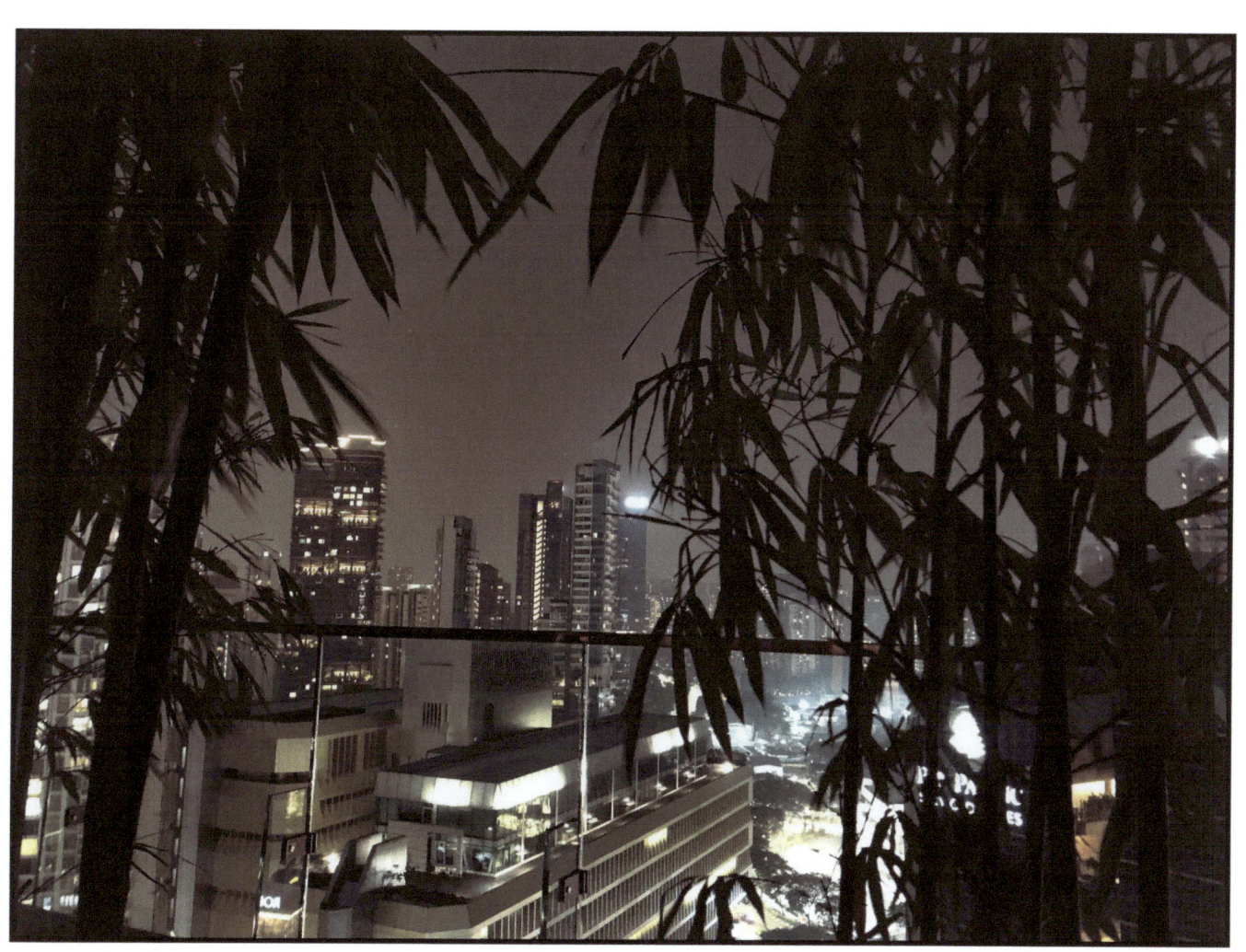

www.ingramcontent.com/pod-product-compliance
Lightning Source LLC
Chambersburg PA
CBHW051144220526
45473CB00003B/656